Celestial Masters

HARVARD-YENCHING INSTITUTE MONOGRAPH SERIES 102

Celestial Masters

History and Ritual in Early Daoist Communities

Terry F. Kleeman

Published by the Harvard University Asia Center
Distributed by Harvard University Press
Cambridge (Massachusetts) and London 2021

The Harvard University Asia Center publishes a monograph series and, in co-ordination with the Fairbank Center for Chinese Studies, the Korea Institute, the Reischauer Institute of Japanese Studies, and other faculties and institutes, administers research projects designed to further scholarly understanding of China, Japan, Vietnam, Korea, and other Asian countries. The Center also sponsors projects addressing multidisciplinary and regional issues in Asia.

The Harvard-Yenching Institute, founded in 1928, is an independent foundation dedicated to the advancement of higher education in the humanities and social sciences in Asia. Headquartered on the campus of Harvard University, the Institute provides fellowships for advanced research, training, and graduate studies at Harvard by competitively selected faculty and graduate students from Asia. The Institute also supports a range of academic activities at its fifty partner universities and research institutes across Asia. At Harvard, the Institute promotes East Asian studies through annual contributions to the Harvard-Yenching Library and publication of the *Harvard Journal of Asiatic Studies* and the Harvard-Yenching Institute Monograph Series.

Library of Congress Cataloging-in-Publication Data
Kleeman, Terry F., 1955–
    Celestial masters : history and ritual in early daoist communities /
Terry F. Kleeman. — 1 [edition].
        pages cm. — (Harvard-Yenching Institute monograph series ; 102)
    Includes bibliographical references and index.
    ISBN 978-0-674-73716-7 (hardcover : alk. paper)
    ISBN 978-0-674-25122-9 (paperback : alk. paper)
    1. Taoism—China—History. I. Title.
    BL1910.K54   2016
    299.5'1409—DC23   2015018475

Index by the author

First paperback edition 2021

♾ Printed on acid-free paper

Last figure below indicates year of this printing
28   27   26   25   24   23   22   21

Contents

Illustrations

Acknowledgments

This book was a decade in creation and was only possible because of the previous work of many distinguished scholars, the personal aid of colleagues and mentors over the years, and the institutional support of both my home university and a number of funding agencies and research institutions around the globe.

My predecessors and colleagues in the study of Celestial Master Daoism provided a foundational understanding of the Daoist church, its institutions, and its history that I have relied upon repeatedly without being able to fully document this influence. Central to my research were the studies of Chen Guofu 陳國符, Ōfuchi Ninji 大淵忍爾, Kristofer Schipper, Michel Strickmann, Ursula Angelika Cedzich, Stephen Bokenkamp, Franciscus Verellen, and Maruyama Hiroshi 丸山宏. Strickmann and Schipper were also my teachers, from whom I learned how to do research and understand Chinese religion. Other mentors in subjects related to the current work included Edwin G. Pulleyblank, Miyakawa Hisayuki 宮川尚志, Kusuyama Haruki 楠山春樹, Fukui Shigemasa 福井重雅, Yasui Kōzan 安居香山, and Edward H. Schafer. The first readers for my manuscript were Nathan Sivin, Barbara Hendrischke, and Chang Chaojan 張超然, and I received helpful comments on the entire manuscript from Robert Campany and Gil Raz (who read it for the press), as well as aid on specific problems from Stephen Bokenkamp, Maruyama Hiroshi, Lü Pengzhi 呂鵬志, John Lagerwey, Zhang Zehong 張澤洪, Bai Bin 白彬, Kikuchi Noritaka 菊地章太, Wang Zongyu 王宗昱, Hsieh Tsung-hui 謝聰輝, William Baxter, Andrew Chittick, Jan Nattier, Tracy Barrett, and Albert Dien. Editorial support at the Asia Center

Publications Program of Harvard University has been superb, with talented editors led by Kristen Wanner finding my mistakes while indulging my eccentricities. Any remaining errors are the result of my own lassitude or ignorance.

I presented some of the materials treated here as part of two National Endowment for the Humanities Summer Seminars for College and University Teachers, held in Boulder in 2011 and 2014. I got excellent, stimulating comments from the members of both seminars, as well as my co-director Stephen Bokenkamp and consultants Maruyama Hiroshi, Chang Chaojan, and Hsieh Shu-wei 謝世維. I also presented aspects of this material in four conferences (in 2005, 2007, 2009, and 2011) at Humboldt University in Berlin, where Florian Reiter gathered a small group of top scholars of Daoism for focused meetings that proved most helpful. I also gained much from the response of colleagues during invited talks at various institutions of higher learning, for which I thank Liu Yi 劉屹 of Capital Normal University (Beijing), Yu Xin 余欣 of Fudan University, Kenneth Dean, then of McGill University, Wendy Swartz of Rutgers University, Hsieh Shu-wei of National Chengchi University (Taipei), Enno Giele of Heidelberg University, Wolfgang Behr of the University of Zurich, Vincent Goossaert of the Ecole Pratique des Hautes Etudes (Paris), Philip Clart of the University of Leipzig, and Robert Campany of Vanderbilt University.

Although there are themes in this book that date back to my earlier study of the Cheng-Han regimes and its relationship to Daoism in the 1990s, work on the present volume began with a request from John Lagerwey for a survey article on early Daoism, which I presented at a conference in Paris in 2006. I began to write up the current manuscript during an eighteen-month period of research beginning in 2009, when a Mellon Fellowship and a Visiting Fellowship at Clare Hall, Cambridge University, permitted a term at the Needham Research Institute, where John Moffett and his staff provided valuable assistance. A subsequent grant from the Center for Chinese Studies, National Central Library 國家圖書館中國研究中心 (Taipei), permitted me to continue this research in Taiwan, where I was sponsored at the Institute for History and

Philology of Academia Sinica 中央研究院歷史語言研究所 by Professor Poo Mu-chou 浦慕周. A Research in China Grant from the American Council of Learned Societies, funded by the National Endowment for the Humanities, then permitted me to continue my explorations in Chengdu at the Center for Daoist and Religious Studies of Sichuan University, where I was hosted by Professor Li Gang 李剛 and gained much from interactions with Professors Zhang Zehong and Bai Bin. I returned to teaching in Fall 2010 and was unable to devote serious attention to the manuscript until my sabbatical in 2012, which was extended by a yearlong fellowship at the International Consortium for Research in the Humanities at Friedrich Alexander Universität, Erlangen, where I was hosted by Professor Michael Lackner with the able assistance of Ms. Petra Hahm; I gained much from the interdisciplinary discussions at the Consortium, and my research was substantially furthered by their excellent staff. A travel grant from the Center for the Humanities and the Arts at the University of Colorado permitted two weeks during this period to work on manuscripts in the British Library. Throughout, the University of Colorado, the Department of Asian Languages and Civilizations, the Center for Asian Studies, and the staff of its Norlin Library have granted me leave time and supported my research. Finally, none of this would have been possible without the understanding, tolerance, and constant assistance of my spouse, Faye Yuan Kleeman 阮斐娜.

T.K., December 2015

Celestial Masters

HARVARD-YENCHING INSTITUTE MONOGRAPH SERIES 102

Introduction

This book is about an organized, institutionalized religion[1] founded in western China around the middle of the second century of our era.[2] At the time, followers of the religion called it the Way of the Celestial Masters (Tianshidao 天師道) and believed that it was founded upon a Covenant with the Powers (*mengwei*

---

1. "Religion" is one of the most contested terms in academia. Campany (2003) has an excellent review of the various emic terms used in China for what we would call "religion" and concludes that it is best understood as an etic term referring to a "repertoire of resources" for the discursive creation of an imagined community. Here I intend a self-identified group of people who employ such a repertoire.

2. This study would have been impossible without the contributions of many preceding scholars. Chen Guofu (1963 [1949]) pioneered the study of the Daoist canon and assembled the basic sources that have made the modern study of early Daoism possible. Ōfuchi Ninji (1964, 1991, 1997) gave the first comprehensive account of the Celestial Master movement. Rao Zongyi (1991 [1956]) and Ōfuchi (1978–79) identified the key Dunhuang manuscripts for the study of early Daoism. Angelika Cedzich (1987, 1993, 2001, 2009) and Maruyama Hiroshi (1986, 2004) gave the first detailed account of Celestial Master ritual and continue to illuminate much about that tradition. Peter Nickerson (1996, 2000, 2006) introduced in English much of the material concerning the spread of Daoism to South China, including archaeological evidence. Franciscus Verellen (2003b, 2004) has provided insight into the Daoist system of parishes and the use of petitions. Stephen Bokenkamp (1997) provided the first extended translations of Daoist scriptures, including several used extensively below.

盟威) that was both correct or orthodox (*zheng* 正) and unique in the world (*yi* 一), giving rise to another term for the religion still in use today, the Correct and Unitary (Zhengyi). Outsiders who noticed that each family was responsible for an annual tithe of five pecks of rice (roughly nine liters) referred to the movement as the Way of the Five Pecks of Rice; some seeking to deny its legitimacy referred to believers as "rice bandits" (*mizei* 米賊).[3] It was not the only such movement at the time; history records other movements like the Way of Great Peace that erupted in revolt a few decades later in eastern China, and there were, no doubt, dozens if not hundreds of similar new religious movements centering on a charismatic founder with a religious message during the early medieval period that arose and disappeared without attracting the attention of Chinese historians.[4]

Over the ensuing centuries, the movement grew and transformed, absorbing a diverse body of practices and beliefs, many of which originated with other religious movements or esoteric traditions. From the beginning, adherents spoke of its tenets as the "teachings of the Dao" (Daojiao 道教), and eventually this became the accepted reference for the movement itself, whereas its religious officiants, initially called "libationers" (*jijiu* 祭酒), came to be called "gentlemen of the Dao" (Daoshi 道士). In English, the religion has most commonly been rendered as "Daoism," and its religious professionals have been dubbed "Daoist priests." I will use these terms throughout this book.

Unfortunately, in English we have a limited range of terms to use with regard to traditional China, and this use of "Daoism" has been contested.[5] The term is also applied regularly to certain philosophers from the Warring States era (479–220 BCE), especially those who preserved their thoughts in books called the

3. For a translation and analysis of these early records, see chapter 1. Earlier studies of these events include Eichhorn 1955; Stein 1963; and Ōfuchi 1991:39–76.
4. Seidel 1969–70, 1983; Tang Changru 1983.
5. Sivin 1978 provides a clear assessment of the various uses of this term, which has no counterpart in Chinese. See Sivin 2010 for an application of these insights to some recent publications on Daoism.

Laozi 老子 or *Master Lao* and the *Zhuangzi* 莊子 or *Master Zhuang*, and which were grouped together in a bibliographic category called the "lineage of the Dao" (*daojia* 道家) around 100 BCE. The figure of Master Lao was revered by the Celestial Masters as a deity called Lord Lao, and the book *Laozi* was given a distinctively religious interpretation in the Celestial Master commentary,[6] but the ideas animating the Celestial Master movement were for the most part quite at variance with the Warring States teachings of either book. The movement stressed explicit norms of moral conduct and the performance of sacred ritual, both of which the two books openly rejected. If one insisted on finding the true origins of the movement in Warring States thought, Confucianism and Mohism are better candidates.

A broader argument has also been advanced, claiming that any group or text that concerns itself with the Dao ("the way") deserves the epithet "Daoist."[7] Since a wide variety of thinkers and groups referred to their preferred way to live or act as their "way," this expands the term to the point where it loses much meaning or utility. Moreover, it puts the modern historian of religion in the position of lumping together groups that clearly saw themselves as distinct. Thirty-five years on, it is high time to agree with Michel Strickmann's pronouncement that Daoism "came into social being with the Way of the Celestial Masters in the second half of the second century AD, and continues under the aegis of its successors and derivatives at the present day" (1977:2).

The early Daoists saw their world as comprising two types of people: the Daoist or the profane (*su* 俗). In our earliest texts, like the *Xiang'er* commentary to the *Laozi*, we already see the Daoist (Daoren 道人), sometimes referred to optimistically as the transcendent gentleman (*xianshi* 仙士), contrasted with the "profane person" (*suren* 俗人). Both are mortal and fear death, for example, but the would-be transcendent gentleman "believes in the Dao

---

6. The *Xiang'er* 想爾, meaning (the personified Dao is) "thinking of you," is discussed in chapter 2.

7. See Raz 2004:22, which cites the identifying criterion of these groups as "a view of the Dao as an overarching and effective force."

and keeps the precepts" (*xin Dao shou jie* 信道守戒) and is thus able to "unite with life" (*he yu sheng* 合於生), whereas the profane are fated to "shed this mortal coil before their time" (*weiyang tuisi* 未央蛻死). Daoism offered salvation from an unsavory posthumous fate where the demonic agents of the Earth Office might seize the deceased and subject him or her to torture-filled interrogations followed by a variety of punishments, as we see in this third-century passage from a spirit revelation:[8]

> The Daoist and the profane person are indeed distant from each other! Why do I say so? The Daoist is pure and correct, and his name belongs up in the Heavens. The profane person is impure and defiled; when he or she dies, they belong to the Earth Office. Is this not distant? When foolish people keep to the profane and give no thought to serving the Dao, they can be called greatly deluded.
>
> 道人與俗相去遠矣。何以言之。道人清正，名上屬天。俗人穢濁，死屬地官。豈不遠乎。愚人守俗，不念奉道，可謂大迷也。

The purity claimed by Daoists derived from their refusal to participate in the most central of traditional Chinese religious rites, the offering of blood sacrifice to deities no different in kind from dead humans, gods who depended on the sustenance of regular offerings of meat and wine, and repaid the sacrificer with divine blessings that assured health, wealth, and good fortune.[9] Daoists worshipped the Dao as a personified yet abstract deity who could temporarily manifest as a supreme deity, first the Supreme Lord Lao and later a trio of Heavenly Worthies, the Three Pure Ones (*sanqing* 三清). These manifestations of the Dao required nothing of humans and accepted no offerings. They evaluated human conduct, reported by a variety of spirits both within

8. From the *Commands and Precepts for the Great Family of the Dao* (*Da Daojia lingjie* 大道家令戒), dated 255. *Zhengyi fawen tianshi jiao jieke jing* 11a4–6.

9. For an analysis of the role of sacrifice in the Chinese common religion, see Kleeman 1994b. For a perceptive account of why Western scholarship has until recently failed to recognize the existence of this common sacrificial religion, see Barrett 2005.

the body of the Daoist and in an external bureaucratic network throughout the natural world, against a code of precepts that were tailored to the individual's level of spiritual development as reflected in religious rank. Their judgments could be swayed only by meritorious action or the ritualized submission of appropriate official documents.

Each Daoist in the early Celestial Master movement held a specific rank within a universal priesthood of believers, conferred through an ordination ritual that transmitted a document called a register (*lu* 籙). The register installed a group of protective spirits in the believer's body and imposed a code of precepts, both of which increased with rank. Children of either sex and any social class could be accepted as novices (*lusheng* 籙生), where they progressed through a number of stages, learning to read and compose official documents destined for the Heavens while gaining control of progressively larger cohorts of divine protectors and emissaries. Upon completion of the program, novices became libationers (*jijiu* 祭酒), who could gather their own followers and establish their own parishes (*zhi* 治). Each household contributed an annual grain tithe to the parish and made pledge offerings to demonstrate sincerity when requesting ritual services; both tithe and offerings were not offerings to the gods but contributions to the operating expenses incurred by the ritual activities of the religion. Each household was supposed to maintain a distinct ritual structure for daily devotional activities and to wear distinctive clothing when engaged in these activities. I follow earlier scholars like Anna Seidel in referring to this self-cognizant, organized, clearly delimited social group as a church.[10]

In this book, I treat the origins and development of this Daoist

10. See Girardot 1983:279; Seidel 1984:168. It is difficult to apply the oft-cited criteria of Ernst Troeltsch (1912) for the Christian church to Daoism, but, by the end of the second century, Daoism was clearly a mass movement drawing followers from all levels of society; it was a dominant force in West China to the point that all in the region felt obliged to belong; it generally enjoyed good relations with the state, sometimes even being favored as the state religion; and, except for rare periods of rapid expansion, most members at any given time had been born into it.

church from its establishment in the mid-second century through the Period of Disunion, ending the inquiry with the reunification of China at the beginning of the seventh century. By then, the Daoist message had been elaborated and transformed in many ways, with the revelation of new gods, scriptures, and liturgies, and a monastic institution was beginning to form. Daoist communities retaining the ancient social organization survived into the Tang dynasty (618–907) and perhaps far beyond; the modern Yao 瑤 ethnic minority of South China and northern Southeast Asia retains a communal Daoism remarkably reminiscent of these original groups.[11] Throughout most of China, however, Daoism eventually evolved into a religion of priests without a lay congregation. They were and still are called on by communities to celebrate specific periodic festivals or by individuals to deal with specific needs on an ad hoc basis.[12] They act as caretakers of the broader common religion, overseeing its sacrificial observances and confirming the official positions of its gods through esoteric Daoist rites that maintain a clear distinction between ritual activities directed toward popular gods and the pure rituals dedicated to the eternal deities of the Daoist pantheon. Even today, Daoist troupes across the breadth of China and in Chinese communities around the world maintain a ritual program that preserves theological concepts, liturgical forms, and divine appellations that originated in the period treated in this book.

This book is divided into two parts: one dedicated to the historical origins and development of the Daoist church, the other describing the ritual activities of its members. The historical section begins by examining in detail outsiders' accounts of the founding and early years of the Celestial Master movement, when it was still largely confined to West China, including the theocratic state that existed briefly (ca. 191–215) in the Hanzhong region of modern southeastern Shaanxi and northeastern Sichuan provinces. Our primary sources are the dynastic histories of China, a uniquely detailed and continuous source, which, however,

---

11. On Yao Daoism, see Strickmann 1982a; Alberts 2006; Hirota 2007.
12. On this transformation, see Kleeman 2005b.

is limited by its court-centered, elite nature and by generic conventions that limit its reporting of religious phenomena not controlled by the state. The second chapter looks at this same period from the viewpoint of Daoist sources, revealing the way members of the church conceived their founding and early history. A careful dating and sensitive reading of surviving materials reveals a narrative that in some ways confirms the testimony of conventional sources but also sheds new light on the significance of early church institutions and activities. The third chapter makes use of three early sources that can be confidently dated to the third century to trace the development of the church after the fall of the Hanzhong state and the subsequent great diaspora of 215, when church members were scattered across the breadth of North China, the central administration was disrupted in unknown ways, and many believers were left to their own devices. During this fecund period, huge numbers were converted to the faith at the same time that new practices and institutions evolved to cope with changed circumstances. The fourth chapter treats the fourth through sixth centuries. In West and North China we see a series of attempts to reconstruct the Daoist theocracy of the Hanzhong period. Meanwhile, as a result of the disruptions at the beginning of the fourth century, Northerners of all classes flood into South China, bringing with them Celestial Master Daoism. We can trace best the elite families who played significant roles in government, but rebellions like that of Sun En 孫恩 (?–402) demonstrate the prevalence of Daoism among peasants and tradesmen, as well.[13] During this period several new scriptural revelations incorporated elements of southern occult traditions and Buddhism into Daoism. In both North and South China we see evidence of an increasing contestation between Daoism and Buddhism for government patronage.

The second half of the book looks at ritual life within the Daoist

---

13. Nickerson (2000) argues that the transmission must have been earlier to have become so widespread among all classes by the end of the fourth century. This is not impossible, but the migrations involved huge numbers of people of all classes, and religions can spread quickly over the course of almost a century.

church, drawing on a body of liturgical and normative sources that accreted throughout this period, mixing authentically early materials with later additions.[14] Chapter 5 introduces Daoist architecture and apparel, describing the oratory and parish buildings that were the site of almost all Daoist ritual and the specialized ritual garb that people wore during ritual performances. Chapter 6 focuses on the Daoist citizen (*daomin* 道民), the most basic level of Celestial Master society. I describe the audience ritual that the head of household performed each morning and evening, bringing him or her directly into contact with potent Daoist deities. I also consider the kitchen-feast, Daoism's answer to the traditional communal sacrificial banquet, which had the same function of exhibiting status distinctions while affirming one's participation in the community. Chapter 7 focuses on the novice or register-student, who learned how to write formal documents to Daoist deities and how to perform the intricate rituals that presented them to the Heavenly Bureaus. There is a detailed description of the ordination as well as an examination of the role of women and those of mean birth within the church. Chapter 8 is about the libationer or parish priest. It introduces the various functions of the libationer as evangelist, director of spirit revelations, judge, and pastor. Here I also present a new interpretation of the development of the parish system, arguing that it transformed from a fixed number of geographically based administrative centers, staffed by a large number of male and female officers with diverse responsibilities, to a diffuse system of smaller units led by a single libationer that functioned as a ranking system. I also look closely at the procedures for composing and submitting ritual documents like the petition and for drawing talismans that assure ritual efficacy. Finally, I describe the understanding of and ritual responses to death in Daoist communities.

I have adopted this dual structure, in part, because the nature of the sources dictated it. The first half of the book relies on datable sources and puts events in a clear chronological framework.

---

14. On accretion or layering in traditional texts, see Farmer, Henderson, and Witzel 2000.

Evidence from the standard histories is written by and for elites from a perspective close to that of the state, but even the Daoist sources exploited in this section were produced by church leaders, sanctioned and promulgated by the central administration of the religion. By combining these two types of sources, I hope to produce a much fuller historical account that preserves multiple voices and relates events as both the profane world and members of the church perceived them. Still, this material alone falls short of the sort of thick description that is the standard for studies of religion and society in a post-Geertzian world.[15]

The materials informing the description of ritual life in the second section were used, to be sure, by church leaders and elite Daoists, but they were equally the property of village priests and peasant Daoist citizens. Before being edited into their final form, they went through a long process of manuscript transmission, handed down by generation after generation of local practitioners who added or deleted items according to need. A similar process has generated the handwritten scriptures (*shouchao ben* 手抄本) that Daoist priests across today's China use. Each surviving liturgical manual or precept list is thus the product of a specific lineage of practitioners. The identity and geographical location of these transmitters is lost to history. This rules out a comprehensive overview of the ritual practice of any specific region of China. Nor can we limit our description to a specific period within the five centuries under examination. We can only claim that the social structures, ritual practices, and modes of interaction with the divine described here were broadly typical of the Daoist church during its formative period. But it is only these sources that can give us a sense of Daoism as a dynamic, vital lived religion,[16] to which millions of Chinese over these centuries devoted their lives and pinned their hopes of divine aid and ultimate

15. See Geertz 1973.

16. For the concept of lived religion as a model for religious enquiry, see Orsi 2003, 2005; McGuire 2008. For the broader question of the use of social science methodology in the study of religious history, see Beyer 2011. Unfortunately, the texts that survive from this early period of Daoism, with their problems of provenance, date, and point of view, can only reveal a partial and

salvation in a time of near constant political and military strife, foreign invasion, natural disaster, and epidemic disease.

Religion in the Eastern Han

Since the first chapter opens with historical accounts of the early Celestial Master movement, I offer here some background to the religious milieu of the second century CE.[17] The Eastern Han (23–220) was a particularly fecund period in Chinese religious history, when the religious world of imperial China began to take form. There were changes to every aspect of religious life, and some of these were directly involved in the birth of Daoism as an organized religion.

Two developments are closely tied to the interregnum between the Western and Eastern Han (6 BCE–23 CE). The first is the rise of the oracular literature most commonly referred to in English as the Aprocrypha (in Chinese, *chenwei* 讖緯, or prognostications and weft texts).[18] Although these texts are best known for their use as political propaganda by the usurper Wang Mang 王莽 (45 BCE–23 CE) and later claimants for the Han throne, they are rich in religious imagery and metaphor. Many of the deities and icons that would be prominent in Daoism are first mentioned in these texts, and their continuing revelation over a number of decades accustomed the populace to the idea of spirit revelation as an important source of religious truth.[19]

The other development at this time is the first recorded popular religious movements. In 3 BCE, near the end of the Western Han, a prophecy appeared in northeast China, claiming that the Grandmother of the West, a goddess connected with death and

---

somewhat tenuous reconstruction of early Daoism that pales in comparison to the vibrant living religions depicted by these modern scholars.

17. For a more detailed account of these events, see Kleeman 1998:63–66.

18. On the Apocrypha, see Seidel 1983; Yasui 1984; Lippiello 2001. "Weft" is a fabric metaphor based on the fact that they supplement and complete the classics, which are called "warp" texts (*jing* 經).

19. Csikszentmihalyi (2002) discusses revealed texts during the Han dynasty.

immortality, would manifest in this mortal world.[20] Thousands left their homes to make a pilgrimage to the capital, singing and dancing in a carnivalesque celebration of the coming divine epiphany. They transmitted plaques that they claimed were imperial commands (*zhao* 詔) guaranteeing salvation. Some two decades later, in 18 CE, we hear the first reports of the Red Eyebrows, members of a communal religion worshipping Prince Jing of Chengyang Liu Zhang 城陽景王劉章 (d. 177), who had suppressed the rebellion of Empress Lü 呂后 and hence represented the restoration of the Han royal house.[21] Interpretations of the their distinctive eyebrows differ, with some claiming that coloring them with cinnabar represented long life, whereas others thought they were red for the fire element that was thought to rule the Han royal house.[22] Members of this uprising traveled with their families in communities and took the titles of their leaders from those of village leaders, much like the later Celestial Master libationers. They were guided by a local spirit medium who conveyed commands from Prince Jing and were able to briefly install a direct descendant of Prince Jing as emperor.

There were also more prolonged manifestations or epiphanies of a deity. The primary figure associated with such beliefs is the divinized Laozi. The *Scripture of the Transformations of Laozi* (*Laozi bianhua jing* 老子變化經), studied by Anna Seidel (1969), traces the appearance of avatars of Laozi under a variety of names and guises up through the middle of the second century CE. The last recorded incarnation is in the Sichuan region, close to the founding revelation of the Celestial Masters both geographically and temporally. The text suggests that Laozi might return in the future, and, indeed, the appearance of these messianic manifestations continued for many centuries, sparking numerous popular rebellions.[23] A parallel development was the appearance of popular

20. See Dubs 1942; Cahill 1993:21–23.

21. On the Red Eyebrows, see *Hou Han shu* 11/477–86; Hendrischke 2000: 135–36; Zhang Huasong 2004.

22. See Zhang Xiangwen 1996.

23. Seidel 1969–70, 1984. For an overview of these many manifestations, see Hendrischke 2000.

temple structures (*fangsi* 房祀, *fangmiao* 房廟) dedicated to dead humans. Although periodically suppressed by the government and attacked by Daoists, such popular cults to local heroes or those suffering an abnormal death became the norm and allowed the masses to access divine powers once restricted to elites.[24]

There is a significant change in burial practices during the Eastern Han. We find in tombs from that period land contracts (*maidiquan* 買地券) as well as grave-quelling texts (*zhenmuwen* 鎮墓文) that tell us much about popular understandings of death.[25] The land contracts record the purchase of the subterranean space occupied by the tomb, which is often described in religious terms ("to the limits of the four directions" and so on), and secure the soul of the deceased in that space, often with the stipulation that the dead will remain separate from the living. Grave-quelling texts (also called "infusion-releasing texts," or *jiezhuwen* 解注文) invoke a powerful deity like the Heavenly Thearch 天帝 or the Yellow God 黃神 to absolve the deceased from any blame incurred through the construction of the tomb. Both reveal a highly bureaucratized world of the dead and a fear of otherworldly curses on the living by or through their deceased relatives. Although the specific methods and deities were not prominent among early Daoists, worry about such matters led many to seek the protection of the Daoist church.

The concept of a utopian world of Great Peace (*taiping* 太平)

24. See *Hou Han shu* 7/314, 57/1841, 76/2470. The use of *fang* 房, "building," in these terms indicates that permanent structures for the worship of divine beings was new in the Han; Six Dynasties texts simply refer to *miao* and *ci* 祠, "shrines." For Daoist officers and gods assigned to battle these demonic figures, see the entry for the Great Director of Attacks in the list of parish offices in chapter 8 and DZ 421 *Dengzhen yinjue* 3/21b. Disrespect for these cults was not limited to the Celestial Masters; Ge Hong remarks that he consistently ignores such shrines yet has never suffered misfortune as a result. See Wang Ming 1985:9/158.

25. For land contracts, see Kleeman 1984; Seidel 1987. On grave-quelling texts, see Wu Rongceng 1981; Zhang Xunliao 1996; Bai Bin 2010. I do not share Zhang and Bai's view that these grave-quelling texts are Daoist or even a direct antecedent to Daoism. For a fuller treatment of Daoist views of death, see chapter 8.

was an important inspiration for the early Daoists. A text with this term in the title was presented to the Han throne twice in the late first century BCE and again in the mid-second century.[26] Questions concerning the dating, stratification, and filiation of the transmitted text(s) are also complex, but large portions seem early, likely of Han date, and as closely related to Eastern Han philosophical works as to anything found in early Daoist texts. It is equally uncertain if the text reflects the beliefs and practices of a distinct religious community or just personal revelations to one or more inspired individuals. It does seem that some version of this text was known to and used by Zhang Jue 張角, who led a religious rebellion in late-second-century East China known as the Yellow Turbans (*huangjin* 黃巾) for their distinctive headgear.[27] The Yellow Turbans shared with the Celestial Masters a belief in the origin of illness in misconduct, the efficacy of confession of sins, and the use of talismans. It is likely that they shared an aspiration for the advent of an age of Great Peace, when social conflicts would be lessened and all peoples would be dealt with equitably, and they may well have thought this would only be attained after an apocalyptic period of social upheaval. There is no evidence, however, that they thought of themselves as "seed people" who would repopulate the world, or that they practiced a sexual ritual like the Merging the Pneumas rite as a prerequisite to such salvation.[28] The *Commands and Precepts for the Great Family of the Dao* of 255 makes clear that Zhang Jue was not considered favorably by the Celestial Masters.[29]

The most far-reaching development during the Eastern Han

26. It is uncertain if these were in any sense the same text or to be identified partially or wholly with the extant *Scripture of Great Peace*. The literature on the *Scripture of Great Peace* is substantial, including important articles by Kaltenmark (1979), Mansvelt-Beck (1980), and Petersen (1989–90), plus the many publications by Barbara Kandel/Hendrischke. For the most recent studies, see Espesset 2002a, 2002b, 2004; Hendrischke 2004, 2006, 2009, 2012.

27. On the Yellow Turbans, see Eichhorn 1957; Michaud 1958; Fukui 1974.

28. See Petersen 1990 for an argument that the *Scripture of Great Peace* does not advocate messianism.

29. See chapter 3.

was the entry of Buddhism, but the extent of its immediate influence is uncertain. In 65 CE, an imperial prince in modern Jiangsu was already hosting public Buddhist rituals with thousands of participants; in 165, the emperor offered official sacrifice to the Buddha. In both cases, the Buddha was associated with Laozi and the pursuit of immortality.[30] By the late second century, we know of several teams of Buddhist monks and laymen in Chang'an translating Buddhist scriptures into Chinese. Although these translators sometimes turned to Daoist terminology to express unfamiliar Buddhist concepts, no one reading these translations would have failed to notice their alien character. Distinctively Buddhist terminology in a Daoist source is a reliable indication of later composition.[31] Still, several features of the new religious movements of the second century are shared with Buddhism, especially the practice of the confession of sins. Moreover, Buddhists, like the Celestial Masters, rejected blood sacrifice, though their rationales for doing so were different. Buddhism may well have stimulated the rise of Daoism. By the mid-second century, Daoists were claiming that Buddhism was a degraded form of Daoism and the Buddha himself just another avatar of a divine Laozi. By the late fourth century, Buddhism had exerted an undeniable influence on Daoist ritual practice and theological conceptions, and was competing with Daoism for official patronage.

All of these changes came together in the rise of Daoism. The fall of the Western Han and the lengthy, strife-torn interregnum had awakened all to the fragility of the Chinese imperial state. Political instability brought warfare, famine, and epidemic disease, leading to large-scale movements of population. Among these frightened and dislocated individuals, a variety of new forms of religious expression arose. The Celestial Masters were one such group. Driven by a revelation from Lord Lao that established a new covenant and guided by ongoing revelations from his

30. The best account of Buddhism's entry into China remains Zürcher 1959.

31. Only in the *Demon Statutes of Lady Blue*, dated to the second half of the third century, do we find a few Buddhist terms, and then only ones with a special resonance for Chinese society. See chapter 3.

representatives as well as deceased leaders of the movement, their teachings on sin as the origin of illness and misfortune, disaster as an apocalyptic punishment for an immoral age, ritualized confession and penance as an effective response to such dangers, and the promise of a utopian age of Great Peace resonated with the masses. Like the new foreign faith of Buddhism, the Daoism they fashioned in Sichuan had a broad appeal, winning converts across China until it was a truly national religion that provided a satisfying answer to the questions of its day. Daoism proved adaptable to changing circumstance, developing new rituals for the salvation of all the living and all the dead, and remains to this day a vital part of the Chinese religious landscape.

Conventions

It remains to guide readers through a few pertinent conventions used in referring to and translating materials from medieval China. Located at the far eastern end of the Eurasian continent, China had traded with the West since Neolithic times but was not significantly influenced by the currents of history that prevailed in the Mediterranean world and later Western Europe. It developed unique ways to understand and describe the natural world and the imagined other world, populated by the dead and the divine, that its East Asian neighbors came to share but were seldom communicated to the Indian subcontinent, the Near East, or Europe. For this reason, translating the vocabulary of early Daoism into a Western language poses certain challenges. In the interests of making this book accessible to scholars of religion and history with no background in Sinology, I have sought approximations in English for every Daoist technical term and conception. Lest these be misunderstood as true equivalents, I note here some of the key problems.

I have followed Bokenkamp (1997) in translating as "pneuma" the word *qi* 氣/炁, which seems etymologically to have referred to the steam of cooking grain but came to mean everything from essence to energy, scent, air, feeling, and spirit. In the Daoist context, it sometimes means a force within the body that can be manipulated, but it often refers to noncorporeal beings, and sometimes these usages are difficult to distinguish. The goal of much Daoist endeavor was the status of *xian* 仙/僊, which originally referred to nonhuman winged beings who could be found only in mountain fastnesses or divine realms but came to refer to humans who had attained some form of physical longevity or immortality.[32] I translate this as "transcendent" because the word is etymologically related to words meaning "to ascend" and because many *xian* were not truly "immortal," the other common translation. For the early Daoists, this status was awarded by heavenly bureaucrats in return for exemplary moral conduct and proper ritual actions. Later, internal and external alchemy as well as various physical regimens were also employed. Another key term is *zhen* 真, which later came to mean simply "real, true" but originally designated a class of divine beings untouched by vulgar desire or impurity. I follow many others in rendering this as "perfected" in both nominal and adjectival usage, a nod to the austere Perfecti of the Cathar tradition, who eschewed both meat and sex. In Daoism, the perfected are the class of beings above the transcendents and just below the Daoist gods (*shen* 神).[33]

Words for deity in Chinese are vexing. It is standard to render *shen* as "god" and *gui* 鬼 as "demon" or "ghost" depending on the context, but *guishen* was a common locution for divine beings in general. We will see in chapter 2 that even the high god of the Daoists was sometimes called a *gui*. I have tried to sort these out, translating appropriately for context, but have sometimes resorted to the ambiguous "spirit" for either term. The high god during the

32. Campany 2009 has shown that the term often referred to real-world ascetics and renunciants who were credited with wonder-working and divine healing.

33. These gods are primordial transformations of the pneumas of the Dao who have never taken human form. They are to be distinguished from the many lower-level, quasi-demonic spirits worshipped by the common people as well as the various body gods populating key spots in the physical form and the register spirits employed in Daoist ritual.

Shang dynasty (ca. 1500–1045 BCE) was called simply *di* 帝,[34] and this remained a popular term for exalted deities, sometimes singular but often plural, throughout Chinese history. Beginning in the third century BCE, it was appropriated by temporal rulers, giving rise to the unfortunate translation "emperor." In an attempt to recapture the sense of a divine ruler, I regularly translate this term as "thearch." Other translation problems are noted as the terms come up.

Although there have been a number of Daoist canons, beginning in the fifth century, the only one to have survived is from the fifteenth.[35] Transmission of these scriptures has been less than ideal, resulting in numerous textual variants. Moreover, up until recently, all Daoist texts were transmitted without punctuation, and only a minuscule number of texts have been published in modern critical, collated editions. For all these reasons and to aid readers interested in the source behind my translations, I have included a punctuated, corrected Chinese text in traditional characters for all of them. Citation is to the 1923–26 Hanfenlou photo reprint of the original Ming edition, cited by chapter, page, recto (a = front) or verso (b = back), and then line number if necessary.[36] Citations of Buddhist works include the serial number of the scripture in the Taishō edition preceded by the letter "T," followed by the volume, page, and register (a, b, or c) on the page. Citations of the classics are to the 1815 *Shisanjing zhushu* edition reprinted by Yiwen Publishing in 1974. Citations of the dynastic histories are to the Zhonghua shuju punctuated editions, and other works are as noted in the bibliography.

34. The etymological meaning of this character is obscure, but, because the graph in oracle bone script looks like a rope tying a bundle of sticks or reeds together, it has been related to the character *di* 締, "to bind," suggesting that it might originally have referred to a sort of super-ancestor who "bound" all the branches of the royal family together.

35. On Daoist canons, see Ōfuchi 1979; the article by Judith Boltz in the *Encyclopedia of Taoism* (Pregadio 2008:1, 28–33); and the introduction to Schipper and Verellen 2004.

36. The bibliography also gives the serial number (beginning with DZ) of the scripture according to the enumeration in Schipper 1975b.

PART I

History

ONE

The Founding of the Celestial Master Church: External Evidence

The foundational period of any religion is key to understanding its significance both in its original historical milieu and in its later development. I will look systematically at all surviving external testimony for this period of Daoism's history in this chapter and then, in the following chapter, take up evidence from Daoist sources. There are four historical sources that provide information on the first few decades of Daoism's history. The earliest integral source is the *Record of the Three Kingdoms* (*Sanguozhi* 三國志), compiled by Chen Shou 陳壽 (233–97), which treats the period from the last few decades of the Latter Han (25–220 CE) until the final defeat of the Wu state in 280.[1] Much of the information in this source is also found, repeated with some variation, in the *Book of the Latter Han* compiled by Fan Ye 范曄 (398–445). Both relied on documents compiled by historians during the Latter Han. There is an early commentary to the *Record of the Three Kingdoms* written by Pei Songzhi 裴松之 (372–451) and a somewhat later one to the *Book of the Latter Han* by Li Xian 李賢

---

1. Chen's work was not completed until sometime after 280 and not presented to the throne until after his death, but the section on Wei, which is most relevant for its account of the Celestial Masters, may have been written as early as the 260s. See Cutter and Crowell 1999:63.

(654–84), both of which cite another important early source, the *Summary of the Archives* (*Dianlüe* 典略) by Yu Huan 魚豢 (fl. 220–32).[2] Chang Qu 常璩 (ca. 291–ca. 361) wrote the earliest surviving regional history of China, the *Record of Kingdoms South of Mount Hua* (*Huayangguo zhi* 華陽國志), focusing on Sichuan and surrounding areas. Finally, there is a biography of Zhang Ling 張陵 (fl. 142 CE) from the *Traditions of Divine Transcendents* (*Shenxianzhuan* 神仙傳) attributed to Ge Hong 葛洪 (283–343), part of which must be considered external and part of which looks to be based on internal testimony. I will first take up the account of Chen Shou, comparing it to that of Fan Ye, then consider the testimony of Yu Huan, and finally look at what Ge Hong has to tell us about Zhang Ling. I will be selective in drawing from Ge Hong, however, because he is late as well as physically remote from Sichuan and because parts of his account are simply not credible.[3]

2. Yu Huan's *Dianlüe* is listed in the bibliographic chapter of the *Sui shu* (33/961) as having eighty-nine chapters; Yu is described as a court gentleman (*zhonglang* 中郎) during the Wei, but almost nothing else is known about him. The *Dianlüe* is frequently cited in commentaries to the *Sanguozhi*, as is his *Weilüe* 魏略, which is presumed to be some portion of the larger work dealing specifically with the Wei state. The *Weilüe* is recorded in the *Jiu Tangshu* bibliography (46/1989) in thirty-eight chapters. Liu Zhiji 劉知幾 (661–721) tells us that the *Weilüe* ends during the reign of Emperor Ming 明帝 (226–39), and Chavannes concludes from this that the work was probably written between the end of that reign and the end of the dynasty, that is, between 239 and 265 CE. A similar date for the *Dianlüe* seems highly likely. See Chavannes 1905: 519–20.

3. Ge Hong clearly had some information concerning the Celestial Masters and had some books in his library that look to be from the Celestial Masters, but, in his expository work on transcendence, the *Master Who Embraces Simplicity* (*Baopuzi* 抱朴子), he makes no mention of them. Moreover, he was a dedicated proponent of alchemy, and this is reflected in his biography of Zhang Ling just as in his biography of Laozi. Finally, roughly two-thirds of his Zhang Ling biography is given over to a tale of Ling testing a disciple named Zhao Sheng that fits the pattern of a seeker of personal immortality rather than the communal salvation pursued by the Celestial Masters. See the further discussion of Ge Hong's biography of Zhang Ling below.

The *Record of the Three Kingdoms*

Chen Shou was a native of Anhan 安漢 (near modern Nanchong 南充) in Baxi 巴西 commandery, which was administered from modern Langzhong 閬中. This was in the heart of the area from which Zhang Lu 張魯 (?–215) drew many of his followers of Ba ethnicity. Chen was a student of Qiao Zhou 譙周 (ca. 200–270), a prominent local historian.[4] He should consequently have been intimately familiar with the area and had access to local historical sources. He was not himself, however, a follower of the Celestial Masters or of Ba ethnicity. This is evident in the account of Zhang Lu translated below and must be kept in mind when evaluating the information he provides. Chen placed his biography of Zhang Lu in the *Book of Wei* because of Lu's ties to the Cao family. I will first examine what that account tells us of political and military history, and then compare it to other surviving accounts, before considering evidence for the local community, its beliefs, and its practices:[5]

> Zhang Lu, cognomen Ziqi,[6] was a man of Feng in the kingdom of Pei.[7] His grandfather Ling had sojourned in Shu, studying the Dao in the Swan-Call Mountains. He fabricated books of the Dao, using them to beguile the commoners. Those who received the way from him would contribute five pecks of rice, and, for this reason, men of the day called them "rice bandits." When Ling died, his son Heng propagated his way. When Heng died, Lu continued to propagate it. Pastor[8] of Yi Province Liu Yan made Lu Marshal Supervising

4. On Qiao Zhou, see the detailed study of the man and his historiography in Farmer 2001, 2007.

5. *Sanguozhi*, Weishu 8/263–64.

6. The modern *Sanguozhi* gives Lu's cognomen as 公祺, but the *Hou Han shu* gives the homophonous form 旗, and the Tang Li Shan commentary to *Wenxuan* 44/13a quotes the *Sanguozhi* with the character used in the *Hou Han shu*, so it is difficult to know which to follow.

7. Modern Feng county, Jiangsu.

8. For translations of official titles, I make use of the system of translations developed for Kleeman 1998:211–15, based largely on the usages in the University

Volunteers (*duyi sima* 督義司馬).[9] Together with Marshal of the
Alternate Division Zhang Xiu, he led troops to attack Su Gu, the
Grand Warden of Hanzhong. Lu then ambushed Xiu and killed
him, stealing his force. When Liu Yan died, his son Zhang was established in his place. Because Lu did not obey him, Zhang killed
Lu's mother and family members. Lu then occupied Hanzhong. He
instructed the citizenry in his demonic way and called himself "Lord
Master" (*shijun* 師君). . . . He held Ba and Han by force of arms for
almost thirty years. In its last days, the Han dynasty did not have
the power to campaign against him, so they honored Lu as Leader
of Court Gentleman Quelling the Barbarians,[10] with the added title
of Grand Warden of Hanning.[11] All he had to do was send in tribute. A citizen found a jade seal in the ground, and all Lu's under-
lings wanted to elevate Lu to be King of Hanning. The merit officer
Yan Pu of Baxi remonstrated with Lu, saying, "The citizens of the
Han River valley number more than a hundred thousand households; they are wealthy, the earth is fertile, and the area is protected
on all four sides by strategic passes. If you support the Son of Heaven
above you, you will be [a hegemon] like Duke Huan of Qi (r. 684–
643 BCE) or Wen of Jin (r. 636–628 BCE);[12] at the worst you will be

---

of California Press's Chinese Dynastic Histories Translations series. These translations try to maintain the semantic content of the original rather than opting for
the functionalist translations of Hucker 1985. Pastor is an older alternative title
for provincial governor (*cishi* 刺史) that implied more independence of action.

9. This newly created title should be compared to terms like *yiding* 義丁, *yi-
bing* 義兵, *yijun* 義軍, and *yishi* 義師, all of which refer to irregular, private mi-
litias organized in response to a specific threat. Here the sense is that Zhang is
supplying his own troops. Note also the usage of the character *yi* in Zhang Lu's
charity huts (*yishe* 義舍) and the charity rice (*yimi* 義米) they offered travelers.

10. Following the reading of the *Hou Han shu*. The text originally read
"quelling the citizenry" (*zhenyi* 鎮民). Ren Naiqiang remarks on this curious
title, which also occurs in *Huayangguo zhi*, and suggests that the *Hou Han shu*
version is correct (1987:72). See Hucker 1581.

11. It is uncertain when the commandery was renamed Hanning. It may have
been instigated by Liu Yan or Zhang Lu and only affirmed in this appointment,
or it may have been an innovation of the Han court at this time. When Cao Cao
conquered the region in 215, he changed the name back to Hanzhong.

12. Huan and Wen are famous as hegemons (*ba* 霸) during the Spring and
Autumn period (771–469 BCE) who, during a period when the Zhou king had
already lost effective power, gathered the Chinese states together to fend off
external threats.

the equal of Dou Rong (16 BCE–62 CE)[13] and will not fail to be rich and honored. If you accept the appointment in this proclamation, your position will be sufficiently powerful to cut off lines of communication. You need not trouble yourself to become a king. I request that you not proclaim this [royal title]; do not take the first step toward disaster." Lu followed this advice.

張魯字公祺，沛國豐人也。祖父陵，客蜀，學道鵠鳴山中，造作道書以惑百姓。從受道者出五斗米，故世號米賊。陵死，子衡行其道。衡死，魯復行之。益州牧劉焉以魯爲督義司馬，與別部司馬張脩將兵擊漢中太守蘇固。魯遂襲脩殺之，奪其眾。焉死，子璋代立。以魯不順，盡殺魯母家室。魯遂據漢中，以鬼道教民，自號「師君」。。。。雄據巴、漢垂三十年。漢末，力不能征，遂就寵魯爲鎮民中郎將，領漢寧太守，通貢獻而已。民有地中得玉印者，群下欲尊魯爲漢寧王。魯功曹巴西閻圃諫魯曰：「漢川之民，戶出十萬，財富土沃，四面險固；上匡天子，則爲桓、文，次及竇融，不失富貴。今承制署置，勢足斬斷，不煩於王。願且不稱，勿爲禍先。」魯從之。

This account begins the tale with Zhang Lu's grandfather Ling, who first came to the Sichuan region and there founded a religion with sacred texts and a tithe of five pecks of rice. This faith was continued by Lu's father, Heng, and leadership of the movement passed on to Lu when his father died. Fan Ye and Chang Qu largely repeat this information, but Chang records a new title for Ling, "Mysterious and Primordial of Great Purity" (*taiqing xuanyuan* 太清玄元), which we can find attested in early Daoist sources.[14] Also, both locate Ling's place of study in the Crane-Call Mountains, rather than Swan-Call, which, as we shall see below, agrees with later Daoist sources.

13. Dou Rong had independent control of the Gansu region at the beginning of the Latter Han. When he submitted to Emperor Guangwu 漢光武帝 in 29 CE, he became an important official, and members of his family achieved positions of great power in the newly reestablished Han dynasty.

14. *Hou Han shu*; Ren Naiqiang 1987:72. We find this term as an appellation of the supreme Dao in *Nüqing guilü* 2/1a, *Chisongzi zhangli* 4/9a, 5/3b, and many other early Celestial Master scriptures. It may be that Chang misunderstood this expression.

In the context of the great military upheavals at the end of the Han dynasty, Zhang Lu associated himself with Liu Yan 劉焉 (?–194), a member of the royal house who had been appointed provincial governor, or "pastor," of the region.[15] His title, "marshal supervising volunteers," no doubt recognizes the fact that his religious followers also constituted a private army, much as the warlords of the day had at the core of their forces a body of relatives and dependent retainer families.[16]

We get a slightly different idea of their relationship in the biography of Liu Yan, where we read:[17]

> Zhang Lu's mother originally had the demonic way and also possessed a youthful appearance. She often visited Yan's home. For this reason, Yan sent Lu as marshal supervising volunteers, to be stationed in Hanzhong, there to cut off the way from [Bao] Valley to [Sword] Pavilion and kill the emissaries of the Han [court]. Yan submitted a letter saying that the rice bandits had cut off the road and that he could no longer communicate [with the court].
>
> 張魯母始以鬼道，又有少容。常往來焉家，故焉遣魯為督義司馬，住漢中，斷絕谷閣，殺害漢使。焉上書言米賊斷道，不得復通。

Chinese historians often use this device of including mutually contradictory information in different parts of the same book. One way to look at it is as a means of dealing with evidence that contradicts or does not fit together neatly with other passages. In Liu Yan's biography, we see the story from his perspective. There it is Zhang Lu's mother, not his father, Heng, who is important in

---

15. Liu Yan had in fact suggested this title for himself. Traditionally, provinces were headed by a regional inspector, who was charged with investigating and overseeing the actions of the grand wardens of the commanderies within his region but actually ranked below them and hence had little power. The title "pastor" (*mu* 牧), in contrast, was superior to the grand warden and conveyed real administrative authority. See Hucker 4041.

16. Ren Naiqiang points out this sense of "volunteer" (1987:74, n. 3).

17. *Sanguozhi*, Shushu 31/867.

gaining support for the family and its nascent religion. Although this reference to the mother's "youthful appearance" might at first glance appear to suggest some sexual appeal, it probably indicates the results of self-cultivation. Cao Pi 曹丕 (187–226) tells of two individuals who, because they were adept at circulating pneumas, "are old but have youthful appearances" 老而有少容.[18] Moreover, as we will see below, the wives of the three founding leaders of the movement enjoyed a special role in early Celestial Master ritual. Fan Ye, however, plays up the erotic aspect of the relationship, saying that Lu's mother had an "alluring appearance" (*zise* 姿色).[19] It is perhaps significant that Fan appends Zhang Lu's biography to Liu Yan's, rather than associating him with the Cao family.

This passage makes clear that Liu Yan's intent in sending Zhang Lu to Hanzhong was to provide an excuse for his own refusal to comply with central government directives; by interposing a military force that he could disown as religious extremists between himelf and the capital, Liu Yan hoped to remain independent from the Cao Cao–controlled court without risking open rebellion. This passage also confirms that Zhang Lu's "volunteers" are in fact his religious followers, whereas the troops under Zhang Xiu's command would have been loyal to Liu Yan, either the remnants of the Yellow Turban rebels or "soldiers from the Eastern Provinces" discussed below. Chang Qu's account of Sichuan under Liu Yan is much more explicit concerning his plans to rebel.

18. See the Pei Songzhi commentary, quoting Cao Pi's *Dianlun* 典論 at *Sanguozhi*, Weishu 29/805, n. 1. Ren Naiqiang makes a similar point, arguing that it was probably Liu Yan's wives and daughters who had converted to Celestial Master Daoism (1987:74, n. 4). Female novices in the church were indeed expected to study with a female master (see *Zhengyi fawen taishang wailu yi* 2a), supporting the suggestion that the primary object of proselytization for Zhang Lu's mother was the females of the household, but if the rite of Merging the Pneumas was first practiced by an initiate and a master of the opposite sex (see chapter 3), then this female Daoist priestess's presence in Liu Yan's court might have suggested a more intimate bond with him personally.

19. *Hou Han shu* 75/2432.

Zhang Xiu and Liu Yan

We must at this point confront the conundrum of Zhang Xiu 張脩. He occurs in Chen Shou's biography of Zhang Lu as another marshal who joined Lu in his attack on Hanzhong, then was killed by Lu, who incorporated his troops into his own forces.[20] A Zhang Xiu also occurs as a religious leader in the Basic Annals of the *Book of the Latter Han* for the year 184:[21]

> Autumn, seventh month. The wicked spirit medium Zhang Xiu of Ba commandery rebelled, plundering the commanderies and counties.
>
> 秋七月，巴郡妖巫張脩反，寇郡縣。

The commentary to this entry quotes the following passage from Liu Ai's 劉艾 *Record of Emperors Ling and Xian* 漢靈獻二帝紀, which may indeed be the primary source for Fan's record:

> At the time, the spirit medium Zhang Xiu of Ba commandery was healing illness, and those he healed would contribute five pecks of rice. He was called a master of the Five Pecks of Rice.
>
> 劉艾紀曰：「時巴郡巫人張脩療病，愈者雇以米五斗，號爲『五斗米師』。」

The most substantive account regarding Zhang Xiu is found in a passage from the *Summary of the Archives* of Yu Huan, quoted with minor variation in the commentaries to both the *Record of the Three Kingdoms* and *Book of the Latter Han* biographies of Zhang Lu:[22]

> During the Xiping reign period (172–78) wicked demonic bandits arose in great numbers. In the Three Auxiliaries region [around the former capital Chang'an], there was Luo Yao. During the Guanghe

20. An almost identical passage occurs in Fan Ye's biography of Zhang Lu. See *Hou Han shu* 75/2432.
21. *Hou Han shu* 8/349.
22. See *Hou Han shu* 75/2463, n. 5; *Sanguozhi*, Weishu 8/264, n. 1.

reign period (178–84), in the east there was Zhang Jue and in
Hanzhong there was Zhang Xiu. Luo Yao taught the citizens the
Method of Distancing [Oneself from] Concealment,[23] Jue created
the Way of Great Peace, and Xiu created the Way of Five Pecks of
Rice. In the Way of Great Peace, the master held a nine-segment
staff while creating talismans and spells, told those suffering illness
to kowtow and contemplate their transgressions, then gave them
talisman-infused water to drink. For those who had only suffered
their illness for a few days and recovered, he would say, "This person has faith in the Dao." Those who did not recover were then
those who did not have faith in the Dao. Xiu's methods were
roughly the same as Jue's. He also established quiet rooms and had
the ailing stay in them, contemplating their transgressions. He also
caused people to be unauthorized prefects [called] libationers. The
libationers were in charge of using the Five Thousand Characters of
Laozi, having [the followers] practice it together. He called these
unauthorized prefects "demon clerks." They were in charge of
praying on behalf of the ailing. The method of prayer was to write
the ailing person's full name and explain that they intended to accept their sin. They would make three copies, one of which would
be sent up to Heaven by placing it on a mountain, one of which
would be buried in the Earth, and one of which they would cast
into Water. He called them the Personally Written Missives to the
Three Offices. He caused the family of an ailing person to give five
pecks of rice as a constant practice and for this reason was called
the Master of Five Pecks of Rice. In fact, this was not effective in
curing illness; it was just licentious dissipation, but the menial people are benighted and stupid, and they vied to serve him. Later Jue
was executed and Xiu also died. At the time that Zhang Lu was in
Hanzhong, since its citizens believed in and practiced Xiu's system,
he augmented and embellished it. He taught them to establish charity

23. Little else is known about Luo Yao, and this term is obscure. Ren Naiqiang suggests, plausibly given the content of other movements of the time,
that it involved the confession of concealed evil action (1987:74, n. 6). Yamada
(1999:175) and Lü Pengzhi (2008:18) interpret *mian* as "to contemplate,"
linking it to the "contemplation of faults" 思過 that this passage attributes to
Zhang Xiu, but this definition is late and examples are ambiguous. *Ni* 匿 (= 慝)
in the sense of "concealing faults" is found in early sources like the *Erya* and Gan
Bao's 干寶 fourth-century *Chronicle of Jin* 晉記. See *Hanyu dazidian* 2333.

huts and placed rice and meat in them to draw in travelers. Those who had hidden small transgressions were to repair the road for a hundred paces, after which their sins would be expunged. He also, in accord with the Monthly Commands,[24] prohibited killing in spring and summer. He also prohibited alcohol. Migrants who took up residence in his territory did not dare refuse to follow this [faith].

典略曰：熹平中，妖賊大起，三輔有駱曜。光和中，東方有張角，漢中有張脩。駱曜教民緬匿法，角爲太平道，脩爲五斗米道。太平道者，師持九節杖爲符祝，教病人叩頭思過，因以符水飲之。得病或日淺而愈者，則云此人信道，其或不愈，則爲不信道。脩法略與角同，加施靜室，使病者處其中思過。又使人爲姦令祭酒，祭酒主以老子五千文，使都習，號爲姦令。爲鬼吏，主爲病者請禱。請禱之法，書病人姓名，說服罪之意。作三通，其一上之天，著山上，其一埋之地，其一沉之水，謂之三官手書。使病者家出米五斗以爲常，故號曰五斗米師。實無益于治病，但爲淫妄，然小人昏愚，競共事之。後角被誅，脩亦亡。及魯在漢中，因其民信行脩業，遂增飾之。教使作義舍，以米肉置其中以止行人；又教使自隱有小過者，當治道百步，則罪除。又依月令，春夏禁殺。又禁酒。流移寄在其地者，不敢不奉。

This passage is the earliest mention of many practices later associated with the Celestial Masters, but here they are attributed to Zhang Xiu, and Zhang Lu is only credited with adopting and expanding this existent cult. The passage also implies that Zhang Xiu was already dead, and not by Zhang Lu's hand, when Lu adopted his teachings. Pei Songzhi found this discrepancy troubling and suggests: "Zhang Xiu should be Zhang Heng. If this is not a mistake on the part of the *Summary of the Archives*, then it is a copyist's error" 臣松之謂：張脩應是張衡，非典略之失，則傳寫之誤. Note that in that passage Yu Huan, following Liu Ai, refers

---

24. The *Monthly Ordinances* is a genre of early calendar or almanac that sets out the activities proper to each month of the year. One example is preserved in the *Record of Rites* 禮記 (chapters 14–17 of the *Shisanjing zhushu* edn.), and a somewhat later example, the *Monthly Ordinances of the Four Estates* 四民月令 (mid-2nd c. CE), survives only in quotations and reconstructions. We cannot be certain what *Monthly Ordinances* is referred to here, but the *Record of Rites* records a prohibition on the "killing of young beasts" for the first month of spring. See *Liji zhushu* 14/23b.

to Zhang Xiu as a "master" (*shi* 師), the standard term within the church for a libationer who heads a parish and teaches novices, rather than a "lord master" (*shijun* 師君), the term that Chen Shou attributes to Zhang Lu and that is used in Daoist scriptures to refer to the first three leaders of the movement.[25]

It is interesting to note that Chang Qu, who had served under the Daoist rulers of the Cheng-Han state (302–47), also attributes all aspects of the religion to Zhang Lu and refers to Zhang Xiu only as a "subordinate" (*dangxia* 黨下) whom Lu sent to attack Hanzhong. Ren Naiqiang points out that there was a rebellion of followers of Zhang Jue's Way of Great Peace in the Sichuan area (1987:76, n. 11), which is dated 184 in *Huayangguo zhi* but 189 in the *Book of the Latter Han*. He suggests that Zhang Xiu was in fact part of the Yellow Turbans and that official recordkeeping was skewed because Liu Yan was only able to take up his post in 189, and he reported all intervening events to the court at the same time.[26] In the section on the Banshun Man barbarians, Fan Ye records: "In the fifth year of Zhongping [189] when the Yellow Turban bandits of Ba commandery arose, the Banshun Man barbarians took this opportunity to rebel again, raiding the cities" 至中平五年，巴郡黃巾賊起，板楯蠻夷因此復叛，寇掠城邑.[27] Thus, it seems that Liu Yan assumed command in Chengdu only in 189 and that Sima Guang was correct in placing the expedition against Hanzhong in 191.

There have been other responses to this rather confusing material. Some have suggested that the 184 spirit medium is not the same Zhang Xiu who accompanied Zhang Lu to Hanzhong. Zhang

---

25. See, for example, *Chisongzi zhangli* 3/9b, which refers to the "three lord masters and their wives" (*san shijun furen* 三師君夫人).

26. Supporting this, the first date in Yan's biography following his appointment is 191. Moreover, *Hou Han shu* 75/2432 attributes the raid on Ba commandery in 184 to Ma Xiang. Ren's comments are unfortunately colored by his claim that the Yellow Turbans were in fact an offshoot of the Celestial Masters. This is almost certainly incorrect; their rituals and deities were quite distinct, and we have the testimony of the *Da Daojia lingjie* 大道家令戒 of 255 disparaging Zhang Jue. See *Zhengyi fawen tianshi jiao jieke jing* 14b.

27. *Hou Han shu* 86/2843.

Xiu is a common name, and there is another Zhang Xiu alive at this time, operating in the Shaanxi area.[28] Liu Lin argues that Chang Qu identified the two because, in his account of Zhang Xiu killing the grand warden of Hanzhong Su Gu, he describes him as the "rice bandit Zhang Xiu."[29]

Some have even on this basis gone on to question the role of Zhang Ling and Zhang Heng in the origins of Celestial Master Daoism. In this interpretation, the Way of the Five Pecks of Rice created by Zhang Xiu was taken over by Zhang Lu, who owed his position solely to his beguiling mother, and the early history of the movement was fabricated.[30] This view ignores important evidence: The Zhang Pu 張譜 stele of 173, discussed below, records a group of Celestial Master libationers receiving a set of sacred scriptures and pledging to propagate the Way of the Celestial Masters. This stele antedates all of the recorded religious rebellions in Sichuan and was found southwest of Chengdu, far from the Ba region and near Swan-Call or Crane-Call Mountain, where Zhang Ling received his revelation. Moreover, Celestial Master documents record the creation of a system of twenty-four parishes to minister to the faithful by Zhang Ling (see fig. 1). The distribution of Celestial Master parishes is centered on the Chengdu plain and has only one outlying parish in Ba territory and three in Hanzhong, also reflecting a movement that began in western Sichuan and spread to the east and the north, rather than in either Hanzhong or Ba territory.

Ōfuchi Ninji accepts that Zhang Xiu was a libationer in the Celestial Master organization and suggests that he was probably assigned to the Yuntai parish in the foothills near Langzhong,

28. In 179 this Zhang Xiu, who held the rank of Leader of Court Gentlemen and was an emissary to the Xiongnu, was convicted of peremptorily beheading the Xiongnu ruler and executed. See *Hou Han shu* 8/343, 89/2964. Yet another Zhang Xiu was active as a military officer in 265. See *Sanguozhi* 4/153.

29. *Huayangguo zhi* 10b: Ren Naiqiang 1987:602; Liu Lin 1984:120, n. 7.

30. This is, for example, the argument of Liu Ts'un-yan (2002), who thinks that the "demonic Dao" is in fact the name of the faith taught by Zhang Ling, Heng, and Lu before taking over Zhang Xiu's movement. Lü Pengzhi (2008:17–19) also adopts this position.

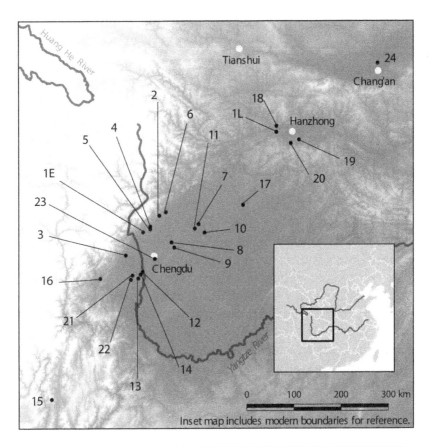

1	Yangping Zhi	9	Changli Shan Zhi	17	Yuntai Zhi
2	Lutang Zhi	10	Linshang Zhi	18	Jinkou Zhi
3	Heming Shan Zhi	11	Yongquan Zhi	19	Houcheng Zhi
4	Liyuan Shan Zhi	12	Choujing Zhi	20	Gongmu Zhi
5	Gegui Shan Zhi	13	Beiping Zhi	21	Pinggang Zhi
6	Gengchu Zhi	14	Benzhu Zhi	22	Zhubu Zhi
7	Qinzhong Zhi	15	Mengqin Zhi	23	Yuju Zhi
8	Zhenduo Zhi	16	Pinggai Zhi	24	Beiming Zhi

GIS data: CHGIS, Version 5. © Fairbank Center for Chinese Studies & the Institute for Chinese Historical Geography at Fudan University, Dec 2010. Made with Natural Earth free raster and vector data @naturalearthdata.com

FIGURE 1. Map of the original twenty-four parishes (*ershisi zhi* 二十四治) established by Zhang Daoling. Map by Angela R. Cunningham.

the later administrative center of Baxi commandery. In his view, Zhang Xiu did indeed lead a Celestial Master–centered uprising in this region in 184, coinciding with but unrelated to the activities of the Yellow Turban rebels.[31] He points out that the Ba tribesmen of this region are recorded as having rebelled against the state repeatedly around this time and that many Ba were followers of the Celestial Masters. When this uprising was suppressed and Liu Yan finally reached Sichuan in 189, he established relations with the former rebels and thus took Zhang Xiu into his service.[32] It was then at the instigation of Zhang Lu's mother that Lu was sent to Hanzhong and a fellow believer, Zhang Xiu, was sent to support him.

This resolves some issues but raises other questions. The Celestial Masters had been able to coexist with representatives of the state throughout Sichuan for quite some time; why would they rise in rebellion only in this region, and why did other parishes not come to their aid? Moreover, if Zhang Xiu was indeed head of a Celestial Master parish, why did he abandon it to come to Chengdu? Further, whereas Zhang Lu was given a very irregular appointment indicating that he commanded a force of his own religious followers, Zhang Xiu was given a normal army appointment, the same title given to one of Liu Yan's sons, and presumably commanded government-organized troops.[33] If he was truly Lu's subordinate in the church, why did he hold an equal rank?

It is significant that Chen Shou never refers to Zhang Xiu as a member of the Celestial Masters, and Chang Qu only calls him a "rice bandit" when he was operating under the direction of

31. See Ōfuchi 1991:6–49.

32. *Hou Han shu* 75/2432 tells us that Liu Yan "soothed and accepted those who had rebelled" 撫納離叛.

33. See *Sanguozhi* 31/867. Zhang Xiu's troops may have been drawn from the refugees who poured into Sichuan at this time and were organized by Liu Yan into a force colloquially referred to as "soldiers from the eastern provinces" (*dongzhou bing* 東州兵). After Liu Yan's death, these soldiers oppressed the locals, leading in 200 to a major rebellion of the elites of Ba commandery, which was suppressed with great difficulty. This was also the year that Liu Zhang killed Zhang Lu's mother and relatives, perhaps because Lu was unwilling to aid Zhang in combatting the rebellion. See *Hou Han shu* 75/2434.

Zhang Lu in Hanzhong. Chang in fact attributes the rebellion in Ba commandery to representatives of the Yellow Turban leader Ma Xiang 馬相, with no mention of Zhang Xiu at all, and we have seen that Fan Ye in at least one account blames Yellow Turbans from Ba. The accounts that associate Zhang Xiu with the Five Pecks of Rice movement are by Liu Ai and Yu Huan, neither a native of Sichuan and both writing from the capital. Although their accounts are early,[34] they can only be based on official reports to the court. Moreover, the earliest account of Zhang Xiu, describing events before Liu Yan's arrival in Sichuan, calls him an "evil spirit medium" (*yaowu* 妖巫). It seems likely, then, that Zhang Xiu was either a follower of the Yellow Turbans or simply a local religious leader who took advantage of the confusion to gather some discontents and rebel. If he was once a Celestial Master libationer, this rebellion would have marked a break with the church, which is why we find him in Chengdu serving Liu Yan. Yan needed the support of Zhang Lu's troops to be sure of conquering Hanzhong, with its natural strategic location, but he sent Zhang Xiu to watch over him and to make sure that the government representatives in the region were killed. We are told that Liu Yan, in sending Zhang Lu and Zhang Xiu to Hanzhong, instructed them to kill any court emissaries bound for Chengdu and then used this as an excuse for disobeying court directives. As we read in Yan's biography, however, he did find some way to report this to the court, and in the above missive he claimed that the "rice bandits have cut off the road."[35] It is likely this report that is the source of all the confusion. It is clear from Chang Qu's detailed account that it was Zhang Xiu and not Zhang Lu who was in the van and directly responsible for killing the grand warden Su Gu as well as his subordinates. In his report, Yan would undoubtedly have portrayed Xiu as a religious fanatic, operating as a member if not the leader of the "rice bandits." He may well have included some information concerning the beliefs of this

34. This is no doubt why Fan Ye accepts their viewpoint in the *Hou Han shu.*

35. See *Sanguozhi*, Shushu 31/867, translated above.

group of putative religious deviants, which we thus find in Yu Huan's *Summary of the Archives* attributed to Zhang Xiu. Chen Shou and Chang Qu, being based in Sichuan with access to local records, are not deceived and clearly attribute leadership of the "Way of the Five Pecks of Rice" to Zhang Ling and his descendants. Thus, Zhang Xiu was labeled the leader of the Celestial Masters, and a number of authentic Daoist practices were attributed to him by Liu Yan in order to blame the Daoists for Liu's own disloyal actions.

Such an interpretation answers many questions. It explains why Zhang Lu killed Zhang Xiu. We do not know if Zhang Lu really sanctioned the murder of Su Gu and his subordinates, but it seems likely that conflict would have arisen eventually with Zhang Xiu when court emissaries arrived. We know that, once Zhang Xiu was out of the picture, Zhang Lu did communicate with the court, offer tribute, and accept an appointment from the court as leader of court gentlemen and grand warden of the region. Moreover, Hanzhong was part of the original scope of the Celestial Master religion, with parishes established from the time of Zhang Ling. Zhang Lu no doubt sought to protect his followers and convert those not yet adhering to the faith, which would again have conflicted with Zhang Xiu's directives to watch out for Liu Yan's interests. Zhang Lu's mother and family members were still in Chengdu, ministering to his many followers in that region, so an open break with Liu Yan was avoided, but Zhang Xiu had to be eliminated, and his troops were not so much "stolen" as assimilated into the larger community. This also explains why all historical accounts of the group refer to it by an outsider's term, the Way of the Five Pecks of Rice, or even more derogatorily as "rice bandits." The tithe of five pecks was important, to be sure, as we shall see, but the Daoists called themselves the "Way of the Celestial Masters" in the 173 stele, and other church documents speak of the "Correct and Unitary Way of the Covenant with the Powers" (*zhengyi mengwei zhi dao* 正一盟威之道). The names used in historical sources confirm that these records were based on the account of a hostile outsider.

It is still somewhat remarkable that Yu Huan could produce a detailed account with such significant misattributions.[36] It seems likely that the account is a synthesis of two different sources of information. The first derived from a time when the court still knew only about Zhang Xiu as the conqueror of Hanzhong and representative of the "rice bandits." The second involved more accurate information about the movement, perhaps from Zhang Lu's reports to court, perhaps from the expansion of the movement itself into the capital region. Information concerning the Celestial Master movement reached the court in two stages. When Zhang Lu moved to Hanzhong, he was able to extend the reach of the Celestial Masters to the Wei River valley, and we see a new parish established there. After Cao Cao conquered Hanzhong in 215, great numbers of Celestial Master Daoists were moved to the area around Ye, where Cao Cao had his capital, as well as to the Wei River valley. Yu Huan must have learned more about the Celestial Masters, compared this to an earlier account that only reflected certain aspects of the movement, then concluded that the earlier version represented Zhang Xiu's creation and what he learned later, Zhang Lu's embellishment.

The Hanzhong Theocracy

Can we learn anything else about the Hanzhong community from conventional historical accounts of its relations with other states? A bit. We know that Liu Yan secretly hoped to establish himself as an independent power in the Sichuan basin. To this end, in 194 he sent five thousand troops to aid the rebellion of Ma Teng 馬騰 (d. 211) and Han Sui 韓遂 (d. 215), involving his two eldest sons, then in the capital Chang'an, in a plot to capture the capital.

---

36. There is another example of faulty information in Yu Huan's accounts related to Celestial Masters. He claims at one point that Liu Bei's son and heir, Liu Shan 劉禪 (207–71), was separated from him as a small child and sold as a slave, ending up in the area ruled by Zhang Lu, where he was discovered by a subordinate of Liu Bei and reclaimed. Pei Songzhi points out that this tale does not fit with the dates involved and Liu Shan's age at the time. See *Sanguozhi* 33/893–94.

When this plot failed, his sons were both executed. Soon thereafter lightning set his stronghold in Chengdu afire, burning it to the ground, and after that a boil appeared on his back, of which he eventually died. It seems likely that Yan believed there was a supernatural cause behind these events and blamed Zhang Lu.

Liu Yan had drawn upon the support of two groups, local Sichuan elites like Zhao Wei 趙韙[37] and a large contingent of refugees from central China, led by the father-in-law of Liu Zhang's eldest son, Pang Xi 龐羲, who had rescued many of Liu Yan's grandchildren after the debacle of 194.[38] When Yan died, they joined in nominating his son Zhang to replace him because he was considered malleable,[39] but by the year 200 the two groups were at loggerheads:[40]

> In the beginning several tens of thousands of people had entered Yi province from Nanyang [Henan] and the Three Auxiliaries [the Chang'an region]. Yan gathered all of them to be his troops, calling them "soldiers from the eastern provinces." Zhang was by nature pliant and easygoing, lacking in both authority and ability to plan. The men from the eastern provinces were aggressive and violent, posing a worry for the citizens, and Zhang could not control them. Many of his former officers were estranged and resentful. When Zhao Wei had been stationed in Ba, he had been very popular with the masses, and Zhang had entrusted him with authority. Because the sentiments of the people were unsettled, Wei secretly allied with the major clans in the province and, in the fifth year of Jian'an [200],

37. Zhao Wei, a native of Baxi commandery, had held a significant appointment as prefect of the imperial granaries (*taicang ling* 太倉令; see Hucker 6230) before resigning it to follow Liu Yan to Sichuan. Chen Shou describes him as a "high clerk" (*dali* 大吏) in Yan's provincial administration, but Chang Qu calls him a marshal in Yan's administration who was appointed leader of court gentlemen campaigning to the east and sent to attack Liu Biao at the same time that Zhang was appointed to succeed his father. See *Sanguozhi* 31/865, 867; Ren Naiqiang 1987:341.

38. See *Sanguozhi* 31/867, 870.

39. Chen Shou says that they "desired Zhang's warm benevolence" 貪璋溫仁. *Sanguozhi* 31/967.

40. *Hou Han shu* 75/2433.

returned [to Chengdu] to attack Zhang. Shu, Guanghan, and Qian-wei commanderies all rebelled in support. The men of the eastern provinces feared that they would all be executed, so they joined together and united their forces, fighting to the death for Zhang. They thus defeated the rebels, advanced, attacked Zhao Wei at Jiang-zhou [modern Chongqing], and beheaded him.

初，南陽、三輔民數萬戶流入益州，焉悉收以爲衆，名曰「東州兵」。璋性柔寬無威略。東州人侵暴爲民患，不能禁制。舊士頗有離怨。趙韙之在巴中，甚得衆心，璋委之以權。韙因人情不輯，乃陰結州中大姓，建安五年，還共擊璋。蜀郡、廣漢、犍爲皆反應。東州人畏見誅滅，乃同心幷力，爲璋死戰，遂破反者，進攻韙於江州，斬之。

It is in this context that we should read the next record from Chang Qu, which is repeated in Fan Ye's *Book of the Latter Han*:[41]

Zhang Lu gradually grew arrogant in Hanzhong; the Ba barbarians Du Huo, Pu Hu, and Yuan Yue rebelled and went over to Lu. Liu Zhang was angry and killed Lu's mother and younger brother[s]. He dispatched Leader of Court Gentlemen Pang Xi, of Hede [Henan province], to campaign against Lu, but Xi did not prevail. The Ba people rebelled daily, so he made Xi grand warden of Ba command-ery, stationing him in Langzhong to repel Lu.

張魯稍驕於漢中，巴夷杜濩、朴胡、袁約等叛詣魯。璋怒，殺魯母弟，遣和德中郎將龐羲討魯。不克。巴人日叛。乃以羲爲巴郡太守，屯閬中禦魯。

Chen Shou says simply that Zhang Lu refused to obey Liu Zhang's commands and relates that Zhang Lu repeatedly defeated Pang Xi. He places both events in the year 200, and it seems very likely that they are related.[42] The Ba clans that Zhao Wei drew on for

41. Ren Naiqiang 1987:5/346.
42. *Zizhi tongjian* (chapters 63–64) mentions the murder of Lu's mother before the rebellion of Zhao Wei and Wei's defeat only in the third month of 201, but none of the primary sources give exact dates, and this order is highly unlikely. Pang Xi had to first defeat Zhao Wei before he could be spared to attack Zhang Lu.

support in his rebellion may well have included the Han tribal leaders Du, Pu, and Yuan; certainly they were behind the rebellions that Pang Xi was assigned to suppress. The command that Lu refused to obey is never stated, but most probably it was a call from Liu Zhang to support him in his battle against Zhao Wei, or, if the Daoists were not allied with Wei, the Ba tribesmen, who, we will see, were followers of Celestial Master Daoism. It is significant that, after suppressing this rebellion in Ba, the leader of the "eastern province" forces Pang Xi was stationed in Ba and was repeatedly ordered to attack Lu.

Zhang Lu also became involved in the Liangzhou rebellion at a later stage. At that point Ma Teng had accepted a position in Cao's government but left his son Ma Chao 馬超 (176–222) in charge of his troops.[43] In 211, Cao sent his general Zhong You 鍾繇 (151–230) at the head of a force ostensibly to attack Zhang Lu, but, as soon as they entered the Wei River valley region, Ma Chao and Han Sui, fearing they were its real targets, rose in rebellion. They were defeated and fled, but Cao had Ma Teng and all members of his family executed. When Ma Chao was finally defeated in 214, he fled to Hanzhong, where Zhang Lu honored him with the title of lecturing libationer (*dujiang jijiu* 都講祭酒).[44] At this point, Zhang Lu also sent his general with ten thousand troops to support Ma Chao in an unsuccessful counterattack.[45] The most complete account preserved is the following passage from the *Summary of the Archives*:[46]

43. For a summary account of this complicated series of battles and alliances, see Haloun 1949. For specific incidents mentioned below, see *Hou Han shu* 72/2343. Ren Naiqiang sorts out some of the varying accounts, pointing out numerous errors (1987:342, n. 6).

44. In the traditional imperial academy, the lecturer (*dujiang*) aided the erudite in explaining the text to students. Later Buddhists adopted the term to refer to one who chants the scripture before the ritual master expounds upon it. In later Daoist ritual, the lecturer was a key member of the troupe that performs the ritual. It is uncertain, at this early date, where to locate the office along this line of development, but it was clearly an office with considerable ritual significance.

45. *Sanguozhi* 25/701.

46. *Sanguozhi* 36/946, n. 2.

Duke Cao campaigned to the west, battling with Ma Chao at the juncture of the Wei and Yellow Rivers. Chao and company were defeated and fled. Reaching Anding,[47] Chao then took flight to Liangzhou. There was a rescript ordering the arrest and extermination of Chao's family members. Chao was again defeated at Upper Long [eastern Gansu] and then fled to Hanzhong. Zhang Lu made him lecturing libationer and wanted to marry his daughter to him. Someone remonstrated with Lu, saying, "If there is someone who does not love their own relatives to such a degree, how can they love others?" Lu then desisted. Previously, before Chao had rebelled, Zhong, the younger brother of his concubine, had remained in the Three Auxiliaries. When Chao was defeated, Zhong entered Hanzhong before him. On the first day of the new year, Zhong wished Chao a long life. Chao beat his breast and vomited blood, saying, "My entire family, one hundred people, all shared the same fate in one day. Should we two now be congratulating each other?" Afterward, he repeatedly implored Lu for soldiers, wanting to take Liangzhou to the north. Lu sent them, but they were unsuccessful. Also Lu's general Yang Bai and others sought to disparage Ma Chao's ability, so Chao fled through Wudu into the Di area, then fled to Shu. This was in 214.

曹公西征，與超等戰於河，渭之交，超等敗走。超至安定，遂奔涼州。詔收滅超家屬。超復敗於隴上。後奔漢中，張魯以爲都講祭酒，欲妻之以女。或諫魯曰：「有人若此不愛其親，焉能愛人？」魯乃止。初，超未反時，其小婦弟种留三輔，及超敗，种先入漢中。正旦，种上壽於超，　超搥胸吐血曰：「闔門百口，一旦同命，今二人相賀邪？」後數從魯求兵，欲北取涼州，魯遣往，無利。又魯將楊白等欲害其能，超遂從武都逃入氐中，轉奔往蜀。　是歲建安十九年也。

Ma Chao, having returned to Hanzhong in defeat yet again, heard that Liu Bei 劉備 (161–223) had besieged Liu Zhang in Chengdu. He secretly contacted him and fled there to serve Bei. This apparently enraged Zhang Lu, who perhaps thought that Ma's conversion to the Celestial Master faith had been sincere because, when Ma Chao's son fell into his hands, it is said that Lu

47. North of modern Jingchuan 涇川, Gansu.

personally killed him.[48] This seems to be the only example of
Zhang Lu interceding in matters outside his own state. It may be
that he felt a common bond with Ma Chao because in 211 Ma had
attacked Cao Cao's force that was headed to invade Hanzhong. It
is also said that Chao enjoyed the support of many of the non-
Chinese peoples of the northwest, and this may have appealed to
Lu, whose religion encompassed many non-Chinese.

The Hanzhong state was an island of tranquility in the nearly
continuous warfare at the end of the Han. Hanzhong itself was
naturally defended by the Qinling mountains to the north and the
Ba mountains to the south, with the narrow Yangping Pass at its
western end the only entry point for a sizable armed force. It sat
across trade routes through the mountains linking Sichuan with
the Wei River valley to the north. Moreover, it was enriched by the
headwaters of the Han River. Traditionally the population numbered around a hundred thousand households, perhaps as many
as five hundred thousand individuals. We are told that several
tens of thousands of households (perhaps 150,000 to 250,000
people) fled the Wei River valley because of the Liangzhou rebellion, taking refuge with Zhang Lu. As we see in his biography, his
followers encouraged him to declare independence, but he resisted;
whether out of strategy or because he truly felt an allegiance to the
Han royal house, we cannot say.

At one point in 211, both Cao Cao and Liu Bei thought to
invade this rich oasis, but both were distracted by more urgent
situations elsewhere. Cao's forces encountered the uprising of Ma
Chao and Han Sui. Liu Bei established himself at Jiameng but in
217 was forced to come to the aid of Sun Quan 孫權 (182–252)
who was being threatened by Cao Cao. In abandoning his campaign against Zhang Lu, Liu Bei acknowledged that Lu presented
no threat, saying: "Lu is a bandit who just takes care of himself.
He is not worth worrying about" 魯自守之賊，不足慮也.[49] Although Zhang Lu aided Ma Chao and resisted the forces of Cao
Cao, he was inclined to favor Cao Cao over Liu Bei, as we see in

48. *Sanguozhi* 36/948, n. 3.
49. *Sanguozhi* 32/881.

this anecdote from a lost biography of Han emperor Xian 漢獻帝 (r. 189–220):[50]

The left leader of court gentlemen Li Fu sent a memorial to the king of Wei [i.e., Cao Pi], saying, "Long ago, when the former king [Cao Cao] had first established the state of Wei, those outside the border hearing this did not look into the matter, and all thought that he had been appointed king. Li Shu and Jiang He of Wudu were visiting Hanzhong, and they said to me, 'Surely he has become duke of Wei. It is not yet the right time to take the kingship. The one who secures the empire will be Cao Pi of Wei. He is the one whom the gods have charged with the mandate, and he will correspond with the talismans and prognostications to fill the position between Heaven and man.' I spoke of He's statement to General Quelling the South Zhang Lu. Lu also asked Jiang He if he knew the origin of this statement. He said, 'This is the jade tablet of Confucius. The reign years of the Son of Heaven can be known, though it be a hundred generations in the future.' A bit more than a month later, a refugee arrived who could write out a copy of the decree, and it was indeed just as Jiang He had said. Jiang He was adept at esoteric learning and was famous east of the passes. Although Lu was concerned in his heart for the country, he was mired in the vicissitudes of a heterodox way and in the end did not realize [the truth of] He's words. Later, when he was secretly discussing plans with his officials, the people of his state were not in agreement, some wanting to communicate with [Liu Bei in] the west. Lu then angrily said, 'I would rather be a slave of the Duke of Wei than a high retainer of Liu Bei!' In saying this he expressed his torment, and there truly was a reason for this."[51]

左中郎將李伏表魏王曰：「昔先王初建魏國，在境外者聞之未審，皆以爲拜王。武都李庶、姜合羈旅漢中，謂臣曰：『必爲魏

50. *Sanguozhi* 2/62–63, n. 2. The *Huayangguo zhi* specifies the date. See Ren Naiqiang 1987:347. Howard Goodman (1994) discusses this passage in considerable detail, but he misunderstands a couple of key phrases, in particular mistaking the nature of the confirmation supplied by the refugee and thus the overall significance of the document.

51. There is evidence that Lu's preference was widely known. When Sun Quan proposed that he and Liu Bei join in attacking Sichuan, he noted that "the rice bandit Zhang Lu occupies Ba and Han[zhong], acting as Cao Cao's eyes and ears, with designs upon Yi province." See *Sanguozhi* 32/880, n. 2.

公，未便王也。定天下者，魏公子桓，神之所命，當合符讖，以
應天人之位。』臣以合辭語鎮南將軍張魯，魯亦問合知書所出？
合曰：『孔子玉版也。天子曆數，雖百世可知。』是後月餘，有
亡人來，寫得冊文，卒如合辭。合長於內學，關右知名。魯雖有
懷國之心，沈溺異道變化，不果寤合之言。後密與臣議策質，國
人不協，或欲西通，魯即怒曰：『寧爲魏公奴，不爲劉備上客
也。』言發惻痛，誠有由然。」

Finally, in 215, Cao Cao was able to focus on Hanzhong. He
personally led an army out the San Pass 散關 but first had to deal
with the remnants of the Liangzhou rebellion, as we see in this
passage from Chen Shou's annals of the Wei state:[52]

In the third month, the duke campaigned against Zhang Lu in the
west. Reaching Chencang, he was about to enter the Di regions from
Wudu. The Di blocked the road. He sent Zhang He, Zhu Ling, et al.,
ahead to attack and break them. In summer, the fourth month, the
duke emerged from Chencang through the San Pass, reaching Hechi.
The Di king Dou Mao had a force of over ten thousand men. Relying
on his strategic position, he would not submit.[53] In the fifth month,
the duke attacked and slaughtered them. With the west pacified, the

52. *Sanguozhi* 1/45. Much of the following can be confirmed by a contemporary source, the "Announcement to the Wu Generals, Colonels, and Troops" 檄吳將校部曲文, written by the famous poet Chen Lin 陳琳 (d. 217) and preserved in the *Wenxuan*. There we read, "When we advanced and approached Hanzhong, then Yangping could not be defended, and a force of a hundred thousand crumbled like dirt and decomposed like fish. Zhang Lu escaped, fleeing into Ba. Grateful for mercy and repenting his transgressions, he sent in hostages and returned to surrender. King of the Ba Pu Hu and Marquis of Cong Town Du Huo, each leading their tribes, turned over Ba commandery and accepted positions from the king" 進臨漢中，則陽平不守，十萬之師，土崩魚爛，張魯逋竄，走入巴中，懷恩悔過，委質還降；巴夷王朴胡賨邑侯杜濩，各帥種落，共舉巴郡，以奉王職. See *Wenxuan* 44/13b.
53. Ren Naiqiang argues that it was because the Di were firm adherents of Celestial Master Daoism that they were willing to defend Hanzhong at the cost of their lives (1987:77, n. 19). If it were true that the faith had already spread to the non-Chinese peoples of the northwest, that might explain Zhang Lu's willingness to aid Ma Chao, but the fact that it took Cao over a month to move from the site of this battle to Yangping Pass suggests that the Di might just have objected to Cao moving a large army through their territory.

generals of Jincheng, Qu Yan, Jiang Shi, et al., joined together to behead Han Sui and sent his head [to Cao Cao]. In autumn, the seventh
month, the duke reached Yangping. Zhang Lu sent his younger
brother Wei and his general Yang Ang to defend Yangping Pass. They
built a wall between the mountains, extending more than four kilometers. They were attacked but could not be routed, so [Cao] with-
drew the army to return. When the bandits saw the great army re-
treat, they let down their guard. The duke then secretly sent Xie Piao,
Gao Zuo, and others to use the defiles to strike them at night and
won a great victory. He beheaded their general Yang Ren and advanced to attack Wei. Wei and company fled during the night.

三月，公西征張魯，至陳倉。將自武都入氐，氐人塞道。先遣張
郃、朱靈等攻破之。夏四月，公自陳倉以出散關，至河池。氐王
竇茂眾萬餘人，恃險不服。五月，公攻屠之。西平、金城諸將麴
演、蔣石等共斬送韓遂首。秋七月，公至陽平。張魯使弟衞與將
楊昂等據陽平關，橫山築城十餘里，攻之不能拔，乃引軍還。賊
見大軍退，其守備解散。公乃密遣解儵、高祚等乘險夜襲，大破
之，斬其將楊任，進攻衞，衞等夜遁。

Pei Songzhi quotes a collection of memorials (*biao* 表) to the
effect that Zhang Lu had already fled, but Wei refused to surrender.[54] Cao had brought a force of a hundred thousand troops and
was told the mountains at Yangping were too far apart to be defended, but he did not count on the fortifications. There was apparently a protracted battle, leaving many wounded, and his large
force was running short of food.[55] Cao was on the point of withdrawing when Zhang Wei's camp was first disrupted by a large
herd of several thousand elaphure (*mi* 麋) that ran through it. Then
a troop of Cao Cao's soldiers led by Gao Zuo 高祚 that had got lost
in the mountains at night happened into the camp. When Gao

54. *Sanguozhi* 8/265, n. 1.
55. In Liu Ye's 劉曄 biography we read: "When they reached Hanzhong, the
mountains were steep and the army's food was quite short. [Cao Cao] said: 'This
is a cursed kingdom. What can I do to possess it? My army lacks food. It would
be best to quickly go back'" 既至漢中，山峻難登，軍食頗乏。太祖曰：「此妖
妄之國耳，何能爲有無？吾軍少食，不如速還。」. Liu is said to have convinced
Cao Cao to continue the attack, which succeeded through concentrated volleys
of crossbow fire. See *Sanguozhi* 14/445.

sounded the drums and horns to gather his troops, Zhang Wei thought Cao Cao's army had ambushed him and surrendered. We learn a bit more about Lu's surrender in his biography, including the fact that Lu initially intended to surrender but was stopped twice, by his younger brother and by Yan Pu 閻圃:[56]

> When [Cao Cao] reached Yangping Pass, Lu wanted to surrender Hanzhong. His younger brother Wei was unwilling and led a force of several tens of thousands to hold the pass, resolutely protecting it. [Cao Cao] attacked and broke them, thus entering Sichuan. When Lu heard that Yangping had fallen, he was about to kowtow [in surrender].[57] Yan Pu said: "If you go now under compulsion, you will certainly receive slight credit for it. It would be better to rely upon Du Huo and go to Pu Hu to hold him off, and only later offer hostages. The credit you receive will be greater." Thereupon he took flight through the southern mountains and entered the central Ba region.[58] His attendants wanted to burn all the treasures and goods in the storehouse. Lu said: "I originally wanted to pledge my fate to the state but was unable to realize this intention. Now I flee to avoid the sharp blade [of the assault]. It is not that I have evil intentions. The storehouse of treasures and goods belongs to the state." He then sealed it up and left.
>
> 建安二十年，太祖乃自散關出武都征之，至陽平關。魯欲舉漢中降，其弟衞不肯，率眾數萬人拒關堅守。太祖攻破之，遂入蜀。魯聞陽平已陷，將稽顙，圃又曰：「今以迫往，功必輕。不如依杜濩赴朴胡相拒，然後委質，功必多。」於是乃奔南山入巴中。左右欲悉燒寶貨倉庫，魯曰：「本欲歸命國家，而意未達。今之走，避銳鋒，非有惡意。寶貨倉庫，國家之有。」遂封藏而去。

It seems that the Ba region was an important center of support for Zhang Lu throughout this period. In 200 CE, Chang Qu tells

---

56. *Sanguozhi* 8/264–65.

57. Following Lu Bi in rejecting the addition by the Zhonghua edition editors of the two characters *guixiang* 歸降. There is no need and no support for emending the text in this way. See Wu Jinhua 1990:58–59.

58. Liu Bei's biography specifies that he fled to Baxi. See *Sanguozhi* 32/894.

us, the Ba kings Du Huo,[59] Pu Hu, and Yuan Yue had supported Zhang Lu in his quest for vengeance.[60] Fan Ye relates that, when Liu Zhang sent the general Pang Xi to attack Lu, it was because Lu "had most of his armed troops in the land of Ba" (*buqu duo zai Ba tu* 部曲多在巴土) that Lu was able to defeat Pang and come to "dominate Ba and Han[zhong]" (*xiong yu Ba Han* 雄於巴漢).[61] Now threatened by Cao Cao's troops, he turned to the Ba again, taking refuge in Bazhong. Ren Naiqiang speculates that he first offered Pu as a hostage and only surrendered when he saw him well treated, but surviving texts cannot confirm this detail. Liu Bei also sent his general Huang Quan 黃權 to seek Zhang Lu's allegiance but was too late. Lu and the Ba kings all submitted to Cao Cao:[62]

Consequently, Lu entrusted hostages to [Cao Cao], who appointed Lu General Quelling the South and enfeoffed him as Marquis of Xiangping. He also enfeoffed his five sons as nobles. At the time, [Liu Bei] had gone east to Gong'an (Hunan).[63] Ba and Han[zhong] submitted. [Cao Cao] appointed the kings of the Ba Du Huo, Pu Hu, and Yuan Yue as grand wardens of the three Ba commanderies. He left General Campaigning in the West Xiahou Yuan and Zhang He as well as Regional Inspector of Yi Province Zhao Yu to protect Hanzhong and transferred its citizens to Guan[zhong] and Long[xi] [Shaanxi and eastern Gansu].

遂委質魏武。武帝拜魯鎮南將軍，封襄平侯。 又封其五子，皆列侯。 時先主東下公安。巴、漢稽服。魏武以巴夷王杜濩、朴胡、袁

59. Du is elsewhere identified as marquis of Cong town 賨邑侯.

60. Ren Naiqiang 1987:72. Ren believes that Du was from modern Dianjiang, where there was a "Cong King city" 賨王城, whereas Pu was the closest to Hanzhong, based in modern Pingliang 平梁 in Bazhong county, and suggests that Yuan Yue may have been from Xuren 朐忍 (west of modern Yunyang 雲陽, Sichuan), where a seal engraved "Han Marquis of Cong Town" 漢賨邑侯 was discovered (1987:76, n. 14). *Zizhi tongjian* reads Ren Yue 任約 for Yuan Yue 袁約.

61. *Hou Han shu* 75/2434.

62. Ren Naiqiang 1987:73.

63. Following Liu Lin in reading Gong'an for Jiang'an 江安. Ren would emend to Jiangzhou 江州. See Liu Lin 1984:120, n. 1.

約爲三巴太守。留征西將軍夏侯淵，及張郃、益州刺史趙顒等守
漢中。遷其民於關隴。

Cao Cao's dominance in the area was short-lived. Huang
Quan later defeated Du and Pu and killed Xiahou Yuan, taking
Ba and Hanzhong for Liu Bei.

Chen Shou tells us a bit more about Zhang Lu's fate. Hanzhong was famous for its wealth and bounty. Cao Cao was impressed that Lu had sealed his storehouse for Cao's use:[64]

> When [Cao Cao] entered Nanzheng, he was very pleased by it. He
> also thought that Lu originally had good intentions and sent some-
> one to console and encourage him. Lu brought his entire family out
> [to surrender]. Cao welcomed him and appointed Lu General Paci-
> fying the South. Treating him with ceremony appropriate to a guest,
> he enfeoffed him as marquis of Langzhong with an appanage of ten
> thousand households. He enfeoffed Lu's five sons and Yan Pu, mak-
> ing all of them marquises. He took Lu's daughter as wife for his son
> Pengzu. When Lu died, he was given the posthumous title of For-
> given Marquis, and his son Fu succeeded him.
>
> 太祖入南鄭，甚嘉之。又以魯本有善意，遣人慰喻。魯盡將家出，太
> 祖逆拜魯鎮南將軍，待以客禮，封閬中侯，邑萬戶。封魯五子及閻
> 圃等皆爲列侯。爲子彭祖取魯女。魯薨，諡之曰原侯。子富嗣。

The Basic Annals places the surrender of the three Ba kings in the
ninth month of 215, with Zhang Lu surrendering only in the eleventh month.[65] Either Zhang Lu wanted to see how they would be
treated, or he hoped to improve his position by sending his allies
to Cao Cao first.

---

64. *Sanguozhi* 8/265. Again we find contemporary confirmation of this in
Chen Lin's "Announcement": "Lu, Hu, and Huo all enjoyed enfeoffments of
ten thousand households. Lu's five sons each received an appanage of one thousand homes. The sons and younger brothers of Hu and Huo, as well as their
generals and colonels were made nobles, more than a thousand people from
the rank of general on down" 魯及胡濩皆享萬戶之封。魯之五子，各受千室之
邑。胡濩子弟部曲將校爲列侯、將軍已下千有餘人. See *Wenxuan* 44/14a.

65. See *Sanguozhi* 1/46.

Cao Cao was famous for showing magnanimity toward those who surrendered, but the favor shown Zhang Lu, extending to all five of his sons, was remarked on widely by contemporaries. There is evidence that Lu's second son, Guang 廣, was a special favorite of Cao Cao and married a woman of his family. The eldest, Fu, succeeded to Lu's fief and presumably leadership of the movement as well.[66] Although the Cao family was known to enforce strict laws against some forms of religious activity, the Celestial Masters seem to have thrived under the Wei, and it may be that they shared a common cause in opposing practices that the Daoists, as we shall see in the next chapter, condemned as "false arts."[67]

Cao Cao also showed special favor to Lu by marrying Cao Yu 曹宇, also known as Pengzu 彭祖, to Zhang Lu's daughter. Yu was Cao Cao's son by Lady Huan 環氏 and was especially close to his nephew Cao Rui 曹叡, canonized Enlightened Thearch 明帝, who ruled from 226 to 239. Yu held a variety of enfeoffments, culminating in King of Yan, and in 238 was named Cao Rui's successor but declined the honor and returned to Ye.[68] His son Huan 奐 (245–302) eventually reached the throne, ruling as the last emperor of the Wei from 260 to 264, and was canonized at death as the Primordial Thearch 元帝. It seems unlikely that Huan was the son of Zhang Lu's daughter since he was born thirty years after she was married. It is interesting to note that Cao Yu's sobriquet Pengzu 彭祖 links him to an individual famous for extreme longevity, which might imply a link to his Daoist marital relations, but such sobriquets are usually given in adolescence, and we do not know Cao Yu's age at betrothal.[69]

66. See *Taiping yulan* 518/3b–4a; Tang Changru 1983:222, n. 2.
67. Tang Changru (1983) has difficulty in understanding how a Cao law against certain types of sacrifice and skepticism on the part of some members of the Cao family toward seekers after immortality could have not included the Celestial Masters, but he admits that the movement seems to have grown during this period.
68. See *Sanguozhi* 14/459, 20/582.
69. It is said that Cao Yu's friendship with Cao Rui was because they grew up together. If they were about the same age, Yu might have been only around ten at the time of his betrothal, and it would seem more possible that the sobriquet

Even less is known of Zhang Lu's daughter, but a legend recorded in the *Commentary to the Scripture of Rivers* 水經注 associated a complex of sacred sites in Hanzhong with a daughter of Zhang Lu:[70]

> The river to the south empties into the Han River. South of this is Lady Mountain, and on the mountain is the Lady's Tomb. Seen from a distance, the mountain tomb is lofty and imposing. When you come to the place, one sees it has the shape of a tomb. On the mountain there is a straight road that descends, devoid of trees or bushes, and people today call it the Lady's Road. Below it is the Lady's Temple and the Pounding Clothes Stone. It is said to be a temple to the daughter of Zhang Lu. There is a small stream that flows north, emptying in the Han River, and it is called the Lady's River.
>
> 其水南注漢水。南有女郎山，山上有女郎塚，遠望山壇，嵬嵬狀高，及即其所，裁有墳形。山上直路下出，不生草木，世人謂之女郎道。下有女郎廟及搗衣石，言張魯女也。有小水北流入漢，謂之女郎水。

Thus, although her name has not been transmitted to us, legends say that a daughter of Zhang Lu was eventually buried in Hanzhong and commemorated there. Various recent sources cite Sima Biao's "Record of Commanderies and Kingdoms" (*Junguo zhi* 郡國志) stating that the lady had been washing clothes when she was impregnated by a mist, then killed herself out of shame, after which a dragon appeared from her womb. This topos is often associated with a royal birth. Even if this tale in some sense relates to Zhang Lu, the lady was clearly not the daughter married to Cao Yu. More likely, the story simply testifies to the continuing fame of Zhang Lu in the Hanzhong area some centuries after his death.

The staunch defense of Hanzhong put up by Zhang Wei without the support of Zhang Lu, and perhaps after he had already

---

referred to his Daoist connections. It is curious that the sobriquet seems unrelated to his name.

70. See Wang Guowei 1984:27/879–80; Zhang Zehong 2012:123 lists other early references to the legend.

fled to the south, convinced Cao Cao that to avoid future trouble he had to break up the Celestial Master community. One target of these transfers was the Wei River valley and the Gansu corridor, that is, regions to the northwest. Pu Hu, Yuan Yue, and Li Hu 李虎, all members of the Cong 賨 ethnic group, were moved to the area north of Lüeyang.[71] It was from this area that Li Hu's descendants would lead Celestial Master migrants in a return to the Sichuan region at the beginning of the fourth century to establish the state of Cheng-Han.[72] Another major focus of resettlement was to the east, to the region around the Cao base at Ye (modern Handan city, Hebei) and Luoyang, where at least eighty thousand persons were moved.[73] Although Zhang Lu was granted a marquisate at Langzhong, it seems that he and his family moved to Ye with their new in-laws. Tao Hongjing 陶弘景 (456–536) tells us that Zhang Lu died soon thereafter, in 216, and was buried to the east of Ye.[74] When his son Fu succeeded to his fief, he no doubt also succeeded to his position as head of the Celestial Master church. The net effect of Cao Cao's transfers was to spread the Celestial Master faith across North China. By the time the Wang family of Langya migrated south after the fall of the Western Jin in 317, they had been Celestial Master Daoists for generations.

Daoist Institutions and Life in Hanzhong

Having examined the events preserved in early secular histories concerning the Celestial Masters, I now turn to what these same sources can tell us about the ritual practices and institutions employed by

71. Ren Naiqiang 1987:483. See *Sanguozhi* 15/472, which records the transfer of "several tens of thousands of households," which might indicate a group twice as large or greater, to this region at the urging of Zhang Ji 張既.

72. See chapter 4.

73. *Sanguozhi* 23/666. One good example is the family of Zhao Qin 趙廞, who was pastor of Yi province at the beginning of the fourth century; he was originally from Baxi and was moved to the east together with the Zhang family. See Ren Naiqiang 1987:447.

74. *Zhen'gao* 4/14b6.

Zhang Ling, Zhang Heng, and Zhang Lu. Since analysis of the passages referring to Zhang Xiu indicated that they represent a misattribution of authentic material concerning the Celestial Masters—whether through the willful deception of Liu Yan or because Zhang Xiu had indeed at one point been a local libationer in the movement who happened to come to the attention of authorities through his involvement in a local rebellion—I will treat this material as applying to the organization founded by Zhang Ling. I begin, as before, with the biography of Zhang Lu in Chen Shou's *Record of the Three Kingdoms*, which sets this material clearly within a tradition beginning with Zhang Ling:[75]

> He [Zhang Lu] instructed the citizenry in his demonic way[76] and called himself "Lord Master." Those who came to him to study the way at first were all called "demon troopers." When their initiation into the main body of the way was confirmed, they were called "libationers." Each had charge of a division of troops. Those whose troops were many became great libationers at the head of a parish (*zhi*). All of them taught to be honest and not to deceive. If one had an illness, he would confess his transgressions. In general, they resembled the Yellow Turbans. The libationers all set up "houses of charity," which were like the neighborhood relay stations today. They would also place "charity rice and meat" there, hanging them in the houses of charity so that passersby could, gauging their hunger, take an adequate amount. If they took too much, the demonic way would inevitably inflict illness upon them. Those who broke the law were forgiven three times, and only after this were they punished. He did not establish magistrates and clerks, using the libationers to administer all affairs. Both the citizens and the barbarians found this convenient and were pleased.
>
> 以鬼道教民，自號「師君」。其來學道者，初皆名「鬼卒」。受本道已信，號「祭酒」。各領部眾，多者爲治頭大祭酒。皆教以誠信不欺詐，有病自首其過，大都與黃巾相似。諸祭酒皆作義舍，如今之亭傳。又置義米肉，縣於義舍，行路者量腹取足；若

75. *Sanguozhi* 8/264.
76. Or perhaps "about the demonic Dao." See the discussion below.

過多，鬼道輒病之。犯法者，三原，然後乃行刑。不置長吏，皆
以祭酒爲治，民夷便樂之。

This passage tells us a good deal about the organization of the early church. Most worship groups in the Chinese common religion are diffuse and voluntary. If you live in the vicinity of a temple, you are usually considered a patron of that temple and expected to contribute to its periodic ceremonial observances, but there is no clear list of adherents, and individuals choose to patronize different temples and address their requests to different deities based on a variety of factors, including proximity, the nature of their problems, the specialization of the deity, and the deity's reputation for divine efficacy (*ling* 靈). The Celestial Masters at this early point in their history seem to have functioned differently. One formally entered the church, was initiated, and was given a specific designation, then progressed through a hierarchy, gaining new titles. The church thus provided a basic social organization for its communities distinct from that of traditional society.

The term cited here for new believers is unusual; there is no surviving Daoist scripture, inscription, or other document that refers to believers as "demon troopers." That term does occur with some frequency in the Daoist canon, but always in reference to large bodies of netherworld troops used to arrest and execute malicious, disobedient demons and monsters of various sorts. Later Daoists refer to the common mass of believers as "citizens of the Dao" (*daomin*). In the Zhang Pu stele of 173, Hu is a "demon soldier" (*guibing* 鬼兵) in service to the Heavenly Elder, a Daoist deity; he does not seem to be a living mortal. The passage from Yu Huan's *Summary of the Archives* mentions "demon clerk" (*guili* 鬼吏) as an alternative term for the libationer, whom he characterizes as an illegitimate prefect."[77] This term *guili* is also found

77. This passage has given rise to considerable confusion and may be defective. The versions in the *Hou Han shu* and *Sanguozhi* differ slightly, and here I follow Fan Ye. I read it: "He also made people illegitimate prefect

in the Daoist canon but always refers to an underworld official, usually one who oversees the dead in the hells. It is possible that the earlier church used these terms metaphorically, but if so, they seem to have fallen out of use quickly. It seems also possible that an outsider, hearing a Daoist ritual or catching sight of a document, might have misunderstood references to spirits employed by the Daoists.

The title used for the basic level of religious leader is "libationer" (*jijiu* 祭酒), a usage widely attested in Daoist scriptures and inscriptions from the second century to the fifth. The term originally referred to a local elder or notable chosen to make the opening oblation at the village communal banquet to the god of the soil (*she* 社). Although it was used by the Han government as an honorific title for the chancellor of the Imperial Academy (Taixue 太學), it was also used to refer to country gentlemen.[78] The text then introduces the "parish-heading great libationer." This exact term is not otherwise known, but one of our earliest sources, the revealed exhortation titled *Yangping Parish*, addresses itself to a variety of early officers of the church, including a group called "parish-heading libationers" (*zhitou jijiu* 治頭祭酒).[79]

The head of this alternate system of organization was a hereditary member of the Zhang family. Zhang Ling had established the position by claiming the title of Celestial Master. To distinguish their position in the founding of the church, his son Heng was frequently referred to as *sishi* 嗣師, or "inheriting master," and his grandson Lu was known as *xishi* 系師, or "successor

libationers. . . . He called these illegitimate prefects 'demon clerks'" 又使人爲姦令祭酒…號姦令爲『鬼吏』. "Prefect" 令 was the normal term for the head of a county under the Han, and it is precisely these people who the libationers replace in Hanzhong. *Shuowen* defines *jian* 姦 as *si* 私 "private"; the *Guangya*, as *wei* 僞, "false"; and it is used in the Han to refer to counterfeit coin (*jianqian* 姦錢). Some have tried to understand *jianling* 姦令 as "prefects [who control] evil," but this seems strained, and I can find no example of a similar usage.

78. See Hucker 542. Ōfuchi gives numerous examples of Han-period teachers and elders down to the level of the village (*li* 里) being referred to as libationers (1991:149–50).

79. *Zhengyi fawen tianshi jiao jieke jing* 20b. This text was composed in or shortly after 220.

master." In this passage we see a general term by which early Celestial Masters were known within the community, *shijun* 師君, or "lord master." The title "master" alone was much more widely applicable, being used for any libationer who instructed novices.[80] A typical invocation of the founding three generations can be found, for example, in *Master Redpine's Petition Almanac*:[81]

> I kowtow and reverently announce upwards to the Supreme Lord Lao, the Celestial Master, the Inheriting Master, the Successor Master, the wives of the three lord masters, and the administrators in their service.
>
> 稽首謹上啓太上老君、天師、嗣師、系師、三師君夫人、門下典者。

Here we should note that the spouses of the first three Celestial Masters were also honored as potent deities. We will look at the role of women in the early church more closely below, but this fact helps explain the prominent role of Zhang Heng's widow at the court of Liu Yan.

Chen Shou's account further notes that Zhang Lu used libationers to administer his government in place of the traditional prefect or elder (*zhang* 長). Here we see that Hanzhong under Zhang Lu was a true theocracy, with a single class of official dealing with both temporal and religious matters. The Celestial Masters had a uniquely religious system of organization as well, the parish. I will examine the system of parishes in greater detail below, but for now note that Celestial Master communities were defined in a way that was at variance with the political system of provinces, commanderies, and counties maintained and manned by the Chinese empire. Within this theocracy, at least nominal membership in the church must have been almost universal. Yu

---

80. See, for example, the petitions in *Zhengyi fawen taishang wailu yi*.

81. *Chisongzi zhangli* 5/9a. This sort of invocation is found many places in the canon with minor variations in wording. Sometimes Zhang Ling's wife is mentioned immediately after him, and the wives of his son and grandson are only implied. This example, with its single invocation of a single deity, seems to me particularly early.

Huan notes that "migrants who took up residence in his territory did not dare refuse to follow [the faith]."[82] It does not, however, seem that the movement was predicated on theocratic rule. After the dissolution of the Hanzhong theocracy, libationers must have maintained special authority within communities where Celestial Master believers predominated, but they functioned alongside traditional government officials, just as they had before Hanzhong and as they did during the half-century of the Daoist-led Cheng-Han state.

The histories also record a charitable institution that seems to have been unique to the early decades of the church, the "charity huts" (*yishe* 義舍). There is no mention of them among surviving Daoist sources, so we have only these historical accounts to rely on. Our text compares them to the relay stations (*tingzhuan* 亭專) established by the government.[83] These stations were set up every ten *li* (roughly 2.5 miles) to provide lodging and food for government representatives and messengers. They also extended the government into local communities, providing public safety functions as well as overseeing registers of population and land tenure for tax purposes. It seems that nonofficials could also stay there for a fee. Since they were staffed by locals rather than centrally appointed and dispatched officials, they were also the closest and most intimate level of government. The charity huts were intended to replace this vital institution. Their primary innovation was that they were open to anyone without cost. At a time of war and epidemic, when large segments of the population were forced to leave their native places, such an institution must have been very inviting to both travelers and migrants. We can see the proselytizing function of these hostels in the warning that, if anyone took more food than needed, the "demonic way" would punish him or her.[84] No doubt the charity huts provided a location where

82. See the passage from the *Summary of the Archives* translated in full above.

83. On relay stations, see Ōfuchi 1991:163–69.

84. Yu Huan puts a negative connotation on this, saying that the hostels "put rice and meat there in order to cause travelers to stop."

the libationer could come into contact with nonbelievers, and the charity provided there demonstrated the compassionate, moralistic aspect of the faith. The word I translate "charity," *yi* 義, also has the sense of "righteous, according to one's duty," and Yu Huan applies it to the rice and meat as well.

The rice placed in the charity huts no doubt derived from the tithe that each household was supposed to contribute. Every source mentions the "five pecks of rice" in connection with the movement, and this was so identified with the Celestial Masters that, as we have seen, every outsider term for them, from the rather neutral "way of the five pecks of rice" to the openly derogatory forms like "rice bandits" or "rice spirit mediums" (*miwu* 米巫), alludes to the tithe. One reason for this is no doubt that rice was something of a luxury good over most of China, which was too dry for paddy rice and lacked the excellent irrigation system of the Chengdu plain. The term we translate "five pecks" is actually equal to around ten liters in the Han dynasty, or about 1.1 U.S. peck, a bit more than forty cups—a modest amount.[85] We will see below that this tithe was regularly collected at the second (7/7) or, at the latest, the third (10/5) of the three annual Assemblies, and a certain portion of it was to be sent on to the central administration of the Celestial Master, while the rest was retained at the local level to feed the libationers and be redistributed through periodic communal banquets.

At this point we must take up the testimony of Ge Hong in his biography of Zhang Ling. Unique among our sources, he does not refer to the religion by an outsider's name like Way of the Five Pecks of Rice, nor does he mention terms like "demon trooper" not found in extant scriptures. Instead, after telling of the office of libationer, he mentions some of the duties of the believers:[86]

---

85. At the beginning of the Han, Chao Cuo 晁錯 (d. 154 BCE) had argued an average family farming one hundred *mu* of land (roughly eleven acres) would produce around one hundred *dan* 石 or one thousand "pecks"; hence this tithe would represent 0.5 percent of an average year's production. See *Han shu* 24A/1132. Schipper claims this is 25 kilos of rice (2000:29).

86. *Taiping guangji*, ch. 8, entry 3. Cf. Campany 2002:349–56.

He also established an itemized code by which his disciples, according to the matter, would contribute rice, silk, vessels, paper, brushes, firewood, and miscellaneous objects.

并立條制，使諸弟子，隨事輸出米絹器物紙筆樵薪什物等。

Here we see the traditional contribution of rice listed alongside a variety of other goods. Most can be found in texts like *Master Redpine's Petition Almanac* in lists of pledge offerings (*xinwu* 信物, *guixin* 賄信). These are objects contributed by the petitioner as attestation of their faith and to defer the cost of the ritual. Most are objects actually used in writing the documents that are central to the ritual, like silk, paper, and brushes. The "vessels" may be jars to hold ink or vermilion for sealing. Firewood is not found among these lists but was a common fine for offenses. Thus, in this passage Ge Hong seems to be providing some insight into the workings of the church based on real scriptures.

Since the Hanzhong church assumed governmental responsibilities, it had to deal with lawbreakers. Chen Shou tells us that the Daoist government was unusually lenient is prosecuting bad conduct: "Those who broke the law were forgiven three times, and only after this were they punished."[87] Fan Ye and Chang Qu repeat this point. Ge Hong does not record the three forgivenesses but does mention that the Celestial Master focus was on preventing misconduct through shame:[88]

Ling also wanted to govern people using integrity and shame. He was not fond of employing corporal punishment and fines, so he established a system that caused people who suffered an illness to write down every sin they had committed since they were born. They then threw this handwritten document into the water and entered into a covenant with the gods that they would not again offend against the law, pledging their own death to secure the bond. There-

87. See the passage from his biography of Zhang Lu under "Daoist Institutions and Life in Hanzhong" above.
88. *Taiping guangji*, ch. 8, entry 3.

upon, every time the common people encountered an illness, they were always to confess their transgressions so that, first, they might get better, and, second, they would be ashamed and regretful and would not dare offend again, reforming themselves out of a fear of Heaven and Earth. Thenceforth, all who disobeyed or offended would reform and be good.

陵又欲以廉恥治人，不喜施刑罰，乃立制，使有疾病者，皆疏記生身已來所犯之皋。乃手書投水中，與神明共盟約，不得復犯法，當以身死爲約。於是百姓計愈邂逅疾病，輒當首過，一則得愈，二使羞慚，不敢重犯。閱畏天地而改，從此之後，所違犯者，皆改爲善矣。

This perceptive comment gets to the heart of the Celestial Master program of justice. Other sources give more detail about the ritual confessions. Chen Shou says merely that "all [libationers] taught to be honest and not deceive. If one had an illness, he would confess his transgressions." Yu Huan gives the most complete description:

> [The libationers] were in charge of praying on behalf of the ailing. The method of prayer was to write the ailing person's full name and explain that they intended to accept his or her sin. They would make three copies, one of which would be sent up to Heaven by placing it on a mountain, one of which would be buried in the Earth, and one of which would be cast into Water. They called them the Personally Written Missives to the Three Offices.
>
> 主爲病者請禱・請禱之法，書病人姓名，說服罪之意。作三通，其一上之天，著山上，其一埋之地，其一沉之水，謂之三官手書。

This is the beginning of the tradition of petitioning Heaven. I will explore these personal confessions in a later chapter.[89] In addition, there was an institution called the "quiet room" or oratory, where "sick people were to stay and contemplate their transgressions" 加施靜室，使病者處其中思過。 Eventually, if not at this point,

89. See chapter 6.

every family was expected to have an oratory in which to perform its ritual obligations.

There was also a type of public service or good works that one did as penance. Yu Huan says: "They taught that if there was one who had hidden a minor transgression, he or she should repair a road for one hundred paces, then the sin would be absolved" 教使 自隱有小過者，當治道百步，則罪除. Ge Hong mentions the same practice, but treats it as a public duty rather than penance:

> [Ling] led the people in repairing and restoring the roads, and all those who did not participate he would cause to get sick. If in the county there were a bridge or road that needed repairing, the commoners would cut the grass or clean out the muck. There was nothing they would not do at his behest.
>
> 領人修復道路，不修復者，皆使疾病。縣有應治橋道，於是百姓 斬草除溷，無所不爲，皆出其意。

The claim that Zhang Ling would cause the person misbehaving to fall ill seems a bit out of place, but Chang Qu does say that, if someone took more than what would satisfy one's hunger at the charity hut, "the demons would make him or her sick" 鬼病之 Chen Shou had said that the "demonic Dao" (guidao 鬼道) would do this. This is the same demonic Dao about which Zhang Lu taught the people of Hanzhong. It is difficult to understand the term with precision because this is its first usage in this sense.[90] One sense of the term *dao* for the early Celestial Masters was a personified high god who spoke directly to Daoists in the words of the *Laozi*. "Demon" was rather ambiguous. The Three Offices (*sanguan* 三官) to whom one addressed petitions administered both a recordkeeping system where good and evil acts were recorded and hell-like realms of the dead where punishment was applied for evil acts. They employed demons in both capacities. Whether *guidao* referred to a "demonic

90. In the Former Han the term had been used to refer to the eight spirit paths by which gods would come to feast on the offerings at the suburban sacrifice. See *Shiji* 12/456. This usage does point out the similarity of the terms for "ghost" and "god" during the Han.

way" or system in which evil was requited with sickness, misfortune, and ultimately postmortem punishment, or to a demon-employing Dao who was the ultimate overlord of that system, it would be a frightening prospect for evildoers.[91]

The texts tell us a bit more about general ethical rules. Chen Shou says that Zhang Lu taught his followers "to be honest and not to deceive." Chang Qu says regarding the regulation of commerce that "the merchants in their markets charged equitable prices" or else they ran the risk of demon-inspired illness.[92] Yu Huan tells us that the Daoists "in accordance with the *Monthly Ordinances* prohibited killing in spring and summer" and "prohibited wine." The *Monthly Ordinances* survives as a chapter of the *Record of Rites* but was also a series of principles cited regularly in divergent forms by Han period rulers.[93] The prohibition on killing, which extended to animals, during the seasons of growth and reproduction makes a certain ecological sense but was really founded on a more involved idea of acting in harmony with natural rhythms understood as alternations of the forces of yin and yang. Ōfuchi points out that "prohibitions" on wine were common at that time (even Cao Cao, who elegized wine often in his poems, did it) and probably referred only to a prohibition on the sale of wine.[94] Such a prohibition seems problematic in light of the use of wine in the Daoist communal banquets known as "kitchens."[95] Finally, though it is not men-

91. If I am correct in speculating that one reason for the rift between Zhang Lu and Liu Zhang was suspicions that Liu Yan's fatal illness was linked to the Celestial Masters, this aspect of the movement would have been behind those doubts.

92. Ren Naiqiang 1987:72. Liu Lin (1984:116, n. 7) cites the *Zhengyi fawen jingzhang guanpin* (1/18a–b), which mentions a god with 120 assistants whose responsibility it is to butcher those who sell wine, open shops to sell to the poor, or use inaccurate weights and measures to cheat their customers.

93. There is also an early version preserved in the *Lüshi chunqiu*, on which see Knoblock and Riegel 2000:39–41.

94. Ōfuchi 1991:149–51. The *Taipingjing* also prohibits the sale of wine (69/7a).

95. A later Buddhist source says that the Daoists were known for "limiting wine" (*zhijiu* 制酒). *Taishō daizōkyō* 2102, T52:49a.

tioned as a value, interethnic harmony seems to have been an important part of the ethos in early Celestial Master communities. Chen Shou, Fan Ye, and Chang Qu all mention that both Chinese and non-Chinese found the faith appealing, and Zhang Lu, in particular, seems to have relied on various Ba-minority groups repeatedly. Daoism is still popular today among many non-Chinese minorities in southern China and mainland Southeast Asia.[96]

The historical texts do not say much about the foundations for these teachings, other than Yu Huan mentioning that the libationers "were in charge of using the Five Thousand Characters of Laozi, having [the followers] practice it together" 主以老子五千文，使都習.[97] It is also said that Zhang Ling created some sort of Daoist text(s) in twenty-four scrolls, but nothing is said of their contents. In the next chapter I will explore these issues and try to fill out our understanding of the early church through internal documents created by the Celestial Masters themselves.

96. On the role of Daoism as an alternative form of Chinese cultural identity for non-Chinese groups, see Kleeman 2002.

97. The *Laozi*, also known as the *Scripture of the Way and Its Virtue* (*Daodejing* 道德經), is conventionally said to be five thousand characters long, but most versions are a bit longer. It is thought that the Daoist version was exactly five thousand characters. There has been a debate as to whether this term *duxi* 都習, which I have translated "practice," signified choral recitation or merely explanation and study. Unfortunately, the term is so rare, occurring nowhere else in the histories and nowhere in the Daoist canon, that it is difficult to answer this question definitively.

TWO

The Founding of the
Celestial Master Church:
Internal Documents

We have determined, on the basis of clearly dated historical sources, that there was an organized religion based in the Sichuan region of western China by the 190s CE. It was referred to by outsiders as the Way of the Five Pecks of Rice as well as pejorative related terms like "rice bandits." It had a distinctive religious hierarchy with uniquely named religious offices, a hereditary succession of leaders spanning three generations, and a clearly defined body of believers who practiced distinctive rituals. Moral conduct was central to the group's ethos, and an important ritual focused on the confession of sin, with absolution being won through the submission of written documents. The faith used the text of the *Laozi* as one source of its teachings but also had its own scriptures of some sort. The Celestial Masters were able to establish a theocratic state in the Hanzhong region of northwest China that lasted nearly thirty years in which religious officiants called libationers replaced traditional state officials, enforcing a particularly lenient code of laws, maintaining a network of communal charitable institutions, and regulating commerce in the interests of the common good.

Thus was the foundation laid for one of the great world religions, which commanded the allegiance and inspired the conduct of vast numbers of believers over the following eighteen centuries and continues to be a vital element of Chinese culture wherever it is found. In this chapter, we will look at this foundational period as the Daoists understood and recorded it in their scriptures.

The Revelation to Zhang Ling

The historical sources we looked at in the last chapter had very little information on Zhang Ling. We learned that he was originally from Feng in the kingdom of Pei, in eastern China (modern Jiangsu province) and had come to Sichuan during the reign of Emperor Shun (126–44 CE) to "study the Dao" in the Swan-Call or Crane-Call Mountains.[1] He is said to have created books about the Dao (Fan Ye says "books of talismans" or perhaps "talismans and books," *fushu* 符書) in order to "beguile the masses" and to have demanded the famous five pecks of rice from those who chose to follow him. None of the historical accounts even tell us his cognomen, which is what all but his closest family members would have called him.

Ge Hong, who seems to have had access to some internal documents, is the only early external source to tell us more, but much of what he says is not credible:[2]

> Zhang Daoling, cognomen Fuhan, was a man of Feng in the kingdom of Pei. He was originally a student in the Imperial Academy and was broadly conversant with the Five Classics. Late in life he sighed, saying, "This will not add to my lifespan." Consequently, he studied the way of longevity. He obtained the *Yellow Thearch's Nine Cauldron Elixir Method*[3] and wished to compound the elixir, but the

---

1. Most commentators assume both terms refer to the same place.

2. *Taiping guangji*, ch. 8, entry 3. For a full translation of this biography, see Campany 2002:349–56, and for detailed notes on variant versions of the tale, 531–33.

3. On this basic scripture of alchemical lore, see Pregadio 1991. It is worth noting that the scripture claims to have been revealed to the Yellow Thearch by the Mystic Woman, both figures whose teachings on arts of the bedchamber are specifically condemned in the *Xiang'er* commentary to the *Laozi* (see below).

ingredients required much cash and silk cloth. Ling's family was poor. Though he wanted to make a living, he was not good at either tending the fields or raising animals, so he never completed the process. He heard that most of the people of Sichuan were pure and generous, and easy to teach, and that there were many famous mountains, so he entered Sichuan with his disciples. He lived on Swan-Call Mountain and composed books of the Dao in twenty-four fascicles.

張道陵者，字輔漢. 沛國豐人也。本太學書生，博通五經。晚乃歎曰，此無益年命，遂學長生之道。得黃帝九鼎丹法，欲合之，用藥皆糜費錢帛。陵家素貧，欲治生，營田牧畜，非已所長，乃不就。聞蜀人多純厚，易可教化，且多名山。乃與弟子入蜀，住鵠鳴山，著作道書二十四篇。

Much of this seems at best the stuff of legends. Ge is the first source to record the name Daoling, with the addition of the character *dao* to indicate his religious status. The cognomen Fuhan means "assists the Han dynasty," which would suggest that he aspired to an important historical role, but cognomens normally are related to the name, and it is difficult to see how this could be related to his name, which means "hill, tumulus" or, as a verb, "to ascend."[4] If he had indeed been a student at the Imperial Academy, trained in the classics, that fact would surely have been noted by earlier, more conventional sources. The statement that he was poor, with his only options being farming or raising livestock, also contradicts this claim. Moreover, if Zhang Ling had dropped out of the Imperial Academy, where elite youth were groomed for a life of government service, why was it already "late in life"? And where did he acquire a company of disciples, and what did he teach them? Given that he traveled to Sichuan in search of famous mountains, it is not inconceivable that he had a yearning for long life, but in early Daoist materials there is no trace of alchemy, which, as Sivin has shown and this passage admits, was

4. For example, the Han period Li Ling 李陵 had the cognomen Shaoqing 少卿, or "young minister" (meaning he would rise in office early); Jin period king Sima Ling 司馬陵 had the cognomen Zishan 子山, "baby mountain"; and Shen Yue's son Ling was styled Jinggao 景高, "shining heights." See *Han shu* 54/2450; *Jin shu* 37/1113; *Song shu* 100/2445.

always a rich man's pursuit and, as Strickmann has revealed, often resulted in preplanned suicide.[5]

As noted in the previous chapter, Ge Hong does seem to have had some information on the religious community established by Zhang Ling, but, after quickly passing over that material, he dwells at great length on a tale that portrays Ling as a standard aspirant for personal transcendence. He is credited with magical powers like the ability to appear in dozens of different locations at once. He is said to have succeeded in creating an elixir of immortality but took only half to avoid immediately ascending to Heaven. We see one reason for this portrayal in Ge Hong's assertion that Zhang Ling used the same formulae that Ge possessed, merely "changing the order here and there." He is said to have entrusted his alchemical secrets to only two disciples, Wang Chang 王長 and a man named Zhao Sheng 趙昇, whose time of arrival and physical appearance Ling had predicted in advance. Ling then tests Zhao Sheng seven times, berating him for forty days, tempting him with gold and women, frightening him with tigers, seeing if he will feed and clothe a destitute beggar, and finally demanding he throw himself off a cliff to get his master some peaches. All through this story, there is not one mention of religious activities like being appointed libationer or parish-heading libationer, writing talismans, composing petitions, confessing sins, or praying and performing penance. In this regard, this account resembles closely Ge Hong's biography of Laozi, which also records religious belief in Laozi as a deity manifesting repeatedly in this world under various guises to lead the people and the state to salvation but explicitly rejects such beliefs in favor of a view of Laozi as a normal mortal who practiced alchemy and attained

5. See Sivin 1976, 1978; Strickmann 1979. In rejecting this image of Zhang Ling, I thus deny Robinet's speculation that he might have been a normal independent quester after immortality whose grandson established the Celestial Master movement (1984:72–73). Such a reading of history does not accord with the Zhang Pu stele of 173, which shows an organized religion before Zhang Lu's time, nor with the biography under discussion, which has him as a religious founder, but only as a method to gain the money for his alchemical pursuits. See also Strickmann 1979:167, n. 131.

immortality. If Ge Hong did not make up the Zhang Ling story himself out of whole cloth, he has chosen a tale about a transcendence seeker named Zhao Sheng, who may have claimed a lofty but poorly understood pedigree linking him to Zhang Ling, and made that the center of the biography.[6]

Just as Ge Hong had recorded accounts of Laozi that he ultimately did not accept, he also includes a tale of a revelation to Zhang Ling that fits poorly with the image of an alchemist and transcendence seeker. This we can accept as an authentic piece of church lore, perhaps not historical in a strict sense but authentically part of the traditions passed down through the church organization concerning Zhang Ling and Swan-Call Mountain:

> He concentrated his thought and refined his intentions. Suddenly there were men descending from the Heavens and cavalry astride tigers and golden chariots with feather canopies pulled by teams of dragons too numerous to count. One figure was announced as the Scribe Below the Pillar, another as the Lad from the Eastern Sea. They bestowed upon Ling the Newly Emerged Correct and Unitary Dao of the Covenant with the Powers. Having received this, Ling was able to heal illness. Thereupon commoners flocked to serve him as their teacher. His disciples came to number several tens of thousands of households.
>
> 乃精思鍊志。忽有天人下乘騎，金車羽蓋驂龍駕虎，不可數。或稱柱下史，或稱東海小童。乃授陵以新出正一明威之道。陵受之，能治病。於是百姓翕然奉事之以爲師。弟子戶至數萬。

"Scribe Below the Pillar" refers to Laozi as the historian of the Zhou royal court; the Lad from the Eastern Sea is a southern god not otherwise found in Celestial Master scriptures but a key figure in the transmission of alchemical texts.[7]

The most significant phrase in this account is "Newly Emerged Correct and Unitary Dao of the Covenant with the Powers." It

6. For a view of transcendents not as supernatural beings but as human mystics making contentious claims in seeking fame and patronage, rather like medieval Christian eremites, see Campany 2009.

7. On the Lad from the Eastern Sea, see Kroll 1985 and Campany 2002:356.

embodies many of the ideas that make the Celestial Masters distinctive. "Correct Unity" (*zhengyi* 正一)[8] is still today a common way of referring to Celestial Master priests, liturgy, scriptures, and so on. It implies that the Celestial Masters are the one and only correct way to approach the gods. The covenant is equally important, an idea that high gods descended and entered into a new relationship with human beings. One aspect of this covenant is embodied in the confession ritual discussed in the previous chapter, wherein members of the church admit to committing sins and undertake to never repeat them, in return for which they are absolved of guilt and pardoned from any punishment. Another element, we shall see below, is a pledge not to offer blood sacrifice to profane deities.

This is perhaps the most majestic surviving account of the initial meeting between Zhang Ling and a heavenly host that results in the establishment of the new religion. It is not, however, the earliest. That is found in *Yangping Parish*, a revealed teaching from the spirit of Zhang Ling himself, which dates to sometime between 220 and 231 CE:[9]

> On the first day of the fifth month of the Han'an reign period [June 11, 142 CE], I received the Dao from the divine pneuma of the August Thearch-King of the beginning of the Han. Taking five pecks of rice as a pledge of faith, I want to allow all worthy people capable of transcendence to ascend to salvation.
>
> 吾以漢安元年五月一日，從漢始皇帝王神氣受道，以五斗米爲信，欲令可仙之士皆得升度。

Here we see an affirmation of the importance of the rice tithe for the movement. Moreover, this statement, recorded less than thirty years after the confrontation between Zhang Lu and Zhang Xiu, provides excellent support for the contention that Yu Huan's

8. Note that I use the adjectival form "unitary" to translate this term in this phrase but adopt the nominal "unity" in subsequent references to the group.
9. *Zhengyi fawen tianshi jiao jieke jing* 20b. On this text, see Bokenkamp 1997:149–85 and the full translation in the next chapter.

attribution of the practice of collecting five pecks of rice to Zhang
Xiu is mistaken. Individuals alive at that time would certainly have
been among the audience for this document and would have known
if the claim that the rice tithe dated to the beginning of the movement was false. The term given here for the revealing deity is
unique in the canon and may represent a textual corruption. The
closest parallel is to the description of the aspirants to the registers
in the ritual formulae recorded in the *Most High's Correct and
Unitary Ritual Registers of the Covenant with the Powers*, who is
said to have "previously borne on my person the divine pneumas
of the newly emerged Lord Lao, the Most High Exalted August
Thearch-King" 素被新出老君太上高皇帝王神氣在身.[10] Given the
unanimity of other references to this event, it seems safe to assume what is intended is some reference to the divinized Laozi.

There is a second revealed text, the *Commands and Precepts
for the Great Family of the Dao*, dating to the middle of the third
century (255 CE), that also refers to Zhang Ling's revelation:[11]

On the first day of the fifth month of the Han'an reign period, at
Redstone Castle in Qu district of Linqiong county of Sichuan, the
Dao created the Way of the Correct and Unitary Covenant with the
Powers in order to seal a contract with Heaven and Earth, establish
the twenty-four parishes, and distribute the Mysterious, Primordial,
and Inaugurating pneumas to govern the citizens.

道以漢安元年五月一日，於蜀郡臨邛縣渠停赤石城造出正一盟威
之道，與天地券要，立二十四治，分布玄元始氣治民。

These two precious sources, revealed to a community of believers
including some who had experienced the Hanzhong theocracy,

10. See, for example, the Adolescent One General Register rite at *Taishang
zhengyi mengwei falu* 1b. There is very similar language, omitting the reference to the "newly emerged Lord Lao" at *Taishang zhengyi yansheng baoming
lu* 1a. Bokenkamp points out that Lord Yellow Stone at the beginning of the
Han was identified with Laozi in Han apocrypha and was the master of Zhang
Liang, who is claimed as Zhang Ling's ancestor (1997:171). Perhaps this is the
figure referred to obliquely here.

11. *Zhengyi fawen tianshi jiao jieke jing* 14a–b.

give us an exact date and place for the revelation. Zhang Ling is said to have come to Sichuan during the reign of Emperor Shun 漢順帝 (126–44), and we have a stele from 173 showing considerable organization in the church, so this date is credible. Linqiong county was administered from modern Qionglai 邛崍, roughly 65 kilometers southwest of Chengdu. Today Crane-Call Mountain is identified, plausibly, with a site due north of this, roughly 50 kilometers due west of Chengdu.

The second passage records three important elements in the founding of the faith. First it specifies that the "covenant with the powers" was indeed a sort of contract linking mortals to the cosmic powers of Heaven and Earth. Second, it records the establishment of the system of twenty-four parishes at the founding moment of the church. No doubt it took some time to actually bring this system into being, but the distribution of parishes accords with an origin in the Chengdu area.[12] Finally, it lays out the basic Celestial Master cosmology of three pneumas still evoked in Celestial Master ritual today.

The revealing deity of the *Commands and Precepts* is the Dao itself, a personified supreme deity. Earlier in the revelation, this is explained in more detail:[13]

When the age of the Han had already been fixed, the last successor ran roughshod and the populace chased benefit, with strong and weak contesting passionately. The Dao grieved for the lives of the citizens, which, once lost, could not be restored. For this reason, he caused Heaven to bestow a pneuma to govern the citizens, calling it the Newly Emerged Demon Lao. Why do we speak of demons? People only fear demons; they do not believe in the Dao. Therefore it was the Demon Lao who bestowed upon Zhang Daoling the position of Celestial Master, most revered, most divine, and he thus became the master of the people.

漢世既定，末嗣縱橫，民人趣利，強弱忿爭。道傷民命一去難還，故使天授氣治民，曰新出老鬼。言鬼者何？人但畏鬼，不信道。故老鬼授與張道陵爲天師，至尊至神，而乃爲人之師。

12. For a more detailed description of the parish system, see chapter 8.
13. *Zhengyi fawen tianshi jiao jieke jing* 14a.

Here we see that the Dao was moved by the war and destruction of the Latter Han to first produce an avatar of himself and use this to transmit the position of Celestial Master to Zhang Ling, who is here already honored with the style Daoling. In this translation I have emended the transmitted text, which calls the Dao's manifestation "the newly emerged Lord Lao" 新出老君. As Liu Zhaorui (2005) has pointed out, the following sentence makes no sense with that reading but perfect sense as an explanation of the term "Demon Lao" 老鬼.[14] The Liu Ji 劉覬 land contract of 485, excavated in 1956, begins with a charge to a long list of underworld officials prefaced "By command of the talisman of the newly emerged Demon Lao, the Supreme Lord Lao" 新出老鬼太上老君 符勅.[15] Here "Demon Lao" is clearly an alternate term for the Most High Lord Lao.

There are two other Daoist scriptures with strikingly similar language. In the *Demon Statutes of Lady Blue* 女青鬼律, which I will argue dates to the late third century, we read:[16]

The Heavenly Dao uses demons to aid gods in deploying pneumas. People fear demons; they do not fear gods, so [the Dao] deceptively employs a name from among them [i.e., demons] to refer to its own position.

天道以鬼助神施炁，人畏鬼，不畏神，詭託名於彼，自號其位。

14. Bokenkamp provides an elegant English translation of the text as it stands (1997:171), but the grammar does not support his reading. He also takes the Dao, rather than the people's fate, as the subject of the clause "once lost could not be restored," understanding it as a reference to the Dao withdrawing from the world, but it is unclear why the Dao would find it difficult to return. Finally, he takes "most revered, most divine" to be a reference to the qualifications of Zhang Ling rather than the office of Celestial Master, which is possible but seems a bit forced.

15. Liu Zhaorui 2005:173. Liu's article is flawed in many respects, misunderstanding the 173 stele, misdating Daoist scriptures, granting unquestioned credence to the historical accounts and Buddhist polemics, and making unwarranted assumptions concerning the social background and level of education of Celestial Master believers, but his central argument is sound.

16. *Nüqing guilü* 1/8b.

The fifth-century *Scripture of the Inner Explanation of the Three Heavens* 三天內解經 invokes the Supreme Lord Lao in the following terms:[17]

> The Most High during the time of Emperor Shun of the Han chose an imperial emissary to pacify and rectify the rule of the Six Heavens, sort out the true and the false, and illuminate the pneumas of the superior Three Heavens. On the first day of the fifth month of the first year of Han'an, a *renwu* year [sexagenary year 19], Lord Lao met with the Daoist priest Zhang Daoling in a stone chamber on Mount Quting in Shu commandery and led him to visit the newly emerged Most High at the great parish at Kunlun. The Most High said: "People of this age do not fear the true and correct but fear deviant demons. For this reason I have called myself the newly emerged Lord Lao." Thereupon Zhang was appointed Correct and Unitary Equanimity Pneuma, Master of the Three Heavens, and entrusted with the Way of the Correct and Unitary Covenant with the Powers as well as the administration of the newly emerged Lord Lao.

> 太上以漢順帝時選擇中使，平正六天之治，分別真偽，顯明上三天之氣。以漢安元年壬午歲五月一日，老君於蜀郡渠亭山石室中，與道士張道陵將詣崑崙大治，新出太上。太上謂世人不畏真正而畏邪鬼，因自號爲新出老君。即拜張爲太玄都正一平氣三天之師，付張正一明威之道，新出老君之制。

In order to make sense of this passage, each occurrence of "newly emerged Lord Lao" should be "newly emerged Demon Lao."[18]

---

17. *Santian neijie jing* 1/5b–6a. This scripture makes reference to the advent of the Liu Song dynasty and therefore can be safely dated to around 420. It preserves information that derives from the mainstream of the Celestial Master tradition and is therefore valuable, but it also includes elements that mark it as representing a splinter movement, like its treatment of early history and of Buddhism, and therefore cannot be used uncritically as a source reflecting the state of the Celestial Master church at the time of its composition. See Bokenkamp 1997:186–229 and the article by Cedzich in Schipper and Verellen 2004: 1, 124–25.

18. Liu Zhaorui provides other examples of passages that were changed by later copyists in response to Buddhist polemical attacks.

This passage introduces a number of new concepts that will be treated below, such as the Three Heavens and the Six Heavens, as well as official titles within the church administration.

Although "demon" sounds quite frightening, and these texts testify that the term was chosen for just this reason, during the Han, Three Kingdoms, and Six Dynasties periods there was not the clear division we find in later dynasties between gods and demons. The god of the hearth, for example, who watched over the household while reporting on misconduct, was sometimes called the "hearth demon" (*zaogui* 竈鬼),[19] and we should probably understand "demon" in these contexts as a godlike figure who was closer to this world and hence perhaps more approachable than a deity. The important question was whether the demon worked for the good or was "deviant" (*xie* 邪) and hence evil.

Since the revelation to Zhang Ling was such a seminal event, it is not surprising that later Daoist scriptures attributed more content to the transmission from the divinized Laozi. One obvious possibility was scriptures. By the early fifth century, a wide variety of scriptures were traced back to this source:[20]

> The *Code of the Great Perfected* says, "On the first day of the fifth month of the first year of the Han'an reign period, the Supreme Lord Lao at Crane-Call Mountain bestowed upon Zhang Daoling the scriptures of the Correct and Unitary Covenant with the Powers in nine hundred thirty scrolls and talismans and charts in seventy scrolls, altogether one thousand scrolls. He also bestowed upon the Celestial Master the *Perfected Scripture of the Great Grotto* in twenty-one scrolls, to be bestowed upon those who had already become perfected."
>
> 《太真科》曰：太上老君以漢安元年五月一日，於鶴鳴山授張道陵正一盟威之經九百三十卷、符圖七十卷，合一千卷，付授天師《大洞真經》二十一卷，授於已成真人。

19. *Shiji* 12/458. On the cult to the god of the hearth, see Chard 1995.

20. *Yaoxiu keyi jielü chao* 1/2a, citing the now lost but widely cited *Taizhenke* 太真科 of ca. 420 CE. For a study of the *Taizhenke* and a reconstruction of its contents, see Ōfuchi 1997:409–505.

The perfected here are a class of divine being, higher than transcendents but below gods. In this passage, a pedigree going back to Zhang Daoling is claimed for a core scripture of the Shangqing 上清 revelations (364–70 CE). We see a similar claim in the *Cavern Perfection Yellow Book (Dongzhen huangshu* 洞真黃書), a Shangqing version of a scripture concerning the sexual rite known as Merging the Pneumas (*heqi* 合氣).[21] The paragraph claiming that the eight scrolls of the *Yellow Book* were revealed during the years 142 and 143 contains many elements that are inappropriate for a Celestial Master context, including references to Ge Hong's tale of Zhao Sheng and Wang Chang, the consumption of alchemical and rare substances (*fushi* 服食), choice of recipient through physiognomy (*ze qi gu* 則其骨), geomantic concepts like the Nine Palaces 九宮, and a revealing deity called not Demon Lao or Lord Lao but rather Laozi. Still, we cannot assume from this that attributions of the Merging the Pneumas rite to the Celestial Masters is incorrect, as we shall see from the earliest concrete evidence of the movement, discussed in the next section.

The Zhang Pu Stele of 173

We are fortunate indeed to have preserved a Song transcription of a stele inscription created by members of the Celestial Master church in 173 CE, only some thirty years after the legendary founding of the group. The stele itself no longer survives, nor do any rubbings of it, but we have a careful transcription of the text by the Song epigrapher Hong Kuo 洪适, who recorded it in his *Continued Clerical Script.*[22] It already shows a religious organization with clearly defined priestly offices and rituals. The text of the stele reads:[23]

21. *Dongzhen huangshu* 1b–2a. On Merging the Pneumas, see below.

22. *Lixu* 隸續 3/8–9.

23. Hong Kuo 1983:3.8a–b. This stele no longer survives, and we are forced to rely on Hong's Song era transcription. He clearly misunderstands the document, identifying the god Hu with a newly enrolled member of the church. This is incompatible with the text, in which Hu "summons" (*zhao* 召, a term

Second year of the Xiping era, third month, first day [April 1, 173]. Hu Jiu, spirit soldier (*guibing*) of the Heavenly Elder,[24] [announces]: You have followed a path to transcendence and your Dao is complete; the mystic dispensation has extended your lifespan.[25] The correct and unitary pneumas[26] of the Dao have been distributed

---

always used by superiors to inferiors) the libationers and presents them with scriptures. Two characters are missing after the emissary's name. One may be a second character of his personal name or cognomen, but one or both must convey the idea that he is communicating (e.g., *yue* 曰, *yan* 言, and so on) and introduce the pronouncement to the libationers.

24. I read *tianlao* where others have read *tian biao* 天表. The character on the stele, after Hong Kuo's transcription, is a graphic variant and does not exactly resemble any known character. The lower portion does resemble that of *biao*, but I can find no example of *biao* written with only one horizontal crossbar in the upper portion of the character. Moreover, the character *lao* 老 on the Cao Quan stele 曹全碑 is close in both appearance and time, and the Wang Xizhi cursive form is also similar and is from a known Celestial Master Daoist. Both can confirm this identification. See *Zhongguo shufa dazidian* (Taipei: Datong shuju, 1970), pp. 978–79 and 1101–2. Zhang Xunliao and Bai Bin describe the normal form of *lao* found in Northern Wei Daoist stelae as "a *xian* 先 character with a *ren* 人 in the hook on the lower right," which also closely approximates our graph. See Zhang Xunliao and Bai Bin 2005:3, 691.

25. The mystic dispensation is also mentioned in this line from the Petition Expressing Gratitude (*xie'en zhang* 謝恩章) presented by the novice after receiving promotion to the One Hundred Fifty Generals Register: "I have received a great grace 大恩. Joy and trepidation arise in turn. The mystic dispensation 玄施 is vast and deep. Truly I must exhort myself to progress!" (DZ 1243 *Zhengyi fawen taishang wailu yi* 6a). Lü Pengzhi has suggested quite plausibly (personal communication) that the term 玄施 refers to the Merging the Pneumas rite, which by some interpretations was completed at the time of reception of the One Hundred Fifty Generals Register. See also *Chuanshou sandong jingjie falu lüeshuo* 1/3b, where we are told that the Transcendent type of Seventy-Five Generals Register governs men and the Numinous type governs women so that, "when men and women unite, these two registers are called the Transcendent Numinous One Hundred Fifty Generals Register" 此二籙，男女合，名仙靈百五十將軍籙也.

26. I read the shortened form of *wu* 无 in Hong's transcription as a shortened or archaic form of the Daoist character for "pneuma," *qi* 炁. The old form of the graph cited by Xu Shen is almost identical and similarly lacks a fire radical at the bottom of the character. In chapter 10 of the *Xiang'er* commentary, Gu Baotian and Zhang Zhongli read the graphically similar *yuan* 元 as *qi* 炁, providing a close parallel reading from the same time and milieu. See Gu Baotian and Zhang Zhongli 1997:37. Other possible readings are *yuan* 元 or *tian* 天, but neither

among the hegemonic pneumas,[27] and it has been decided to summon the libationers Zhang Pu, Meng Sheng,[28] Zhao Guang, Wang
Sheng, Huang Chang, and Yang Feng to come to receive[29] twelve
scrolls of arcane scriptures. The libationers vow to spread the ritual
system of the Celestial Master Dao without limit!

---

seems to make good sense in context. Rao Zongyi reads the graph as an abbreviated form of *qi* 其 (亓), but this leads to an irregular meter. I read the inscription
in four-character phrases as much as possible. See Rao Zongyi 1991:159.

27. Rao Zongyi (1991:160) reads these two characters as *baiqi* 百氣, "the
hundred pneumas," and suggests that *bai* could be a loan for *po* 魄, the earthly
component of the composite Chinese soul (*hunpo* 魂魄). They may be an otherwise unknown official title, like the *lingjue* 領決, or "determiner of pneumas,"
in DZ 1139 *Sandong zhunang* 三洞珠囊 (7.18–19; see also Kleeman 1998:78–
79), who pronounced upon the validity of oracular pronouncements from
spirit mediums 鬼氣男女, but it seems more reasonable to take *bo* as *ba* 霸,
"hegemon, violent," a common variant reading that yields an interpretation
suitable to the historical circumstances of the violent age in which the early
Celestial Masters lived. The reading chosen here is supported by the parallel
to two lines in the *Commands and Precepts*: "Later the pneumas of the Dao
[i.e., the Most High Lord Lao] were to be distributed throughout the four seas"
後道氣當布四海 (DZ 789 *Zhengyi fawen tianshi jiao jieke jing* 13b1) and "[The
Dao] divided and distributed the mystic, originating, and inaugural pneumas
in order to govern the people" 分布玄元始氣治民 (14b1–2). Here it is the pneumas of the Correct and Unitary Covenant that are being distributed to the
faithful. Note also that the fourth-century libationer Du Jiong 杜炅 speaks of
the "pneumas of the Correct and Unitary" 正一之氣 as being the only possible
agent to suppress the "killing and disorder among men and demons" 人鬼殺亂
that prevailed in his day. See *Yunji qiqian* 111/7a, where Du Jiong's name has
been transmitted incorrectly as Du Bing 杜昺.

28. Some have read this name as a title, with *meng* 萌 being a loan for *meng*
盟, "covenant," but there is no example of the term *mengsheng* 盟生 anywhere
in Daoist or secular sources, and the original *meng* is a known surname that,
though rare, is specifically linked to the Sichuan region. See *Hanyu dazidian*
3233, entry 1.7.

29. Although some have read this *shou* 受, "to receive," as the homophonous
graph with the hand radical (*shou* 授, "to bestow"), the pairing of the character
yi 詣, which Wang Li glosses as "to arrive" (usually at the place of a superior,
elder, or revered figure), makes clear that the libationers are lower in status than
the other party and therefore must be receiving rather than bestowing the texts.
Note also that in later ordination texts like the *Taishang wailu yi* and S-203, it is
always a single individual, never a group, who actually bestows the text on the
ordinand. See Wang Li, *Wang Li Guhanyu zidian* (Beijing, 2000), p. 1274.

喜平二年三月一日。天老鬼兵胡九 □□。仙歷道成，玄施延命。
道正一炁，布於伯氣，定召祭酒張普、萌生、趙廣、王盛、黃
長、楊奉等，詣受微經十二卷。祭酒約施天師道法無極哉。

In this inscription the emissary of an exalted Daoist deity, the Heavenly Elder (Tianlao), announces the selection of a group of priests who have made notable progress in spiritual development and rewards their diligence by revealing to them a set of esoteric scriptures. The Heavenly Elder has many possible referents. It may be just another reference to the Supreme Lord Lao, hence the "Heavenly Lao." In the *Scripture of the Conversion of the Barbarians* 化胡經, we read that one of Laozi's avatars, during the reign of King You 周幽王 of the Western Zhou (r. 795–771 BCE), when he also served the Zhou court as "scribe below the pillar," was in fact named Heavenly Elder.[30] We also see Master Redpine addressing a Heavenly Elder Pingchang 平長 in the preface to *Master Redpine's Petition Almanac* (1/1a), and in the second chapter of the same work (2/27b) we see a Heavenly Elder pose questions to the Three Augusts 三皇. In the *Supreme Secret Essentials* 無上秘要, a Heavenly Elder is twice said to "determine the register," suggesting that he has a role in keeping the ledger books of fate.[31] This would be particularly appropriate for a god charged with determining promotions. Whoever this Heavenly Elder is, however, the essential thing is that Hu Jiu is his emissary, hence a divine figure, and definitely not a new convert to the faith, as Hong Kuo speculated and many others have assumed.[32] We cannot confidently supply the missing two characters following Hu Jiu's name, but at least one of them must be a character that introduces a quote like *yue* 曰, "to say"; *gao* 告, "to announce"; or *jiao* 教, "to instruct."[33]

30. Quoted in *Sandong zhunang* 9/7b.

31. See DZ 1138 *Wushang miyao* 98.5a1, 6a4.

32. I was unable to find a single example of a church officer of any rank whose office is preceded by the name of a god.

33. The other character may be an adverb like *xiang* 相, it could be the second character of Hu Jiu's personal name, or it may be that a two-character verbal phrase like *jiangyan* 降言, "sent down words," occupied both spaces.

Thus, we see already in this inscription that heavenly spirits are communicating directly with the group, probably through some form of spirit possession, and that this sort of direct revelation is the ultimate determiner of advancement. Centuries later, suitability for promotion always had to be certified by a group of divine officials called the "lords of interrogation and summoning" (*kaozhaojun* 考召君), though we are equally ignorant of how the master at that time received the answer.

We also can discern that by this time there were at least two different ranks within the church, since this group of libationers summoned by Hu Jiu was already libationers and had just completed a course of study or perhaps merit-making activity beyond that level. There may well have been a different set of scriptures conferred initially when they reached the level of libationer.

We do have one important clue as to the nature of the esoteric scriptures entrusted to them and the significance of the rite as a whole: the term "mystic dispensation" (*xuanshi* 玄施). This would seem to be a reference to the rite of sexual union called Merging the Pneumas. I will treat this rite in greater depth in the next chapter, but for now it is sufficient to note that the rite was of great importance in the early church and that it was often linked to salvation, so it is appropriate that it might "extend [one's] lifespan." There has been debate about when the rite was performed and by whom, but it seems from the inscription above that at this time it was restricted to relatively high officers in the church.

Finally, we should take note of the final clause, which binds the libationers to exert themselves in order to propagate the faith. It was precisely this evangelical ardor that helped the church survive and grow, spreading throughout the Chinese cultural sphere, through the turbulent history of the Period of Disunion.[34]

---

34. We will see this same evangelical spirit below in both the *Xiang'er* and the third-century encyclicals.

The *Laozi* and the *Xiang'er* Commentary

I have noted repeatedly the special role of Laozi in various divine forms for the early Celestial Masters. He founded the religion, appointed Zhang Ling as his representative, established the administrative network of parishes, and perhaps approved its internal personnel decisions. We have also seen that a primary duty of the libationers was to preach the book named after Laozi to their followers, though we cannot be sure if this involved group memorization through choral recitation or simple exposition of its contents.

Among the manuscripts found in a Dunhuang cave at the turn of the twentieth century was a partial edition of the *Laozi* with a commentary interspersed with the text, representing chapters 3 to 37 of the modern edition (see fig. 2). Catalogued in the British Museum as Stein manuscript 6825, it was identified as the long lost *Xiang'er* commentary edition, which Tang Emperor Xuanzong 唐玄宗 (r. 712–57) and the Five Dynasties specialist in Daoist ritual Du Guangting 杜光庭 (850–933) both attributed to Zhang Ling. We have since confirmed that the text of the *Laozi* reflected in this edition is particularly ancient, with close parallels to the early Han manuscripts unearthed in 1973 at Mawangdui.[35] It is also mentioned in and shares some language with the *Commands and Precepts for the Great Family of the Dao*, which is dated internally to 255 CE, and identified as a product through spirit revelation of the disembodied author of that text, who was either Zhang Ling or Zhang Lu, so it is likely that the text was already in use in Hanzhong. Ōfuchi's detailed examination of all references to the text finds that it is most often attributed to Zhang Lu and occasionally to Zhang Ling; Rao suggests an elegant solution to the dispute, that it was written by Zhang Lu based on the ideas of Zhang Ling.[36] Although the text is a commentary on a work

35. See Boltz 1982. On the identification of the text and its dating, see Ōfuchi 1991:247–80 and Bokenkamp 1997:58–62.

36. Rao Zongyi 1991:4. Bokenkamp also accepts that the earlier attributions point to Zhang Lu.

FIGURE 2. The Dunhuang manuscript of the *Xiang'er* commentary to the *Laozi* with details of the beginning and ending sections. Photo courtesy of the British Library, Or.8210/S.6825, ©The British Library Board.

written centuries earlier, we can still use the *Xiang'er* commentary, with due care, to understand the teachings of the Celestial Master Daoists before the dissolution of the Hanzhong community in 215 CE.

As a product of its time, commenting on a Chinese philosophical work of the Warring States period, the *Xiang'er* commentary partakes of a worldview quite distinct from our own and hence requires some explanation. Most readers will probably be familiar with the concepts of yin and yang, negative and positive forces that rise and fall in alternation, such that one is at a peak when the other is at its nadir, and which can be applied to a wide variety of phenomena in the natural and human world. The commentary also draws on the concept of the five agents (*wuxing* 五行), five qualities that succeed each other in two distinctive patterns: mutual production, in which fire gives rise to earth, which produces metal, which yields water, which produces wood; and mutual conquest, in which fire conquers metal, which conquers wood, which conquers earth, which conquers water, which conquers fire. These five agents are correlated with numerous other groups of five, such as the five seasons, the five directions, the five flavors, and, most important for the *Xiang'er*, the five viscera (liver 肝, heart 心, spleen 脾, lungs 肺, kidneys 腎). The commentary also refers to a group of eight phases, sometimes linked to the eight trigrams of the *Scripture of Changes*: *wang* 王 (flourishing), *xiang* 相 (robust), *tai* 胎 (gestating), *mo* 沒 (declining), *si* 死 (dying), *qiu* 囚 (imprisoned), *fei* 廢 (abandoned), and *xiu* 休 (retreating).[37] Finally, it mentions three substances within the body: Pneumas (*qi* 氣) are the energies in the universe, which take forms ranging from fine (air) to turbid (objects); some originate from the Dao itself. Essences (*jing* 精) are the products of the refinement of pneumas into pure substances like semen, which have creative power. Gods (*shen* 神)

37. Oddly enough, there seems to be no standard name for this system, and it is often identified by the name of its first two members, *wangxiang*.

are the result of the coalescence of essence and become body gods who direct and protect the functioning of the body. Having defined these basic terms, let us turn to a consideration of their deployment in the *Xiang'er* commentary.

By the end of the second century CE, the figure of the transcendent (*xian*) had a long history in the Chinese imagination. Transcendents began in the late Warring States era as unworldly figures, equipped with wings and looking rather birdlike, found only in the most remote, inaccessible regions, where they lived lives of extended length and leisure. By the time Ge Hong wrote about them around 320 CE, they were humans who had transformed themselves through various forms of self-cultivation and personal transformation, including macrobiotic diet, breathing exercises, sexual practices, meditation, and alchemy. Campany (2009) has recently given us a picture of aspirants to this status not as remote, divine figures but as the village mystic, engaging in public displays of asceticism and offering various mantic services in a quest for fame and sponsorship.

The Celestial Masters condemned most of these methods and their practitioners as deviant (*xie* 邪) and not in accord with the intentions of the Dao. They specifically condemn, as we shall see below, sexual practices involving the retention and recycling of essence as well as meditative practices involving the visualization of the Dao in a specific form and place within the body (but not the less exalted spirits of the body or the register, as we shall see below). A variety of other practices are subsumed within the blanket condemnation of "false arts of the modern world" (*shijian weiji* 世間偽技). There are occasional hints as to what these might entail, like the visualization of doors and windows within the body, but often we simply do not know what they were referring to. What sort of methods did the Daoists support, and what was the envisioned result of these practices?

The ideal espoused in the *Xiang'er* commentary is the transcendent noble (*xianshi* 仙士), where the second character originally referred to a knight but by this time meant a learned person of high social status. We are told that such individuals "do not value glory, rank, or wealth," "know nothing of profane affairs," "have a taste for the Dao and know nothing of common things," and "close their hearts so as not to be bothered by evil or [the desire for] profit."[38] Like commoners, they "know fear of death and delight in life" but "believe in the Dao, maintaining its precepts and thus joining with life," or again "rejoice only in their faithfulness to the Dao and in keeping its precepts, not in evil." Clearly a key theme here is avoiding any activity that is in conflict with the precepts (*jie* 戒), which I will discuss below. There is a suggestion of physiological practice though, in the following passage:[39]

> They only value "drawing sustenance from the mother"—that is, their own bodies. In the interior of the body, the "mother" is the stomach, which governs the pneumas of the five viscera. The profane eat grain when they have it, and, when the grain is gone, they die. The transcendent nobility eat grain when they have it, and when they do not, they ingest pneumas. The pneumas return to the stomach, which is the layered sack of the bowels.
> 但貴食母者，身也，于內爲胃，主五藏氣。俗人食穀，穀絕便死。仙士有穀食之，無則食氣。氣歸胃，即腸重囊也。

This passage suggests an affinity with practices related to the avoidance of grain, wherein those aspiring to transcendence seek to avoid normal food for progressively more rarified substances, until they subsist only on pneumas.[40] Ge Hong records one version of this practice when he reports of "books of the Dao" that maintain that, "if you want to obtain long life, your bowels must be clear" 欲得長生腸中當清, and "those who eat pneumas are

---

38. Most comments on the transcendent noble are collected in the commentary to chapter 20, and that is the source of the quotations in this paragraph. I follow Bokenkamp (1997:109–12) except for substituting a synonym here and there to maintain consistency in translation, but I translate *xin* 信 in its more common meaning of "believe in" rather than Bokenkamp's "keep faith with." Note that for convenience I cite the *Xiang'er* by the equivalent chapters of the modern text, but the *Xiang'er* itself does not record these divisions.

39. *Laozi Xiang'er zhu*, ch. 20; Rao Zongyi 1991:26–27.

40. On this practice, see Lévi 1983; Eskildsen 1998; Campany 2005.

divinely illuminated and do not die" 食氣者神明不死.[41] However, the statement that Celestial Master transcendent nobles do eat grain when they have it certainly indicates a certain distance between the practices. The retention and use of pneumas and essence are described more fully in an extended metaphor found in the commentary to chapter 21:[42]

> The ancient transcendent nobles treasured the essences to gain life. Today's people lose the essences and die. This is the great proof. Now if one merely congeals essences, can one then obtain life? No! It is essential that one's various actions be complete. This is because essence is a variant form of the pneumas of the Dao. It enters into the human body as the root and the source. I have already explained what happens when one holds only half of them. If you desire to treasure the essences, the hundred actions should be complete and the myriad good deeds should be illustrious. Harmonize the five agents so that happiness and anger are eliminated. Only when one has extra counters on the celestial officers' left tally will the essences be maintained. When evil persons treasure their essences, they trouble themselves in vain, for in the end the essences will not remain but must certainly leak away. If the heart corresponds to the compass, it regulates the myriad matters; thus, it is called the "three paths of the Luminous Hall."[43] While dispersing deviances of yang and injuries of yin, it holds to the center and correctly measures out the pneumas of the Dao. The essences might be compared to the waters of a pond and the body to the embankments along the sides of the pond. Good deeds are like the water's source. If these three things are all complete, the pond will remain intact and sturdy. If the heart does not fix itself upon goodness, then the pond lacks

41. See *Baopuzi neipian* 15/1a–b; Wang Ming 1985:266.

42. Largely following Bokenkamp 1997:113–14, with some alteration to maintain consistency, except where noted. *Laozi Xiang'er zhu*, ch. 21; Rao Zongyi 1991:27–28.

43. The significance of this line is unclear. The Luminous Hall is normally identified with a palace in the head, one inch in from a point midway between the eyebrows, where three lords rule, or it is identified with the spleen. This identification with the heart is much rarer, and I can find no other reference to the Three Paths. See *Dengzhen yinjue* 1/8a–10b; *Shangqing huangshu guoduyi* 19a.

embankments, and the water will run out. If one does not accumulate good deeds, the pond is cut off at its source, and the water will dry up. If one breaches the dike to irrigate uncultivated land, the canal is like a stream or river. Though the dike is there, if the source leaks away, the pond will certainly empty. When the bank[44] becomes scorched and cracked, the hundred illnesses all emerge. If one is not cautious about these three things, the pond will become an empty ditch.

古仙士寶精以生，今人失精以死，大信也。今但結精，便可得生乎？不也。要諸行當備，所以精者道之別氣也。入人身中爲根本，持其半，乃先言之。夫欲寶精，百行當備，萬善當著。調和五行，喜怒悉去。天曹左契，笇有餘數，精乃守之。惡人寶精，唐自苦終不居，必自泄漏也。心應規制萬事，故號明堂三道。布陽耶陰害，以中正度道氣。精並喻像池水，身爲池堤封，善行爲水源。若斯三備，池乃全堅。心不專善，無堤封；水必去，行善不積；源不通，水必燥幹；決水漑野，渠如溪江。雖堤在，源沭[流]泄，必亦空。岸燥炘裂，百病並生。斯三不慎，池爲空坑也。

This extended passage presents some philological problems that cannot be easily resolved, but its general import is clear. The regulation of conduct and the performance of good deeds is the source that supplies the essence, a refined form of the Dao's pneumas. Heavenly recordkeepers, no doubt one or all of the Three Offices of the historical accounts, record all actions in one of two documents, a tally of the left for those with a positive store of merits and a tally of the right for those whose store of merit has been depleted and who thus await misfortune, death, and postmortem punishment. On the basis of one's good or bad conduct, "counters" are added or subtracted from the amount with which one was born.[45] Depletion of this account through evildoing

44. Following Gu Baotian and Zhang Zhongli 1997:106, n. 31, in reading this otherwise unknown character as *an* 岸. Bokenkamp translates "bed of the pond" without explanation.

45. Ge Hong talks about these counters in some detail, but it is unclear if the Celestial Masters assigned the same numerical value to each. See Wang Ming 1985:6/125. Later Daoist ritual often focused on erasing one's name from the right tally and inscribing it on the left. See, for example, *Daomen dingzhi* 7/20b.

makes it impossible to maintain the essence necessary for life. At the same time, the body plays a vital role in maintaining the essence. Bokenkamp suggests that "irrigating the fields" refers to "unbridled sexual intercourse," but it may be broader than that, referring to any time that one of the five agents gains undue dominance, giving rise to strong emotion. The commentary corresponding to chapter 4 specifically warns against anger, which is expressed as antagonism among the five viscera, each of which is ruled by one of the five agents. This can be particularly serious if a "flourishing" viscus and its associated emotion attack and "imprison" one 發王刻囚, which can lead to calamity.[46]

As for one's ultimate fate, the *Xiang'er* does not have a comprehensive discussion, but it does twice speak about what happens after death to a dedicated Daoist, in chapters 16 and 33:[47]

> The Great Yin is the palace where the Dao accumulates and one refines the physical form. There are ages that one cannot abide, and the wise will avoid them by feigning death. They pass through the Great Yin and and are reborn in a new visage on the other side, thus dying without perishing. The profane are unable to accumulate good deeds, and, when they die, it is true death. They enter the custody of the Earth Officer.
>
> 太陰道積練形之宮也。世有不可處，賢者避去託死。過太陰中，而復一邊生像，沒而不殆也。俗人不能積善行，死便真死，屬地官去也。
>
> When a Daoist's practice is complete, the Daoist gods flock to him, he feigns death to avoid the age and, passing through the Great Yin, is reborn; this is to "not perish" and therefore is to be long-lived.

46. This system, which has its origins in the *Huainanzi* and the Apocrypha, is poorly understood.

47. *Laozi Xiang'er zhu*, ch. 16, 33; Rao Zongyi 1991:22, 46. Cf. Bokenkamp 1997:102, 135; Puett 2004:18. My reading of the first sentence is closer to Puett. In the second passage, Bokenkamp and Puett both take the *gui* 歸 causatively, "calls them to return." I follow Gu Baotian and Zhang Zhongli 1997:168. A good parallel usage is found in *Mencius* 1A6, which Legge translates: "Such being indeed the case, the people would flock to him, as water flows downwards" 誠如是也，民歸之，由水之就下 (Legge 1895:137).

The profane have no good merit, so one who dies belongs to the Earth Office; this, then, is to perish.

道人行備，道神歸之，避世託死，遇太陰中，復生去爲不亡，故壽也。俗人無善功，死者屬地官，便爲亡矣。

We do not know much about how the Celestial Masters conceived of the Great Yin. For later Daoists, it was an unfavorable outcome for those who could not attain transcendence, but in these two passages it seems a place of transition to longevity.[48] Bokenkamp describes it as a place where "the last vestiges of dross in corruptible human bodies are refined away through a process analogous to alchemical refinement of base metals to celestial substances in the alchemist's crucible," but this perhaps reads too much into the term *lian* 練, which fundamentally refers to the boiling of silk to make it supple or, with the fire or metal radical in place of the silk radical, the refining of metals for rather more mundane purposes.[49] In the *Xiang'er*, Great Yin is also used as a reference to the kidneys, where essence is congealed both for the purpose of reproduction and to create the gods of the body.

Among the fourth-century revelations preserved in the *Declarations of the Perfected* we find the following explanation of a process similar to that mentioned above:[50]

If someone dies temporarily and proceeds to the Great Yin, visiting briefly the Three Offices, once his or her muscle has rotted, the blood sunk away, and the veins disintegrated, the five viscera will live on their own, the white bones will be jadelike, the seven white souls will

48. For examples from scriptures of the later Celestial Masters, the Shang-qing and Lingbao traditions, see Bokenkamp 1997:220, 330, 428.

49. The two earliest usages of the term "refine the form" are found in the *Traditions of Arrayed Transcendents* 列僊傳 (attributed to Liu Xiang 劉向, 77–6 BCE), which tells of a certain Guifu 桂父 (Father Cinnamon) who constantly ate cinnamon leaves mixed with turtle brains and thereby attained the appearance of an adolescent, and the *Broad Record of Things* 博物志 of Zhang Hua 張華 (232–300), who cites the *Scripture of Shennong* 神農經 to the effect that it is accomplished through the ingestion of five-mineral powder 五石散. See *Wenxuan* 3/15a (六臣 edn.); Fan Ning 1980:4/48.

50. *Zhen'gao* 4/16a–b; Mugitani and Yoshikawa 2000:174–75.

maintain and serve [the corpse], the three cloud souls will protect the household, the three primal [pneumas] will rest for the moment, and the great spirit will seal itself within. After twenty or thirty years, or ten years or three, emerging whenever he or she will, at the time that person is born, he or she will receive new blood and grow muscles, produce saliva that forms mucus, restore substance and complete a form, becoming superior in appearance to before death. This is what is called the perfected refining their forms in the Great Yin and changing their appearance in the Three Offices.

若其人蹔死適太陰，權過三官者，肉既灰爛，血沉脈散者，而猶五藏自生，白骨如玉，七魄營侍，三魂守宅，三元權息，太神內閉。或三十年二十年，或十年三年，隨意而出，當生之時，即更收血育肉，生津成液，復質成形，乃勝於昔未死之容也。真人鍊形於太陰，易貌於三官者，此之謂也。

This seems like a sloughing off of the old form, a sort of hibernation kept alive only by the pneumas in the viscera overseen by one's body spirits, followed by the spontaneous regeneration of the physical body. The Celestial Thearch goes on to praise this method, which Tao Hongjing ties to the ingestion of Five Mineral Oil, as superior to the Nine-Recycled Cinnabar, permitting one to ascend directly to the Heavens as a perfected. This account, then, depends on an alchemical elixir and does not seem to allow a return to the mortal world. We cannot be certain what elements of this mature belief, if any, can be traced back to the early Celestial Masters.

The one real practice we can clearly attribute to the *Xiang'er* commentary seeks a sort of emotional equanimity. This is no doubt what is meant by the repeated references to "pure stillness" (*qingjing* 清靜).[51] Perhaps the best exposition is in chapter 15:[52]

---

51. I eschew the popular translation of *qing* as "clear, clarity." This translation, advocated by Edward Schafer, works well in describing the limpid quality of a mountain stream but does not convey the lack of corruption or defilement that was central to Daoist conceptions of the divine or to contemporary terms like *qingyi* 清議, "pure criticism," and *qingtan* 清談, "pure talk."

52. *Laozi Xiang'er zhu*, ch. 15; Rao Zongyi 1991:29. Cf. Bokenkamp 1997:99. I read some of the grammar a bit differently, reading *shi* 時 as "frequently," not "temporarily," and *qie* 且 as "about to" rather than "and."

When those who seek long life are given something, they do not decline it; when something is taken from them, they have no rancor. They do not follow the common run of people in their shifts and turns. Instead, their thoughts are perfectly directed to the Dao. As they learn to be pure and still, their thoughts will often seem confused and muddy. It is because they are able to be confused and muddy that they are on the point of attaining the simplicity of the uncarved block. After this, they will be pure and still, and able to perceive the many subtleties. Since inside they are spontaneously pure and illuminated, they will not wish to be among the profane. Pure stillness is the great essential. The subtle [pneumas] of the Dao delight in it.

求生之人，與不謝，奪不恨，不隨俗轉移。真思志道，學知清靜，意當時如癡濁也。以能癡濁，樸且欲就矣，然後清靜能睹眾微。內自清明，不欲于俗。清靜大要，道微所樂。

The same passage goes on to explain that, when thunder and wind displace the normal, life-giving humidity, dessication harms living beings, and the pneumas of the Dao hide away so that they are no longer equally distributed. Similarly, human beings should avoid living in withering dryness. Instead, we read.[53]

Therefore, they must not live in a raucous environment. They should constantly strive for pure stillness. At sunrise and sunset the dew rises and descends, and the pneumas within the human body also are distributed. The master sets dawn and sunset [practice] wherein pure stillness is the great essential.

故不得燥處。常清靜爲務，晨暮露上下，人身氣亦布至。師設晨暮，清靜爲大要。

It is uncertain just what practices require this state of mind. Bokenkamp cites a Tang commentator to the *Scripture of the Yellow Court* (*Huangting jing* 黃庭經), an important early Celestial

---

53. Bokenkamp takes the dew as a metaphor for something within the body, but the Chinese clearly draws an analogy between a natural and a human phenomenon.

Master text, who mentions morning and evening ingestion of yang and yin pneumas, respectively, but there is no evidence for such a practice among the early Celestial Masters. It seems more likely that this is related to the audience (*chao* 朝) ceremony that Celestial Master practitioners performed each morning and evening in their oratories or "quiet rooms" (*jingshi* 靜室). We saw in the previous chapter that Yu Huan had spoken of the oratory as a place where the ailing might contemplate their sins and seek redemption. That might well have happened as part of the confessions recorded in the personally written petitions to the Three Offices, and pure stillness would be conducive to this sort of introspection. The oratory had a broader role as a place where each believer might perform his or her daily and periodic ritual activities. Preceding each would have been an audience ceremony to establish a sacred space and welcome the Daoist deities. I will discuss this in greater detail in chapter 6, where I examine ritual life within Daoist communities. For now, it is sufficient to note that one aspect of pure stillness was a state of mind appropriate to the performance of ritual. Since the time of Confucius, ritual in China has been understood to have an aspect of self-cultivation, but it is not primarily a physiological practice.

Other passages comment on this practice of stillness in revealing ways:[54]

Knowing to treasure the root in pure stillness is the constant method to restore the life force.

知寶根清靜，復命之常法也。

To speak seldom and enter into pure stillness is in accord with the self-so, and you can long endure.

希言入清靜。合自然。可久也。

Daoists should value their own essences and gods, and pure stillness is the basis [for doing so].

道人當自重精神，清靜爲本。

54. *Laozi Xiang'er zhu*, ch. 16, 23, 26; Rao Zongyi 1991: 20, 30, 33.

This cherishing of essences, however, is again linked to moral conduct in a warning to those who enjoy fame and respect:[55]

> It is vital to value pure stillness and to uphold the precepts of the Dao.
>
> 務當重清靜，奉行道誡也。
>
> The Dao is constantly free from desire and joy, pure and still, and thereby causes Heaven and Earth to be constantly correct.
>
> 道常無欲樂，清靜，故令天地常正。

Thus, it seems that the practice has definite benefits for the body and the vitality but that these are closely linked to the precepts. What are these precepts?

The manuscript of the *Xiang'er* commentary does not include any associated precepts, but Ōfuchi Ninji has identified in the Daoist canon precepts associated with the *Xiang'er* commentary.[56] They consist of nine exhortations to practice something positive (beginning with *xing* 行, "practice . . ."), divided into three groups of three, and twenty-seven precepts (beginning with *jie* 戒, "you are warned to . . .") detailing conduct to avoid or to carry out, again divided into three groups of nine each. The exhortations can all be found in the text of the *Laozi* itself, whereas the precepts are to be found in the language of the *Xiang'er* commentary. Unlike the *Xiang'er* commentary, which seems to have dropped out of transmission at the end of the Tang dynasty, the exhortations to conduct and the precepts are preserved in four Tang era sources, the oldest version being found in the *Scripture and Statutes of the Most High Lord Lao* 太上老君經律, where they are titled the "*Xiang'er* Precepts to the Revered Scripture of the Dao and Its Virtue" 道德尊經想爾戒.[57] The Nine Practices read:

55. *Laozi Xiang'er zhu*, ch. 26, 37; Rao Zongyi 1991:33, 47.
56. Ōfuchi 1991:25–57.
57. There are parallel texts in the *Taishang jingjie* 太上經戒 and in *Yaoxiu keyi jielü chao* 要修科儀戒律鈔 5/4b–5a. All are cited in Ōfuchi 1991:251–57. Cf. Bokenkamp 1997:49–50.

Practice nonaction	行無爲
Practice supple weakness	行柔弱
Practice preserving the feminine;	行守雌，勿先動
do not act first	
Practice no fame	行無名
Practice pure stillness	行清靜
Practice good deeds	行諸善
Practice no desire	行無欲
Practice knowing to stop at enough	行知止足
Practice yielding	行推讓

We are then told: "If you complete nine practices, you will become a divine transcendent; if six practices, you will double your lifespan; if three practices, you will extend your years and not die before your time."

The twenty-seven precepts are as follows:[58]

Do not delight in deviance;	戒勿喜邪，喜與怒同[59]
delight and anger are the same	
Do not waste essence or pneumas	戒勿費用精氣
Do not harm flourishing[60] pneumas	戒勿傷王氣
Do not eat bloody animals,	戒勿食含血之物，
delighting in their delicious flavor	樂其美味
Do not long for a meritorious	戒勿慕功名
reputation	
Do not practice false arts, pointing	戒勿爲偽技，指形名道[61]
to shapes and calling them the Dao	
Do not forget the rules of the Dao	戒勿忘道法

58. *Taishang laojun jinglü* 1b–2a.

59. Ōfuchi, on the basis of a parallel in the *Zhuangzi*, argues that the text should have originally read: "Do not be angry or delighted; delighting in the deviant is the same as being angry" 勿怒喜，喜邪與怒同 (1991:278, n. 11).

60. These are pneumas that are in the ascendant based on a system of changing patterns of influence described in greater detail below.

61. Reading the character *bi* 彼 as a graphic error for *ji* 技, following Ōfuchi 1991:278, n. 12.

Do not make tentative moves	戒勿爲試動[62]
Do not lust after jewels and goods	戒勿貪寶貨[63]
Do not study deviant texts	戒勿學邪文
Do not lust after lofty splendor, seeking it by force	戒勿貪高榮強求
Do not seek fame and renown	戒勿求名譽
Do not be led into error by ear, eye, or mouth	戒勿爲耳目口所誤
Always dwell in humble lowliness	戒常當處謙下
Do not become irritated easily	戒勿輕躁
Be deliberate in all matters, do not let the heart become flustered	戒舉事當詳，心勿惚恫
Do not indulge yourself in good clothes or fine food	戒勿恣身好衣美食
Do not overindulge	戒勿盈溢
Do not because of poverty and meanness demand wealth and status	戒勿以貧賤強求富貴
Do not perform evil acts	戒勿爲諸惡
Do not observe many taboos	戒勿多忌諱
Do not pray or sacrifice to the spirits	戒勿禱祀鬼神
Do not be obstinate	戒勿強梁
Do not be convinced of your own correctness	戒勿自是
Do not argue with others about who is right; avoid an argument before it arises	戒勿與人爭曲直，得諍先避之

62. Other versions read: "Do not make undisciplined movements" 勿爲妄動 and "Do not be moved by objects" 勿爲物動. Either seems preferable to the current text, but it is difficult to choose between them.

63. The primary text originally had here "Do not kill or say 'kill,'" whereas the two parallel texts had "Do not kill the living" and "Do not kill." This line has no parallel in the *Laozi* and is the only precept with a parallel in the Buddhist Five Precepts, so it is likely a later addition. The precept given is found in the two parallel texts, giving them ten precepts for this section, but was apparently removed in the primary text to maintain the correct number of precepts.

Do not proclaim yourself a sage or claim fame	戒勿稱聖名大
Do not delight in weapons	戒勿樂兵

These precepts are followed by a similar statement promising divine transcendence for one who is able to maintain all of them, doubled longevity for one who can keep eighteen, and extended life for one who can keep as many as nine.

Bokenkamp comments on these precepts that "morality is here defined in such a way as to encompass the necessity of physiological cultivation practices."[64] This evaluation depends on the linking of pure stillness to the ingestion of pneumas and reading the injunctions to "preserve the feminine," avoid "overindulging," and not waste essence as a program of "sexual abstinence" or limited activity. He correctly points out that advice concerning restraining the emotions and avoiding harm to flourishing pneumas might benefit the individual and augment one's general health. But the commentary always returns to observing the precepts as the key to being suffused with the pneumas of the Dao, producing and retaining essence, and using it to create internal body gods. Consider this passage from chapter 3:[65]

The heart is like a compass, and in its midst there are fortune and misfortune, good and evil. The belly is the sack of the Dao, and the pneumas always want to fill it. If the heart is violent and evil, the Dao will leave, and the sack will be empty. When the sack is empty, deviance enters, and then you kill others. If you empty the heart of violence and evil, the Dao will come home to it, and your belly will be full.

心者，規也，中有吉兇善惡。腹者，道囊，氣常欲實。心爲兇惡，道去囊空。空者耶入，便煞人。虛去心中兇惡，道來歸之，腹則實矣。

64. *Laozi Xiang'er zhu*, ch. 3; Rao Zongyi 1991:6. Cf. Bokenkamp 1997: 50–51.

65. Cf. Bokenkamp 1997:78. He takes the "deviance" in the penultimate sentence as the subject of *sha*, "to kill," and assumes that the object, *ren*, refers to the practitioner. I take *ren* in its more common meaning of "other person."

Here it is immoral conduct that drives the Dao away. The Dao naturally wants to fill the body with its pneumas, and humans need only act in accordance with moral principles to be filled with the Dao. They do not need to ingest pneumas, do breathing exercises, perform visualizations, or engage in sexual rituals to obtain these precious breaths of energy.

An impartial evaluation of this list of rules would, I believe, have to conclude that the focus is on one's conduct within society. Moreover, as we have seen, this interpretation of the *Laozi* equates the passages in that work most suggestive of personal cultivation, like those concerning "preserving the One," with the observance of a list of moral injunctions. Thus, the Celestial Master interpretation of the *Laozi* is distinctive within the commentarial tradition in that it turns away from the tradition of physiological cultivation and replaces it with a concern for social conduct.

In a stimulating analysis of the *Xiang'er* commentary deeply rooted in his own studies of Warring States self-divinization movements, Michael Puett (2004) argues that the cosmology of the *Xiang'er* portrays a Dao who has created both the cosmos and humans for the sole purpose of generating gods (he calls them "spirits"). The purpose of the commentary and the Celestial Master movement as a whole is then "an attempt to build a hierarchical community of adepts whose self-cultivation techniques are deemed necessary to bring order to the cosmos." In an abstract sense, there is some truth to this, but it makes unwarranted assumptions about both the nature of the community, which did not consist of adepts but rather priests, and their practice, which was not self-cultivation as Puett understands it from Warring States philosophical texts, but rather, as I have just argued, obedience to a divinely revealed code of conduct. Moreover, the gods produced in an individual's body through strict adherence to this demanding code are not part of a cosmically orchestrated plan of the Dao but, as we shall see in coming chapters, personal protectors and supernatural agents who were used in everyday ritual, completing tasks that were essential for the survival of the Daoists, their families, and the larger community.

Now it is true that, considered as a whole, the individual actions of each practicing Daoist and the communal actions of each local group of Daoists did work toward restoring the supremacy of the good and correct over the evil and deviant, and that these ritual actions combined with the fearful celestial punishments being prepared by the Most High Lord Lao for evildoers—like Puett's aspirants to personal divinity with their "false techniques"— would eventually cleanse the cosmos and bring the advent of Great Peace, but, in this great cosmic battle, the internal body gods generated by individual Daoists together with their essences and pneumas were much closer to ammunition than soldiers, and it was the rituals performed by the Daoists that launched them into the battle.

Daoists and the Profane

One aspect of church life that the commentary gives us insight into is conflicts with nonbelievers, who are both addressed directly as "the profane" (*su* 俗) and alluded to indirectly as practitioners of "false arts" (*weiji* 僞技). The most revolutionary of the *Xiang'er* precepts, the ones most at variance with traditional codes of conduct, are the exhortations to forsake the religious rituals that were at the center of Chinese society, praying or sacrificing to the spirits, and to ignore the taboos that girded and shaped all aspects of life. The first question is taken up in the commentary to chapter 24:[66]

> The correct law of Heaven does not reside in offering foodstuffs and praying at ancestral shrines. Thus, the Dao has prohibited these things and provides heavy penalties for them. Sacrifices and food offerings are a means of commerce with deviant forces. Thus, even when there is excess food or implements [left over from the sacrifices], Daoists will not eat or employ them.
>
> 天之正法，不在祭餟禱祠也。道故禁祭餟禱祠，與之重罰。祭餟與耶通同，故有餘食器物，道人終不欲食用之也。

66. Bokenkamp 1997:119–20.

The passage that immediately follows this one mandates that Daoists should avoid the vicinity of such sacrifices entirely. These sacrifices were the vehicle for a transaction with supernatural beings, who consumed the fragrance of the proffered items, then imbued them with blessings that the mortal sacrificers internalized through a banquet. The Celestial Masters' teaching was summarized in an oath called the Pure Bond (*qingyue* 清約)—"The gods do not eat or drink; the master does not accept money" 神不飲食，師不收錢—which highlighted the fact that it was the transactional nature of this relationship that was objectionable.[67] Only blessings won through the observance of the precepts of the Dao were legitimate.

Bokenkamp rightly points out that such sacrifices were not merely, as is sometimes claimed, to lowly popular gods, but included those made as part of the sacrificial program of the Chinese state.[68] We should note that the "gods" do not include the ancestors since, in its discussion of sexual activity, the *Xiang'er* is careful to state that the Dao wishes ancestral sacrifice to continue, lest the institution of the family be threatened. But sacrifice to the local gods of the soil and hearth defined membership in local communities, and rejection of these cults would have put church members outside of the bounds of local society.[69]

Similarly, if we are to believe the historical accounts, certain seasonal practices, like the avoidance of killing in the spring, were observed by the Daoists, but taboos on the proper timing of actions were ignored. Such taboos were deeply ingrained into Chinese society, as testified to by the presence of hemerological works in most of the hoards of texts excavated by Chinese archaeologists in recent

67. The Pure Bond is only preserved in Celestial Master scripture from the fifth century, but it was understood by Lu Xiujing 陸修靜 as an original element of the church and part of the original covenant on which the faith was founded; he calls it "the true teaching of the pure bond of the covenant with the powers" 盟威清約之正教. See *Lu xiansheng daomenke lüe* 1a, 8a, and *Santian neijie jing* 3a.

68. See Kleeman 1994b; Schipper 2000.

69. Fifth-century Celestial Master documents make allowance for both ancestral sacrifice and worship of local earth gods but only on limited occasions.

years.[70] Open flaunting of these rules as well as taboos on various sorts of pollution must also have been a source of considerable friction with nonbelievers, who might well have seen this as the willful rejection of traditional wisdom that would threaten not just the individual but also the surrounding community.

This was not the only point of contention between the Daoists and nonbelievers. The Celestial Masters represented only one tradition in a religious landscape teeming with both ideas dating back several centuries and new teachings at the heart of nascent religious movements. The *Xiang'er* commentary reflects this rather embattled status, inveighing repeatedly against "deviant texts" and "deviant knowledge." Although they shared many of the same conceptions as other movements of their day and engaged in similar practices, there is no sense of ecumenical goodwill toward competing religious systems or individual teachers. In the commentary to the modern chapter 8, there is a warning against choosing the wrong teacher:[71]

> All people should desire to serve a master and should seek out one with good abilities who knows the true Dao. They should not serve the deviant, the false, or the cunning. Deviant knowledge is arrogant and extravagant.
>
> 人等當欲事師，當求善能知真道者，不當事耶偽伎巧。耶知驕奢也。

Eventually the Daoists evolved an ecclesiastical organization and a system of training that clearly identified who was a proper guide, but the criteria may not have been in place yet when the commentary was written. Even then, as we shall see in the early collections of precepts, there are repeated warnings against individual masters developing innovative ideas or practices and thus "creating their own methods" (*zi zuo yifa* 自做一法).[72]

---

70. On these texts, see Poo 1993; Harper 1999; Kalinowski 2008.
71. Adapted from Bokenkamp 1997:86. Cf. Gu Baotian and Zhang Zhongli 1997:31.
72. See below, chapter 3.

One of the more significant disagreements seems to have been in the area of meditative practices. We have seen that there are perhaps some suggestions but not much explicit proof that the Celestial Masters used physiological self-cultivation practices. The *Laozi* has vague references to a practice called "preserving the One" (*shouyi* 守一), which have given rise to a variety of commentarial traditions over the ages and an equally varied set of practices.[73] The "One" is almost always identified with the Dao, and, for the Celestial Masters, this meant that it was also the Most High Lord Lao. Most practitioners of the day integrated this practice into a detailed set of meditative practices centering on the gods of the body. Ge Hong gives an account of one such practice:[74]

> An ancient scripture of the transcendents says: "If you want to live long, you should understand preserving the One. . . . The One has a surname and a name, and clothing of a certain color. For men, it is nine-tenths of an inch; for women, six-tenths. Sometimes it is in the Cinnabar Field, 2.4 inches below the navel; sometimes it is in the Cinnabar Field between the golden towers of the Scarlet Palace below the heart; sometimes it is between the eyebrows, where, if you proceed inward one inch, it is the Luminous Hall, two inches for the Grotto Chamber, and three inches for the Upper Cinnabar Field."
>
> 故仙經曰：子欲長生，守一當明。。。。一有姓字服色，男長九分，女長六分，或在臍下二寸四分下丹田中，或在心下絳宮金闕中丹田也，或在人兩眉間，卻行一寸爲明堂，二寸爲洞房，三寸爲上丹田也。

The *Xiang'er*, identifying the One with the Most High Lord Lao, explicitly condemns this sort of practice:[75]

73. See Andersen 1981 for an example from the fourth century.

74. *Baopuzi neipian* 18/1b; Wang Ming 1985:323. This passage is cited in Bokenkamp 1997:144–45, n. 26, but he mistakes the size of the One, giving instead heights of nine inches and six inches.

75. *Laozi Xiang'er zhu*, ch. 10; Rao Zongyi 1991:13. Adapted from Bokenkamp 1997:89.

The One does not reside within the human body. Those who attach it to the body are all practicing the false arts of the mundane world. Theirs is not the true Dao. The One exists beyond Heaven and Earth. Entering into the space between Heaven and Earth, it only comes and goes within the human body. It is there everywhere within your skin, not just in a single spot. The One disperses its form as pneuma and gathers in its form as the Most High Lord Lao, whose permanent rule is on Mount Kunlun.

一不在人身也。諸附身者，悉世間常僞伎，非真道也。一在天地外，入在天地間，但往來人身中耳。都皮裏悉是，非獨一處。一散形爲氣，聚形爲太上老君，常治崑崙。

Thus, although the Dao is personified in the *Xiang'er*, there seems to have been concern for overly anthropomorphizing the high god. Another passage, in the commentary to chapter 14, makes a similar point with a bit more detail:[76]

The Dao is the most revered. Subtle and hidden, it has no appearance or form. We can only follow its precepts; we cannot see or know it. Now the false arts of the mundane world point to a form and call it the Dao, giving it a certain color of clothing, a name and a cognomen, an appearance, and a size. This is wrong! It is all merely deviant falsehoods.

道至尊。微而隱，無狀貌形像也。但可從其誡，不可見知也。今世間僞伎，指形名道，令有服色名字狀貌長短，非也。悉耶僞耳。

The incorporeal nature of the Dao seems to have been a key point in Celestial Master theology. It was important to insist on because it affirmed the transcendental nature of the highest level of Daoist deity. This did not mean that other gods had no fixed form or appearance, however. We will see that the gods of the body, formed of essence accumulated through the performance of good deeds and the keeping of the precepts, had precise descriptions and locations. Some of these are described in the *Scripture of the Yellow*

---

76. *Laozi Xiang'er zhu*, ch. 14; Rao Zongyi 1991:18. Cf. Bokenkamp 1997:97. The portion corresponding to chapter 16 has a very similar passage.

Court. However, the practice associated with the *Scripture of the Yellow Court* was primarily recitation, and, although fourth-century Shangqing practitioners may have performed this recitation while visualizing the gods mentioned in the text, there is no evidence that Celestial Master followers also did so.[77]

Sexual practice was another area that revealed significant disagreements with popular practice. It is difficult to know when practices using sexual union to enhance vitality and extend life first arose, but two manuscripts detailing pre-Daoist methods and dating to the beginning of the Han (before 168 BCE) were found at Mawangdui in 1973, and the bibliography of the Han imperial library includes a category for works on the arts of the bedchamber.[78] The *Xiang'er*'s most detailed discussion of this topic is found in the commentary to chapter 6, where it identifies the vagina (the "yin hole") and the penis (the "male stem") as the roots of Heaven and Earth,[79] then comments as follows on the line "gossamer thin, it seems to exist" 綿綿若存:[80]

> The way of yin and yang uses the congealing of essence to create life. When one's age reaches the point of "knowing fate" [i.e., fifty], this should be called "stop yourself." When young, although there is [sexual intercourse], you should stagger it and reduce it. When it

77. See Tao Hongjing's description of the "Method of Reciting the *Scripture of the Yellow Court*" in *Dengzhen yinjue* 3/1a. The possibility of visualizations connected to this text in the early church cannot, however, be categorically denied, given the role of visualizations in the audience ceremony and in receiving, reviewing, and employing the spirits of the register.

78. On the Mawangdui manuscripts, see Harper 1987; for the Han bibliography listing eight titles, see *Han shu* 30/1778–89.

79. Bokenkamp also cites in this regard the line in chapter 16 "When the pneumas of the Dao return to the root, it is even more important to be pure and still" 道氣歸根，愈當清淨也 (1993:48), but in context it seems unlikely that this "root" refers to the genitals.

80. *Laozi Xiang'er zhu*, ch. 6; Rao Zongyi 1991:10. Cf. Bokenkamp 1997:83–84. I translate the *Laozi* line in its more common interpretation. Bokenkamp translates this line "attenuated and so enduring," but the commentary seems to take *ruo* 若 here as a second-person pronoun, so perhaps "you will endure" would be closer. The image *mianmian* 綿綿 (cottony) is of a wispy ball of cotton that you can draw out into a thinner and thinner but seemingly continuous strand.

says "gossamer thin," it means attenuated. If you adopt this attenuated sparsity, then your youth will last long. Now this affair is causing great harm. Why did the Dao create it? The Dao values the
continuation of the ancestral sacrifices so that our kind does not
disappear. It wants to make you unite essences and reproduce;
therefore it teaches the young to practice it seldom but not abandon
it completely. It does not teach them to devote their energies to it.
This plan of devoting one's energy to it is simply the product of the
minds of fools. How can you blame the Dao! Persons of superior
morality, whose intentions and self-control are resolute and strong,
and who are able to avoid falling in love and reproducing,[81] should
cease the practice when young, and their good gods will mature
sooner. One who says this is stating the essence of the Dao.[82] The
fact that [the Dao] has caused Heaven and Earth to have no ancestral shrine,[83] dragons to have no sons, transcendents to have no
wives, and jade women to have no husbands is the great proof of this.

陰陽之道，以若結精爲生。年以知命，當名自止。年少之時，雖
有當閉省之。綿綿者，微也。從其微少，若少年則長存矣。今此
乃爲大害。道造之何？道重繼祠，種類不絕。欲令合精產生，故
教之年少微省不絕，不教之勤力也。勤力之計，出愚人之心耳，
豈可怨道乎！上德之人，志操堅強，能不戀結產生，少時便絕，
又善神早成。言此者，道精也，故令天地無祠，龍無子，仙人無
妻，玉女無夫，其大信也。

The *Xiang'er* reveals what can at best be described as a conflicted
attitude toward sexual congress. On the one hand, it recognizes
that the union of male and female essences is necessary for reproduction and hence for the survival of humanity and the continuation of ancestral sacrifices, just as the essences of yin and yang
must be joined within the body to produce the good corporeal

81. Puett translates this phrase "are able to not unite and produce life"
(2004:16), which seems to misunderstand *lianjie* 戀結, "to become emotionally
attached to."

82. Bokenkamp translates this phrase "These are called 'essences of the
Dao.'" It is, in any case, difficult to construe.

83. Puett translates "ancestral shrine" as "sacrifices," then argues this means
that Heaven and Earth do not need sacrifice (2004:16), but the point of the line
is that they have no offspring to sacrifice to them as ancestors.

deities. On the other hand, it believes the activity should be limited, practiced seldom while young and abandoned after reaching the age of fifty. Moreover, youths with especially firm resolve should refrain from intercourse altogether because it allows their body gods to mature sooner. This does imply that they will never reproduce, but the facts that Heaven and Earth have no children to offer sacrifice to them, dragons produce no offspring, and transcendents and jade maidens take no spouses are mentioned as proof that such a decision is correct.

The *Xiang'er* specifically differentiates its position from the teachings of the bedchamber prevalent in its day, attributed to the Yellow Thearch, the Mysterious Woman, Gongzi, and Rongcheng.[84] It condemns practices of intercourse without ejaculation in hopes of recycling the essense to enrich the brain (chapter 9). Another criticism opposes the idea that the practitioner should "borrow" pneumas from his or her sexual partner, arguing that it is better to conserve one's own essence in the kidneys (*shen* 腎), also called the Great Yin 太陰, which is described as "black":[85]

> For one who knows how to preserve the black, the virtues of the Dao are constantly present. They do not borrow from others. They would certainly have to repay, and this is not as good as possessing it oneself.
> 知守黑者，道德常在，不從人貸，必當償之，不如自有也。

Only a few lines of the texts being criticized survive, and the comments in the *Xiang'er* are at best cryptic, so we may never fully understand the Celestial Master teaching on sex, but the overall import is probably summed up in the following line:[86]

---

84. Works on the arts of the bedchamber attributed to both the Yellow Thearch and Rongcheng are recorded in the *Han shu* bibliographic treatise mentioned above; see *Han shu* 30/1778–89.

85. *Laozi Xiang'er zhu*, ch. 28; Rao Zongyi 1991:38. Cf. Bokenkamp 1997: 125, where Bokenkamp understands *chang* 償, "to repay," as "to give."

86. *Laozi Xiang'er zhu*, ch. 28; Rao Zongyi 1991:38. Adapted from Bokenkamp 1997:125.

Only those who preserve their own [supply of essence], cutting off desires and shutting off yearnings, will be great without limit.

唯有自守，絕心閉念者，大無極也。

I will return to this topic in later discussion of the sexual rite called Merging the Pneumas.

Authority in the *Xiang'er*

Like many religions, the Celestial Master Daoists believed that the world had once been once a much better place than it was in their day.[87] That utopia was labeled "high antiquity" (*shanggu* 上古), whereas their recent history was "lower antiquity" (*xiagu* 下古). In high antiquity, the "Dao was employed," the rulers of the day "personally revered and practiced it" and "made themselves subservient to the Dao," and, since "none of the officials or subjects failed to pattern themselves on their ruler," all "competed with one another in loyalty and filiality." In fact, all people were "benevolent and righteous," and "every family was benevolent and filial" so that that there was no need to distinguish the virtuous. This was all in sharp contrast to the situation in their day, when ministers "all study deviant writings and practice argumentation and deception," all throughout society the "six relations are inharmonious,"[88] and a virtuous person is so rare that "that person is praised by all in contradistinction to others."

The Celestial Masters did not, however, constitute a revolutionary force intent on overthrowing the imperial government. I noted in the last chapter that they coexisted with the secular administration of the empire in the Sichuan region for several decades before Liu Yan ordered Zhang Lu and Zhang Xiu to seize

87. This paragraph quotes passages from the commentary to chapter 18 as translated in Bokenkamp 1997:104–5.

88. The six relations are variously defined but most commonly include the father, mother, older siblings, younger siblings, spouse, and sometimes offspring. See, for example, the commentary to *Shiji* 62/2132, n. 4.

Hanzhong, and that, after that, Zhang Lu was caught between the competing forces of Liu Yan and Liu Zhang, Cao Cao, and Liu Bei, all of whom sought to establish independent kingdoms. We find confirmation of this generally positive attitude toward secular authority in the *Xiang'er*, first in the condemnation of regicide:[89]

> When crazed, deluded[90] people plot to usurp the position of and assassinate [the ruler], Heaven will certainly kill them. You must not do this.
>
> 狂或之人圖欲纂弒，天必煞之。不可爲也。

This is followed by a general sanctioning of rulers as having received the approbation of Heaven, or else they would not survive:[91]

> A kingdom cannot for one day be without a lord. When the essence of one of the Five Thearchs is to be born, the Yellow and the Luo Rivers proclaim his name, the essence appears among the seven lodgings, and the five weft-stars concur with them.[92] Such persons are manifestly appointed by Heaven and charged with rule. They have no other choice. Those who are not entrusted with the realm must not wantonly hope for it.

89. *Laozi Xiang'er zhu*, ch. 29; Rao Zongyi 1991:39. Cf. Bokenkamp 1997: 126.

90. Following Rao (1991:39) in reading *huo* 惑 for *huo* 或.

91. Again *Laozi Xiang'er zhu*, ch. 29; Rao Zongyi 1991:39. Adapted from Bokenkamp 1997:127. Bokenkamp translates the penultimate phrase "not appointed by heaven," apparently regarding the character *xia* 下 as excrescent, perhaps because of the parallel with the next bit of commentary.

92. These are omens that accompany the transfer of the Mandate of Heaven. The [Yellow] River Chart and Luo Writing are magical diagrams said to appear at the beginning of a new reign. The seven lodgings represent one-quarter of the twenty-eight lunar lodgings and hence one quadrant of the sky and one cardinal direction, presumably that of the agent that will dominate during the coming reign. The weft-stars are the five planets visible to the naked eye (Mercury, Venus, Mars, Saturn, Jupiter); the planets pass through and interact with the lodges, forming astrological omens.

國不可一日無君。五帝精生，河雒著名，七宿精見，五緯合同。明
受天任而令爲之，其不得已耳，非天下所任，不可妄庶幾也。

Thus, a secular lord was necessary, but it was still to be hoped that
this ruler would accord with the Dao, for, "when the Dao is employed, officials are loyal and offspring are filial, and the kingdom
is easy to govern." Eventually, such an enlightened ruler will guide
his state to the utopian condition known as Great Peace:[93]

> The lord who governs the kingdom should strive to practice virtues
> of the Dao; loyal officials who aid him should strive to practice the
> Dao. The Dao will become universal, and its virtues will overflow;
> then Great Peace will arrive.
>
> 治國之君，務修道德。忠臣輔佐，務在行道。道普德溢，太平
> 至矣。

One aspect of such a ruler's governance was to act as a barrier
to the circulation of heretical ideas or deviant teachings. This
duty is set forth in the commentary to the *Laozi* passage "Love
the citizens and regulate the state but have no knowledge":[94]

> The lord of the people, desiring to cherish his citizens so as to
> cause their longevity and to govern the kingdom so as to bring
> about Great Peace, should earnestly plumb the intentions of the
> Dao and teach his citizens, causing them to know the perfection of
> the Dao and not allowing them to know of false ways or deviant
> knowledge.
>
> 人君欲愛民令壽考，治國令太平，當精心鑿道意，教民皆令知道
> 真，無令知僞道耶知也。

Here we see the two responsibilities of the Daoist ruler: first, to
assure that his subjects live to an appropriate old age and, second,

93. *Laozi Xiang'er zhu*, ch. 30; Rao Zongyi 1991:40–41, adapted from Bokenkamp 1997:128.
94. *Laozi Xiang'er zhu*, ch. 10; Rao Zongyi 1991:13, adapted from Bokenkamp 1997:90.

to see that the state embodies the ideal of Great Peace, a world where violence of any form is unknown and there is reasonable equanimity among citizens. Given the rather broad range of ideas that were classified as false or deviant by the Celestial Masters, this practically meant that the ruler must be a member of the faith, and in fact an advanced one, to be able to discern the "intentions of the Dao."

Thus, the ruler is essential to the Daoist program of temporal salvation in the face of a deteriorating society in the present. In chapter 35, we read that "the transformative influence of the Dao proceeds down from the top," and, for this reason, "in its rule there are not two lords."[95] Such a ruler, who models himself on the Dao, winning auspicious omens and eventually effecting the arrival of Great Peace, will merit the ultimate designation, that of a Daoist Lord 道君. There is even hope for a ruler of only moderate faith because he will select worthy officials who will "aid him by means of the Dao," but, because so much depends on these ministers, if they should "depart one morning, the kingdom will be in danger of toppling by evening." Achieving order through only the ministers is inherently difficult, like "water flowing to the west," whereas all Chinese rivers flow east to the Pacific. With a truly unworthy ruler, who "discards the Dao," the Dao will visit upon him all manner of natural disasters and demonic sprites as an admonishment, then hide away to watch, returning only when disorder reaches its peak to reimpose the rule of the Dao.

So, in addition to the unique role of the ruler, the minister and other officers of state have an important part to play in the implementation of Daoist governance. Does that mean that the Dao sanctions all social distinctions of a class society? Is there not some sort of program of social leveling inherent in the Daoist teachings?

There are certainly exhortations to be humble and to eschew wealth and glory. The transcendent noble, for example, does not

---

95. The quotations in this paragraph are all taken from Bokenkamp 1997: 136–37.

value "glory, rank, or wealth." Many such ideas are expressed clearly in the text of the *Laozi* itself, so it is not surprising that the *Xiang'er* espouses a healthy suspicion of fame:[96]

> When there is glory, there is bound to be disgrace. Daoists fear disgrace; therefore they do not lust after glory but only set their aspirations on the Dao.
>
> 有榮必有辱。道人畏辱，故不貪榮，但歸志於道。

Still, we find a rationalization given for those in power that Bokenkamp suggests may have functioned to increase the appeal of the commentary, and presumably the movement, to the nobility:[97]

> Kings and lords have succeeded their ancestors and therefore have illustrious names but did not seek them by force. The Dao permits this and desires only that they strive to revere the Dao and practice the precepts, being neither proud nor conceited.
>
> 今王侯承先人之後，有榮名，不強求也。道聽之，但欲令務尊道行誡，勿驕溢也。

It is misguided to look for radical social views in a strongly morality-oriented religious movement that is deeply rooted in Chinese culture. Although the Celestial Master movement condemns significant elements of the Chinese tradition, as we have seen, the values that are central to most streams of Chinese thought, like benevolence, righteousness, filial piety, and loyalty, are enthusiastically championed. We shall see in a later chapter that the movement did offer significant opportunities for social mobility and a unique role, for its time, to female members of the church, but

---

96. *Laozi Xiang'er zhu*, ch. 28; Rao Zongyi 1991:38, adapted from Bokenkamp 1997:125–26.
97. *Laozi Xiang'er zhu*, ch. 32; Rao Zongyi 1991:44; Bokenkamp 1997:133, see second footnote.

we find in the commentary a doctrine promoting acceptance of one's lot in life that reminds one of a classical Confucian author like Xunzi:[98]

> Whether wealthy and exalted or impoverished and humble, all should strive to keep to their own path. For those of utmost sincerity, the Dao will be with them. The poor and humble should not belittle themselves, seeking by force wealth and status. Those who do not seek this by force, because they do not lose their positions, will long endure.
> 富貴貧賤，各自守道爲務，至誠者道與之，貧賤者無自鄙強欲求富貴也。不強求者，爲不失其所故久也。

Wealth and status are really not proper goals for a good Daoist following the teachings of the *Laozi* as explained through the *Xiang'er* commentary. A much more valued goal was the personal attention of the Most High Lord Lao. What I translate here as "keep to their own path" also implies "keeping the Dao." Elsewhere we are told that, "if you abandon deviant learning and only keep the Dao, the Dao will be with you" (chapter 20). The Dao is like water and the believer is a fish so that, if he or she "does not practice the precepts and keep the Dao," the Dao will leave, and the individual will die like a fish out of water (chapter 36). Salvation, then, does not depend on worldly success or on the performance of difficult practices of self-cultivation but simply on being a good person as defined by the precepts of the Dao. This will keep the Dao close to you and "thinking of you," which is the meaning of *xiang'er*.[99]

The Dunhuang manuscript of the *Xiang'er* was copied in the sixth century. Authors through the Tang dynasty cite and quote the *Xiang'er* commentary, so it was in circulation for at least seven centuries. The precepts, arguably encompassing the most

---

98. *Laozi Xiang'er zhu*, ch. 33; Rao Zongyi 1991:45, adapted from Bokenkamp 1997:135.

99. On this point, see Bokenkamp 1997:61–62.

important content of the commentary, circulated independently and were transmitted until today in at least three sources. During these centuries, the *Xiang'er* commentary was an important document for generation after generation of Celestial Master Daoists, and for nearly two millennia Daoists have vowed to uphold its precepts.

THREE

After the Fall: Daoism
in the Third Century

W hen, in 215, Cao Cao conquered the Daoist community in Hanzhong, he transferred large segments of the population to the Wei River valley region in the northwest and to the capital region in the central North China plain. In this way, Celestial Master Daoism was spread across the breadth of North China, a key development in its transformation into China's first national religion (see fig. 3). The population transfers must, however, have disrupted the early church in any number of ways. The system of parishes, tied to the geography of Sichuan, would no longer have been appropriate as an administrative network for the church. It is uncertain to what degree the eastern and western branches of the church remained in communication, or even continued to share a common hierarchy. Tao Hongjing records that Zhang Lu died in 216 and was buried near the Cao family stronghold of Ye, so we can presume that the central administration of the church was now in central China. We do not know who, if anyone, succeeded Lu as Celestial Master. The remark in his *Record of the Three Kingdoms* biography that his son Fu succeeded him presumably refers to his fief as marquis of Langzhong; there is no explicit statement that he also took up his father's ecclesiastical office. In fact, there is a huge gap in our records until the beginning of the fourth century; the only Daoist historical figures we can name for nearly one hundred years are the ancestors of fourth-century believers.

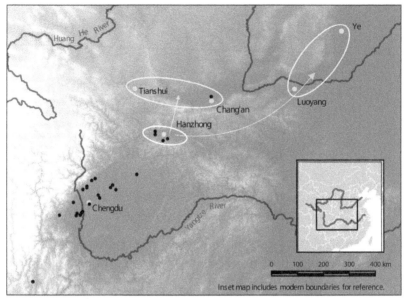

GIS data: CHGIS, Version 5. © Fairbank Center for Chinese Studies & the Institute for Chinese Historical Geography at Fudan University, Dec 2010. Made with Natural Earth free data @naturalearthdata.com

FIGURE 3. The Daoist diapora. Arrows indicate the forced relocation of Daoists by Cao Cao around 215 CE. Map by Angela R. Cunningham.

Three texts that can be reliably dated to the third century will form the basis for this chapter. First, we will take up two oracular revelations that address the members of the church directly. The first of these, titled *Yangping Parish*, is dated internally to shortly after 220 CE. The second, the *Commands and Precepts for the Great Family of the Dao*, is dated to 255. Verellen has characterized the second of these as a "harangue." This fits the first equally well—both are exhortations to the faithful, full of criticism and bile. They might more properly be termed encyclicals, authoritative pro-nouncements from a supernatural source circulated by the central church to all its branches. The third text is the *Demon Statutes of Lady Blue* (*Nüqing guilü* 女青鬼律), which cannot be earlier than 265 in its current form but was composed no later than the end of the third century. It is a unique text that gives us many insights into the Daoist worldview.

Yangping Parish

The Zhang Pu stele of 173 CE was both our first clearly datable piece of evidence for the Celestial Master church and our first evidence for the key role played by spirit revelation in its early history. The first two documents I examine in this chapter are testimony to the continuing vibrancy of this tradition through the third century. When, in the mid-fourth century, we find the first major reforms occurring within the Celestial Master church by incorporating elements of the southern occultist tradition, direct spirit revelation is again the vehicle.

The exhortatory tract *Yangping Parish* 陽平治 announces by its title that the speaker is a Celestial Master. Yangping was the highest of the parishes, led first by Zhang Daoling and, since then, by a lineal descendant.[1] Here it is the now deified Daoling himself who speaks through some sort of medium. The tract is suffused with this authority and is found in a collection of early church literature titled *Ritual Texts of Correct Unity: The Scripture of Precepts and Codes, Teachings of the Celestial Master* 正一 法文天師教戒科經.[2] The term *jiao* 教, "teaching," in this title seems to have been a technical term for spirit revelations from an authoritative source. It is likely that *Yangping Parish* was composed shortly after 220, the latest date mentioned in the text, and almost certainly before 231. The latter is mentioned as the date of a key event in the second encyclical, the *Commands and Precepts for the Great Family of the Dao*, yet is not mentioned here. Here is the text:[3]

---

1. See *Zhengyi fawen chuan dugongban yi* 1b.

2. The four-character introduction to the scriptural title is the name of the first Celestial Master canon, compiled during the Six Dynasties period (265–589), with its first surviving witness being the *Wushang miyao* 無上秘要 of 563 (46/16b–18a). See Schipper and Verellen 2004:9–11. Some surviving scriptures with this designation seem quite early, like the tracts discussed in this chapter, whereas others show clear influence from Buddhist scriptures and must be no earlier than the late fourth century.

3. *Zhengyi fawen tianshi jiao jieke jing* 20a–21b.

The Teaching says: I instruct the Five Pneumas, Central Pneumas, Supervisors of Deities, Circulators of Pneumas of the Four Sectors, Left and Right Overseers of Deities, and Parish-Heading Libationers of the twenty-four parishes, the leaders of the alternate parishes, and the unassigned parish citizens both male and female, young and old. I received the Dao on the first day of the fifth month of the inaugural year of the Han Peace reign period [142] from the royal divine pneuma of the First Emperor of the Han. Taking five bushels of rice as a pledge offering, I wanted to cause all those worthy individuals who could attain transcendence to rise up and be saved. You people are all so difficult to teach. I cannot talk to you. You turn right into wrong and consider bent to be straight. At this confluence of a thousand years, what should I do about you? I have followed the Supreme Lord Lao as he traveled to the end of the earth in all eight directions, traveling amongst the citizens in order to select the seed citizen, but in the end we could find none at all. Neither among the commoners nor all of you was there anyone who qualified to be a seed. You only lust after glory, wealth, money and possessions, grain, silk brocade, and filmy cottons. You think your only concern is to care for your wives and children. You extort the taxes of other [masters'] citizens, collect their cash and goods. You steal the services of the commoners solely to create citizen households. You cultivate agriculture and forge plowshares[4] in order to care for your wives and slaves. You consider yourselves correct and others wrong, hoping to obtain fame for your accomplishments. You adorn your person and make yourself wealthy, lust unrestrainedly for cash and possessions. Your households are not harmonious; jealousy rules them. Men and women, young and old, talk about each other, taking turns to slander and defame. Your loose talk fills the roads, and you say something different when the person's back is turned. If others say something different from you, you turn on them and say they are jealous. You are not prudent in dealing with the spirits, nor do you worry about the Heavenly Dao. You cause the pneumas to be confused and disordered. Who should be accused of these crimes? Each of you claims to have received a secret Teaching, speculating about how to act on the basis of precedents. I cannot stand you people any longer!

4. Reading *xia* 鍜 as a graphic error for *duan* 鍛 and *si* 私 as a graphic/phonetic error for *si* 耜. These are admittedly bold emendations, but, as presently represented, the phrase cannot be construed.

I want to seize you and make you face a bill of indictment. Do you have any idea what that would mean? You libationers and leaders, men and women, young and old, you are all so benighted! You are no different from the profane! You say one thing but think another. You have a human's head but the heart of an animal. You show no moderation in the bedchamber, giving free rein to your lascivious emotions. Men and women, young and old do not correct each other. You are so benighted. As a group your conduct is filthy and defiled, and you have abandoned the path of the master. Lord Lao, the Most High, having projected on the basis of previous events, has established guiding principles and raised high the net [of justice]. Previous actions will be used to assess for punishment those leaders who have been entrusted with responsibilities and libationers who were assigned parishes, executing three or four of every ten, so that they can return to the Heavenly Bureaus to be interrogated and tortured as punishment for their crimes. You people, be wary of this! The pneumas will move quickly. At most a year or two. Within the next three years, you people will hear about it. He is going to make you people see it with your own eyes. Could you fail to be wary of this? Are there still a few old-timers or not among the various libationers and leaders? Since the Jian'an period or the first year of Huangchu [220 CE], all the various leaders and libationers have cited a Teaching to create their own parishes. They no longer obtain them according to the former rules of the Dao. They do not make you people perform [the promotion ritual] according to the Teachings of my Yangping, Lutang, and Heming parishes. These actions you take, are they in accord with former precedents or not? If they are auspicious, why am I so anxious? I am anxious to turn my attention to getting in touch with the people of the parish. The Determiner of Pneumas has sent down teachings, telling you all what Lord Lao, the Most High, has passed on, that he wants to make all of you take care, to earnestly exert yourselves and further to exhort yourselves for the sake of the Dao to maintain all of the principles and to encourage the commoners to convert.

教：謝二十四治、五氣、中氣、領神、四部行氣、左右監神、治頭祭酒、別治主者、男女老壯散治民：吾以漢安元年五月一日，從漢始皇帝王神氣受道，以五斗米爲信，欲令可仙之士，皆得升度。汝曹輩乃至爾難教。叵與共語。反是爲非，以曲爲直。千載之會，當奈汝曹何？吾從太上老君周行八極，按行民間，選索種民，了不可得。百姓汝曹，無有應人種者也。但貪榮富錢財、穀帛錦綺絲綿，以養妻子爲務；掠取他民戶賦，欶索其錢物；掠使百姓，專作民戶；修農鍜私，以養妻奴；自是非他，欲得功名；榮身富己，苟貪錢財；室家不和，妬姤爲先；男女老壯更相說道，轉相誹謗，溢口盈路，背向異辭，言語不同，轉相說姤，不恤鬼神，以憂天道，令氣錯亂罪，坐在阿誰？各言祕教，推論舊事。吾不能復忍汝輩也！欲持汝輩應文書，頗知與不？祭酒主者，男女老壯，各爾憒憒，與俗無別。口是心非，人頭蟲心。房室不節，縱恣淫情。男女老壯，不相呵整。爲爾憒憒，群行混濁，委託師道。老君太上推論舊事，攝綱舉網。前欲推治諸受任主者、職治祭酒，十人之中，誅其三四，名還天曹，考掠治罪。汝輩慎之！氣將欲急，遠不過一年二年，三年之中，當令汝曹聞知，當令汝輩眼見，可不慎之！諸祭酒主者中頗有舊人以不？從建安、黃初元年以來，諸主者祭酒，人人稱教，各作一治。不復按舊道法爲得爾。不令汝輩按吾陽平、鹿堂、鶴鳴教行之。汝輩所行，舉舊事相應與不。吉，吾有何急？急轉著治民，決氣下教，語汝曹輩，老君、太上轉相督，欲令汝曹人人用意，勤心努力，復自一勸，爲道盡節，勸化百姓。

In this tract, the church founder Zhang Daoling inveighs against a series of practices that are against the morality of the Celestial Master church. Many are topics mentioned in the *Xiang'er* commentary. The focus on wealth and goods giving rise to greed and envy is familiar. The accusation that church members pursue sex without moderation is also familiar from that text. The condemnation of deception, slander, backbiting, and hypocrisy is not unprecedented either.

There are other passages, however, that give us new insight into the faith. The claim that believers do not correct each other brings us face to face with the communal religion in a way that at least the surviving portions of the *Xiang'er* do not. The mention of the parishes and a number of officers within the church is our first clear reference in a datable document to these features. I will return to this for a more detailed examination in the next section, but note that there were already disputes within the church about how one should make appointments to one of these offices and how to fill them with believers. The forced conversion of the profane is condemned as "raid[ing] the commoners," but the piece ends with an exhortation to evangelize.

Revelation plays an important role in these developments. Notice the repeated references to Teachings.[5] There are both legitimate Teachings, verified by someone called the Determiner of Pneumas, and unreliable ones, cited by individuals to justify their assumption of a new title or their creation of a new parish without verification from the central church.

Here we see that the dynamism imparted to the movement by the power of direct, unmediated contact with the divine had both positive and negative effects. Zhang Daoling is here speaking to his faithful from beyond the grave, from the divine position that he has assumed at the side of the Most High Lord Lao (or should it here be the Most High Demonic Lao?). His proper Teachings are communicated through the three exalted parishes of Yangping, Lutang, and Heming, verified by the Determiner of Pneumas, and he expects that the faithful will heed and obey them. But he condemns other libationers for claiming that their own Teachings supersede the authority of those central parishes and their officers. Here I think we see the breakdown in central authority caused by the uprooting of the Hanzhong community and the scattering of its inhabitants. One can well imagine that the Daoists dispatched to the northwest, an area that would have taken weeks to communicate with the Celestial Master in Ye, might have found divine forces speaking to them directly in filling church vacancies or crafting new parishes to minister to the faithful in this unfamiliar environment. Surely it is not surprising that they might "speculat[e] about how to act on the basis of precedents." This encyclical is thus issued by the center in an attempt to reclaim control over the widely scattered parishes of the church.

We also have a new and deeper understanding through this document of the utopian world of Great Peace. In the *Xiang'er*,

---

5. I use the capitalized Teaching to refer to spirit revelations from authoritative church figures as opposed to simple doctrinal elements.

this had seemed a realizable goal, dependent on a sage ruler who understood the intentions of the Dao and implemented them through his rule. Here for the first time we hear of the "seed citizens" (*zhongmin* 種民) who are destined to populate that world. They are to be individually selected by the Most High, accompanied by Zhang Daoling, on the basis of personal conduct. It may be that the *Xiang'er* was intended as a more public document that avoided this topic or that it was indeed mentioned in the half of that commentary that has been lost. But it seems likely that, with the dissolution of the Hanzhong community and the promise that it held, the movement has taken an apocalyptic turn. Now it seems that Great Peace will only be reached after millenarian disasters that will kill off 30 to 40 percent of the community as unworthy. Moreover, these disasters are not in some far-off future but will begin "at most within the next year or two [or three]." This is no doubt the reason for the closing comment on continued evangelization.

Church Offices

The *Yangping Parish* encyclical begins with an invocation of its audience through a series of offices, presumably beginning with the highest and proceeding to the average citizen. I am not sure, however, that we are warranted in assuming that this is a comprehensive list of all church offices. At the least, it seems likely that within the "unassigned citizens" that are mentioned last there may well have been finer divisions. Moreover, there is no mention here of the Determiner of Pneumas, who is mentioned in the body of the text as well as the *Commands and Precepts*, or the True Pneumas 真氣 mentioned in that text.

The only sources earlier than this to mention church offices are the historical accounts, which refer only to libationers and parish-heading great libationers, and the Zhang Pu stele, which mentions only libationers. Both libationers and parish-heading libationers (without the "great" but presumably the same office) occur in this source, but none of the alternate names given in historical sources, like "demon clerk" or "demon trooper," are found here or in any other surviving Celestial Master source.

The offices above the rank of libationer are poorly understood. The offices of Five Pneumas and Central Pneumas are mentioned in a passage discussing the seating order at banquets from the otherwise lost *Scripture of the Essential Teaching* 旨教經:[6]

> The seating begins with the Five Pneumas at the head; [next] is the Central Pneumas, then the Correct Parish, then the Inner Parish, then the Alternate Parish and Unassigned Pneumas, then the One Hundred Fifty Generals Register, then the Seventy-Five Generals Register, then the Ten Generals Register, then the Adolescents, then the Transcendent Officers, then the Upper Numinous Officers, then the Renewed Mandates.
>
> 坐起五氣上，中氣，次正治，次內治，次別治散氣，次百五十將軍籙，次七十五將軍籙，次十將軍籙，次童子，次仙官，上靈官，次更令。

This text dates to no earlier than the fifth century, so it is not surprising that there have been some changes, but the church hierarchy seems to be basically the same. We do, however, see much more differentiation at lower levels of the structure. In particular, this source introduces the concept of registers (*lu* 籙), which are ordination documents certifying a level of accomplishment. We will look at registers in more detail in chapter 7.

We are in a better position to explain the next three posts, the Supervisors of Deities, the Circulators of Pneumas for the Four Sections, and the Left and Right Overseers of Deities. The first and third do occur in a list of twenty-four church offices preserved in the Tang Daoist encyclopedia *Sack of Pearls of the Three Caverns*,

---

6. *Yaoxiu keyi jielü chao* 9/8a–b. The scripture quoted here presumably included the liturgy for the Fête of the Essential Teaching 旨教齋, which it was claimed was an early Celestial Master ritual, but Lü Pengzhi (2010) has shown that it was created after the Lingbao revelations of the 390s.

and the second may occur with a slight variation in title.[7] There we read of the duties of the Supervisor of Deities:

> In charge of selecting the wise and worthy, and demoting the false and evil, responding to and assembling the various pneumas. In charge of all those who have offended or disobeyed.
> 主選擇賢良，貶退偽惡，對會諸氣，諸有犯違，盡主之也。

As for the Overseers of Deities, which is divided into posts of the left, occupied by males, and of the right, occupied by females, their duties are as follows:

> In charge of investigating the statements of all offenses committed heretofore, compiling them into a document, examining the benefits and harms [engendered by the offenses], restraining [the faithful] from mistakes and errors, and converting and enlightening concerning the precepts and orders.
> 主考素所犯狀，結文書，開視利害，縛束謬誤，化諭戒勅。

From these descriptions, it would seem that the overseers are lower-level officials who deal with the offenses of the average Daoist citizen, perhaps being directly engaged in the creation of the Handwritten Missives to the Three Offices that we read about in the historical accounts of the foundation period. The supervisors have a similar function in combating evil but are focused on selecting worthy individuals for promotion and office.

The title Circulator of Pneumas does not occur in this list, but we do find a Circulator of Deities:

> In charge of distributing the pneumas and propagating conversion to illuminate the teachings of the Dao.
> 行神職：主布氣宣化，顯明道教。

---

7. *Sandong zhunang* 7/17b–19b. For a full translation of this list of offices, see chapter 8.

Given the description of the duties assigned, it seems possible that an alternate term for this post was Circulator of Pneumas. We can assume that the Four Sections in the encyclical refer to the four cardinal directions, with one officer being assigned to promote converts in each direction.[8]

We have also mentioned the office of Determiner of Pneumas (*jueqi* 決氣), who is mentioned in both *Yangping Parish* and the *Commands and Precepts*. This office does not occur among the twenty-four offices, but there is again one that sounds very similar:

> The Supervisor of Determinations: In charge of demonic pneuma men and women, who are possessed by pneumas and transmit words. Supervises the determination of Teachings, distinguishing among Chinese, Yi barbarian, Hu barbarian, Rong barbarian, Di barbarian, Di' barbarian, and Qiang barbarian, and between authentic and false [pneumas].[9]

8. Although it is not direct evidence, in support of this interpretation we can cite the *Register of the Pneumas of the Most High's Twenty-Four Parishes* 太上二十四治氣籙 in the Tang period DZ 1209 *Taishang zhengyi mengwei falu* 13b–16b. In this text we find the twenty-four posts have been transformed into register spirits and each assigned to a parish, but we do find Circulators of Pneumas of the East, South, and West, though oddly none of the north, as well as a Left and Right Supervisor of the Circulation of Qi 左右領行氣.

9. The various types of barbarian are traditionally associated with different directions, with the Yi in the east, the Hu in the west, and the Di in the north, but the Di' are related to the Qiang tribes in the northwest and were in close contact with the Daoists in Hanzhong (Taniguchi 1976 argues they were converted to Daoism). The Ba peoples are sometimes referred to as Ba-Yi barbarians. The term for Chinese is Qin, the word that is at the origin of most Western names for China. It was used as a general term for Chinese in the northwest from at least Latter Han times. We see these non-Chinese peoples integrated into the Celestial Master cosmology in a petition in *Nüqing guilü* (3/28a), which invokes: "The Green Thearch of the East, Lord of the Nine Yi; the Red Thearch of the South, Lord of the Eight Man; the White Thearch of the West, Lord of the Six Rong; the Black Thearch of the North, Lord of the Five Di; and the Yellow Thearch of the Center, Lord of the Three Chinese" 東方青帝九夷君,南方赤帝八蠻君,西方白帝六戎君,北方黑帝五狄君,中央黃帝三秦君. Given this integration, it is not surprising that spirit communications might be relayed by a non-Chinese figure.

領決職：主鬼氣男女，被氣傳語。領決教，分別秦夷胡戎狄氏羌
真偽。

This is an office specifically dedicated to authenticating spirit communications. Given the multiethnic character of the early Daoist community, it cannot be assumed that a Teaching from a non-Chinese pneuma was necessarily a false one. If the Determiner of Pneumas is not an alternate term for this office, it is perhaps his or her subordinate.[10]

Most of the twenty-four offices, translated in chapter 8, are never mentioned in Daoist scriptures, and we must depend on the brief description preserved in the Tang for our understanding of them.[11] Many seem concerned with recordkeeping for the community, tracking individual conduct as well as that of parish leaders, recording additions through birth to or subtractions through death from individual Daoist families, recording meritorious acts like the performance of ritual, and recommending individuals for promotion on that basis. One office, the Director of Pneumas 都氣, is devoted to organizing the Three Assemblies (see the section below on the ritual calendar) and scheduling requests for healing rituals. The office of Solemn Decorum 威儀 oversees proper etiquette, whereas the Regulator of Pneumas 典氣 makes sure that relations among ranks and offices follow established norms. Interestingly, there is an office called Equalizer of Integrity 廉平 that roots out corruption that would result in differences

10. Cedzich dismisses this identification as having "little reason or evidence" and proposes to read the phrase as verbal but never offers a translation of any of the sentences where it occurs that would show how such a reading could actually be applied to the grammar (2009:25, n. 53). See note 8 above for an example of an office mentioned in *Yangping Parish* to which the prefix "supervisor" has been added. Cedzich also insists that "this by no means endorses spirit-mediumship as a regular praxis" of the Celestial Masters, but this is difficult to reconcile with predominance of spirit-written texts among the surviving documents of the early church and the frequent references to spirit revelation.

11. I have profited much from the comments on some of these offices by Cedzich (2009:22–25). My doubts concerning some of her interpretations are recorded in the notes to the list in chapter 8, but it must be admitted that the language is often obscure and no one can be sure of its proper interpretation.

in the amount of food and drink consumed by members. Some offices are focused on the larger world and even supernatural realms, like the Supervisor of Merit 領功, who evaluates the conduct of profane deities; the Submitter of Pneumas 上氣, who reports upon them to the Heavens; and the Great Director of Attacks 大都攻, who launches assaults on those deemed deviant or evil. It is not surprising that we find three offices, the Circulator of Deities 行神, the Circulator of Teachings 行教, and the Pneuma of the Dao 道氣, responsible for propagating the faith and converting evildoers.

The titles of these offices do not tell us much about their responsibilities, with fully eleven of twenty-four, or nearly half, including the word "pneuma" and the pneumas representing anything from forces within the believer's body to profane spirits, meteorological phenomena, and manifestations of the Dao itself. We are indeed fortunate that this guide was preserved in a Tang era encyclopedia. The original was part of a major text called the *Statutes of the Mystic Capital*, of which only a small portion survives.[12] We do not really know how these offices were distributed: whether each parish was supposed to have one of each office,[13] or perhaps two, male of the right and female of the left, giving a full complement of forty-eight; or whether each post was assigned to a different parish, perhaps then yielding only one or two (male and female) per parish (I propose a historical solution to this problem in chapter 8). In fact, there is an alternate ordering that enumerates only twelve posts but with a left (male) and right (female) version of each and assigns one to each of the twenty-four primary parishes; this is then followed by eight posts assigned to the eight "roving parishes" (see below), for a total of twenty rather than twenty-four posts.[14] This list is credited to Zhang Bian 張辯,

12. DZ 188 *Xuandu lüwen*. The final compilation of the present text was no earlier than the Tang because of continuous additions as the situation within the church changed, but it includes much authentic early material. See Jiang Boqin 1991; Schipper and Verellen 2004:469–70.

13. This is the assumption of Cedzich (2009:22).

14. See *Shoulu cidi faxin yi* 19b–23a. This source credits Zhang Lu with establishing the eight posts in roving parishes. See also Chen Guofu 1963:346–

the thirteenth-generation Celestial Master, who lived during the Liang dynasty (sixth century), but gives no indication of the duties of each post. Some of the more prosaic recordkeeping offices must have been present in each parish. With the transformation of the parishes in subsequent centuries, many of these offices came to be interpreted as divine postings, each associated with a different parish.[15]

The Parish System

I have mentioned the system of parishes several times, but having encountered the first clearly datable reference to this administrative network, it is appropriate here to examine it in greater detail.[16] The character for "parish" can be read as a verb in level tone, *chi* 治, meaning "to govern, administer," and the derived noun *zhi*, in falling tone, meant the administrative center of a governmental unit like a county or commandery. We should first note that a system of twenty-four has several natural analogues within Chinese culture, including the twenty-four seasonal nodes of the solar calendar, which are so vital to farming life because they truly demarcate the seasons, and indeed they are named after seasonal and climatic events (the Chinese lunar calendar varies from year to year by as much as six weeks, making it almost worthless for the purposes of planting or harvesting). Another analogue within the Daoist world was the human body, which

---

51. Chen suggests that the *Statutes of the Mystic Capital* ordering reflects the North after the reforms of Kou Qianzhi, whereas the Zhang Bian ordering reflects the South; however, the example of Li Dong 李東 in the *Zhen'gao* (20/13b) does not accord with the "southern" list and would only make sense if each parish had a full complement of officers. This is explicitly stated for two offices that occur only in the "southern" roving parish list in *Yaoxiu keyi jielü chao* 10/1b. See chapter 8 for full details.

15. See DZ 1209 *Taishang zhengyi mengwei falu* 13b–16b, which Schipper and Verellen date to the Tang (2004:469–70), and the Southern Song DZ 1167 *Taishang ganyingpian* 28/14a–b.

16. For an excellent exposition of the mature system of parishes, see Verellen 2003b.

comprised three distinct levels, centering on the head, the chest, and the abdomen. Each has a set of eight gods inhabiting and regulating it. The parishes are also presented as an upper, middle, and lower set of eight.

The *Statutes of the Mystic Capital* describes the parish in the following way: "The parish is what the nature, fate, soul, and spirit depend upon" 治者，性命魂神之所屬也.[17] The parish provided a variety of functions to the early church communities. Believers went to its ritual center when confronting a personal problem like misfortune or bad health and on fixed occasions like the Three Assemblies, held annually on the seventh day of the first month, the seventh day of the seventh month, and the fifth day of tenth month. The libationers assigned to a parish would respond to individual emergencies by offering a petition to the Daoist Heavens. On the Three Assemblies, they would first preach a sermon, then offer a communal feast for church members. This was also the time when they collected the grain tithe, which supplied the feast and fed the libationers. Rosters of population were maintained in the parish and memorialized to Heaven on these days as well. The parish no doubt also fulfilled a sort of judicial function, resolving disputes within the community.

Given all of these functions, it is curious that the original twenty-four parishes are all reported to have been on mountains. In Sichuan, a paddy rice growing area, the population was highly concentrated on the plains. Even though the relevant mountains were not high, it would have been a considerable trek each time individuals wanted to visit their parish. Given the dense population of the Sichuan region, it seems likely that there were subordinate libationers living much closer to population centers and ministering to daily needs. A trip to the local parish would then have been a rather infrequent outing, perhaps taken only on the Assembly days or when some special need arose.

We have seen that by 255, the time of the revelation of the

---

17. This passage does not appear in the *Xuandu lüwen* found in the canon, which is only a small portion of the original work, but is quoted in *Sandong zhunang* 7/1a.

Commands and Precepts text, church members believed that the original twenty-four parishes were included in the revelation to Zhang Ling by the Most High Lord Lao that began the movement in 142. Only the attestation of the office of libationer and the rice tithe is earlier. Yet it is hard to imagine that the system was more than notional at that time, simply because Zhang Ling did not yet have a network of believers across the rather vast area covered by the parish system. Even if such a system of organization was present before the period of intense evangelization, one can well imagine that originally the twenty-four parishes were laid out on a much smaller grid.[18] Still, no trace of this period survives. Instead, in the earliest records, the parishes are centered, to be sure, on the Chengdu plain but extend north to Hanzhong, south to the Yangzi, east to the Ba region, and west to the foothills of the Tibetan plateau.

The three most exalted parishes, all tied closely to the Celestial Master himself, are grouped in close proximity to the north and west of Chengdu, two in what was at the time Fan 繁 county (modern Xinfanzhen 新繁镇) and one in neighboring Linqiong 臨 邛 county (modern Qionglai 邛崃), both of Shu commandery. In fact, six of the top eight and seven of the twenty-four parishes were in Shu commandery. If you combine Guanghan commandery, which abuts it to the north, and Qianwei, its neighbor to the south, this accounts for nineteen of the twenty-four. We are surely justified in seeing this area as the geographical origin of the movement, especially since one of the three highest parishes (interestingly enough, however, only the third) was on Mount Crane-Call, where the Most High appeared to Zhang Ling, founding the religion. It was Yangping parish, as I have mentioned, that was the seat of the Celestial Master. The leader of that parish, first called "Parish-Leading Libationer" and later "Director of Merit" 都功, was always a lineal descendant of the first Celestial Master, Zhang Daoling.

18. A similar sort of expansion tracking the growth of Chinese civilization is evident in the system of the five marchmounts, in which the northern and southern marchmounts were moved repeatedly. See Robson 2009.

It is uncertain how this system transformed once the Celestial Master no longer physically occupied Yangping parish, moving first to Hanzhong and then to the headquarters of the Cao family in Ye (west of modern Linzhang, Hebei), but the *Commands and Precepts* argues for the continued authority of the top three parishes. One list of the original twenty-four includes one to the west in Yuesui commandery, one to the east in Ba commandery, three in Hanzhong, and one in the capital of Chang'an.[19] We do not know to what degree Celestial Master believers throughout the Sichuan area might have immigrated to be part of the Hanzhong theocracy, but we do have a record of the ancestor of Li Te 李特 (ca. 245–303), who moved there from Dangqu 宕渠 (modern Quxian 渠縣 in southeastern Sichuan) together with five hundred households of relatives and retainers, two thousand or more people.[20] We cannot be sure if they retained their parish identities when they moved, but it seems likely that some members of that group were at least libationers, and this must have had a distorting effect on the parish system. When the inhabitants of Hanzhong were transferred, the disruption would have been even greater.

This may well be why we find a set of four "supplementary parishes" (*beizhi* 備治, although several sources say that they were known as "alternate parishes," *biezhi* 別治, to outsiders) revealed to Zhang Lu through his father, Zhang Heng (who was long dead), at dawn on the day of the first of the Three Assemblies (February 1 by Western reckoning) in 198.[21] This created a group of twenty-eight, which could be aligned one-to-one with the twenty-eight lunar lodges that divide the Chinese celestial equator. Sometimes known as "star-lodge parishes" (*xingxiuzhi* 星宿治), these would have allowed individuals to be assigned to parishes not on the basis of their place of residence, but rather on

19. The last is truly a bit surprising, but perhaps it is the result of missionary activity among the elite. Moreover, the capital region was home to many non-Chinese, and a presence there might explain Zhang Lu's ties to Ma Chao and others from that area, mentioned in the preceding chapter.

20. Ren Naiqiang 1987:483; *Jin shu* 120/3022.

21. *Yaoxiu keyi jielü chao* 7/5b.

when they were born. This arrangement would have been ideal for a situation where individuals from a variety of places were mixing together. It would hardly have been practical to squeeze them all into the three parishes that were actually located in Hanzhong, and such a solution would have left the libationers and other church officers, who could not easily change parish, in a difficult situation. The star-lodge parishes were not, however, a permanent solution. I will return to this topic in chapter 8 on libationers. In fact, some of the tensions that developed in this system were already apparent in the next church encyclical we shall consider, the *Commands and Precepts for the Great Family of the Dao* of 255.

Commands and Precepts for the Great Family of the Dao

The same collection of Celestial Master teachings that preserved *Yangping Parish* contains another encyclical, the *Commands and Precepts for the Great Family of the Dao* 大道家令戒.[22] The date of this text is disputed, largely because scholars did not understand the way "Qin" 秦 is used in the text (and other early documents) to mean Chinese rather than to refer to any specific dynasty named Qin. The text states the date of its revelation, the seventh day of the first month, hence the day of the First Assembly, of the second year of Corrected Prime 正元, or January 31, 255 CE,[23] and there is no reason to doubt this. As Ōfuchi and Bokenkamp have shown, the date fits the contents well and accords with the dates of other pieces in the *Scripture of Precepts and Codes, Teachings of the Celestial Master*. Since Bokenkamp has already offered

22. For an introduction to and full translation of this text, see Bokenkamp 1997:149–85.

23. Bokenkamp gives February 1 (1997:177), off by one day. I base myself on the Academia Sinica online tables at http://sinocal.sinica.edu.tw/ (accessed October 17, 2015). Bokenkamp may have been basing his calculations on the Shu-Han calendar, which started the year one day later in 255.

a full translation of this text, here I will only translate and discuss selected passages.

The piece begins with a recounting of history from a distinctively Daoist perspective. All begins with the Great Dao, which spontaneously produced the universe out of primordial chaos, then ordered it through the production of three subtle pneumas: the Mystic (*xuan* 玄), which is black and represents Heaven; the Inaugurating (*shi* 始), which is yellow and represents Earth; and the Primordial (*yuan* 元), which is white and represents the Dao. They act as the parents of all living creatures. Everything that is eternal, embodying these pneumas, possesses essences and gods. The pneumas gave birth to Heaven, Earth, and Humankind, giving rise to nine pneumas, which are vital to the viscera and organs of the body and must be preserved by performing good deeds and keeping the Dao. Although much of this is reminiscent of the teachings of the *Xiang'er* commentary, it is the first clearly articulated Daoist cosmogony.

Coming to our age of Lower Antiquity, lust led to deviance and falseness, to cravings for wealth and bribes, and hence illness arose. Beginning with the reign of the Yellow Thearch and continuing through the Xia, Shang, and Zhou dynasties, humanity turned to war and violence, which only one person in ten thousand survived. The Dao, valuing human life, first manifested in Langya (modern Shandong, but near Zhang Ling's ancestral home in Jiangsu) to reveal the Way of Great Peace to Gan Ji 干吉. Although the *Xiang'er* often refers to Great Peace, this is the first explicit confirmation that one inspiration for the Celestial Masters was the *Scripture of Great Peace*. Further on, however, the *Commands and Precepts* condemns Zhang Jue 張角, leader of the Yellow Turbans movement that was more directly founded on the *Scripture of Great Peace*.

This initial attempt at conversion met, however, with only limited success because the pneumas were still insignificant. The Way of Great Peace supplied the people with food, which led them to make sacrifices to the gods. In what seems today a rather anachronistic move, the Dao then manifested in the west of China as Laozi. Realizing that the conditions were not sufficient to realize

Great Peace, he provided the "oral instructions of an enlightened teacher" in the form of the Five-Thousand-Character Scripture (i.e., the *Daodejing*). Despite these instructions for the cultivation of one's life and strict prohibitions on conduct, the people were foolish, and few were saved.

Laozi then went into the west to teach the Dao to the barbarians, giving them extremely strict prohibitions that included a ban on sexual activity and killing living beings for food. Because the barbarians could not put their faith in the Dao, he further manifested as a perfected transcendent, at which point they finally shaved their heads and accepted the faith. This is a very positive understanding of Buddhism as a "true Dao," albeit in an altered form adapted for a non-Chinese population. The text says, "This was not merely for the barbarians and not for the Chinese, so that the Chinese would not get the perfected Dao."

This promise was realized with his next manifestation at the beginning of the Han dynasty, when the Dao bestowed the book of the transcendent Lord Yellow Stone on Zhang Liang 張良, an advisor to the Han founder, Liu Bang, who some authors consider an ancestor of Zhang Daoling.[24] Then, in a passage already cited, while the last rulers of the Han were running roughshod over the country, the Dao took pity on the people and appeared to Zhang Daoling as the Newly Emerged Demonic Lao, appointing him Celestial Master. This is, then, the second earliest account (after *Yangping Parish*) of the revelation and records the exact date and place that would be enshrined in church lore from this point forward. The twenty-four parishes were established and the Three Pneumas distributed to them to govern the citizens.

Alas, people still did not reform but merely "competed in lusting after an age of luxury, each claiming higher status than the other, disobeying the Dao and betraying virtue" 競貪高世，更相貴賤，違道叛德. It was this "enjoyment of disorder" that gave rise to

---

24. *Shiji* 55/2034–35 records Zhang Liang's mysterious encounter with an old man named Lord Yellow Stone, who tests Liang and then bestows on him a book, saying, "If you read this, you will become the master of a king." Cf. *Han shu* 40/2024.

the rebellion of the Yellow Turbans. The text asks the faithful, "Do you know who Zhang Jue was?" implying that he had a secret, unsavory identity known only to members of the church.

The next passage is both difficult and important, and opinion is split on how to interpret it, so I treat it in detail:[25]

> The Dao caused the last successors [to the Han dynasty] to divide the pneumas and rule the citizens of Hanzhong for more than forty years. The Dao forbade a genuine Inaugural year. The stories about divine transcendents were promulgated by the Dao. How could you consider the *Xiang'er*, the [*Scripture of the*] *Marvelous Perfected . . .* and the *Seven-Character Verses of the Three Divines* not to be genuine and say the Dao cheats us?[26] Alas, how sad! When our righteous kingdom was toppled, those who died escaping numbered in the tens of thousands, which harmed people's resolve. Ever since the migrations and transfers [of population], you have been spread across the realm. The Dao then saved your lives again and again. Sometimes the Determiner of Pneumas spoke to you, sometimes there were former officers and commanders who corrected you, and yet you still did not believe. This is extremely lamentable. If you want the morning to come, the sun must first set. If you want Great Peace, there must first be disorder. Human evil cannot be eliminated. There must first be warfare, illness, floods, drought, and death. You fellows have an

25. Cf. Bokenkamp 1997:172–73. My translation differs from his in numerous respects.

26. There is a gap of four characters in the text following the mention of the *Xiang'er*, suggesting that originally another scripture was also mentioned in this list. Bokenkamp takes "Marvelous Perfected" to be an epithet of the Most High Lord Lao and hence considers this part of the extended reference to the *Scripture of the Yellow Court* (1997:172, n. 3), but Ōfuchi points out that there was a text called the *Scripture of the Marvelous Perfected* that was closely associated with the *Xiang'er* and shares some of its teachings (1991:268–70). It is cited frequently in sixth-century sources like the *Wushang miyao*. Contra Bokenkamp (183, n. 3), leaving blanks equivalent to the number of missing characters is a common way to indicate lacunae in texts of the Ming Daoist canon (e.g., DZ 335 *Taishang Dongyuan shenzhou jing* 3/9b9–10, where the verse structure makes clear that the two one-character-sized gaps indicate two one-character lacunae) and results in a much more persuasive reading of the entire passage than assuming a paragraph break at that point in the text.

unfortunate fate to have met with this. Although this is so, fortunate people will not be punished. You became Daoists in the past just to prepare for what is coming. For those who die before the arrival of Great Peace, their children and grandchildren will enjoy the grace of Heaven. In the latter days, people are glib and superficial, and not resolute in their hearts. If you citizen households, both new and old, seeing this world and knowing that it is changing, are able to reform your hearts and do good, practice benevolence and righteousness, then this will be good. You will be able to see Great Peace, to survive and escape the calamities and misfortunes, and become the seed people of the age to come.

道使末嗣分氣治民漢中四十餘年。道禁真正之元。神仙之說，道所施行。何以《想爾》、口口口口、《妙真》、《三靈七言》復不真正，而故謂道欺人。哀哉可傷。至義國損顛，流移死者以萬爲數，傷人心志。自從流徙以來，分布天下。道乃往往救汝曹之命。或決氣相語，或有故臣令相端正，而復不信。甚可哀哉。欲朝當先暮，欲太平當先亂。人惡不能除。當先兵病水旱死。汝曹薄命，正當與此相遇。雖然，吉人無咎。昔時爲道，以備今來耳。未至太平而死，子孫當蒙天恩。下世浮薄，持心不堅。新故民戶，見世知變，便能改心爲善，行仁義，則善矣。可見太平，度脫厄難之中，爲後世種民。

Although the first sentence is often understood to refer to Zhang Lu[27] or Han emperor Xian, who resigned his throne in favor of Cao Pi of the Wei dynasty, I believe it refers to Liu Bei and his son Liu Shan, who controlled the Shu-Han state in Sichuan, and the territory of Hanzhong, from 219 on. By 255, this had indeed been almost forty years and fits the next phrase much better than assuming it refers to the twenty-four years (191–215) that Zhang Lu

27. The idea that Daoists would refer to Zhang Lu as the "last successor" (*mosi* 末嗣) is difficult to accept. It would imply that there was no Celestial Master after his death, but we at least know of Zhang Bian (see earlier in this chapter), successor in the thirteenth generation, under the Liang dynasty. Moreover, it seems a disparaging way to refer to a respected former leader. Bokenkamp takes it to refer to Emperor Xian but then breaks the sentence after "divides the pneumas" and attributes this to Zhang Jue, who never had any influence in Sichuan.

was based there. When the parishes had been set up, the Three Pneumas of the Dao were distributed among them. Now the Shu-Han state ruled some of those parishes, thus "dividing" their pneumas off from the main body of the church. The denial by the Dao of a "true, correct Inaugural year," then, refers to the fact that Zhang Lu was never able to claim the title of king or emperor as an independent sovereign. A new reign in China was marked by a new reign name, and the first year was called the Inaugural Year (*yuannian* 元年).[28]

The next passage is important for confirming the association of certain texts with the Celestial Masters. The *Xiang'er* commentary had promised that, with the advent of the age of Great Peace, believers would become transcendents, a lofty goal usually thought attainable only by rigorous self-cultivation or expensive alchemical practices. The *Scripture of the Yellow Court* (*Huangting jing* 黃庭經), a text composed by the Supreme Lord Lao—the Marvelous Perfected—in seven-character verses and treating the three divine cloud souls (*hun* 魂), explained how the body gods congealed out of essence would effect this.[29] The *Yangping Parish* encyclical had begun with Zhang Daoling traveling throughout the world in the company of the Dao, looking for individuals worthy of becoming seed people in Great Peace but finding none. This seems to have been a stopgap way of explaining to people at that time why Great Peace had not yet arrived: the faithful were not worthy. Now, forty years after the dissolution of the community, which spread believers across North China, the prolonged but still unfulfilled wait for

28. This practice was begun by Emperor Wu 武 of Han (r. 140–87 BCE) in 134 BCE. See *Shiji* 12/460. Establishing a new state and beginning a new reign name came to be called "establishing the inaugural," or *jianyuan* 建元. Tang Changru explicitly explains the phrase in this way (1983:228). Bokenkamp punctuates differently and translates this phrase "the origins of the True and Correct" (1987:172).

29. The *Scripture of the Yellow Court*, later renamed the *Outer Scripture* 黃庭外經 when the Shangqing revelations produced a rewritten *Inner Scripture*, has been conclusively shown to be of a similar date and geographic origin to other early Celestial Master texts by Yu Wanli (2001) using phonological analysis.

Great Peace had given rise to a crisis of faith, as people who had expected the advent of Great Peace in their lifetimes were increasingly dying off. There is a remarkable parallel here to the situation in the early Christian church regarding expectations for the Second Coming. Even the most basic scriptures of the movement were being questioned, leading the speaker to reassert that they had been revealed directly by the Dao.

This text is also remarkable for its explicit description of the early church's millenarian teachings. Disasters must arise as a way of ridding the world of profane nonbelievers, and those church members who did not remain steadfast in their faith and constant in their conduct might be swept away with them. The tract goes on to cite the astrological and meteorological omens that had appeared recently, confirming the imminent arrival of these disasters.[30] It is interesting that the text explicitly addresses both old members who had belonged since the Hanzhong theocracy—what the text calls the "righteous kingdom"—and those converted by the ongoing program of evangelization that made Daoism a national faith. It is also intriguing to see that the fount of ongoing spirit revelation through the official Determiner of Pneumas had not been shut off. It is uncertain if the "former officers and commanders" who still spoke to believers were physical survivors or were also communicating through spirit mediums. This text, like *Yangping Parish*, has a rather ambiguous attitude toward such communication. In this passage it is encouraged as a way of guiding those in danger of falling into apostasy, but later on we read of church members who, "listening to the Determiner of Pneumas, [instead] believe the shadowy dreams of their wives" 或聽決氣, 信內人影夢.

In chapter 1, I mentioned the signal treatment that Zhang Lu received from Cao Cao on his surrender, including enfeoffments for himself and his sons, and intermarriage with the Cao family for both his daughter and at least one of his sons. I speculated then that this might have indicated a favored position for the Celestial Master faith within the Wei state, and we find confirmation

30. See *Zhengyi fawen tianshi jiao jieke jing* 16a4–6; Bokenkamp 1997:175.

of this in the *Commands and Precepts*, in a moving passage describing the conditions at the end of the Han dynasty:[31]

Long ago, during the last generation of the Han, warlords ran roughshod, the strong oppressed the weak, the people practiced deception, and men and woman fell easily into debauchery. The government was unable to save them, and families did not prohibit this behavior. Bandits plagued the marketplaces, the small folk were the subject of unjustified resentment, people enslaved each other, and the myriad peoples were gobbled up as if by silkworms. The citizens resented this and longed to rebel; the refractory pneumas drew the attention of Heaven, which therefore caused the five planets to lose their timings, comets to sweep the skies, and the Fire Star to lose its companion.[32] Powerful officials fought amongst themselves and herds of miscreants goaded each other on, for more than a century. The Wei house was authorized by Heaven to drive them out; the calendar demanded this. It was recorded in the River Diagram and the Luo Writing, and images [confirming it] were displayed in the Heavens. Thereupon, in accordance with Heaven and in obedience to the times, I as Master of the Kingdom charged the Martial Emperor with administering the realm.[33] The dead filled

31. *Zhengyi fawen tianshi jiao jieke jing* 16b6–17a7; cf. Bokenkamp 1997: 179–80.

32. Although Bokenkamp takes this as a reference to Mars, it more likely refers to the Great Fire star 大火星, the red supergiant Antares, which was the second star in the Heart asterism. The sighting of Antares on the horizon at dusk around the end of May was a marker of the coming of summer. I am grateful to Dr. Ning Xiaoyu 寧曉玉 of the Institute for the History of Natural Science in the Chinese Academy of Sciences for this explanation. Antares has an emerald-hued companion star, but it is unclear if this is truly visible to the naked eye; otherwise, the reference here may be to the Preceding Star (前星, Gamma Scorpii), which is often said to precede Antares and is associated with the heir apparent. On the astrological significance of Antares, see Schafer 1977:60–61, 73, 117, 208, and especially 128.

33. Bokenkamp translates, "I received the mandate to be Master of the Kingdom. The Martial Thearch launched the empire," thus making two sentences and understanding the title to refer to the Wei, but the grammar indicates the reading given here. This Master of the Kingdom is Laozi who appears generation after generation in this position, as recorded in the fifth-century *Santian neijie jing*, but there is also a tradition, preserved in a Tang encyclopedia but

the ditches. Having brought my state glory, even newborn infants were not harmed, there were repeated bestowals of gold and purple, and individuals obtained extended longevity. Seven sons were granted the five ranks of nobility,[34] becoming the glory of the state, while more than a few generals, ministers, and associates were enfeoffed as marquises, and [bestowals of] silver and copper numbered in the thousands. When the father died, the son succeeded, and, though the younger brother perished, the elder flourished, all bathing in the sage grace.[35] Have you all noted this virtue and realized the source of this perfection? In the old days, the gate was open and you were taught to do good, yet you did not listen. From now on, I am going to avoid the world and entrust you to the Wei. With their pure governance and administration based on the Dao, one can travel along for hundreds of miles, and tigers and wolves will hide themselves in submission, and no one will close his outer gates.

昔漢嗣末世，豪傑縱橫，強弱相陵，人民詭點，男女輕淫。政不能濟，家不相禁。抄盜城市，怨枉小人，更相僕役，蠶食萬民。民怨思亂，逆氣干天。故令五星失度，彗孛上掃，火星失輔，強臣

---

from a sixth-century source, that when conveying to Zhang Daoling the position of Celestial Master, he also granted to him the position of Master of the Kingdom, to be transmitted to his descendants. In any case, it would have been as Master of the Kingdom for the Han that this figure transferred the Mandate to the Wei, so Bokenkamp's speculation about a post given Zhang Lu by Cao Cao is irrelevant. See *Santian neijie jing* 1/3a6; *Sandong zhunang* 7/6b10, citing the *Tianshi ershisi zhi tu* 天師二十四治圖 of Zhang Bian.

34. Bokenkamp and Ōfuchi understand this is as "of [my] seven sons, five were made lords" (Ōfuchi 1991:266), which is not impossible, but *wuhou* is a common term for the five ranks of nobility. Bokenkamp further says that the *Sanguozhi* "mentions only six of Lu's sons, one of whom was murdered by Liu Zhang, whereas the five remaining were enfeoffed upon Zhang Lu's surrender to Cao Cao" (Bokenkamp 1997:180n), but there is no mention of a sixth son in the *Sanguozhi*, and it was Lu's younger brother(s) who was killed by Liu Zhang. See *Sanguozhi* 31/868. Since it seems unlikely that an internal source would get this wrong, perhaps Lu had distaff or adopted sons who were not recorded by the source used by Chen Shou.

35. As Bokenkamp points out, these are probably elliptical references to the Zhang family, but we know so little that we can only guess about their referents. The reference to the father dying and being succeeded by his son may refer to Zhang Lu, or perhaps, if Zhang Lu died in 216, already to Lu's son and grandson.

分爭，群姦相將，百有餘年。魏氏承天驅除，歷使其然，載在河
雒，懸象垂天，是吾順天奉時，以國師命武帝行天下，死者填
坑。既得吾國之光，赤子不傷身，重金累紫，得壽遐亡。七子五
侯爲國之光，將相緣屬，侯封不少，銀銅數千，父死子係，弟亡
兄榮，沐浴聖恩。汝輩豈誌德知真所從來乎？昔日開門教之爲
善，而反不相聽。從今吾避世，以汝付魏，清政道治，千里獨
行，虎狼伏匿，外不閉門。

This passage would seem to be talking about the treatment of
Zhang Lu's family, and it raises the question of who is the speaker.
Bokenkamp argues for a disembodied Zhang Lu, Tang Changru
claims that it is the Dao himself, and Zhang Daoling, who was the
speaker in the *Yangping Parish* encyclical, also seems to be a possibility.[36] I have tried to translate this passage to maintain the
ambiguity, but it does favor Zhang Lu. The problem is that the
text is not very consistent; for example, when mentioning Zhang
Daoling, it does not use the forms of address that his grandson
would use. But perhaps it is expecting too much for a revealed text
to be wholly consistent. There are other problems with the text,
like accounting for the claim of one hundred years since the beginning of the troubles at the end of the Han, or the inconsistency of
the reference to the "last rulers of the Han," which I argued refers
in an earlier passage to the rulers of the state of Shu-Han, Liu Bei
and Liu Shan, rather than Emperors Huan, Ling, and Xian.

Whoever the speaker is, the Hanzhong community is still of considerable importance to him and presumably to the larger Daoist
community. In this regard, we should take a look at another passage that has puzzled many commentators:[37]

Of the various male and female officers whom I had previously
appointed to posts, no more than a few are still there. Ever since
the fifth year of Great Harmony [231 CE], the various postings have
each been self-appointed, and the appointments no longer derive

36. See Bokenkamp 1997:150–51; Tang Changru 1983:225, n. 2.
37. *Zhengyi fawen tianshi jiao jieke jing* 17a5–8; cf. Bokenkamp 1997:
177–78.

from my pneumas, selected by the True Pneumas and the Supervisor of Deities.[38]

諸職男女官，昔所拜署，今在無幾。自從太和五年以來，諸職各各自置，置不復由吾氣，真氣領神選舉。

Here it seems that the centrally administered system of appointment has broken down. The passage goes on to refer to people appealing to the authority of direct revelation, which was perhaps an inevitable response to diaspora. Still, we are led to ask just what happened in 231 to occasion this apparent loss of authority. Bokenkamp, in discussing this issue, mentions the rising tensions between the Cao ruling house and the Sima family that would eventually usurp its position and found the Jin. Sima Yi 司馬懿 (179–251) was already a prominent figure, but it is uncertain if this threat was already evident at this time, when many of Cao Cao's most powerful supporters were still alive.

To understand the reference to 231, we have to look back to the preceding year, when the Wei launched a major offensive to retake Hanzhong.[39] Cao Zhen 曹真 (d. 231), who had proposed the campaign in order to put an end to raids from the Shu-Han

38. The last phrase is difficult to interpret. It may well be that "my pneumas" (*wuqi* 吾氣) is, as argued by Tang Changru (1983:229), a mistake for the Five Pneumas (*wuqi* 五氣) office mentioned at the beginning of *Yangping Parish*. The office of True Pneumas is otherwise unknown, and this may then be a mistake or alternate name for the Central Pneumas (*zhongqi* 中氣) mentioned immediately after the Five Pneumas. Adopting this emendation would make this passage exactly parallel to the *Yangping Parish* enumeration. Another possibility is that the True Pneumas is to be identified with the Sage Pneumas (*shengqi* 聖氣) office, which is "in charge of investigating and comparing the documents to determine merits at the end of the year." This would seem to be an appropriate office to consult in promotions and appointments. I have discussed the Supervisor of Deities, in charge of "selecting the wise and worthy," but have not remarked on the curious title, which suggests that spirit messages played a role in this evaluation. Since this might imply that a deceased Celestial Master like the speaker of this passage was directly involved in the selection of officers for appointment, I have maintained the original "my pneumas" here, while noting other possibilities in this note.

39. The most comprehensive account of this campaign is in *Zizhi tongjian*, chapters 71–72, pp. 2261–68.

state, was dispatched to enter Hanzhong from the north, while Sima Yi attacked up the Han River from the east. From the beginning, there were concerns about how to supply the large force, and they encountered a month of continuous rain that wiped out the corduroy road through the mountains. After a series of memorials criticizing the expedition, Cao Zhen's force was recalled, and, when Zhuge Liang counterattacked into Shaanxi the following spring, it was Sima Yi who was dispatched to fend him off.

Cao Zhen was an adopted son of Cao Cao and had shared the regency during the early years of the reign of Cao Rui 曹叡, the Enlightened Emperor 明帝 (r. 227–39).[40] His eldest son, Cao Shuang 曹爽, was the regent together with Sima Yi during the next reign, of Cao Fang 曹芳, who was deposed by the Simas in 254, having lost all effective support with Shuang's execution in 249. So Cao Zhen and his son were at the center of the Cao family faction contending with the Simas for control of the court. Moreover, Cao Shuang, like Zhang Lu's son-in-law Cao Yu, was said to have been close to Cao Rui when they were growing up.[41] We have to assume that the Zhangs, with multiple members married to Cao men and women, were part of that faction.[42] Moreover, Cao Zhen died in 231. No member of the Zhang family is mentioned in connection with this expedition against Hanzhong, but with so many of them holding fiefs in the region and generals from the Celestial Masters forces being familiar with the terrain, it seems likely that they were involved, and the Zhangs may actually have been behind the campaign from the beginning. In light of the comments in the *Commands and Precepts*, it would seem that the Hanzhong region held special significance for the Celestial Masters, perhaps as the physical location of the eagerly

40. See *Sanguozhi* 9/280–82. Zhen's name and cognomen, Zidan or "Thane Cinnabar," the name of a deity in the *Scripture of the Yellow Court*, suggest a Daoist association.

41. *Sanguozhi* 9/282. This suggests that Cao Yu and Cao Shuang were also close friends.

42. However, Cao Shuang and his compatriots were famous for extravagance, profligacy, and sexual indulgence, all the subjects of criticism in the two encyclicals, so there may also have been tensions in this relationship.

awaited coming realm of Great Peace, and that this failed campaign brought about a loss of prestige and authority for the Zhang family. There is evidence that Hanzhong long preserved a special place within Daoism: despite its comparative remoteness from their center of administration, it was one of the first places attacked by the Li 李 family of Cheng-Han when establishing their new Daoist state at the beginning of the fourth century, and they transferred sizable parts of the local population back to their Sichuan base to shore up their support there; further, the "Treatise on Geography" of the Sui (589–618) dynastic history describes the people of Hanzhong in the following terms: "They esteem and value the teachings of Daoism; the influence of Zhang Lu still survives there" 崇重道教，猶有張魯之風焉.[43]

Most of the *Commands and Precepts* text consists of moral exhortations and condemnations of immorality. In general, these passages promote common Chinese values like loyalty and filial piety and promise a place in the world of Great Peace as a seed person. We see an encouragement to adopt "pure stillness" while performing the basic rituals each morning and evening. Humility is valued, and there is a special warning against the pursuit of fame, which is described as "an axe that hacks away at the body." In general, the faith in the workings of supernatural justice is absolute, as we see in the following passage, which addresses the epidemic diseases that were ravaging the populace at this time.[44]

> In recent years there have been epidemic diseases in all quarters, sweeping away the hordes of evildoers, but they only kill evil people. . . . When a libationer cures an illness, if it returns after having been eliminated, this is an evil person. You are not to treat it any more.
> 從比年以來，四方疾病，掃除群凶，但殺惡人耳。。。。祭酒治病，病來復差，既差復病，此爲惡人，勿復醫治之。

43. See *Jin shu* 121/3036–37; *Sui shu* 隋書 29/829.
44. *Zhengyi fawen tianshi jiao jieke jing* 18a–b; Bokenkamp 1997:181.

Daoist medicine at the time was still founded on the confession of sins and their ritual absolution. An essential part of the confession was an undertaking to sin no more, and a returning illness was understood as a sure sign that this promise to the spirits was not being kept.

Some pronouncements have specific significance for the administration of the movement, such as the prohibition on making unauthorized appointments:[45]

> As for the postings, from this point forward, you must not improperly make appointments to posts on your own. If you disobey me again, you will be harmed; do not blame me.
> 諸職自今以後，不得妄自署置爲職也。復違吾，中傷勿怨。

We also find a reiteration of the *Xiang'er* prohibition on visualizing the Dao as having a definite shape and place in the body but with a novel explanation for why this must be so:[46]

> The Dao does not desire that you point to a form to name it as such. The wise, seeing one instance of it, know that there are ten thousand. This can be compared to someone recognizing a musical key. If the Dao were present in one body, how could it be in the body of others?
> 道不欲指形而名之，賢者見一知萬，譬如識音者。道在一身之中，豈在他人乎。

The point here would seem to be that, just as one trained in music could recognize a given note in a composition but that did not mean that it was the only instance of that note, just so the Dao could manifest in multiple forms and places within each person's body.

45. *Zhengyi fawen tianshi jiao jieke jing* 18b; cf. Bokenkamp 1997:181.
46. *Zhengyi fawen tianshi jiao jieke jing* 16a. I have a slightly different understanding of this passage from Bokenkamp, who does not understand the penultimate clause as conditional and translates the last as a separate sentence: "Why seek to find it in others?" (1997:175–76).

We also find in the *Commands and Precepts* the same concern noted in the *Xiang'er* about "deviant" doctrines. In a passage immediately following upon the condemnation of improperly visualizing the Dao, we read:[47]

In practicing good deeds, you have lost sight[48] of the basis and do not accept the words of the scripture. Teaching each other deviant practices, you pursue the false and abandon the true. I long ago recorded on a short sheet of paper the miscellaneous theories and deviant texts, commanding that all be eliminated. The libationers were feckless and deliberately allowed people to keep them and hide them away. They have been preserved up until now, causing the least learned of the present age to delight in ridiculous theories, pointing to the false and calling it true. All of them offend again the prohibitions of Heaven; you certainly will be harmed and in the end will not attain blessings. They will only exhaust you, nothing more.

汝曹學善，夫根本，不承經言。邪邪相教，就偽棄真。吾昔皆錄短紙雜說邪文，悉令消之。祭酒無狀，故俾挾深藏，于今常存，使今世末學之人，好尚浮說，指偽名真。此皆犯天禁，必當中傷，終不致福也，但勞汝耳。

We cannot be certain just what sort of deviant theories are being discussed here, although the last comment makes one think it might involve sexual practices, given the *Xiang'er*'s repeated injunctions not to exert oneself in sexual matters. We will see some concrete examples of deviant behavior in the twenty-two precepts of the *Demon Statutes of Lady Blue*, discussed later in this chapter.

The encyclical closes with an injunction to the faithful to heed this message and act upon it:

Now transmit my Teaching in order that both new and former citizens will understand my heart, and do not disobey me.

今傳吾教，令新故民皆明吾心，勿相負也。

---

47. *Zhengyi fawen tianshi jiao jieke jing* 16a–b; cf. Bokenkamp 1997:176.

48. Here I follow Bokenkamp in reading *shi* 失, "to lose," for the graphically similar introductory particle *fu* 夫, although Bokenkamp does not explicitly note this emendation.

This injunction is followed immediately by a seven-character poem titled "The Teaching of the Celestial Master." The seven-character verse form, with each line rhyming, is a distinctive genre, closely associated with the Celestial Masters, used also in the *Scripture of the Yellow Court*, to which the *Commands and Precepts* refers twice. It seems likely, then, that the last line does not refer back to the preceding text but that rather the *Commands and Precepts* is in fact a preface to this poem, which is the real Teaching. Here, then, is the Teaching:

TEACHING OF THE CELESTIAL MASTER	天師教
Now I send down a Teaching, composing seven-word verse,	今故下教作七言，
To proclaim to the libationers and male and female citizens.	謝諸祭酒男女民。
Heaven and Earth merged registrations, their pneumas as if married,	天地混籍氣如姻，
The four seasons and five agents rely on each other in turn.	四時五行轉相因。
When Heaven and Earth joined together, there were no people,	天地合會無人民，
Stars and asterisms jumbled together were predecessors of humans.	星辰倒錯爲人先。
Amid the twenty-eight lodges, the chronograms Net and Triaster	二十八宿畢參辰，
Dazzler [Mars] and Great White [Venus] emerged among them.	熒惑太白出其間。
As if there had been an anomaly before the images were displayed.	若有改變垂象先，
Laying the foundations of Great Peace, no time for rest.	太平之基不能眠。

This makes me so frustrated[49]
I cannot express.
To speak, producing a Teaching,
my thoughts are troubled.

是令軸軻不可言，

發言出教心意煩。

Speeding my pneumas to the eight
extremes, then return home,
I observe and inspect the commoners, barbarian and Chinese.
I see no seeds of humankind,
only corpse-citizens.
Giving free rein to desires and
whims, they exhaust essential
gods.
Their five viscera empty and void,
they are corpse people.
Their fate beyond redemption,
they belong to the Earth Office.
Placed in squads of demons,
they enter the Yellow Springs.
If you wish to reform and repent,
follow my words;
You can rise up and cross over
as a transcendent!
Limit carefully yin and yang,
preserve and cherish your gods.
Among the five viscera and six
organs, there are rulers and
ministers,
Accumulating in a tiny place,
they fashion a perfected being.
When gods and thoughts are
forlorn and you cannot sleep,
Frolic with the commoners
amidst the five viscera.

走氣八極周復還，

觀視百姓夷胡秦。

不見人種但尸民，

從心恣意勞精神。

五藏虛空爲尸人，

命不可贖屬地官。

身爲鬼伍入黃泉，

思而改悔從吾言。

可得升度爲仙人，

節慎陰陽保愛神。

五藏六府有君臣，

積在微微爲真人。

神思愁慘不能眠，

遊戲百姓五藏間。

---

49. Reading *kanke* 轗軻 for *zhouke* 軸軻, literally, "axle and axle-tree,"
synecdoche for a chariot.

Then, returning, converse with   還與真人共語言，
    the perfected being,
This perfected one in your heart   心中真人來上天。
    will ascend to Heaven.

Dressed in a singlet of scarlet   絳黃單衣三縫冠，
    and yellow, a three-seamed cap,
A Heavenly jade talisman on his   佩天玉符跪吾前。
    belt, he kneels before me,
To discuss the commoners and tell   陳說百姓道萬民，
    of the myriad Daoist citizens,
Producing a clear text of merit   功過進退有明文。
    and fault for promotion or
    demotion.

This poem recounts many of the basic teachings of the encyclicals in the form of a mnemonic verse. We begin with the cosmogonic origins of the universe, before the appearance of humankind. As Heaven and Earth merge together in a union that is compared to the marriage of Daoist novices through the union of their registers, the cosmic polarities of yin and yang, here expressed as the progression of the four seasons, and the five agents order them. This gives rise to the twenty-eight lunar mansions of the Chinese zodiac, with a special focus on the asterisms of Net and Triaster, which in the allocated-field (*fenye* 分野) system of earth-sky correlations represent the geographical regions of the ancient states of Jin 晉 and Wei 魏, or the location at that time of the Wei capital of Luoyang and the Cao family base at Ye. Mars (fire) and Venus (metal) represent South and West, respectively; hence, their appearance in central China reflects the movement of the Celestial Master from Sichuan to central China, but at the same time both planets also portend war and punishments, a reference to the many battles of that unsettled time.[50] The hope

50. On the significance of Mars and Venus as portents, see Schafer 1977: 214–15.

for security lies in the advent of Great Peace, but, just as he had at the beginning of *Yangping Parish*, the Celestial Master warns that he has traveled throughout the world and found few worthy of populating this new world as seed people. Having fallen into decadence, the people do not nourish their internal gods and are instead headed for the ranks of demons administered by the Earth Office, the fell bureaucracy charged with the dead. The proper course lies in sexual moderation and cultivation of the essences and gods of the body, as mentioned in the *Xiang'er* and detailed in the *Scripture of the Yellow Court*. The Perfected in the Yellow Court at the center of that internal microcosm is your representative, who will ascend to Heaven and make your case for transcendence by reporting all of your worthy actions.[51]

Demon Statutes of Lady Blue

There is one last document that we can date with some confidence to the third century, the *Demon Statutes of Lady Blue* (*Nüqing guilü* 女青鬼律). Most commentators have agreed that this text is early. Many place it conservatively in the fourth century, but recently Yu Wanli has analyzed a lengthy rhymed section of chapter 5, finding it consistent with other early Celestial Master documents like the "Teaching of the Celestial Master" poem and the *Scripture of the Yellow Court* and hence written by someone from northwest China in the third century.[52] It probably cannot be earlier than 265, though, because it mentions Zhong Hui 鐘會 (225–64), the conqueror of Shu-Han for the Wei kingdom. It is possible that there are some other relatively minor additions that

51. This is the perfected Zidan 子丹, mentioned in each of the three stanzas of the original *Scripture of the Yellow Court*. See stanza 1, line 36; stanza 2, line 23; and stanza 3, line 8, in Schipper 1975a:1–6.
52. See Yu Wanli 2001:551–80, esp. 576–77; Lai Chi-tim 2002a. Dudink tentatively dates the work to the third century; see Schipper and Verellen 2004:127–29. The earliest epigraphical reference to the "edict of Nüqing" is on a list of grave goods (*yiwu shu* 衣物疏) dated 352. See Liu Yi 2005:121.

are later, but there is also a significant overlap in vocabulary with the encyclicals and the *Xiang'er*, so we are justified in attributing it to the Daoist church of the third century. We do not have the entire original text; it refers internally to its eight scrolls, but only six survive, and quotations are sometimes not found in the received text of the Ming Daoist canon.

We will not, however, be able to say much about the figure to whom the scripture is attributed. We know next to nothing about Lady Blue other than that she is associated with the Mystic Capital 玄都 and with such things as "statutes" 律, "statutes and commands" 律令, an "edict" 詔書 through which these statutes and commands were apparently issued, and a "prison" 獄 or hell.[53] Lai Chi-tim, who has made one of the most extensive studies of the text (Lai 2002), believes that the edict is distinct from the statutes, and, whereas the former is mentioned in grave contracts protecting the deceased from harm in the underworld, the latter is instead directed to living believers of the church (who one secular source claims were called "demon troops" 鬼卒). The terms "edict" and "statutes" often seem, however, to be used interchangeably in this context, and, although the text does have passages oriented toward the conduct of the living, more of it deals with demons and how to control them.[54] In any case, if there ever was a distinct Edict of Lady Blue, it does not survive, despite its frequent invocation.

The *Demon Statutes* is the lengthiest text I have considered so far, and its content is varied. I will first take up a code of precepts that give unique insight into life in the early church, then consider the significance of the text for early belief in demons, the soteriology of Celestial Master Daoism, and early ritual practice.

53. For a detailed treatment of this question, which suggests that the origin of the name was as a demonifugic herb mentioned in the *Shennong bencaojing* 神農本草經, see Kikuchi 2009:198–202.

54. For example, the *Taishang dongyuan shenzhou jing* (7/8b) refers to "demon statutes, the Edict of Nüqing" 鬼律女青詔書, which would seem to suggest that the edict is also the demon statutes.

Prohibitions and Taboos

The third chapter of the *Demon Statutes* consists primarily of a numbered list of twenty-two rules titled "Prohibitions and Taboos of the Daoist Statutes" 道律禁忌. Each rule ends with a numerical value to be deducted from one's lifespan, conceived as a specific number of units represented by counting rods (*suan* 算).[55] These statutes are thus enforced by the Heavenly Bureaus that maintain the divine record books. They are introduced by the following paragraph:

> The Celestial Master said: "Examining the men and women of the realm, [I find that] in everyday life they are disloyal, and, when a good deed is done, they do not seek to repay it, so that the devastation of disasters arises daily. The interrogations of Heaven, the raids of demons, and the circulation of the Five Poisons all arise from a lack of faith; they give no thought to keeping the One and doing good, and so each person summons his or her own calamity.[56] I am concerned that you will not attain to longevity and immortality. I have received a Teaching of the utmost urgency from the Most High and have been ordered to show it to the Heavenly citizens so

55. The most detailed explanation of this system of counters is found in the *Baopuzi*, where Ge Hong explains that a god in charge of overseeing transgressions constantly follows one, noting infractions and subtracting time from one's allocated lifespan in units of "counters," representing three days or "cycles" (*ji* 紀), representing three hundred days. See Wang Ming 1985:6/125. They are already mentioned in the *Xiang'er* commentary, and therefore we can conclude that they were a foundational teaching of Celestial Master Daoism.

56. We see many of the same figures mentioned in an early petition, the Petition for State Merit and Secure Dwelling, in *Nüqing guilü* 3/27b: "These several people are not secure in their homes, worrying that they might have offended against the otherwordly directors, and have thereby drawn to themselves interrogation pneumas. Because of the annual cycle of this year, the Five Poisons are circulating, harming internally the Heavenly citizens, and making no exception for the worthy and good" 某若干人，住宅不安，慮觸冥司，招延考氣。以今年運，五毒流行，中傷天民，不擇良善. The Five Poisons have various referents, including the five flavors, the five poisonous minerals, and the poisons produced by five insects (scorpion, viper, centipede, toad, and lizard), but the most likely meaning here refers to the five purveyors of epidemic disease.

that they might know the prohibitions and taboos and would not offend against the divine writing of the spirits, the *Demon Statutes of Lady Blue's Mystic Capital*. I allow[57] all of you to hear of it so that the refractory may return to obedience and the evil return to good, reforming their past actions and cultivating those to come, all in accordance with the demonic statutes and commands."

天師曰：視天下男女，日用不忠，行善不報，災害日興。天考、鬼賊、五毒流行，皆生於不信，不念守一行善，身招其禍。念子不得久世長生。吾受太上教勑嚴切，令以示天民，令知禁忌，不犯鬼神靈書《女青玄都鬼律》。令使汝曹皆悉知聞，逆者還順，惡者還善，改往修來，當依鬼律令。

This passage traces the code of conduct that follows to a direct revelation from the Most High Lord Lao to the Celestial Master, though we cannot be sure which one. It is thus a Teaching, much as the two encyclicals discussed above were, and it shares with them a condemnation of improper conduct and an exhortation to good deeds. Although the misfortune is portrayed as widespread, its source is individual misdeeds, not those of the group. The role of demons in this scripture is complex, but note that here they are portrayed as divinely ordained, mentioned in parallel with the "interrogations of Heaven" and the Five Poisons, that is, the five demons of pestilence who are supposed to take the lives of those who have either reached the end of their allotted lifespans or committed sufficient sins to merit immediate death. They are thus portrayed as orthodox forces in the service of Heaven.

Let us now turn to the code of statutes and prohibitions themselves:

1. You must not come and go, entering and exiting from the north, south, east, or west, without announcing when you leave or reporting when you return, in accordance with your own wishes and desires. All this contravenes the statutes and laws. Thirty-two counters will be subtracted.

57. This *ling* 令 may be a graphic error for *jin* 今, which would yield "Now I let you all know about it."

一者：不得自東自西自南自北出入去來，去無所闚，還無所白，任意從心。皆負律令。除算三十二。

2. You must not proclaim that Heaven has no gods or discuss the instructions of your teacher,[58] subvert justice and disrupt governance, argue that you yourself are correct and the words of another[59] are wrong. All contravene the demon statutes. Heaven will deduct 13 counters.

二者：不得呼天無神，言道師旨，敗刑亂政，自言己是，道人言非。皆負鬼律。天奪算一十三。

3. You must not, bearing the truth, enter into falsity,[60] defiling and disrupting the saintly luminaries, drinking wine and eating meat, raising a ruckus and acting in an unprincipled manner. Thirteen hundred counters will be deducted.

三者：不得持真入偽，姦亂聖明，飲酒食肉，呼嗟無道。奪算千三百。

4. You must not spread evil words, discuss other people, recklessly establish your own religion, disbelieve the Heavenly Dao, or speak groundless lies. Heaven will deduct 1,200 counters.

---

58. This phrase, *shizhi* 師旨, can refer simply to the key teachings imparted by one's master, as when one vows after taking ordination that "I would not dare to ignore my master's instructions" (*bu zunyi shizhi* 不遵依師旨; see DZ 1219 *Gaoshang shenxiao yuqing zhenwang zishu dafa* 12/9a), but I wonder if here it is not an abbreviation of "the essential teachings of the Celestial Master" (*tianshi zhijiao* 天師旨教), as when, in the Rite of Mud and Charcoal, one undertakes, "in accordance with the essential teachings of the Celestial Master, to establish this Mud and Charcoal [Rite]," in DZ 1138 *Wushang miyao* 50/1b, 10b, 12a, 18a, 20a.

59. Or perhaps "a man of the Dao" (Daoren 道人). The character *dao* is used often in this code in the sense of "to say," but Daoren, presumably referring to members of the Celestial Master community, is found repeatedly in the *Xiang'er*.

60. This phrase (*chizhen ruwei* 持真入偽) would seem to refer to the introduction of Daoist deities or ritual elements into profane contexts such as rites to non-Daoist, "blood-eating" deities or perhaps simply the participation of a Daoist believer in such rites. Precept 8 of the Ten Perverted Evil Paths (*shi xie dao* 十邪道), in DZ 345 *Taishang dongxuan lingbao jieye benxing shangpin miaojing* 17b, says, "When the masses of sentient beings encounter the faith (*fa* 法), their hearts are filled with perverse views. Turning their backs on perfection and entering into falsity (*beizhen ruwei* 背真入偽), they accept and serve spirits and gods, in form resembling the disciples of spirit mediums."

四者：不得傳宣惡語，道說他人，妄作一法，不信天道，虛
言無實。天奪算千二百。

5. You must not spread lies, speak hypocritically or recklessly,
   express delight or anger with no constancy [of emotion],
   devote yourself to defiance and slaughter, or fail to take care
   in sexual matters. Heaven will deduct 132 counters.

五者：不得傳虛，兩舌妄語，喜怒無常，專行逆煞，不慎陰
陽。天奪算百三十二。

6. You must not treat the aged with contempt or use abusive
   language to your relatives, nor should husband and wife curse
   each other and cause each other harm, or foster evil with a
   poisonous heart, or be unfilial, committing one of the Five
   Rebellions.[61] Heaven will deduct 180 counters.

六者：不得輕慢老人，罵詈親戚，夫妻呪詛，自相煞害，毒
心造凶，不孝五逆。天奪算一百八十。

7. You must not, having received the Dao, transmit it to an inappropriate person with no regard for the careless contempt of
   this act, or accept a profit because of a desire for wealth, taking from others to benefit yourself, or borrow things and not
   return them, making them your private treasure. Heaven will
   deduct 1,800 counters.

七者：受道不知輕慢傳非其人，貪財受利，取人自益，借物
不還，以爲私寶。天奪算一千八百。

---

61. The Five Rebellions 五逆 are mentioned earlier in the *Nüqing guilü* (1/8a)
and again below in precept 18. This term originates with Buddhism and is
found twice in the *Aṣṭāsahasrikāprajñā-pāramitā Sūtra*, both in the translation
by Lokakṣema 支婁迦讖 (fl. 150–80), the *Daoxing borejing* 道行般若經 (translated 179 in Loyang, T224.8.441b and 8.461a), and in that by Zhi Qian 支謙
(fl. 223–52), the *Da mingdu jing* 大明度經 (T225.8.488a and 8.498c). I am indebted to Jan Nattier for these references. The Five Rebellions are defined as
(1) killing one's mother, (2) killing one's father, (3) killing an arhat, (4) causing
the Buddha to shed blood, and (5) harming the harmony of the order of monks.
The fact that this term is prefaced by *buxiao* 不孝, "being unfilial," reveals that
it was the first two elements of this list that caught the imagination of the Chinese and suggests that it may have entered the religion from popular preaching
rather than a scholarly source. See Nakamura 1975:1, 357a; *Foguang dacidian*
(Taiwan: Foguang chubanshe, 1989), 1142.

8. You must not battle with words, or indulge in sex while under the influence, or, pretending to speak for the Great Dao, recklessly pronounce the words of demons, or insistently assemble men and women to drink wine and eat meat. Heaven will deduct 300 counters.

   八者：不得鬪爭言語，因醉淫色；假託大道，妄言鬼語，要結男女，飲酒食宍。天奪算三百。

9. You must not roam about, east and west, everywhere uniting men and women. Though you seek to dispel disaster, you will not gain absolution, and this will result in deviant disorder. Heaven will deduct 13,000 counters, and a deadly curse will flow down for seven generations.

   九者：不得遊行東西，周合男女。消災不解，因成邪亂。天奪算萬三千，死殃流七世。

10. You must not transmit the Dao to adolescent girls, taking this opportunity to enter their "gate of life," harming their gods and transgressing against their pneumas. This is refractory, evil, and unprincipled [literally, Dao-less]. You will die and leave no posterity. You must not turn men into women[62] so that yin and yang are inverted and confused. Heaven will deduct 300 counters.

    十者：不得傳道童女，因入生門，傷神犯氣，逆惡無道，身死無後。不得反男爲女，陰陽倒錯。天奪算三百。

11. You must not have sexual congress in the open, offending against the Three Luminaries, or visit people in order to drink, relying upon your authority to join [sexually] with them. Heaven will deduct 300 counters.

    十一者：不得露合陰陽，觸犯三光，因酒往還，承威相接。天奪三百。

---

62. It is uncertain if this phrase, *fan nan wei nü* 反男爲女, literally, "turning men over so that they become women," is meant as a metaphorical reference to sex roles or indicates an actual physical inversion of the male body in preparation for sodomy. It is the only obvious condemnation of homosexuality that I have found in early Daoist texts.

12. You must not cause the pneumas of one person to live while those of another person die, imposing upon and transgressing against the Perfected.[63] Heaven will deduct 33 counters.

十二者：不得一人氣生一人氣死，逼犯真人。天奪算三十三。

13. The sons of the same father must not live separately, leading to the scattering and dissolution of the home and family. Heaven will deduct 32 counters.

十三者：不得一父子別居，室家離散。天奪算三十二。

14. You must not become attached to that which you desire and hate to lose it, so that you gather together men and women to recklessly speak deviant words. Heaven will deduct 120 counters.

十四者：不得嗜慾惡失，男女聚集，妄道邪言。天奪算百二十。

15. You must not be jealous of your coreligionists, gossip about each other, or put no faith in the Three and the Five,[64] or comment on the strengths and weaknesses of the heavenly pneumas. Heaven will deduct 823 counters.

十五者：不得同法相嫉，更相道說，不信三五，評論天氣長短。天奪算八百二十三。

16. You must not flee from your parents, roaming to the four corners of the earth in order to establish your perfected pneumas and gather together a group. Heaven will deduct 320 counters.

---

63. This obscure passage would seem to refer to a type of disreputable ritual in which the name of the client is removed from the book of death administered by the Perfected and the name of another added in his or her place.

64. This phrase, *sanwu* 三五, or "the three and the five," has many possible referents. It sometimes refers to the legendary divine rulers of antiquity known as the Three August and Five Thearchs (as in *Hou Han shu* 40b:1360, 1361 n. 7), or the Three Regulators (sun, moon, and stars) and Five Phases (*sanzheng wuxing* 三正五行, as in *Hou Han shu* 3b:1060, esp. n. 1), or the Three Cinnabar Fields and Five Viscera, as in the *Inner Scripture of the Yellow Court*. In Daoist scriptures, it often seems to indicate the cosmos, portrayed as having three vertical registers (Heaven, Man, Earth or Heaven, Earth, Water) and five directions. Here it seems to refer to something like the cosmic order.

十六者：不得逃遁父母，遊行四方，位立真氣，自相收合。
天奪算三百二十。

17. You must not destroy what Heaven has created, wantonly
    killing animals or shooting birds; nor should you proclaim
    south to be north, according to the dictates of your heart.
    This is not in accordance with the demon statutes. Heaven
    will deduct 3,000 counters.

    十七者：不得滅天所生，妄煞走獸，彈射飛鳥，指南作
    北，任心所從，不依鬼律。天奪算三千。

18. You must not interfere in the affairs of others or make public
    the matters of other families, concealing their good deeds while
    calling attention to their evil actions, or violate the wives of
    others and plot to steal their husbands, or rebel against the
    Three Luminaries, secretly harm or curse, or act unfilially,
    committing the Five Rebellions.[65] Heaven will deduct 1,220
    counters.

    十八者：不得干知人事，宣布他家，藏善出惡，姦人婦
    女，謀圖人壻，逆戾三光，陰賊呪詛，不孝五逆。天奪算千
    二百二十。

19. You must not, on a day when you will perform a ritual to
    the Dao,[66] lust after sex with a lascivious heart, circulate the
    pneumas too long, indulging ceaselessly in self-gratification,
    or enter into a secret pact. You will thereby give birth to an
    unfilial son, who harbors an evil heart among his five viscera
    and does not possess the Dao. Heaven will take away 30,000
    counters.

    十九者：不得行道之日貪色淫心，行氣有長，自解不已，私
    共約誓，因生不孝，姦心五內，無道之子。天奪算三萬。

---

65. On the Five Rebellions, see n. 61 above.

66. This presumably refers to performance of the *heqi* ritual, but the term
xing Dao, literally, "perform the Dao," seems to have a wide range of referents,
involving any sort of ritual performance in a Daoist context. In the *Xiang'er*,
it is linked with observing the precepts (ll. 17, 180), "returning to simplicity"
(l. 433), and obtaining life (ll. 137, 374). In the first chapter of the Lingbao
Scripture of Salvation, it is equated with "reciting this scripture." See DZ 87
Yuanshi wuliang duren shangpin miaojing sizhu 1/30a6.

20. You must not visualize a [profane] god and not report it,[67] then circulate living pneumas, seize and bring down primordial pneumas, and spend all day and night with limbs entwined in lust and sexual desire. Such conduct is unprincipled. Heaven will take away 342 counters.

   二十者：不得思神不報，因行生氣，取降元氣，貪淫愛色，手足不離，彌日竟夕。如此無道。天奪算三百四十二。

21. You must not carelessly transmit the red pneumas[68] to profane persons so that mouth, hand, breast, and heart each come into contact in turn. This is to abandon the Dao and rebel against one's one master—to be without religion. Heaven will take away 300 counters.

   二十一者：不得以赤氣妄傳俗人，口手胸心更相交接，委道自叛師主無法。天奪算三百。

22. You must not carelessly transmit a scriptural document to the profane, speak the taboo names of your mother or father, or reveal to the profane the essentials of the Perfected or the secret oral instructions. Heaven will take away 300 counters.

   二十二者：不得妄以經書授與俗人，道父母名諱，泄漏真要訣語俗人。天奪算三百。

The prohibitions are followed by four separate Teachings of the Celestial Master related to them. The first is the most general in nature:[69]

> I have received an essential teaching from the Most High. His prohibitions and taboos are extremely severe. You men and women have since birth been so benighted and up until now have not

67. The meaning of this passage is obscure, but John Lagerwey points out (personal communication) that the character *bao* occurs repeatedly in the description of the Heqi rite in DZ 1294 *Shangqing huangshu guoduyi*. There, after invoking cosmic forces or performing various breathing regimens, one retreats and "reports." There seems to be no direct tie there to the visualization of deities.

68. Presumably these red pneumas are the living pneumas produced in the Merging the Pneumas rite.

69. *Nüqing guilü* 3/3b–4a.

known how to restrain yourselves. By establishing your own faith, you have become estranged from Heaven. If the interrogation reaches the leaders, after Heaven has stripped you of your counters, I fear it will be painful for you! You will not see Great Peace. If there are leaders,[70] libationers, or Daoist officers who have achieved merit in evangelization, your merits will redeem your transgressions. If the citizens do not observe [these prohibitions], but you still wish to evangelize, you should reform your past actions and cultivate those to come, then concentrate upon the nourishment of your nature. In this way you will be able to survive the three disasters and the nine cyclical dangers.[71] If you only practice evil disobedience and do not practice loyalty and filiality, I fear that your life cannot be preserved. Thinking of you makes me sad. It is truly fortunate that I can warn you again.

天師曰：吾受太上旨教，禁忌甚重。汝男女憒憒，生來至今，不知禁制。自作一法，與天相違。考至主者，天奪子筭訖，恐將可痛。不見太平。生者及祭酒道士，宣化有功，功過相贖。民若不用，故有宣化之心，可自改往修來，專一養性，可度天三災九厄。子唯行惡逆，不行忠孝，恐子年命不自保。念子可傷，幸復重囑丁寧甚也。

The implicit threat for misconduct is punishment, but the greatest punishment is still denial of entry into the utopian world of Great Peace. Misconduct can be redeemed by good deeds, but the best is still spreading the faith. The remaining passages touch on the sexual ritual of Merging the Pneumas, so I will discuss them below under that rubric.

These precepts are problematic in several ways. First, a single precept often addresses more than one topic. This may reflect their origin in spirit revelation, like the meandering, repetitive style of the encyclicals discussed earlier in this chapter. Similarly,

70. Reading *zhuzhe* 主者 for the graphically similar *shengzhe* 生者.
71. These terms are frequently found in Daoist scriptures but never explained. In Buddhist sources, the three disasters are disasters of water, fire, and warfare or of warfare, pestilence, and famine. The nine cyclical dangers are in Buddhism identified with nine specific incidents in the life of the historical Buddha. See Nakamura 1975:1, 256a, 463b–c.

the punishments specified for the offenses vary widely, from 13 to 30,000, and it is difficult to correlate the degree of the punishment with the severity of the offense. This suggests that the code was rather archaic, reflecting an early stage in the formulation of church doctrine, taking form over time through accretion, and did not remain in common use long enough to pass through a process of rationalization and regularization. The presence of a single, perhaps somewhat misunderstood Buddhist concept (prohibitions 6 and 18, see n. 61) would support such a conclusion.

Some of the more general moral exhortations are familiar from the text of the *Xiang'er*, the *Xiang'er* precepts, and the encyclicals. The warning against expressions of "delight and anger" (prohibition 5) echoes a repeated injunction in the *Xiang'er* (chapters 4, 21, 33, and the first of the twenty-seven precepts).[72] The condemnation of unfilial behavior, though linked to a more general Buddhist rule that condemned acting against those with authority, is also familiar from the *Xiang'er* (see especially the commentary to chapters 18 and 19). The broader injunction to maintain harmony within the family, both among relatives and between spouses, in precept 6 seems in keeping with this condemnation. The emphasis on an extended family maintaining a single dwelling (prohibition 13) is a common Chinese ideal but seems to be new to Daoist sources. The condemnation of desire in prohibition 14 recalls the *Xiang'er* precept against "lust[ing] after jewels and goods," and the condemnation of killing wild animals or birds in prohibition 17 can be linked to the *Xiang'er* precept "Do not eat bloody animals."

Many of the prohibitions deal specifically with the Daoist community, church theology, or religious practice. The very first prohibition limits free movement, although it is unclear if one must report each departure from or return to the community to church officials or the overseeing deities.[73] Harmony among members of the faith is stressed in prohibitions 4 and 15. The same two

72. For the twenty-seven precepts, see chapter 2.
73. In Kleeman 2007a, I had assumed that this reflected a strict control of movement within the community by its leaders, but Chang Chaojan suggests

articles condemn the expression of doubt toward Daoist deities and attempts to split the congregation by establishing one's own sect or faith. Prohibition 3 addresses contacts with the profane sacrificial religion, interdicting believing Daoists from participating in their rituals or partaking of their sacrificial feasts, another element found in the *Xiang'er* commentary.[74] There are also strictures on blasphemy (prohibition 2), defiling the true faith (prohibition 3), and misusing the powers entrusted to the faithful in order to effect someone's death (prohibition 12). A surprising number of the prohibitions (7–11, 19–21), however, seem to focus on matters of sexual conduct, specifically a rite of transmission or initiation that involved sexual congress and provided opportunities for abuse. Because this theme receives attention elsewhere in the *Demon Statutes*, I will examine this issue in greater detail.

The Merging the Pneumas Rite

We have seen that the *Xiang'er* commentary was quite concerned with sexual conduct, but primarily in a negative vein, condemning the traditional forms of self-cultivation through techniques of the bedchamber, advocating the limitation of sexual activity for most believers, and praising sexual abstinence for a select few who chose to redirect this energy into nourishing the internal deities of the body. Both of the revealed encyclicals treated above made a special point of condemning sexual excess.

Our earliest hard evidence for the Celestial Masters, the Zhang Pu stele of 173, records the conferral of texts that seem to be connected to a sexual ritual, the "mystic dispensation," on worthy libationers. Daoist reformers of the fourth and fifth century and Buddhist polemicists of the fifth and sixth are also unanimous in attributing to the early Celestial Masters this sexual

---

that the reporting may be to the gods inhabiting each believer's oratory (personal communication, June 2010).

74. See the discussion in chapter 2.

practice, most commonly calling it the Merging the Pneumas (*heqi* 合氣) rite.[75] It is also referred to as the Yellow and Red rite because the text describing its performance, the *Yellow Book* 黃書, was written on yellow paper with a red border, and those qualified to perform it were given a document called the Yellow Book Contract 黃書契令 (occasionally Yellow and Red Contract 黃赤券契), to be worn belted at the waist.[76] The rite was also sometimes referred to by the numerical sequence of yang numbers 3–5–7–9 because, in the course of the rite, participants orchestrate their breaths in such a pattern while invoking the twenty-four (3 +5 +7 +9) gods of the body. The *Demon Statutes* provides our earliest datable evidence for the role of this ritual in the early church and reveals some of the problems that accompanied its practice.

I have mentioned the utopian realm of Great Peace that was the aspiration of the early church as well as the status of seed person that was key to surviving the contemporary dangers from war, pestilence, and misfortune in order to live until and participate in the world of Great Peace. In *Yangping Parish*, we saw the Celestial Master go searching for those worthy to be seeds, with little success, whereas the speaker in the *Commands and Precepts* tried to reassure the faithful that Great Peace would indeed become manifest, if not for them, then for their descendants. A passage in the *Demon Statutes* reveals that participation in the Merging the Pneumas rite was an important qualification for making it to Great Peace:[77]

You must not let yourself go, grasp your heart!
If you do not practice the 3 and 5, it is just evil lust.
They say Heaven is a Great Dao and does not prohibit [sex?];

75. There have been many studies of this ritual, most of them inconclusive. See Wang Ka 1997; Bo Yi 1999; Ge Zhaoguang 1999; Raz 2008.

76. Contracts in traditional China were created in two halves, shared between the two parties to the contract, and it is to be assumed that the other half of this contract was submitted to the heavenly bureaucracy.

77. *Nüqing guilü* 5/1a–b.

The rulers of the Three Offices are picking the seed people.
They will pick those who have merged pneumas, eighteen
    thousand.
How many have there been from the beginning until now?
The great limit has not been reached, strive for it!
Changing your heart and bowels, become a Perfected of the Dao.
An oral secret from your master shows you are worthy,
Those who wear my contracts will all be first,
Will get to see the Divine Transcendent Lord of Great Peace,
Who, leader of the Five Thearchs, will transmit the secret words.

勿得任意唯捉心，不行三五唯邪淫。言天大道而不禁，三官主者
擇種民；取合炁者萬八千，從來至今有幾人。大限未足子勤身，
改心易腸道真人。師受口訣以見賢，佩吾券契一爲先。得見太平
神仙君，五帝主者傳祕言。

Thus, according to the third-century understanding, there was
a finite limit on the number of people who might survive to see
Great Peace, and the selection was ongoing. Supernatural officials were rigorously examining every aspect of behavior. They
are mentioned in the second Teaching to follow the code in chapter 3:

The Celestial Master says: You men and women of the realm who,
seeing the text of these worthy precepts, are unable to follow them,
who only want to pursue what you desire, teaching others to act
improperly, running about getting into arguments, only promoting
the teachings of demons, whether old or young, you are unfortunate. This momentary pleasure of the world will lead to a calamity
that will last one thousand years; it is an axe that hacks at the body,
a spear that extinguishes your life force. You who already know the
Dao, as well as those who do not yet know it, seeing my Demon
Statutes with new and old provisions, all are to follow them. On the
day of the 3–5–7–9 [ritual], be careful in circulating the living pneumas. You should do it according to my diagram, and do not offend
against the Three Pneumas; if you are able to become a transcendent,
you will convert a thousand citizens. If you do not know the true
name of the Father and Mother of the Dao, you are just a profane
person. Though a Daoist knows of the contract of the *Yellow Book*,

if you do not know the twenty-four gods, you are just a pretender. When the Dao reaches the extreme, the numbers cease; Heaven has its three and five [structure]; if you do not know this, how can you say the Dao is not divine? If you do not know the Dao, how can you say the pneumas do not shine? Hearing something a hundred times is not as good as seeing it once. Why do you not reform your own heart, change your gut, and enter into my living pneumas so that you can become a Perfected and, on the day of Great Peace, fly up to Heaven? Even if you do not fly, you will live out your lifespan and not die [prematurely]. You will then become an earth transcendent and get to see Great Peace. If you pass day after day in angry frustration, not believing, not loyal, your only practices lacking the Dao, you will not see Great Peace. Though I think about you deteriorating on your own, why should I torment myself?

天師曰：天下男女，見善戒之文，不能從用，唯欲從其所欲，教人行非，走作口舌，專作鬼教，老小凶凶。天下一時之樂，千年之禍，伐身之斧，滅命之爰也。子已知道，及未知者，見吾鬼律，新故科文，皆可從用。三五七九之日，慎行生兂。子依吾圖局，不犯三兂，如可仙，化民一千。不知道父母真名，故爲俗人。道士雖知黃書契令，不知二十四神人，故爲僞人。道極數訖，天有三五，子自不知，何得言道不神？子不知道，何得言兂不明？百聞不如一見，子何不自改心易腸，入吾生兂，得爲真人，太平之日飛舉上天。子只復不飛，壽終不死，便爲地仙，得見太平。子日一日，憤悶憤悶，不信不忠，唯行無道，不見太平，念子自衰，吾當何苦。

Note here the reference to new and old elements of the prohibitions; a recent expansion of this code might explain the unusual number of entries (twenty-two) as well as the disparity in the punishments allotted for different infractions.[78] Note also the esoteric knowledge necessary for the proper performance of the rite, such as knowledge about the twenty-four gods and the true name of

78. For example, if we considered each offense meriting a deduction of more than one thousand counters to be late (prohibitions 3, 4, 7, 9, 17, 18, 19), we would be left with a group of fifteen. All of these are religious in character, dealing with relations with profane believers or the practice of ritual. See Kalinowski 1985.

the father and mother of the Dao.[79] The following two Teachings are just short warnings to follow all the rules while practicing the ritual so as to avoid misfortune.

There is much that remains uncertain concerning the Merging the Pneumas rite. Below I will examine it in greater detail in the context of the ritual activities of the libationer, looking particularly at who was involved in the ritual and how it might have been understood to function. For now, note that during the third century it was already an indispensable part of the Celestial Master church's ritual program and its performance was deemed essential to surviving the coming apocalyptic disasters and attaining salvation.

But why would participation in a sexual ritual qualify one for Great Peace? Although surviving texts are too fragmentary and difficult to understand to give a definitive answer, their exploration will provide some clues.

Let us begin with a hostile, outsider's account from the sixth-century Buddhist mathematician and anti-Daoist polemicist Zhen Luan 甄鸞 (ca. 535–66), who claims to have participated in the rite as part of his initiation into Daoism at the age of twenty:[80]

> When your servant was twenty years of age, I was fond of Daoist arts and went to an abbey to learn them. First they taught me the Way of the *Yellow Book* and Merging the Pneumas in which men and women copulate to the timing of 3–5–7–9. With four eyes and two tongues facing each other, they perform the Dao in their Cinnabar Fields. Those who perform this survive cyclical calamities and extend their

79. There are multiple sets of twenty-four gods, but the most likely array is the eight gods occupying each of three registers within the human body. There is no reference outside this scripture to the "true names of the father and mother of the Dao," but the Dao father and Dao mother seem to have multiple interpretations, placing them in the body in the Yellow Court or in the Cavern Chamber 洞房 palace in the head, and perhaps identifying them with the Grandfather of the East 東王公 and the Grandmother of the West 西王母 (they are paired with the Thearchs of the North and South). See *Chisongzi zhangli* 2/9a–b.

80. *Xiaodaolun* 笑道論 in T2103 *Guang Hongmingji* 52.152a27–b3. See Kohn 1995:149–50.

lives. They teach husbands to exchange their wives with sex as the first consideration. Fathers and brothers stand before them, with no sense of shame. They call this the "true art of the central pneuma." Nowadays Daoist priests often practice this ritual, using it to seek the Dao. There is something there I cannot understand.

臣年二十之時，好道術就觀學。先教臣黃書合氣三五七九男女交接之道。四目兩舌正對。行道在於丹田。有行者度厄延年。教夫易婦，惟色爲初。父兄立前，不知羞恥。自稱中氣真術。今道士常行此法。以之求道，有所未詳。

This passage makes several claims: that the merging of pneumas was taught to beginners new to the faith, that it involved an exchange of partners among married couples, and that close relatives participated in some way. Although the ritual was enacted physically, it occurred symbolically within the Cinnabar Fields of the participants and was linked to the "central pneuma(s)." Moreover, the goal of the practice was to survive periods of potential misfortune and extend the lifespan. Zhen Luan also quotes a passage from a now lost *Statutes of the Dao* 道律 that warns against personal preference in selecting partners:[81]

> The Daoist statute says: "Circulate the pneumas according to the sequence. You may not reject the ugly to go to the one you favor as you like, thus circumventing or skipping through the sequence."
> 道律云：行氣以次。不得任意排醜近好抄截越次。

Although this could be interpreted as referring to a sort of round-robin of couplings among church members, it might also be a directive to masters, who had to schedule initiations among the local community, to not show favoritism among parishioners. In any case, if authentic, this passage suggests that someone was actually performing the rite with multiple partners.

81. See T2103, 52/0152a. Another passage quoted in this context, about male and female disciples paying their respects to their master on the days of the full and new moons, does not seem to refer to sexual activity at all, and it is uncertain how Zhen Luan understood the passage.

The Supreme Purity revelations of the mid-fourth century transmitted the teachings of a group of perfected beings, who communicated new techniques of individual self-cultivation through visualization and the ingestion of pneumas. Their scriptures accepted that the traditional Merging the Pneumas rite had originated with Zhang Daoling but dismissed it as a technique of limited utility and considerable potential danger, as we see in this passage:[82]

> The Perfected of Pure Vacuity bestowed a writing that said: The Way of the Yellow and Red, a method of mixing the pneumas, was taught to Zhang Ling to promote conversion. It is merely a technique of the seed people, not a matter for the Perfected. I have frequently seen individuals who ended their lineage by practicing this; I have never seen one who attained life by planting this seed. Among a million, there is not one who was not interrogated and punished for it. Among ten million there might be one who attains it by mistake, but attaining it would only lead to not dying. It was just something that Zhang Ling received to teach the people of his era.
>
> 清虛眞人授書曰。黃赤之道。混氣之法。是張陵受教施化。爲種子之一術耳。非眞人之事也。吾數見行此而絕種。未見種此而得生矣。百萬之中。莫不盡被考罰者矣。千萬之中。誤有一人得之。得之遠至於不死耳。張陵承此以教世人耳。

The Lady of Purple Tenuity then chimed in, saying (2/1b) that, although it was a "secret essential for long life," it was in fact only a "lesser art" that even practiced successfully qualified one only "to hold the brush for the Water Officer and beat the drums for the Three Offices" 適足握水官之筆，鳴三官之鼓耳. Another scripture from the Supreme Purity corpus, the *Scripture of the Bright Code of the Four Extremes*, gives a bit more detail about the procedure, including the sort of dangers that accompany its practice:[83]

---

82. *Zhen'gao* 2/1a.
83. *Taizhen yudi siji mingke jing* 太真玉帝四極明科經 1/11b. Isabelle Robinet dates this scripture to the Six Dynasties and argues that the "bright" (*ming* 明) in the title should in fact be "covenanted" (*meng* 盟). See Schipper and Verellen 2004:1, 192–93.

The Yellow Book with Red Border, the way of the Perfected One. This is a minor art of sexual intercourse, but it is also a secret matter among Daoists. Its principle is subtle but vital, all tied in with the two simulacra [yin and yang] separating and uniting, the Three Pneumas harmonizing together, dispelling[84] disaster and releasing from cyclical misfortune. By returning the essence, you nourish the gods, letting you avoid death. Those who have received this rite do violence to their correct pneumas, develop attachments and desires, mix in the muck with no restraint, become jealous and suspicious, attack their teachers, and slander and defame each other. That is why the prohibitions [surrounding it] are particularly heavy. Should anyone commit this sin, they themselves and their seven generations of ancestors would all be sentenced to serve as the left and right guards. Treading through the mountains eating fire, carrying rocks to fill the river, they suffer the five torments of the three [unfortunate] paths.

黃書赤界真一之道。此交接之小術，亦道手之秘事。其理妙嶮。皆二象離合，三氣相和，濁災解厄。還精養神，令人不死。受此法者有虧損正氣，心生愛慾，混濁不節，嫉妒疑貳，攻伐師本，更相讒訕。其禁尤重。有犯此罪，己身及七祖同充左右二官之罰。履山食火，負石填河，三塗五苦。

Here again we see the claim that the rite can rescue from disaster, presumably the apocalyptic disasters preceding the advent of Great Peace. The danger seems to be that it arouses attachment to one's partner and jealousy among others, including one's teacher. If Zhen Luan is correct that the rite involved sexual congress in public, especially if it included partners other than one's spouse, it is not surprising that feelings of jealousy might arise. There is one source that suggests that this is in fact the purpose of the rite, a passage in the *Scripture of Divine Spells Piercing the Abyss*. This part of the scripture dates from around 420, the founding of the Liu Song dynasty.[85]

84. Reading *xiao* 消 for the graphically similar *zhuo* 濁 of the text.

85. *Taishang dongyuan shenzhoujing* 20/24a–b. The Piercing the Abyss (Dongyuan 洞淵) movement was openly millennial, with a firm expectation for world calamity followed by a new world order. It was their contention that,

The Dao said: From this time on, I announce to all people of later ages, when you receive the Dao, husband and wife must receive it as a pair; it cannot be just one of them. Now when you receive the *Yellow Book*, you should be initiated by the three masters; then the Dao will confer the Yellow Contract. If you are not initiated, you personally will be tortured and in future incarnations will not be reborn into human bodies. How much more is this true about pursuing transcendence. You certainly cannot deceive people. If you worship the Dao but do not offer up incense and candles, you will personally experience torture, and the torture will extend to your descendants. Once there were two families who lived near each other. Each received the *Yellow Book* with the Great Inner and Outer Contracts. One family had the three masters initiate them, and they performed the Dao every day. A Daoist priest dispelled disasters, everything they encountered turned out to be an auspicious day, and all went according to their desire. When the husband and wife ascended as transcendents, the heavenly beings protected them. The other family also received [the *Yellow Book*] but did not go through initiation, nor did they have the three masters. They became jealous of each other and consequently did not perform the Dao. They did not live out their natural lifespan. Within two years, all members of the household had perished. The heavenly beings executed them. When you receive the Dao, you must follow every line of the scripture.

道言：自今以去，告後世人：汝等受道，夫妻對受，不得偏也。夫受黃書，三師過度，道受黃契。不過，身考，後世不復人身也。況復求仙也。亦不得誑人也。奉道不香火，身必有考，考及子孫。昔有二家相近，都悉受黃書內外大契。一家得三師過度，日日行道。道士消災，觸事好日，不違人意。夫妻上仙，天人護之。有一家，亦受而不過度，而無三師。自共相妒嫉，遂不行道。不終天壽，二年中皆滅門族。天人誅之矣。受道須一一順其經文也。

This passage is very informative. First we see that receiving the Dao is done in couples and that married couples must receive it

---

after a certain point, Merging the Pneumas was no longer needed in this new world because the Heavens were directly in control. Therefore, there are also passages in the work that disparage Celestial Master adherents as "Yellow and Red Daoists" and warn against associating with them.

together. The *Protocol of the Outer Registers* confirms this, telling us that one had to marry someone with the same rank of register, and in preparation for this there were forms to raise the rank of the lower party quickly.[86] According to this passage, the norm was for married couples to practice the rite. Here we should note that, on the basis of surviving portions of the *Yellow Book* (discussed below), Kristofer Schipper assumes that Merging the Pneumas was something like a Daoist marriage ceremony, but Chang Chaojan, analyzing the same material, argues that it describes instead a ritual performed by a single initiate and a master.[87] The example of the two families here suggests that the entire family should receive initiation, including the blessing of the Three Masters, and practice Merging the Pneumas daily. The family that did not receive initiation fell into jealousy and never practiced the rite together, then came to a very bad end. Thus, jealousy is an undesirable factor that might prevent one from performing the rite. Perhaps an important objective of the rite was to desensitize participants to emotions surrounding sexual union to help them attain the state of constrained emotions that the *Xiang'er* calls "pure stillness."

One more early source provides a useful perspective on the rite, the *Scripture of the Intoned Precepts of Lord Lao* 老君音誦戒經. This scripture was revealed in the early fifth century to Kou Qianzhi 寇謙之, who sought to revive and transform Celestial Master Daoism with himself as a new Celestial Master. Merging the Pneumas was one element of traditional practice that he criticized directly:[88]

> In the teachings of the bedchamber, as transmitted through the scriptures and contracts of the Yellow and Red, there are one hundred twenty methods, yet, as for connections with the teachings of my gate and hall,[89] there is not a single point of intersection. Ever since the

86. *Zhengyi fawen taishang wailu yi* 2a.
87. See Schipper 1993:151–52; Chang Chaojan 2003.
88. *Laojun yinsong jiejing* 17b–18a; Yang Liansheng 1956:51–52.
89. Reading *she* 涉 for the graphically similar *bu* 步. The phrase remains difficult to construe. Perhaps Kou intends to declare it alien to his upbringing;

Connected Celestial Master Daoling rose up as a transcendent, there
has only been the scripture[90] abroad in the world. Who was there
who understood it? How many people have there been who [follow-
ing it] attained eternal life and flew off as transcendents? The most
essential elements within the body, the oral instructions for guiding
the pneumas,[91] are all in the mouth of the teacher, whereas the teachings of brushes on placards are to regulate people's hearts. If there is
one who understands this and has faith in it, who upholds the scripture with all her heart so that, surrounding herself with incense and
fire, she refines her essence and achieves success, moving and awakening to the perfected deities so that she can sport with the transcendents, such a person can obtain the ultimate oral teaching. Now
people lie and cheat, acting arrogantly toward the Dao and becoming
jealous of the gods, embellishing the words of scripture, reforming
and confusing the rules and methods, recklessly innovating without
limit, creating all those false practices that then become customary.
I exhort and instruct all of you men and women throughout the
realm who have received and worn the contract and transmit it to
each other in ignorance: you cannot control yourselves, yet you take
charge of disciples, misleading and deluding the commoners. Those
who have committed sins are many, and they will summon down
upon themselves disastrous interrogations. Defiling the teachings of
the Dao with desire, they will destroy their dharma body. My *Intoned
Precepts* will interdict and reform the Yellow and Red, cultivating
in its place a purified, exceptional method that will have the same
merit with the Dao. As for male and female officers and novices
who wear the contract of the Yellow and Red, from the promulga-
tion of these precepts on, those who wear it will be inauspicious. If
there are those who do not practice it with care, the Perfected Officers of Earth and Pneuma Injectors of the place where they live as
well as the overseers and emissaries of the oratory or parish will
assess and record it independently. I shall visit upon them a disastrous
interrogation, and, when they die, they shall enter the earth prisons.

---

such a reading would make sense if Kou was raised in a Celestial Master family, but that would raise other questions.

90. This likely refers to the sexual manual otherwise known as the *Yellow
Book*.

91. *Daoyin* 導引, literally, "guiding and pulling," is a system for conducting
pneumas through the body that is still practiced today.

Should their souls be reincarnated, they will be reborn as insects, barnyard animals, pigs, or goats. They will never be able to fully redeem their sins. I have observed the husbands and wives of the world practicing the Yellow and Red; there was not a single regulation that they observed from the *Heavenly Officer's Essentials*. . . . However, the bedchamber is the basic place to seek life. Moreover, the scriptures and contracts encompass over one hundred methods, and they are not among the prohibited practices. If a husband and wife delight in the rite, let them strive to ask a pure and upright teacher, then do as he says. Choose whatever you like; to transmit any one rite can be sufficient.

房中之教，通《黃赤經契》有百二十之法，步門庭之教，亦無交差一言。自從係天師道陵昇儛以來，唯經有文在世，解者爲是何人？得長生飛仙者，復是何人？身中至要、導引之訣，盡在師口，而筆諜之教，以官人心。若開解信之者，執經一心，香火自縈，精練功成，感悟真神，與仙人交遊，至訣可得。今後人詐欺，謾道愛神，潤飾經文，改錯法度，妄造無端，作諸僞行，遂成風俗。勸教天下男女受佩契令，愚闇相傳。不能自度，而相領弟子，惑亂百姓，犯罪者眾，招延災考。濁欲道教，毀損法身。吾《誦誡》斷改黃赤，更修清異之法，與道同功。其男女官籙生佩契黃赤者，從今誡之後，佩者不吉。若有不慎之人，所居止土地真官注氣、靖治典者使者，當自校錄，吾與之災考，死入地獄，若輪轉精魂、蟲畜、豬羊而生，償罪難畢。吾觀世人夫妻修行黃赤，無有一條按天官本要。。。。然房中，求生之本，經契故有百餘法，不在斷禁之列。若夫妻樂法，但懃進問清正之師，按而行之，任意所好，傳一法亦可足矣。

It is often said that Kou advocated the prohibition of the rite, but that is not what this passage is saying. It seems, rather, that by his time the rite had diversified into many parallel practices, and he was concerned that some were leading the faithful astray. He stresses again the esoteric nature of the teaching and the need for a master who can impart the true method. This, then, is a much more familiar type of criticism, similar to that of the Supreme Purity scriptures and echoing, in a sense, the warnings of the *Xiang'er* that sex was necessary and proper for procreation but should not be overdone. Moreover, Kou has clearly adopted the goals of the southern occultists for physical immortality that make the promised fruits of the Merging the Pneumas rite insignificant and not worth the dangers associated with incorrect practice. Like them, he offers higher rewards.

Two texts in the Ming Daoist canon claim to be parts of the otherwise lost *Yellow Book*. Both by their titles are associated with the Supreme Purity revelations, which should give us pause given what I have just said concerning Shangqing attitudes toward the rite. The *Cavern Perfection Yellow Book* (*Dongzhen huangshu* 洞真黃書) is suffused with practices of the southern occultist tradition, including alchemy and physiognomy, that mainstream Celestial Masters eschewed. The *Supreme Purity Yellow Book of the Rite of Initiation* (*Shangqing huangshu guoduyi* 上清黃書過度儀), in contrast, has many of the features and the language of a Celestial Master scripture. Many passages are cryptic—we lack the oral instructions on how to interpret them—but the Three Pneumas described in the *Commands and Precepts for the Great Family of the Dao* are central to the practice, and they are visualized by a pair of participants engaging in some sort of physical ritual. Here is the invocation by the supervising priest that introduces the participants and explains the reason for conducting the ritual and what they hope to achieve. It begins by naming the sponsor, then invokes the gods and spirits necessary to accomplish the ritual and makes the specific request of the deities assembled.[92]

> Respectfully, there is a male or female novice X, from _____ commandery, county, township, and village, who is _____ years old, and who loves the Dao and delights in the transcendents. Now he or she has come humbly to your servant, begging to be initiated. He or she will follow the yin and yang, the five agents, and the Three Pneumas—the first born from the Middle Prime, the second from the Upper Prime, and the third from the Lower Prime, which bound together, constituting the Dao. I would like to ask the Lord of Conversion Who Inspects the Inner and Outer and his clerks; the Lord Who Returns the Spirit, Restores Color, and Replenishes the Pneumas and his clerks; the Divine Lord of Central Conversion Who Guards the Region, his generals, and his clerks; and the various Lords of Inter-

92. *Shangqing huangshu guoduyi* 4a.

rogation and Summons, serving the Three Offices of Heaven, Earth, and Water, their generals, and their clerks, on behalf of your servant and X, to dismiss all interrogation and arrest warrants, erase us from the roster of death, and inscribe our names on the Jade Calendar of Long Life so that we may be members of the seed people. I request that, for both your servant and X, our essential spirits will be focused and stable, living pneumas will spread through us and pervade us, and our four limbs and five viscera will each be without problem. What we seek we shall obtain, those we initiate will cross over, slander will subside. When the matter is complete, we will make a statement of merits and will not fail to keep our pledges.

謹有某郡縣鄉里男女生某甲，年如干歲，好道樂仙。今來詣臣，求乞過度，奉行陰陽，五行三炁。先從中元一生，上元一生，下元一生，三炁相結，共成爲道。願請監察內外開化君吏、還神復色補炁君吏、營域中化神君將吏、天、地、水三官考召諸君將吏，當爲臣及甲，解釋三官考逮，撤除死籍，著名長生玉曆，得在種民輩中。願臣及甲，精神專固，生炁布染，四支五藏，各得無他。所求者得，所過者度，口舌伏匿，事竟言功，不負效信。

The gods invoked are charged with overseeing personal conduct and reporting on it to the heavenly bureaucrats. The goal of the ritual is to attain salvation, which is realized by the recording of one's name in the roster of those fated to live eternally. This qualified one to become a seed person and live on into the world of Great Peace.

Although the details of the ritual are obscure, with euphemisms for certain actions and body parts that we cannot be certain we are interpreting correctly, we can get some feel for the rite and the cosmological significance with which it was infused from the following passage:[93]

Self-guided: Imagine that your pneumas and spirits have all taken complete form. X then takes the hand and guides himself. Taking his left hand, he touches from the side of the left nipple to the foot, saying, "To the left, the Supreme," three times, then stops. Again, taking the right hand, he touches from the side of the right nipple

93. *Shangqing huangshu guoduyi* 14a–b.

to the foot, saying, "To the right, the Mystic Elder," then stops. Next, using the left hand, he touches from the forehead directly down to the Cinnabar Field and [says:] the Most High, then the right hand follows it. In this way, he touches three times and speaks three times, then rising, rides on the Dipper and travels like a dragon, with no [ties] from the three vertical and five horizontal directions. Getting up, he uses the right hand to rub the lower Cinnabar Field three times, then proceeds to the Gate of Life. With the right hand, he opens the Golden Door, with the left raises up the Jade Flute, and makes it ejaculate on the Gate of Life. Again, using the left hand to support Kunlun and the right hand to rub the Gate of Life up-and-down and across three times, he says:

> The waters flow to the east
> Clouds return to the west,
> Yin nourishes yang,
> The pneumas subtle and fine.
> The mystic essence and clear saliva,
> Proceed on up to the Master's Door.

X then incants:

> The Divine Man holds the pass,
> The Jade Maiden opens the door.
> Dispatch pneumas from the yin,
> Bestow your pneumas on me.

Y then incants:

> Yin and yang bestow transformation,
> The myriad things are born from it.
> Heaven covers and Earth supports.
> I request that you bestow your pneumas on this servant's/
>   maidservant's body.

自導：思氣神都畢，甲因以手自導。以左手將左乳邊至足，言「左無上」三過。止，又以右手將右乳邊至足，言「右玄老」三過。止，次以左手將額上直下，下至丹田，「太上」，右手隨之。如此三將三言之，便乘魁起，不受三五龍行。上復以右手摩下丹田三，便詣生門。以右手開金門，左手挺玉籥，注生門上。又以左手扶崑崙，右手摩命門縱橫三。言：「水東流，雲西歸，陰養陽，氣微微，玄精滋液，上詣師門。」甲又咒：「神男持關，玉

女開戶，配氣從陰，以氣施我。」乙咒：「陰陽施化，萬物滋
生，天覆地載，願以氣施 臣/妾 身。」

This passage clearly describes sexual foreplay and perhaps actual
sexual congress in the context of the rite. Since Y's final chant can
be that of a male or a female, it seems either could be the active
partner in this rite.

Having surveyed surviving evidence for the practice of Merging the Pneumas, let us look again at the prohibitions and taboos
to see what they can tell us about its use and abuse during the
third century. The first sort of problem focuses on overindulgence. Prohibition 9 criticizes the indiscriminate practice of the
rite with a large group of unrelated partners in hopes of averting
calamity. Our sources repeatedly tell us that avoiding disaster
was a primary benefit of the rite, so we can imagine that it was
practiced more frequently and more widely when circumstances
looked threatening, whether from epidemic, natural disasters like
flood or drought, or political upheavals and warfare. Prohibition 19 also warns against overindulgence, but here it is length of
time and energy devoted to the ritual that is problematic. Although such a coupling might result in progeny (the only mention
in our material of what must have been a goal of the ritual), the
resulting son or daughter would be morally tainted. Prohibition
20 is more difficult to understand but also involved overindulgence in some form. The rituals in the *Yellow Book Initiation
Protocol* require that after each set of actions the participants
"report" (*bao* 報), and it would seem this prohibition involves not
merely overuse but also practicing the visualizations of deities
that are part of the rite without this vital step. Prohibition 11 may
refer to unritualized sexual union but would no doubt also have
applied to the Merging the Pneumas rite, interdicting its practice
in the open or while imbibing alcoholic drinks.

The second issue centers on the rite as an instrument of initiation into the group. We have seen that the rite was an important
initiation, bringing membership in the group and the protection
of its gods, but prohibition 10 warns against using these benefits
to seduce underage women. If we are correct that the rite involved

conferral of an upper-level register, underage women would not have possessed the requisite level of register to participate. Prohibition 21 is similar, forbidding the performance of the rite with non-Daoists, which is considered an offense against both the Dao and one's personal master, who was the source of one's own transmission.

Considering these provisions in the context of the controversies mentioned above, it seems that the rite was not at this time practiced primarily at the time of a marriage, nor was it confined to married couples. Although the presence of one's master might have been required for the initiatory performance, it was not required for subsequent practice. In terms of the salvific promise of the ritual, it may well have been linked to one's eventual selection as a seed person, but it seems likely that the avoidance of disaster it ensured was more often directed to the everyday existential calamities that threatened the health and well-being of the individual and the household. Because the rite promised both sexual gratification and the benefits of self-cultivation, abuse could manifest in the amount of time devoted to it, the frequency with which it was practiced, the individuals who were found to act as partners in the rite, and the indulgence in alcohol and feasting before or during performance. These abuses accord with the dangers that Supreme Purity sources as well as Kou Qianzhi imputed to the rite. In view of the esoteric nature of the master's oral instructions during the initiatory performance of the rite and the multiple forms into which it was elaborated, we cannot understand the nature of the rite in greater detail than this. Moreover, given the esoteric nature of the rite itself, its mode and frequency of employment may have varied considerably over time or space.

Demons and the Dao

The code of prohibitions and taboos and the material concerning the Merging the Pneumas ritual are valuable early sources for our understanding of the Celestial Master church, but the primary function of the *Demon Statutes* is as a demonography, listing a wide variety of demons and advising believers on how to deal with them. The key bit of information for each demon is its true name, which gives the knower power over the demon, but the text is also important because it allows one to predict which demon to guard against. We find an instruction on how to use these esoteric names at the end of chapter 1:[94]

> If among the unassigned citizens of the realm there are individuals who are filial, obedient, loyal, and faithful, they can write the names of the demons of the sixty days [of the sexagenary cycle] and keep them in a black sack. At midday on the first day of the first month of each year, they should personally proceed to their master's home to receive them, tying them on the left and right arm. If you take them when you travel, demons will not dare interfere. When the realm reaches Great Peace, you can return them to your home parish. If you fear encountering evil while traveling at night, you can swallow the demon's name, and the demon will not dare to face you. If people do not realize that the spirits govern themselves, they will personally encounter disasters for no reason. If you do not understand the correct technique, through the three times six years,[95] you will yourself perish.

> 天下散民中有孝順忠信者，可書六十日鬼名，著烏囊貯之。常以正月一日日中時以身詣師家受之，係著左右臂。以此行來，鬼不敢干。天下太平，送還本治。夜行恐逢惡，可服其鬼名，鬼不敢當。人不知鬼神自治，空身受災。不達義方，通三六之年，子自滅亡。

This passage suggests a primarily apotropaic use for the names of demons. The sexual rite also had its place in managing the relationship of humans and demons. Although the mechanism is not completely clear, it would seem that the generation of "living

94. *Nüqing guilü* 1/9a–b.
95. The meaning of this sentence is uncertain. Three sixes is usually a way of saying eighteen, but later sources do mention a "three-six hell." In referring to the days of a month, the "three sixes" refers to the sixth, sixteenth, and twenty-sixth days of the month. See *Yuanshi tianzun shuo Fengdu miezui jing* 2b.

pneumas" in the context of the rite was an important element, as we see in the following passage, which repeats many of the themes we have seen in this early literature:[96]

When humans are born into this world, they are originally allotted a life of one hundred years, but being born in the morning gives no guarantee they will see the sunset; those who die are many, and those who live are few. Rebellious killer demons roam throughout the human world, madly propagating the hundred ailments. Confronting the diseased pneumas of the Five Rebellions,[97] chills, fevers, and headaches, concretions forming in the stomach, vomiting, regurgitation, and shortness of breath, feelings of fullness in the five internal [viscera], distorted vision, dumbness, deformities of the hands and feet, inability to concentrate, [threats to] the life force loom each day and night, and ill-omened demons come to watch over them. Men and women of the realm, you can examine the names of these demons in my illustrated text and employ my lower talisman of Great Mystery, then send up the living pneumas of the Three Heavens produced by the 3–5–7–9 practice in order to join with the citizens of Heaven. The citizens of Heaven die and are reborn. I have personally seen the men and women of the realm, ever since the Great Beginning,[98] use demonic craft, not putting faith in my Perfection. For this reason, I had hidden this scripture, but those who died were too numerous to count. I have suffered grief contemplating this, and now I have again sent down the statutes and commands, with the surname and name, clothing, color, and size of each spirit in the realm. If you know the *Statutes* and summon the pneumas of Correct Unity, you can know their names by the day, and the myriad demons will not dare to interfere with you.

人生於世，元百年之生，朝不保暮，死多生少。逆煞之鬼，流布人間，誑作百病。五逆疾炁，寒熱頭痛，或腹內結堅，吐逆短炁，五內脹滿，目視顛倒，口唵手足孿縮，不自知慮，命在日夕，凶鬼

96. *Nüqing guilü* 1/8a–b.
97. On the Five Rebellions, see n. 61, above.
98. The Great Beginning refers to the origin of the cosmos, when yin and yang had been differentiated and the myriad things were produced. It is the last of four stages of creation in the "Heavenly Auspicious Signs" 天瑞 chapter of the *Liezi* 列子. See *Chongxu zhide zhenjing yijie* 沖虛至德真經義解 1/2b.

來守。天下男女，汝曹自可按吾圖書視鬼等名，施吾太玄之下符，上三天生炁，三五七九之生，以與天民，天民死而更生。自見天下男女，從太始以來鬼黠，不信吾真，故隱祕斯經，而死者不可勝數。念之傷悼，今重下律令，天下鬼神姓名、衣服、綵色、長短。知律，至正一之炁，子可隨日名，萬鬼不敢干。

We have seen that the early historical accounts of the founding characterize its teachings as "the demonic Dao," that our earliest epigraphical evidence for the cult concerns a conferral of texts announced by a figure called a "demon soldier," and that the high god of the religion was sometimes referred to as the Most High Demon Lao. One would expect from this that the faith's attitude toward demons would be somewhat ambivalent. This question has special significance because some Daoist sources characterize the gods of the Chinese common religion as demonic. The condemnation of demons thus encompassed the objects of worship of both the diffuse religious practices of families throughout China as well as the more organized activities of the Chinese state; both offered bloody victuals to supernatural beings in return for blessings. The *Demon Statutes of Lady Blue* provides key evidence for understanding how the Celestial Master Daoists conceived of and dealt with demons.

The secondary literature reveals a split on this question of the nature of demons and their equation with popular deities, especially the deities whose worship was undertaken by the Chinese state. Rolf Stein (1979), in a paper presented at the Second International Conference on Daoist Studies, held in Tateshina, Japan, and published eventually in *Facets of Taoism*, argued that Daoism made common cause with the Chinese state in condemning certain popular cults as "excessive." Thus, for the Daoists, "between their own practice and those of the prohibited popular cults there was not a difference of nature, but only of the degree, not of quality, but only of quantity," and the Chinese state shared this same distinction in its own labeling of certain types of practice as "licentious cults" (p. 59). Wang Zongyu (1999), for his part, has claimed that this condemnation was directed not just toward popular cults but also toward the high gods of the state. He points to figures in the *Demon Statutes of Lady Blue* that can be credibly linked to figures from the state cult. Thus, the "Hundred-Thousand-Foot-High Demon of High Heaven" 高天萬丈鬼, who is surnamed Huang 皇 (imperial), can, according to Wang, be identified with the central figure of the state cult, the Supreme Thearch of Lofty Heaven 昊天上帝, and the Keeper of the Talisman Demons of the Five Directions is to be identified with the Five Thearchs 五帝. These gods are arguably the most exalted deities of the state cult, ruling over the Six Heavens as identified by the Latter Han commentator Zheng Xuan 鄭玄. Moreover, even if these identifications are challenged, it is difficult to deny the presence in the text of other figures normally found in the state cult, like astral deities, the five marchmounts 五嶽, the three rivers 三河, and the four streams 四瀆. Their listing in the text does not, however, mean that all were treated as evil opponents of the Dao and of Daoists. Angelika Cedzich (2009), in an analysis based primarily on a lost text called the *Protocol of the Twelve Hundred Officials* 千二百官儀, argues that "Daoist liturgy was not limited to merely opposing the sacrificial model of both state cult and popular religion, but also involved the active attempt of transforming these cults according to its own legal, bureaucratic, and ethical standards."[99] All three scholars cite the *Demon Statutes of Lady Blue* but conclude variously that Daoism is basically in agreement with, in opposition to, or intent on assimilating through transformation the traditional deities of the state cult and local religion. There is some support for each position, but the dominant response of the early church was rather an accommodation of existing religious authority within a new framework.

Much as the *Commands and Precepts for the Family of the Great Dao* had depicted the cosmos as having formed from the differentiation of the primordial Three Pneumas, which were then

---

99. The *Qian erbai guan yi* is a lost work known only through a relatively small number of quotations, but many think it is substantially preserved in the *Zhengyi fawen jing zhangguanpin* 正一法文經章官品. See the article by Cedzich in Schipper and Verellen 2004:1, 133–34, and the collation of the text by Wang Zongyu (2009b).

corrupted by human desire, giving rise to the immorality and squalor of Lower Antiquity, the *Demon Statutes of Lady Blue* relates a historical process that explains the opposition of demons to the will of Heaven, which is further elaborated in later Daoist scriptures. Let us first look at the historical progression as depicted in the opening passage of the *Demon Statutes*:[100]

> When Heaven and Earth first were born, the primordial pneumas were propagated and circulated, and the myriad gods distributed the pneumas; there were no ugly, rebellious, wicked, deviant, incorrect demons. Men were filial and women were chaste, lords were courteous and officials loyal. The Six Seams[101] were as one, and there was neither trouble nor harm. Since the inaugural year of the Heavenly August reign period, gradually the hundred skills were born; [humans] stopped believing in the Great Dao; there was rebellion and murder in every quarter; epidemic pneumas began to arise. Tigers, wolves, and the myriad beasts, receiving the pneumas, grew large; and the hundred bugs, snakes, and imps increased day by day. Heaven has sixty days, and each day has a god on duty. On each day, there were a thousand demons flying about who could not be restrained or stopped. The Great Dao did not restrain them, the Celestial Master did not command them, so they had free access to the realm, one ill-omened creature following after another. They were allowed to kill the populace, and the dead numbered in the billions. The Most High Great Dao could not bear to see [this devastation]. At midday on the seventh day of the seven month of the second year [of the Han'an reign period], he sent down these *Demon Statutes* in eight scrolls, recording the surnames and names of the spirits of the realm as well as the techniques of fortune and misfortune. He charged the Celestial Master Zhang Daoling with them, causing him to command the spirits, so that they would not be able to wantonly move to the east, west, south, or north. Since then, when men or women of the Dao see my secret scripture and know the surnames and names of demons, all will be auspicious. The myriad demons will not interfere with them, and the thousand gods will submit to them like guests.

100. *Nüqing guilü* 1/1a–b.
101. The Six Seams (*liuhe* 六合) refer to Heaven above, the Earth below, and four directions, hence the three dimensions of space. See *Zhuangzi* 2.

天地初生，元氣施行，萬神布氣，無有醜逆祅邪不正之鬼。男孝
女貞，君禮臣忠，六合如一，无有患害。自後天皇元年以來，轉
生百巧，不信大道，五方逆殺，疫氣漸興。虎狼萬獸，受氣長
大，百蟲蛇魅，與日滋甚。天有六十日，日有一神。神直一日，
日有千鬼飛行，不可禁止。大道不禁，天師不勅，放縱天下，凶
凶相逐。唯任殺中民，死者千億。太上大道不忍見之，二年七月
七日日中時下此鬼律八卷，紀天下鬼神姓名吉凶之術，以勅天師
張道陵，使勅鬼神，不得妄轉東西南北。後有道男女生，見吾祕
經，知鬼姓名，皆吉，萬鬼不干，千神賓伏。

In this passage we are told that the primordial cosmos was perfect
and free of harm but gradually began to decay with the creation
of "skills." This accords well with the *Xiang'er* commentary,
which links skills with the "false techniques" of the profane. A
passage from the beginning of chapter 2 of the *Demon Statutes*
speaks about the primordial age before the decline:[102]

> The Statutes of the Most High of the Upper Three Heavens of Great
> Purity, Mysterious and Primordial, charge the Leaders of the Three
> Offices of Heaven, Earth, and Water: "When August Heaven was
> first born, only gods were honored. The current age is benighted,
> evil, and disordered. There are no perfected deities to be seen, only
> demons who disrupt the lives of humans. Now you should record
> and distinguish the names of the demons in order to establish the
> gods of the three levels and five directions to control the demons."
> 太清玄元上三天太上律勅天地水三官主者：皇天初生，唯神爲
> 尊。今世憒憒，邪亂紛紛，不見真神，唯鬼亂人。今當紀別鬼
> 名，定立三五神以治鬼。

It would seem that in the beginning there was still no distinction
between proper and improper ritual practice. It is only with the
decline and the proliferation of demons that Daoism becomes
necessary.

We find a more detailed description of this historical development in the fifth-century redaction of a Celestial Master ritual

102. *Nüqing guilü* 2/1a.

code by Lu Xiujing, *Master Lu's Abridgement of the Daoist Code*
陸先生道門科略:[103]

For the Great Dao is empty and silent, cut off from all shapes or appearance. His supreme sagacity is embodied in his actions and lodged in his words and teachings. The Most High Lord Lao observed that in late antiquity there had been a descent into violence, so that purity was defiled and simplicity lost; the universe had lost direction, and men and ghosts mixed in confusion; the stale pneumas of the Six Heavens claimed exalted office and assembled the hundred sprites as well as the ghosts of those who had suffered severe injuries, the dead generals of defeated armies, the dead soldiers of armies in disarray; the men claimed to be generals, and the women called themselves ladies. Leading ghostly soldiers, they moved as armies and rested in camps, roaming freely about Heaven and Earth, wantonly wielding authority and dispensing blessings, attacking the temples of others, seeking the sacrifices offered to them. They stirred up the populace, who slaughtered the three sacrificial animals at a cost that had to be counted in the tens of thousands, until they squandered their wealth and exhausted their possessions, yet did not receive [the gods'] protection but rather suffered their harm, so that those who died innocently or before their times were incalculable. The Most High was saddened that this had come to pass and for this reason bestowed upon the Celestial Master the Way of the Correct and Unitary Covenant with the Powers, with its prohibitions, precepts, statutes, and codes, in order to oversee and report upon the obedience or disobedience, blessings or calamities, merits or transgressions of the multitudes so that they might know good and evil. He established twenty-four parishes, thirty-six quiet huts, two thousand four hundred inner and outer Daoist priests. He sent down the *Twelve Hundred Officers* and ten thousand petitions so they might use execution talismans to attack temples, killing demons and preserving the lives of humans, to purge the universe and clearly rectify the cosmos so that throughout the Heavens and Earth, there could no longer be licentious, evil

103. *Lu xiansheng daomenke lüe* 1a–b. Note that I do not accept Nickerson's contention (1996b) that this text can be divided into a primary text by Lu Xiujing and a commentary perhaps by one of his disciples. Current printed editions of the text do not distinguish such layers, and Nickerson's divisions cut across clear metrical patterns.

demons. He banished all thoughts of interdictions and ruled the citizens with the Pure Bond: "The gods do not eat or drink, the master does not accept money."

夫大道虛寂，絕乎狀貌；至聖體行，寄之言教。太上老君以下古委懟，淳澆樸散，三五失統，人鬼錯亂。六天故氣稱官上號，構合百精，及五傷之鬼、敗軍死將、亂軍死兵，男稱將軍，女稱夫人，導從鬼兵，軍行師止，遊放天地，擅行威福，擾亂人民，宰殺三牲，費用萬計，傾財竭產，不蒙其祐，反受其患，枉死橫夭，不可稱數。太上患其若此，故授天師「正一盟威之道」、禁戒律科，檢示萬民逆順、禍福、功過，令知好惡。置二十四治、三十六靖，廬內外道士二千四百人，下千二百官、章文萬通，誅符伐廟，殺鬼生人，蕩滌宇宙，明正三五，周天匝地，不得復有淫邪之鬼。罷諸禁心，清約治民：「神不飲食，師不受錢。」

Here blame is attributed to the "stale pneumas of the Six Heavens," who lead assorted fell spirits who have died in battle. The Six Heavens were the primary object of worship of the Han state sacrifices, at the pinnacle of the continuum of sacrificial practice that constituted the Chinese common religion; hence this marks an explicit break with that tradition. Although this documentation is late, it was already implicit in the condemnation of sacrifice in the *Xiang'er* commentary and the description of the Daoist Three Heavens in the *Commands and Precepts*. The Pure Bond may well have been a feature of the movement since its inception, a sort of shorthand description of the Covenant with the Powers.[104] But a careful reading of this passage shows that this is not a blanket condemnation of all spirits who receive blood sacrifice. After all, there are legitimate spirits whose temples these miscreants attack, and surely some spirits respond to sacrifice with the protection for which their worshippers pray. Moreover, although some "died innocently or before their times," logically there were always those who died because of their transgressions or at the end of their natural lifespans. The spirits who effected their deaths in such cases would have done nothing wrong and hence would not need to fear the execution talismans of the Daoists.

104. On the Pure Bond, see Schipper 2000.

The full development of this idea of a primordial fall is visible in the *Dongyuan Scripture of Divine Spells* (*Taishang dongyuan shenzhou jing* 太上洞淵神咒經), the earliest stratum of which can be dated to the early fifth century.[105] This apocalyptic scripture preaches of an impending millenarian catastrophe caused by hordes of unrestrained demons, which must be controlled by the forces of orthodoxy. The origins of the problem are explained in the following passage:[106]

The Primordial Heavenly Worthy was in the Palace of Eternal Joy in the Land of the Hall of Great Blessings together with the Divine King of Flying Devas of Limitless Great Sagacity, both seated on thrones of seven-colored precious mist in order to transmit the Great Exorcistic Scripture of Divine Spells Piercing the Abyss. He summoned the Samadhi Divine Spell Kings of the ten directions and the Flying Mysterious Marvel Great Heavenly Perfected Great Gods to appear before their thrones. The Heavenly Worthy announced to the Most High Lord of the Dao: "I have heard quite often that in the regions bordering on the Land of the Hall of Great Extreme Joy and Blessings demons and devils are being produced wantonly who invade and harm the male and female sentient beings. Do you often hear their sad and suffering voices or not?" The Lord of the Dao said: "This region for seven billion five hundred thousand kalpas was a world of extreme joy, where there were no sad sounds of crying. Since the Dragon Han, the commoners, male and female, have all given rise to violent, evil killing and have brazenly prayed to the various gods and devils, wantonly seeking their survival. Since this awakening, for seven billion five hundred million kalpas, the commoners have been impoverished and suffering, their human forms suffering aging and illness; whether male or female, all shared the same dedication to cajoling and imploring evil demons. The stale pneumas of the Six Heavens allowed the nine uglies, tree sprites, and wicked goblins to enter their hearts; their thoughts

105. I accept Christine Mollier's argument that the last two chapters of the scripture should be seen as roughly contemporaneous with the first ten and not of Tang date, like chapters 11 through 18. See Mollier 1990; Cedzich 2009:75, n. 208.

106. *Taishang dongyuan shenzhou jing* 19/1a–2a.

turned to violent rebellion; and they killed the innocent so that evil gods came to thrive." At this time, the Heavenly Worthy proclaimed that the Five Venerable High Thearchs should summon and command the Great Devils of the Ten Heavens, the leaders of the Three Realms, and the Perfected Divine Great Soldiers of the Most High, numbering in the billions and trillions, to collect and seize all demons who had escaped from their rosters. Why? Because they have harmed the living, causing the territory to lack Great Peace, so that the living have many debts and are born and die without peace or happiness. The perfected kings of the Three Heavens together with the divine perfected of the ten directions and the great soldiers of the Three Heavens will patrol along the borders of the state, healing illness for all of the people, aiding the correct pneumas of heaven, exterminating evil sprites, and saving the lives of the sentient beings so that all can count on the power of the Dao to live out their heavenly ordained lifespans.

元始天尊於大福堂國土長樂宮中，與無極大聖飛天神王，俱坐七色寶蘊之座，度洞淵神呪大驅經，召十方三昧神呪王，飛行玄妙天真大神俱詣座下。天尊告太上道君曰：「頗聞大極樂福堂國土十方邊界，有鬼魔妄生，侵害眾生男女，常聞悲苦之聲否？」道君曰：「此境七百五千萬劫，是極樂世界，無有悲哭之聲。自龍漢之後，百姓男女之人，皆生兇惡，殺害婬祝，向諸神魔，妄求生活。自覺以來，七百五千萬劫，百姓貧窮困苦，人形衰老疾病，是男是女，皆同一心，諂求邪鬼。六天故炁承九醜木精妖魅入心，心生兇逆，殺害無辜，邪神轉盛。」是時，天尊告五老上帝，召命十大大魔、三界主者、太上真神大兵，億億萬眾，收取世間一切脫籍之鬼。何者？爲害生民，致使國土無有太平，生民多債，生死而無安樂者矣。三天真王與十方神真三天大兵，遊行國界，爲一切人治病，佐天正炁，殺滅邪精，救度眾生之命，俱得道力，全其天命。

In this passage, which shows clear influence of Buddhist ideas that entered Daoism through the Lingbao 靈寶 scriptures, the fall from original purity is traced back into the remote past, and the entire historical era of China's past is portrayed as a period of unremitting suffering and misrule. But note that leading the forces of Heaven to suppress the evildoers and restore a world of peace and tranquility are the Five Venerable Supreme Thearchs, who seem to be analogues of the Five Thearchs at the top of the state cult. Moreover, although the enforcing powers are led by Perfected figures from the Three Heavens, they include fearsome spirits like the devil kings.

The beings that cause evil in the world do not do so because it is their basic nature but rather because higher demons in service to the Daoist Heavens fail to control them. They are characterized as "demons who have escaped from the rosters" (*tuoji zhi gui* 脫 籍之鬼). There is a somewhat more detailed description of this process in the first chapter of *Scripture of Divine Spells*:[107]

> When there are illnesses, trouble with officials, disputes, or the impoverishment of households, proclaim this scripture and its precepts and command the devils with a divine spell. If there is a single demon who fails to depart and wantonly proclaims himself a great god, and if those receiving tutelary sacrifices in the wilds, the masters of popular temples, the dead generals of defeated armies, or demons who have escaped from the rosters come to aid this evil king, causing illness and pain to the common people and refusing to obey the great law, the killing gods of the ten directions will collect them together and execute them. If they obstinately return, indulging in violence and devoting themselves to spreading suffering, poison, and harm, the demon kings will behead them and the devil kings personally smash them into a myriad pieces. They are not permitted to pardon them. Do this speedily, in accordance with the statutes and commands.
>
> 若有疾病、官事、口舌、宅中虛耗，聞此經誡，勅魔神呪。若一 鬼不去，妄稱大神，山林社祀，世間廟主，壞軍死將，脫籍之 鬼，來助邪王，病痛世人、不從大法者，十方殺神收而誅之。若 復故來，縱暴專行苦毒害者，鬼王等斬之，魔王等身作萬分，不 得恕之。急急如律令。

Here we see demons who have escaped the control of their leaders, the devil kings, linked with local earth gods and the gods of popular temples. They are not condemned categorically as evil but rather chastised for refusing to submit and accept regulation by the Heavens and their representatives, Daoist priests. They assume titles that have not been authorized by the Heavens and

---

107. *Taishang dongyuan shenzhou jing* 1/9a.

cause death and misfortune that has not been properly adjudicated. The divine spell does not itself compel obedience but rather invokes authority.

The scriptures of the Shangqing revelation counsel a similar approach to demons, asserting the Daoist master's authority in order to compel them to return to acceptable norms of behavior. The following spell can be used when passing through a region where malefic spirits pose a danger:[108]

> I am a disciple of the Most High. Below, I command the Six Heavens. The palaces of the Six Heavens are subordinate to me. Not only are they assigned to me; they are ruled by the Most High. I know the names of the palaces of the Six Heavens, and, for this reason, I will live forever. If there is one who dares to accost me, the Most High will behead you. The name of the first palace is . . .
> 吾是太上弟子，下統六天，六天之宮，是吾所部，不但所部，乃太上之所主。吾知六天之宮名，是故長生，敢有犯者，太上斬汝形。第一宮名。。。

This passage claims that knowledge of the names of the six palaces at the center of the Six Heavens confers power over the nefast forces. Although the demons are threatened with physical punishment, it is a rather sedate response when compared to the violent exorcisms often used in traditional contexts when confronting such malefic spirits. We might see this as a systematized, routinized response to supernatural threats. The counterpart for the early church was the esoteric names of the demons conveyed through the *Demon Statutes of Lady Blue*.

Looking more closely at the demons whose secret names are revealed in the *Demon Statutes*, we find a number who present a threat only because they are part of the justice system of the Heavens, which centers on oversight, recording of conduct, and punishment for misdeeds. I have already mentioned the Hundred-Thousand-Foot-High Demon of High Heaven.[109] For the past

108. *Dengzhen yinjue* 2/13a.
109. *Nüqing guilü* 1/1b.

thirty-six thousand years, he has ascended to Heaven once a month to "respond to questions about interrogations and punishments" 對問考罰. He is followed in the list by the South-Facing Thrice-Venerable Demon, colloquially referred to as the Demon of the Five Paths, who is in charge of the rosters of the dead as well as "the interrogation and calculation of the sins of the living" 考計生人罪.[110] Many of the demons are enforcers keeping the evil demons under control, like the seven killer spirits of the Dipper 斗綱加煞, in charge of killing "the wicked, deviant, and rebellious demons of the realm" 天下姦邪逆鬼.[111] Others are assigned to normal humans like the Celestial Thearch's Demons in Charge of the Constant Supervision of Transgressions 天帝常司過鬼, who descend to listen to human conversations so that they can discover sins before they are committed and return to inform the interrogating killer spirits. Another set of three demons hide in the corners of dwellings and report on "married couples who act immorally and do not accord with yin and yang" 夫婦無道不順陰陽, presumably referring to some sort of sexual misconduct.[112] When they report, the humans are removed from the roster of the living. These demons are clearly in the service of the forces of good. Presumably, they might make mistakes, so the Daoist is given a way to control them, but they do not seem to be the sort of out-of-control demons who have escaped from their registers and are plaguing humankind. Moreover, some only manifest as demons in certain circumstances, like the Earl of the Gate 門伯 and the Door Attendant 戶丞, who "during the day are gods who bless the dwelling, at sunset turning into demons" 白日爲神福室，暮作鬼.[113]

The demons recorded so carefully in the *Demon Statutes of Lady Blue* are a mixed group, including both evil beings, who serve no function other than bringing misfortune, illness, and death to humanity, and loyal servants of the Daoist Heavens, who aid in administration of justice. Although in the Celestial Master system

110. *Nüqing guilü* 1/1b–2a.
111. This demon and the next are both found in *Nüqing guilü* 1/4a.
112. *Nüqing guilü* 4/2a–b.
113. *Nüqing guilü* 4/2b–3a.

all misfortune is ultimately caused by the actions of demons, some misfortune is deserved and just, or fated and inevitable. Faith in the Dao and proper ritual action can sometimes forestall or deflect the actions of these supernatural agents, but ultimately only proper conduct, or confession and sincere repentance for misconduct, can assure fortune and longevity.

The instrument for confession was the Personally Written Missive to the Three Offices, mentioned in historical accounts of the movement. In fact, the agents of the Three Offices would seem to be quite similar to the demons mentioned in the *Demon Statutes*. Although they are good and in service to the Dao, there is reason to think that they are in fact part of what later sources call the Six Heavens. In the "Teaching of the Celestial Master," translated above, we read that the "corpse people" who are beyond redemption belong to the Earth Office. The first essay in the *Scripture of Precepts and Codes, Teachings of the Celestial Master*, affirms this:[114]

> People of the Dao are pure and correct; their names belong to Heaven above. The profane are defiled and impure; when they die, they enter the custody of the Earth Office. How could they not be distant from each other?
>
> 道人清正，名上屬天；俗人穢濁，死屬地官，豈不遠乎。

From this pronouncement we can see that, although early church documents condemn evil elements of the pre-Daoist sacred world in scathing terms, this criticism was only intended for those figures who rejected the commands of the Daoist Heavens. Other figures, such as the Three Offices and their many agents, worked in concert with the Dao, forming an indispensable part of the entire system of supernatural justice and retribution.[115] They

114. *Zhengyi fawen tianshi jiao jieke jing* 11a4–6. Although this essay is not quite as early as the encyclicals that follow it, it still seems to be an authentic document from the early church, inspired by the same spirit of devotion.

115. On this ambiguous character of Daoist demons, see Seidel 1988:202–3; Lai 2002a:271; Sasaki 2009.

oversaw the actions of mortal beings and the dead, and recorded their good and evil conduct. When misconduct merited punishment, they were also the enforcers of that punishment, imposing upon both the living and the dead sentences of misfortune, illness, and penal servitude. Living mortals often had to die so that sanctions could be imposed in the other world. Moreover, as overseers of the dead, fearsome spirits functioned as a first court of appeals for the dead who thought they had been wronged and had lodged sepulchral plaints against the offenders or their descendants. For the living, even the administrators of the netherworld were fearsome, demonic beings who were the proximate cause of all bad things in their lives. Their agents of punishment, in particular, were often only semihuman demons, the denizens of nightmares who attack in the dark with fell weapons and choking miasmas.

The early Celestial Master church promised protection from such figures through its rituals and through the spirit generals, clerks, and troops whose control the registers of church rank conveyed to initiates. This protection was undoubtedly an important inducement when convincing the profane to convert. At the same time, such protection was limited and came at a price. Misconduct had to be redeemed through confession and penance. The only way to keep threats permanently distant was by rigorously observing a strict code of conduct that regulated all aspects of life. Membership in the church brought with it the assurance of a personal relationship with the Dao, but with that came increased scrutiny by a deity with very high standards for his flock. The severity of that scrutiny is evident in the excoriating criticisms that characterize the two encyclicals with which I began this chapter, *Yangping Parish* and *Commands and Precepts for the Great Family of the Dao*. It must have been reflected in many more spirit messages that have not been preserved as well as in regular interaction with libationers and other members of the church community.

FOUR

Daoism under the Northern and Southern Dynasties

In the preceding chapters we have examined the founding of Celestial Master Daoism on the basis of external and internal sources, then traced to the degree possible the development of the church through the tumultuous third century, following the great diaspora of Daoist believers in 215. We turn now to the fourth through sixth centuries, a period when the rule over Chinese territories was fragmented, with a succession of short-lived Chinese dynasties in the south vying for survival against a variety of non-Chinese invaders who ruled most of northern and western China. During this period, Buddhism grew in support throughout China and frequently received official governmental recognition in North China, but there were also attempts to revive a Daoist administration in Sichuan under the state of Cheng-Han (r. 302–347) and in the North China plain under the Northern Wei (386–534) and the Northern Zhou (557–581). In the south, although Daoism never approached the power of a theocracy, many of the highest officers of state and large swaths of the aristocracy were members of the Celestial Master church, and the rebellion of Sun En 孫恩 (d. 402) provided a dramatic example of the power of Daoism among the populace. I begin with the case closest to the founding of Daoism, the resurgence of political Daoism in Sichuan at the beginning of the fourth century.

The Li Family and the Cheng-Han State

Ancient Sichuan was home to two peoples, the Shu 蜀 in the Chengdu plain, settled farmers who were heirs to the bronze age Sanxingdui 三星堆 civilization, and the Ba 巴 in the Jialing river basin and southwestern Hubei, riverine hunter-gatherers known for their fierceness in battle.[1] By the Latter Han, the Shu had been fully assimilated, but the Ba maintained a distinct ethnic identity, identified primarily by the tribal name Cong. The Celestial Masters evangelized among these Cong and gained many converts, who were attracted to the Daoists' mastery of spirit armies (*guidao* 鬼道) and the protection they offered from demonic attack.[2] As we saw in chapter 1, when Zhang Lu established his theocracy in Hanzhong, he relied on the military support of the Cong from their traditional homeland to the south. Many came to settle in the Hanzhong area to participate in the coming age of Great Peace. Among them was a tribal leader from Dangqu 當渠 (northeast of modern Qu 渠 county) named Li Hu. After the surrender of the state to Cao Cao, he and his followers, around five hundred households, were transferred to the area north of Lüeyang, Gansu, where he was made a general in the Wei forces. His son Li Mu 李穆 served as Eastern Qiang-Hunting Commander (*dong Qiang lie jiang* 東羌獵將) as did his grandson Li Xiang 李庠.

Another grandson, Li Te, was a man of uncommonly tall stature who served in a variety of offices under the Western Jin. The 290s was a tumultuous decade, especially in the northwest, where local rebellions, famines, and epidemics eventually led to a mass migration that included many members of the Celestial Master church. As the band of migrants grew, Li Te distinguished himself

1. The primary sources for the history of Cheng-Han are chapters 8 and 9 of the *Huayangguo zhi* 華陽國志 of Chang Qu 常璩 (ca. 291–361), who was an official in the state at the time of its demise, and *Jin shu* 121. A more complete account of the state by Chang, called *Li Shu shu* 李蜀書 or *Cheng-Han zhi shu* 成漢之書, existed until the Tang and is reconstructed in Kleeman 1998.

2. Taniguchi Fusao (1976) argues that the Di 氐 were also among these early non-Chinese converts.

as a leader, caring for the ill and starving along the way. The group, now numbering hundreds of thousands, first returned to Hanzhong, hoping to find succor in the former Daoist homeland. When the resources there proved insufficient to sustain the migrants, they moved on to the Chengdu plain, where they allied themselves with the governor of Yi 夷 province, Zhao Xin 趙廞, a Daoist whose family had also been part of the Hanzhong kingdom. Many among the migrants were skilled fighters, adept at cavalry warfare, and formed an important support for Zhao. When Zhao defied a court order to take up a position at court, he also turned on the migrants, but a military ambush was thwarted, and eventually the migrants hunted him down, killed Zhao Xin, and transmitted Zhao's head to court in an act of loyalty that won Li Te and his brother appointments as generals.

They now controlled northern Sichuan. The governor of Liang province, Luo Shang 羅尙 (d. 310), was transferred to Chengdu, initially receiving the support of the migrants. When a central government edict ordered the migrants to return to their native place, local elites conspired to confiscate the migrants' possessions and force them on their way. Li Te won the allegiance of the migrants by repeatedly petitioning for a delay in their departure. He is said to have issued a simplified legal code in three articles and amnesties on existing debts. An attempted ambush of the migrants was unsuccessful, but Li Te was killed in a subsequent battle in 303.

This brought to the fore his son, Li Xiong 李雄, a devout Daoist. The migrants had previously been resupplied by the Daoist Fan Changsheng 范長生 (248–318), who led a community of more than a thousand households, no doubt his parishioners, on the slopes of Mount Greencastle 青城山, northwest of Chengdu.[3] When Li Xiong's aides encouraged him to claim the throne as king, he first offered the position to Fan, hoping to re-create the

3. Fan, also called Jiuchong 九重 and Yanjiu 延久, wrote a commentary to the *Yijing* in ten scrolls under the name Talent of Shu (Shucai 蜀才). Originally from Fuling 涪陵, in southeastern Sichuan (now Chongqing city), he may have been of Cong ethnicity. See Kleeman 1998:83; Wang Liqi 2002:17/440; *Sui shu* 32/910.

Hanzhong theocracy in which his great-grandfather had been a participant. Fan declined, saying:

> If one [by divination] projects forward to the Grand Beginning, the five phases converge in the *jiazi* year. The throne will go to the Li clan. It is not the proper time for me to rule.
> 推步太元，五行大會甲子。祚鍾于李。非吾節也。

Fan came to the capital riding in a white cart. Li Xiong met him at the gate and led him to his seat, where he appointed Fan chancellor, with the honorific title Fan the Worthy 范賢. Two years later, when Xiong claimed the title of emperor, he honored Fan with the title Great Master of the Four Seasons, Eight Nodes, Heaven and Earth (*sishi bajie tiandi taishi* 四時八節天地太師), which recalls the titles used by the first three Celestial Masters.[4] Xiong took as the name of his state Great Perfection (*dacheng* 大成), a reference to a poem from the *Odes* (Mao 179) that had been linked during the Latter Han to the establishment of a realm of Great Peace.[5]

Fan Changsheng served the state as chancellor until his death in 318. At that time, his son, Fan Ben 范賁, replaced him, serving until the demise of the state in 347. Even after that, a failed attempt to reestablish the state centered on Fan Ben. Given the family-based model of membership in Celestial Master Daoism, we can assume that Fan Ben was also a high official in the church.

It is remarkable, then, that the historical accounts of the Cheng-Han state in both the *Record of States South of Mount Hua* and in the official *Book of Jin* fail to mention the activities of the prime minister or the Daoist allegiance of its leaders. As Anna Seidel pointed out over four decades ago, it is likely that the Li

---

4. See *Zizhi tongjian* 86/2721, kaoyi 考異. The current *Huayangguo zhi* shortens the title to *Tiandi taishi*.

5. See Seidel 1969–70:219; *Shijing* (H-Y Index edn.) 39/179/8; *Hou Han shu* 7/295. Zheng Xuan's commentary to this passage (7/296, n. 6) says: "Great Perfection refers to the attainment of Great Peace" (*dacheng wei zhi taiping ye* 大成謂致太平也).

family gained support because of prophecies foretelling the rise of a Daoist leader surnamed Li who would bring about a world of Great Peace that was in some sense a restoration of the Han dynasty.[6] Thus, even the change of dynastic name to Han in 338 has significance in this regard.[7] Cheng-Han featured a limited and comparatively lenient legal code and charitable institutions for the poor. In comparison to the turmoil that shook the rest of China during the first half of the fourth century, the state was an island of peace, security, and good government.

This was particularly true during the reign of Li Xiong (r. 304–34), who seems to have been the state's most devout Daoist. The historian's assessment of his reign in the *Book of Jin* characterizes him as "generous and sincere" and notes that he "reduced punishments and simplified the legal code," pardoned his enemies, established schools, and reduced taxes and corvée labor so that, although "the entire world within the seas was in great disorder, Shu alone was without troubles." Even the criticism that "rank and seniority were not distinguished; nobility and commoners did not differ in their clothing and insignia" may have reflected the different social structure and more egalitarian nature of Daoist communities.[8] This eliding of Daoist elements in mainstream Chinese historical sources adds to the difficulty of determining the role of Daoism in Chinese history.

North China: The Northern Wei and Northern Zhou

In the preceding chapter, all of our evidence for Celestial Master Daoism during the third century came from North China, but, during the fourth century, the focus of Daoism shifted to the south.

6. See Seidel 1969, 1969–70; Kleeman 1998:61–86.
7. The fourth ruler, Li Shou 李壽 (r. 338–43), had been given the title King of Han when he conquered the Hanzhong region that was the site of Zhang Lu's millennial kingdom.
8. See Kleeman 1998:179–80, translating *Jin shu* 121/3040.

This was largely the result of the migration of numerous elite Daoist families to the south after the Revolt of the Eight Kings (291–306), the destruction of the Western Jin dynasty (317), and the invasion of North China by several seminomadic, horse-riding peoples. But Daoism certainly survived in the north, as evidenced by the Buddho-Daoist stelae that began to appear in the mid-fifth century. These show that at the village level there were still libationers, novices, and Daoist citizens playing significant roles in the community. Another key piece of evidence is the role of the Daoist Kou Qianzhi at the Northern Wei court.[9]

The Toba family that established the Northern Wei dynasty was attracted to and supported both Buddhism and Daoism. Emperor Daowu 北魏道武帝 (Tuoba Gui 拓拔珪, r. 386–409) was particularly interested in alchemical means to attain immortality. During the Tianxing reign period (398–404), he established a Transcendents Workshop (xianfang 仙坊) and appointed Transcendent Erudites (xianren boshi 仙人博士) to staff it.[10] They were given West Mountain as a place to create their elixirs and were permitted to test them on criminals sentenced to death. Emperor Mingyuan 魏明元帝 (Tuoba Si 拓拔嗣, r. 409–23) continued these endeavors, as did his son, Emperor Taiwu 魏太武帝 (Tuoba Tao 拓跋燾, r. 424–52). Emperors Daowu and Mingyuan both died of elixir poisoning.[11]

Kou Qianzhi was the second son of an illustrious northern family originally from close to modern Beijing, who traced their lineage back to the Han dynasty official Kou Xun 寇恂 (d. 36 CE).[12] His elder brother Kou Zan 寇讚 (d. 348) was rewarded with high office by the Northern Wei for settling there refugees from his

9. Primary sources for Kou are the Treatise on Buddhism and Daoism of the Book of Wei 魏書釋老志 and the Scripture of the Intoned Precepts of Lord Lao (Laojun yinsong jiejing). For a list of recent articles dealing with Kou, see Zhuang Hongyi 2010:23–25. Lagerwey (2007:29) is correct in noting that the only substantial study of Kou (prior to his own) was Yang Liansheng 1956.

10. Weishu 114/3049.

11. Weishu 2/44; 3/62.

12. Kou claimed to be Xun's descendant in the thirteenth generation, but Liu Yi (2002) calculates it must be the eleventh.

adopted home in Shaanxi. Kou Qianzhi spent thirty years as a recluse on Mount Hua and Mount Song, the western and central Sacred Peaks, searching for the secret to immortality.

The *Book of Wei* records the encounter of Kou with a "demoted transcendent" (*zhexian* 謫仙) named Chenggong Xing 成公興.[13] This figure, who was working as a simple laborer, so impressed Kou Qianzhi with his hard work that Kou hired him to perform his corvée labor duties. One day when Kou was stumped by an astronomical calculation, Chenggong Xing showed him how to solve it. Kou, realizing this was no ordinary laborer, then asked to become his disciple, but Chenggong instead demanded to study under Kou. Leading Kou to dwell in a cave on Mount Hua, Chenggong collected herbs to feed him. This continued for seven years, after which Chenggong Xing announced his impending departure and apparently died. The next day, two youths appeared at the cave bringing ritual garments, a begging bowl, and a staff. Chenggong came back to life, donned the clothing, took up the bowl and staff, and left. This story is related in our source to an earlier tale of a man named Wang Huer 王胡兒, who, once on one of the subsidiary peaks of Mount Song, happened upon an abandoned mansion with "golden rooms and jade halls" that bore a plaque titling it "Mansion of Chenggong Xing." His uncle had told him that Chenggong was a transcendent who had been demoted for setting fire to seven rooms of a heavenly building and sentenced to serve Kou Qianzhi as a disciple for seven years. This is a common story of an encounter with an immortal and seems to have no connection to Celestial Master Daoism.

The primary revelation to Kou Qianzhi is said to have occurred in 415, when the Supreme Lord Lao, riding a cloud pulled by dragons and accompanied by an entourage of spirits, transcendents, and jade maidens, alit on a peak of Mount Song.[14] He tells Kou:

> In the preceding forty-eighth sexagenary year [411], the Master of the Quelling Spirits Assembling Transcendents Palace submitted an

13. *Weishu* 114/3050.
14. *Weishu* 114/3050–51.

announcement to the Heavenly Bureau, saying: "Ever since the Celestial Master Zhang Ling died, this earthly office has been vacant,[15] and those who cultivate goodness have had no master to teach them. The Daoist priest of Mount Song, Kou Qianzhi of Shanggu, is upright and principled of character, his conduct is in accord with the spontaneous, and his talent is sufficient to be the first model. He can hold the position of Master." So I have come to observe you, to confer upon you the position of Celestial Master,[16] and to bestow upon you the *Precepts of the New Intoned Code among the Cloud* in twenty scrolls, with the appellation "Dual Advancement."

往辛亥年，嵩岳鎮靈集仙宮主表天曹，稱：自天師張陵去世已來，地上曠職。修善之人，無所師授。嵩岳道士上谷寇謙之，立身直理，行合自然，才任範首，可處師位。吾故來觀汝，授汝天師之位，賜汝《云中音誦新科之誠》二十卷，號曰并進。

The author of the announcement recommending Kou is presumably Chenggong Xing. The scripture is now lost except for one poorly transmitted chapter, preserved in the Daoist canon under the title *Scripture of the Intoned Precepts of Lord Lao* (*Laojun yinsong jiejing*).[17] The term Dual Advancement is nowhere explained but perhaps refers to the dual cultivation of morality, by observing the precepts, and immortality, through the ingestion of herbs and drugs, mentioned below. Lord Lao further instructs Kou as follows:

These scriptural precepts of mine, since the creation of Heaven and Earth, have never been transmitted in the world. Now, according to the cycles of fate, they should appear. You will disseminate this *New Code* of mine in order to purify and correct Daoism, eliminating the false methods of the Three Zhangs: the rent rice and cash tax as

15. Following the *Guang hongmingji* in reading *zhi* 職 for *cheng* 誠. See n. 41 in the Zhonghua edn., p. 3061.

16. Following the quotation in *Cefu yuangui* 冊府元龜 53, cited by the Zhonghua editors in ibid., n. 42.

17. See Yang Liansheng 1956 for an attempt to decipher this problematic text. The many incorrect characters may just be the result of poor transmission, but such errors and the colloquial character of the text are consistent with an origin in spirit revelation.

well as the technique of men and women merging the pneumas. The Great Dao is pure and empty. How could it countenance this sort of affair? [Daoists] should place only matters of propriety at the fore and supplement them with the ingestion of elixirs and breath cultivation.

吾此經誡，自天地開闢已來，不傳于世。今運數應出。汝宜吾《新科》，清整道教，除去三張僞法，粗米錢稅，及男女合氣之術。大道清虛，豈有斯事。專以禮度爲首，而加之以服食閉練。

There was a second revelation almost a decade later, toward the end of 423. In this case, the revealing spirit was a self-proclaimed great-great-grandson of Laozi, Li Puwen 李譜文, who claimed to have attained the Dao during the reign of Han Emperor Wu (r. 141–87 BCE). He noted that Kou had spent ten years in service of the Dao when he was still a youth,[18] and twelve years when, "though you had no great achievements in moral transformation, you did exert yourself in transmitting [the Dao] to a hundred others" 教化雖無大功，且有百授之勞. Li granted Kou authority over an area controlled by Mount Song that is "a myriad *li*[19] square" as well as a series of registers:

I bestow upon you promotion into the Inner Palace and four registers: the Most Perfected Most Treasured Perfected Master of the Nine Continents, the Controlling-Spirits Master, the Controlling-Citizens Master, and the Succeeding to Heaven Master Register. Because you continued to strive without failing, you were promoted again. I bestow on you the Heavenly-centered Register of the Three Perfecteds' Great Text, which investigates and summons the hundred gods, to confer upon your disciples. There are five grades of text registers:[20] The first is called the Great Officer of Yin and Yang; the second is called the Perfected Officer of the Correct Head-

18. Reading *tongmeng* 童蒙 for the graphically similar *jingmeng* 竟蒙.
19. A *li* was at the time roughly 400 meters.
20. Throughout this text I understand *lu* 錄 as *lu* 籙, a convention common in Six Dynasties and Tang manuscripts. The conventional Celestial Master register system is examined in detail in chapter 7 below. See Zhang Zehong 2005:42.

quarters; the third is called the Perfected Officer of the Correct Chamber; the fourth is called the Unassigned Officer of the Night Palace; the fifth is called the Master of the Register of Dual Advancement. Each differs as to the position of the altar, the [object of] worship, the robe and cap, and the rites. Altogether there are more than sixty scrolls, which are called the *Perfected Scripture of Registers and Charts.*

今賜汝遷入內宮，太真太寶九州真師、治鬼師、治民師、繼天師四錄。修勤不懈，依勞復遷。賜汝《天中三真太文錄》，劾召百神，以授弟子。《文錄》有五等，一曰陰陽太官，二曰正府真官，三曰正房真官，四曰宿宮散官，五曰并進錄主。壇位、禮拜、衣冠、儀式各有差品。凡六十余卷，號曰《錄圖真經》。

This text is the basis for the establishment of a new Celestial Master religion, with four exalted registers possessed solely by the new Celestial Master and five graded registers to be conferred upon a body of disciples. It was intended for use in support of the northern Perfected Lord of Great Peace (*beifang taiping zhenjun* 北方太平真君), a term adopted as a reign name by Emperor Taiwu in the year 440.

The revelation also included architectural specifications for a Heavenly Palace employing the Quiet Wheel method (*tiangong jinglun zhi fa* 天宮靜輪之法), the successful construction of which would allow the Celestial Master to create perfected transcendents. As for lay men and women, they faced an impending apocalypse (*mojie* 末劫) that made the propagation of this religion difficult. Most need only erect buildings with altars and worship morning and night (presumably a reference to the audience ceremony held in the oratory)[21] to gain merit for themselves and any worthy ancestors. A select few could aspire to greater things:

Those among them who can cultivate their bodies and create an elixir, learning the arts of longevity, will become the seed citizens of the Perfected Lord [of Great Peace].

其中能修身練藥，學長生之術，即為真君種民。

21. See chapter 6.

With this second revelation, the foundation was complete for a new theocratic state, including sacred buildings, a hierarchically organized priesthood, a trained laity, and a heavenly ordained ruler who would lead them all into a grand new age of Great Peace. At the center of this movement would be the newly appointed Celestial Master. Kou claimed that no Celestial Master had existed since the first, Zhang Daoling, conveniently ignoring not only his son Zhang Heng and grandson Zhang Lu, who had established the first Daoist theocracy in Hanzhong, but all the Daoists of the intervening three centuries, as we see in this passage from the *Intoned Precepts*:[22]

> Since [Zhang] Ling crossed over, his office has long been empty, and no one was appointed Connected Celestial Master. I had the perfected tutelary officers of the various provinces, commanderies, and counties inject their pneumas in order to administer ghostly matters and control the population rosters of the mortals; I made no use of the defiled, disordered method of having mortal libationers govern the citizens.
>
> 從陵昇度以來，曠官真職，來久不立係天師之位。吾使諸州郡縣土地真官注氣治理鬼事，領籍生民戶口。不用生人祭酒理民濁亂之法。

This brazen claim was no doubt necessary in the face of a living Daoist church with an active priesthood serving across the breadth of North China according to ancient rules of ordination and promotion, which also directly communicated with the church founders through spirit communication.[23] Previous studies have assumed that Kou grew up in a traditional Celestial Master family on the basis of the statement in the *Book of Wei* that he

---

22. *Laojun yinsong jiejing* 2a.

23. See below, chapter 8, for details of the organization of the Celestial Master priesthood. For evidence of the survival of these church offices in North China stelae of the fifth through seventh centuries, see Bokenkamp 1996–97, 2002; Hu Wenhe 2004; Zhang Xunliao 2010.

"when young cultivated the techniques of Zhang Lu, ingesting elixirs and herbal medicines" (*shao xiu Zhang Lu zhi shu fushi eryao* 少修張魯之術服食餌藥), but we have seen above that such practices had no place in the Daoist church. This statement is simply a mistaken conflation of Kou's early history as a seeker of immortality and an outsider's misunderstanding of the nature of Daoism. In light of the preceding claim that no Celestial Master had succeeded to Zhang Daoling's position as well as the portrayal of Kou in the *Book of Wei* as a conventional seeker after immortality through alchemy and especially the role Kou played as an advocate of blood sacrifice to Mount Hua and Mount Song recorded in stelae dedicated to each mountain,[24] it is unlikely that Kou grew up in a traditional Celestial Master family, much less that he was a descendant of a member of the original Hanzhong theocratic kingdom.[25]

Kou presented his revealed scripture, though perhaps not the *Intoned Precepts*, to the throne in 424. Emperor Taiwu was initially not convinced, though he appointed him to the Transcendent Workshop, but Kou did gain the ear of the aristocrat Cui Hao 崔浩 (d. 450), who had established a reputation as an expert in astrology and the *Book of Changes*. Cui became Kou's disciple and studied his arts. He repeatedly recommended Kou to the emperor, arguing that the appearance of such an eminent recluse in his court unbidden was a testament to the young emperor's sterling virtue. The emperor's response was to make a sacrifice of jade, silk, and a trio of animals (*tailao* 太牢) to Mount Song and to welcome Kou's cohort of disciples from the mountains. This group of 40 Daoists eventually grew to 120, who followed Buddhist practice in praying six times a day and offered huge kitchen-feasts feeding thousands of people every month.

Kou actively supported the emperor's plan of conquest, accompanying him on campaigns and arguing for the precedence of

24. On these stelae, see Shao Mingsheng 1962; Liu Yi 2002.

25. See Liu Yi 2002 for a convincing refutation of such theories, especially as expressed in Chen Yinke 1950.

martial over civil virtues in order to install the emperor as the Perfected Lord of Great Peace. Two buildings were built at his request in the capital (modern Datong, Shanxi).[26] The first was a Daoist temple with a three-layered altar, atop which was placed a round platform, with a throne atop that. Northeast of this was the Quiet Wheel Palace, an exceptionally tall building perhaps modeled on a Buddhist stupa, on which construction began in 431.[27] It was supposed to be "so high that one could not hear the crowing of roosters or the barking of dogs, so that one could connect above with the gods of Heaven" (*gao buwen jiming goufei zhi sheng, yu shang yu tianshen jiaojie* 高不聞雞鳴狗吠之聲，欲上與天神交接). Despite a labor force of over ten thousand, it was not completed after a year. A Buddhist source claims that in this same year Daoist temples with priests were established in all the provincial capitals of the Northern Wei empire, but this is not recorded in any government or Daoist source.[28] It was only in 440 that the emperor changed the reign name to Perfected Lord of Great Peace. In 442, Emperor Taiwu finally accepted a Daoist ordination register from Kou, a custom continued by later emperors, despite their support for Buddhism, until the end of the dynasty in 534. When Kou died six years later, he was buried with the rites of a Daoist priest.

It is unclear to what degree we should see Kou Qianzhi's movement as a reformation of Celestial Master Daoism as opposed to a new scriptural movement like the Supreme Purity (Shangqing 上清) or Numinous Jewel (Lingbao 靈寶) movements that arose a few decades earlier in the south. In a sense, the departure from Celestial Master practice was more radical: Supreme Purity and Numinous Jewel followers received registers that they thought more exalted and powerful than their Celestial Master registers,

---

26. The most detailed description of these buildings is in the *Shuijing zhu* 水經注 of Li Daoyuan 酈道元 (ca. 470–527). See Wang Guowei 1984:13/427–28.

27. This according to Liu Zhaorui 2004. Lagerwey translates this as the Revolving Palace (2007:53, 54, n. 57), without explanation, but Liu argues that the name refers instead to the Quiescent Wheel of the Dharma (*jijing falun* 寂靜法輪) mentioned in contemporary Buddhist scriptures.

28. Mather 1979:141; Lagerwey 2007:54.

but Kou's followers had their traditional Celestial Master registers replaced with new documents predicated on a radically different church structure and understanding of the role of the libationer.

Like the Supreme Purity revelations, Kou's *Scripture of the Intoned Precepts of Lord Lao* does not approve of the Merging the Pneumas rite, saying of married couples who practice the rite, "there is not one who does it according to the essentials of the heavenly officers" (*wu you yitiao an tianguan benyao suo xing* 無有一條按天官本要所行).[29] Still, he does not condemn it:[30]

> However, the bedchamber is the basic place to seek life. Moreover, the scriptures and contracts encompass over one hundred methods, and they are not among the prohibited practices. If a husband and wife delight in the rite, let them strive to ask a pure and upright teacher, then do as he says. Choose whatever you like; to transmit any one rite can be sufficient.
>
> 然房中求生之本。經契故有百餘法不在斷禁之列。若夫妻樂法，但蔥進問清正之師，按而行之，任意所好，傳一法亦可足矣。

The same is true for hereditary succession to Daoist parishes. Kou condemns the practice but ultimately admits that the son should only be barred from succession if he is manifestly incompetent. This should probably be seen as a concession to the popularity of the Merging the Pneumas rite and the resilience of the parish structure.

Kou's "reforms" sought to strip libationers of their traditional pastoral role in Daoist communities. His claim that the Supreme Lord Lao had never made use of libationers, instead relying on local spirits of the earth to directly minister to the people, negated the legitimacy of the traditional parish structure, which was based on libationers listing and updating their parishioner households on fate rosters (*mingji* 命籍). Acceptance of his new

29. *Laojun yinsong jiejing* 18b.
30. *Laojun yinsong jiejing* 19a. Cf. Yang Liansheng 1956:22; Lagerwey 2007:47–48.

system of registers, administered by the local divine bureaucracy, would have eliminated the raison d'être and the primary source of revenue for libationers.[31]

The traditional role of the master as judge, who assesses the conduct of his parishioners against a graded set of precepts and imposes penances upon them, was also usurped by the gods of the parish and oratory, who report not to the master but to the Supreme Lord Lao himself. For example, those who offend against his new restrictions on the Merging the Pneumas rite face punishment:[32]

> The perfected officers of the earth and their pneuma injectors, the administrators and emissaries of the oratories and parishes will collate and record them. I will visit upon them disaster and torture so that they die and enter into the hells.
>
> 所居止土地真官、注氣、靖治典者、使者，當自校錄。吾與之災考，死入地獄。

In this final threat to banish the disobedient to the hells, we see evidence that Buddhism was the source of many of these changes.[33] The competition with Buddhism at the Northern Wei court was significant. Cui Hao, perhaps with Kou's assistance, was responsible for the first major persecution of Buddhism in Chinese history.[34]

A simplified ordination procedure was promulgated for use by all, regardless of previous rank in the Daoist church, centering on a written copy of the code, which had to be sung, probably in imitation of Buddhist chants (*fanbai* 梵唄):[35]

---

31. *Laojun yinsong jiejing* 2a.

32. *Laojun yinsong jiejing* 18b. Cf. Lagerwey 2007:32.

33. Mather emphasizes the influence of the newly imported Buddhist *vinaya* code on the *Intoned Precepts*, relating this to Kou's supposed contact with Buddhist missionaries in Chang'an (1979:111).

34. Mather (1979) discounts Kou's role in these events, but Buddhists laid much of the blame at his feet. See *Fozu tongji* 佛祖統紀, T2035, 49:354b.

35. *Laojun yinsong jiejing* 1b. I adopt several emendations to the text suggested by Yang Liansheng (1956:38).

Daoist officers or novices: When receiving the precepts for the first time, you should face the precept scripture and bow eight times. Then stand upright facing the scripture. A master or friend will hold the scripture and intone it using the eight notes music.[36] You, the recipient, should prostrate yourself, pausing after finishing the scroll. Then bow eight times, and you are finished. If you do not understand intoned chanting, just do the normal chanting. The scripture should be stored in a container like a box and should be frequently reverenced. If you in turn bestow the scripture on friends or disciples, you should transmit it according to this rite.

道官、籙生，初受誡律之時，向誡經八拜，正立經前。若師若友，執經作八胤樂，音誦。受者伏誦經，竟卷後訖。後八拜，止。若不解音誦者，但直誦而已。其誡律以函若箱盛之。常當恭謹。若展轉授同友及弟子，按法傳之。

There seem to be few restrictions on who could transmit or to whom the scripture could be transmitted, and no pledge offerings, purifications, or other preparations were specified.

The twenty-four parishes of the early Celestial Masters were, according to Kou's account, abandoned after Zhang Daoling's ascension to a heavenly office and were replaced by twenty-eight parishes based on the lunar lodges. This meant that the traditional parishes constituted by libationers through membership recorded on their fate rosters were null and void. Moreover, the ordinations into these parishes, which conveyed to their owners a body of generals, clerks, and soldiers that did their bidding, were similarly invalid. Daoist libationers simply imagined that they controlled these spirits:[37]

The Daoist officers and libationers transmit to each other out of foolish benightedness, bestowing upon each other parish registers. They fool themselves by requesting thousands of generals, clerks, and soldiers. It is false to request them recklessly. They receive no protection whatsoever from these clerks and soldiers.

36. The meaning of the original *bayin* 八胤 is unclear. Here I follow Yang Liansheng's speculation.
37. *Laojun yinsong jiejing* 8b.

道官祭酒愚闇相傳，自署治籙，爲請佩千部將軍吏兵相惑，亂請
之僞。吏兵衛護，盡皆無有。

As a consequence, the libationer had no gods to externalize and consequently could not send petitions to the Heavenly Bureaus. Instead, they would just accumulate in the office of the local earth god.

Under Kou's new system, Daoist believers could make an oral request (*kouqi* 口啓), but, other than this, their only recourse was the offering of a kitchen-feast. Further, since Lord Lao had abolished the grain tithe that libationers used to supply their parish-sponsored kitchen-feasts at the time of the Three Assemblies, the kitchens depended on private or government sponsors. The *Book of Wei* tells us that the biggest sponsor was the Northern Wei state, which sponsored kitchen-feasts for thousands of people every month. In fact, stripped of their parishes, parishioners, and grain tithes as well as the pledge offerings that went with the submission of petitions, libationers were left with no source of income. This was a thoroughgoing plan to destroy communal Daoism at its roots and replace it with a state-sponsored system that closely resembles the pattern of patronage of northern Buddhism. The seed citizens of an earlier age, who needed only to perform the Merging the Pneumas rite to be assured a chance at salvation, were replaced by elites who could afford the ruinous costs of alchemical elixirs. Lord Lao, who had appeared to peasants across China in the guise of Li Hong 李弘, was revealed to have stayed in Heaven ever since the worldly demise of Zhang Daoling in the mid-second century, ignoring the petitions of all libationers and caring only for the offerings of elites to local earth gods. The millenarian lord of the new age of Great Peace, who was to bring fairness, equality, and peace to all in the land, was revealed to be the hereditary ruler of an existing, highly aristocratic state.

It remains to ask to what degree this system was ever put into practice and how far its influence extended. Lagerwey paints a picture of a "nation-wide system of state-supported Daoist temples" blanketing the territory of the Northern Wei and lasting until the end of the dynasty (2007:54). Mather suggests that the influence of these reforms on the grass roots of Daoism was difficult to assess, but probably "negligible" (1979:104). Daoist stelae from North China confirm this assessment (see fig. 4); they incorporate many new ideas about the Daoist Heavens and deities but continue to reflect a community structure of libationers, novices, and Daoist citizens similar to that described in our sources from South China.[38] Kou Qianzhi did, however, succeed in creating a form of Daoism that could be integrated with the state, and this paved the way for the imperial support of Daoism during the Tang. His example of a Daoist-imperial theocracy as well as the persecution of Buddhism that he encouraged found their immediate successor in the Northern Zhou.

The rulers of the Northern Qi dynasty (550–77) that succeeded to most of the Northern Wei empire were devout Buddhists. They did not receive Daoist registers when enthroned and stopped all formal support for Daoism. Buddhism grew until there were three million monastic Buddhists, who did not pay taxes or perform corvée labor, out of a population of perhaps thirty million.[39] This was an unsustainable burden on society.

The Northern Zhou (557–81) originally controlled only regions in northwest China but supplanted the Northern Qi in 577. It reinstituted governmental support for Daoism on a par with Buddhism. With the accession of Emperor Wu 北周武帝 (r. 561–78), Daoism came to the fore. The emperor claimed to favor an ecumenical approach, supporting Daoism, Buddhism, and Confucianism, but Lagerwey argues that his syncretism was centered on Daoism (1981:5–6). In 567, the Daoist priest Zhang Bin 張賓 convinced the emperor of the superiority of Daoism, leading him to accept ordination, receiving a Daoist talisman register and donning Daoist ritual garb.[40] Further evidence for this is found in

38. On Daoist stelae, see Li Song 2002; Hu Wenhe 2004; Zhang Xunliao 2010.

39. Gang Li 2010:264.

40. *Guang hongming ji* 8, T2103, 52:136a; Lagerwey 1981:19.

FIGURE 4. This votive statue of Lord Lao was created in 587 by the Daoist citizen Su Zun. *Votive image of Laojun*, Chinese, Sui dynasty, A.D. 587. Carved limestone with inscription; 24 × 15 × 11.5 cm (9 ⁷⁄₁₆ × 5 ⁷⁄₈ × 4 ½ in.). Museum of Fine Arts, Boston, Special Chinese and Japanese Fund, 07.732.

the name of the institution established to create this all-inclusive religion under the direction of the emperor, the Pervasive Dao Abbey (Tongdao guan 通道觀). It was there that Daoism's first encyclopedia, the *Supreme Secret Essentials* (*Wushang miyao*), was edited. Lagerwey (1981) argues that this compilation, which centers on texts of the Numinous Jewel tradition, wholly avoids the Celestial Master canon precisely because Emperor Wu intended to forge a new Daoism in his own name. Thus, despite the privileged position accorded Daoism at court, it is uncertain what this meant to the Celestial Master tradition.

Emperor Wu is famous for the second great religious persecution in Chinese history, in 574. He intended originally to suppress only Buddhism, but this engendered fierce debate, and eventually both Buddhism and Daoism were attacked. Daoist priests were compelled to return to secular life, Daoist temples were given to court officials, and images were burnt.[41] It is likely that this suppression affected only Daoists gathered in abbeys rather than the bulk of priests living among the people in local communities.

South China: Gentry Daoism and Sun En

Disruptions at the end of the Han began a large-scale migration to the region south of the Yangzi River, resulting in the preservation there of Han period occult traditions that were eclipsed among the northern elite by Mysterious Learning (*xuanxue* 玄學) and the Teaching of Names (*mingjiao* 名教).[42] During the third century, Daoism also spread throughout North China, aided by the forced relocation of Daoist households by Cao Cao in 215, which I refer to as the Great Diaspora, and by a missionary fervor promoted by the role of evangelization as the primary means of attaining promotion. Daoism was always a broad-based movement encompassing all social classes, but it seems that at this time it made striking inroads among elite families. The millenarian elements

41. *Zhou shu* 5/85; Gang Li 2010:266.
42. On these movements, see He Qimin 1978; Tang Yongtong 1991.

within Daoism, promising salvation tied to performance of the Merging the Pneumas sexual ritual, played an important part, as we saw in chapter 3. Another element seems to have been family traditions of allegiance to the Yellow Turbans and their promotion of Great Peace, which predisposed many in the northeast to take up the new religion.[43]

When first the internal warfare of the Disorders of the Eight Kings (291–306) and then the invasion of numerous seminomadic horse-riding peoples known as the Five Hu Barbarians 五胡 brought about the downfall of the Western Jin in 317, this set off a huge migration of Chinese to the South. The populations of entire counties, facing famine, epidemic, and foreign rule, picked up and moved. They brought Daoism with them. By the end of the fourth century, northern and southern elites and commoners had adopted the faith in large numbers, and Daoism had become a truly national religion.

We are best informed about the elite members of society, who figure prominently in the standard histories of the period. Among the most prominent Daoist families, we can cite the Wang clan of Langya 瑯琊王氏 and the Xie clan of Chen commandery 陳郡謝氏.[44] Wang Dao 王導 (276–337) was a key figure in the southern transition, serving in the highest offices—as prime minister, regent, and grand marshal—for two decades, and is credited with preserving the Jin dynasty through multiple perils. He was instrumental in putting down the rebellion of his elder cousin, the general Wang Dun 王敦 (266–324), who almost succeeded in

43. The classic article by Chen Yinke (1932) is wrong in conflating the Yellow Turbans with the Celestial Masters but correct to point out the number of prominent fourth- and fifth-century Celestial Master families whose roots could be traced to places where the Yellow Turbans once thrived, especially Langya 瑯琊 county (modern Linyi, Shandong), which was about as far as you could get from Sichuan within the Wei kingdom.

44. Both clans were destroyed in the mid-sixth century when they refused to intermarry with the rebel Hou Jing 侯景 (d. 552) and were slaughtered en masse. The Tang poet Liu Yuxi 劉禹錫 (772–842) commemorated this dramatic fall with the line "Of old a swallow in the halls of the Wangs and Xies/Flew into the home of a normal commoner" 舊時王謝堂前燕，飛入尋常百姓家. See *Quan Tang shi* 365/4117.

usurping the throne. His nephew Wang Xizhi 王羲之 (303–61) is widely considered China's best calligrapher. Among his most famous works was a copy of the *Scripture of the Yellow Court*, discussed in chapter 3. (See figure 5.) Members of the Wang clan continued to hold high office until the mid-sixth century.

The Xie clan hailed from Chen 陳 commandery (modern Taikang, Henan) before migrating to Guiji 會稽 (modern Shaoxing, Zhejiang). Members held high office at the time of the transfer to the South. Xie An 謝安 (320–86) was one of the most prominent figures of his day. Famous from childhood as a model of style and deportment, he lived most of his life as a recluse, consorting with his social peers in elegant soirees and outings like the famous Meeting at the Orchid Pavilion.[45] He also played a key role in government, rising to the office of prime minister. He is renowned for his composure under pressure, fending off an internal threat from Huan Wen 桓溫 (312–73) and an external one from Fu Jian 苻堅 (338–85) in the 370s and 380s.[46] A preserved letter reflects his Daoist identity, beginning "Daoist citizen An" 道民安.[47] An's great-grandnephew Xie Lingyun 謝靈運 (385–433) was one of the most prominent poets of the early medieval period, famous for landscape poetry.[48] Born just ten days before the death of his illustrious grandfather Xie Xuan, he was raised until the age of fifteen in the parish of the Celestial Master libationer Du Mingshi 杜明師.[49]

45. On this poetic gathering, see the classic study by Obi (1955).

46. Huan Wen is best known as a military leader. He was responsible for conquering the Cheng-Han state in 347, reintegrating Sichuan into Jin, and three times launched unsuccessful campaigns to retake North China. See *Jin shu* 98. Fu Jian, ruler of the Former Qin, was on the point of reunifying China when defeated at the Battle of Feishui, where Xie An and his nephew Xie Xuan 謝玄 (343–88) played key roles. See *Jin shu* 79; Rogers 1968.

47. See Yan Kejun 1958; *Quan Jinwen* 83; *Zhongguo shufa quanji*; *Songtuo Chunhuage tie* 宋拓淳化閣帖 2/114–15; *Shiwen* 2/31.

48. Mather says he was "in his own generation and for some centuries thereafter the most popular poet of the age" (1958:67).

49. Chen Yinke 1932:157, citing the *Shipin* 詩品 of Zhong Rong 鍾嶸 (468–518). This lodging is nowhere explained but, given the proximity of his birth to his grandfather's death, may have been due to a perceived incompatibility of

Even some emperors seem to have been members of the Daoist church. During the Eastern Jin, Sima Yao 司馬曜 (362–96), who reigned as Emperor Xiaowu 晉孝武帝 (r. 372–96), and his younger brother Sima Daozi 司馬道子 (364–403), who controlled the government for a period, were both Daoists.[50] Liu Yu 劉裕 (363–422), canonized as the Martial Emperor 宋武帝 (r. 420–22), who founded the succeeding Song dynasty, was promoted in both the *Scripture of Divine Spells* and the *Inner Explanations of the Three Heavens* as the one destined by the Daoist Heavens to restore the Han dynasty.[51] Xiao Yan 蕭衍 (464–549), known to history as Emperor Wu of Liang 梁武帝 (r. 502–49), is most famous as an advocate for Buddhism and a proponent of vegetarianism, but he was raised as a Daoist and, even after ascending the throne in 502 (at age thirty-seven), submitted his own memorials to the Daoist gods.[52] He must have held at least a Ten Generals Register, if not the status of full libationer. Similarly, Chen Baxian 陳霸先 (503–59), who founded the subsequent Chen dynasty (Emperor Wu 陳武帝, r. 557–59), was also a member of the Daoist church.[53] Thus, rulers of both North and South, including many of the most effective and most militarily active (as noted by posthumous titles including the character *wu* 武, or "martial"), were not merely patrons of Daoism but active initiates.

One of the most prominent Daoist practitioners of the period was Du Jiong 杜炅 (fl. 365), who was master of a parish in Qiantang

---

Lingyun's birth date and time (according to the sexagenary cycle) and that of other members of his family.

50. Chen Yinke concludes on the basis of events surrounding their births as well as their style names that both were raised in a Celestial Master environment (1932:157). The incident concerning Sima Daozi's patronage of a woman who dressed as a Celestial Master priest (see chapter 5) confirms this.

51. On references to Liu Yu in the *Dongyuan shenzhou jing* 洞淵神咒經, see Mollier 1990:56–58; for the *Santian neijie jing*, see Bokenkamp 1997:187–88.

52. *Sui shu* 35/1093. One wonders if his imposition of vegetarianism on Buddhism did not find an inspiration in the meatless Daoist kitchen-feast.

53. *Sui shu* 35/1093. Chen came to prominence through his suppression of the rebellion of Hou Jing, who, as noted above, decimated the two most prominent southern Daoist lineages.

錢塘 (modern Hangzhou).[54] The *Biographies of Cavern Transcendents* says of him:[55]

> Daoists and the profane from near and far came to him for conversion [in groups as thick] as clouds. Within ten years, the households contributing grain numbered in the tens of thousands.
>
> 遠近道俗，歸化如雲。十年之內，操米戶數萬。

This record of a parish of more than a hundred thousand parishioners may be exaggerated but certainly indicates a group comprising very large numbers of new converts as well as existing Daoists. In addition to his many commoner parishioners, Du often ministered to members of the elite in nearby Guiji, like Wang Xizhi and Xie An, healing them when possible by submitting petitions. When Du Jiong died, his parish was taken over by his disciple Sun Tai 孫泰 (d. 398) and later by Tai's nephew, Sun En.[56] Both Tai and En are said to have been "respected [by their parishioners] as if they were gods." Sima Daozi exiled Tai to Guangzhou 廣州,[57] which only succeeded in expanding his following into that region. The emperor then recalled him on the suggestion of people close to his nephew, Daozi's eldest son. Toward the end of the fourth century, the court was threatened repeatedly by attacks from the devout Buddhist Wang Gong 王恭 (d. 398)[58] and the military leader Huan Xuan 桓玄 (369–404). Tai raised troops from among his followers to oppose them. Seeing the Jin house in such a weakened

54. On Du Jiong, see *Song shu* 100/2445; *Nan shi* 57/1405; *Zizhi tongjian* 103/3248; *Sandong zhunang* 1/1a–b; Bumbacher 2000:161–69.

55. *Yunji qiqian* 111/7a–b, citing the *Dongxian zhuan* 洞仙傳. That text is now lost but is first recorded in the *Sui shu* bibliographic chapter (33/979), so it should be no later than the end of the Six Dynasties.

56. On Sun Tai and Sun En, see *Jin shu* 100/2631–33; Eichhorn 1954; Miyakawa 1971.

57. Guangzhou comprised most of modern Guangdong and Guangxi provinces, with its administrative center at Panyu 番禺, modern Guangzhou city.

58. Wang Gong is famous for publicly humiliating Sima Daozi for allowing at his table a woman who liked to dress in Daoist ritual attire. See chapter 5.

state, Tai continued to gather his forces, until he was seized, along with his sons, and executed as a potential usurper on the command of Sima Daozi.[59] Sun En escaped to an island off the coast and regrouped. In 399, he gathered his forces and marched on the capital, attacking first the kingdom of Guiji. The seneschal of the kingdom was Wang Ningzhi 王凝之 (d. 399), son of Wang Xizhi, who was a famous calligrapher in his own right and a devout Daoist:[60]

> When Sun En attacked Guiji, the aides [of Ningzhi] requested that defensive preparations be made for them. Ningzhi did not follow this advice; he just entered his oratory and offered a prayer. Emerging, he said to his generals and aides, "I have already made a request of the Great Dao, who has promised demon soldiers to aid us. The bandits will be destroyed by themselves." He made no preparations and consequently was killed by Sun En.

> 孫恩之攻會稽，僚佐請爲之備。凝之不從，方入靖室請禱，出語諸將佐曰：「吾已請大道，許鬼兵相助，賊自破矣。」既不設備，遂爲孫恩所害。

Eight commanderies rose up in support of Sun En, killing their officials and uniting with Sun until his force numbered in the tens of thousands. Battles seesawed over the next couple of years, with Sun withdrawing to offshore islands when attacked, then coming ashore elsewhere. Liu Yu proved the decisive force, hounding him up and down the coast until Sun's forces were depleted. In 402, Sun En threw himself into the ocean, followed by hundreds of his most faithful followers, who were convinced he had become a water transcendent (*shuixian* 水仙). The rebellion continued intermittently over the next decade, led by En's brother-in-law, named Lu Xun 盧循 (d. 411), who seems to have also had Daoist roots but was

59. His followers, insisting this was a ruse and that he had actually become a transcendent, went out onto the ocean to make offerings to him.

60. See *Jin shu* 80/2102–3. Liu Yi's claim (2011) that this action is inconsistent with Celestial Master practice and therefore must represent a non-Daoist ritual is wholly unfounded.

not the same sort of religious leader. The remarkable aspect of this rebellion was the number of elite and commoner Daoists of both northern and southern origin on both sides. Here we see that Celestial Master Daoism could be used by a charismatic leader to inspire rebellion but that many Daoists interpreted their faith as supporting the established power structure.[61]

The mixture of northern and southern religious culture in South China during this period provided a fertile environment for religious innovation. Two Daoist movements came to have great influence. The Supreme Purity movement was based on revelations from exalted Daoist deities to members of an old southern family, the Xus, who had been among the first Southerners to accept Celestial Master Daoism.[62] Initially appearing to Xu Mai 許邁 (300–49), the gods found a better vehicle in the medium Yang Xi 楊羲 (330–86), who relayed messages from a variety of divine figures to Mai's younger brother Xu Mi 許謐 (303–73) and Mai's son Xu Hui 許翽 (341–ca. 370) over the years 364 to 370. The gods transmitted scriptures as well as a variety of personal messages, introducing new, more exalted gods and new ritual techniques. Although almost everyone associated with the movement came from a Celestial Master background, and one of the most important revealing deities had been a Celestial Master libationer while alive, the Supreme Purity gods claimed to have superseded the Celestial Master tradition. For example, they rejected the Merging the Pneumas rite as a method of limited efficacy that could bring misfortune if misused and advocated a more ethereal practice of uniting with the essence of divine beings called Pairing the Phosphors (*oujing* 偶景). Similarly, the revelations introduced a new Inner or Esoteric version of the *Scripture of the Yellow Court* (*Huangting neijing* 黃庭內經) that focused on elaborate visualizations of the gods of the body. Although the

---

61. Miyakawa (1971) points out that Sun Tai and Sun En were related by marriage to Cui Hao, who was the most important supporter of Kou Qianzhi.

62. On the Supreme Purity movement, see Strickmann 1977, 1979, 1982b; Robinet 1984; Bokenkamp 1997:275–306; 2007. The Xus had migrated south at the end of the Han.

Supreme Purity revelations were to have great appeal to elite Daoists of later centuries, the manuscripts were closely held for at
least a century after the revelation and only became widely available in the mid-sixth century or later.

Tao Hongjing played a key role in their dissemination by
gathering and editing the miscellaneous revelations into a work
called the *Declarations of the Perfected* (*Zhen'gao* 真誥). As the
teachings gained popularity, a lineage of patriarchs was retroac-
tively created in which Tao held the ninth place. The Supreme
Purity "school" had very little influence on the period treated in
the present book and never held much appeal for nonelite practitioners. Among the books produced by Tao Hongjing was an extensively annotated work called the *Hidden Instructions for Ascending to Perfection* (*Dengzhen yinjue* 登真隱訣), which preserves
much information concerning Celestial Master religious practice,
as does a Supreme Perfection ritual code called the *Code of the
Great Perfected* (*Taizhenke* 太真科) that is dated to ca. 420.[63]

This was also the period when Buddhism began to make substantial inroads into Chinese society.[64] Like Daoism, Buddhism
appealed to the elite and vied for patronage from the powerful.
Originally, Buddhism had been understood as a form of Daoism
or an adaptation of Daoism for non-Chinese peoples. Now, as
understanding deepened and Chinese intellectuals became advocates of the foreign faith, some elite families chose it while others maintained their allegiance to Daoism. Families like the Chis
were split, with Chi Yin 郗愔 (313–84) and his younger brother
Chi Tan 郗曇 (320–61) upholding the Way of the Celestial Masters, whereas his son Chi Chao 郗超 (336–77) became a famous
advocate of Buddhism.[65] One reason the two faiths successfully
competed for elite allegiance was their common rejection of the
sacrificial practices of the Chinese common religion. Beginning in

---

63. On the *Secret Essentials*, see Cedzich 1987; on the *Code of the Great
Perfected*, see Ōfuchi 1997:409–505. Both works are cited extensively in part 2
of this book.

64. On Buddhism's entry into China, see Zürcher 1959.

65. See *Jin shu* 67/4713.

the fifth century, advocates of Daoism and Buddhism launched a series of polemics against each other.[66] Although this might seem to reflect a growing antagonism between the two religions, in the Tang dynasty both were supported by the state and experienced rapid growth. The adoption of Buddhist terms, concepts, and practices by Daoists was a distinctive feature of the fourth through sixth centuries.[67]

The most prominent example of this appropriation was the rise of the Numinous Jewel scriptural tradition.[68] Although some of these scriptures are attributed to the third-century occultist Ge Xuan 葛玄, Tao Hongjing tells us that the initial wave of Numinous Jewel scriptures was actually created by Ge Chaofu 葛巢甫 in the 390s.[69] Others were produced in the early fifth century. The corpus was ordered and delimited by Lu Xiujing 陸修靜 (406–77), who catalogued it in 437.[70] These scriptures introduced rituals dedicated to the universal salvation of all humanity and the deliverance of all the dead from reincarnation, in contrast to Celestial Master rites for specific individuals or households. They also included rites for the protection and deliverance of the state that proved popular with rulers. These new rites were organized into lavish multiday rituals called purificatory feasts (*zhai* 齋) and offerings (*jiao* 醮). All of these new ritual forms proved popular and are still practiced today.

Other scriptural traditions also emerged during this period and even into the Tang, such as the Piercing the Abyss movement or that associated with the *Guide to the Golden Lock and Flowing Jewels* (*Jinsuo liuzhu yin* 金鎖流珠引).[71] Most have left behind at

66. These debates are preserved in T2102 *Hongming ji* 弘明集 and T2103 *Guang hongming ji* 廣弘明集. The only Western work to treat them extensively is Kohn 1995.

67. An important study of this process is Bokenkamp 2007, which looks at Daoist acceptance of the concept of reincarnation.

68. On the Lingbao tradition, see Ōfuchi 1974; Bokenkamp 1997:373–92; Yamada 2000.

69. See *Zhen'gao* 19/11b; *Daojiao yishu* 2/6b confirms this date.

70. On this catalog, see Bokenkamp 1983.

71. On Piercing the Abyss scriptures, see Mollier 1990; on the Golden Lock movement, see Tsai 2005.

most a handful of liturgical texts and some hagiographical material. It does not seem that any of them actually presented a substantial alternative to the social reality of the Celestial Master
church. They were all integrated into the Celestial Master system
of registers, forming new, more exalted levels that promised increased spiritual power and access to newly discovered regions
of the sacred realm.[72] The Celestial Master system of registers
was compressed and the novitiate shortened, but they were never
displaced, and no pastoral religion ever replaced Celestial Master
Daoism on the local level. Only with the appearance of a syncre-
tistic monastic movement in the twelfth century, the Complete
Perfection school (Quanzhen pai 全真派), did a real alternative to
Celestial Master Daoism arise, and it was only in the late Ming
and early Qing (sixteenth and seventeenth centuries) that it actually became an important presence in the Chinese religious
world.[73]

72. On the mature Tang system of registers, see Schipper 1985; Kobayashi
2003.

73. On Quanzhen, see Esposito 2000, 2001; Goossaert 2001, 2004, 2007.

PART II

Ritual and Community

FIVE

Ritual Life

R itual permeated all aspects of life in Daoist communities. As
we shall see in part 2 of this book, every household maintained a sacred space where they conducted solemn Daoist rites at
least twice a day, and, even when not engaged in the performance
of ritual, there were extensive ritual codes delineating proper
grooming, dress, and comportment. In a larger sense, Celestial
Master Daoism was essentially a method of intervening in and
directing the course of events through the proper employment of
a set of ritual formulae by trained officiants, who had participated
in an ordination rite and who observed a strict code of ritualized
conduct. Even the act of sexual congress was properly performed
only within the context of the Merging the Pneumas rite. Part 2
of this book is devoted to the ritual life of Daoist communities during the first five centuries of Daoism's existence. This ritual life
was certainly not static, but, because surviving liturgies and ritual
manuals accreted over time as they were transmitted from master
to master, reaching their final form only toward the end of the Six
Dynasties period, we are presented with what seems a static system, within which we can only sometimes see internal evidence
of historical development. For this reason, I present here the mature ritual system of early medieval Daoism with only occasional
remarks as to how it may have evolved over time.

In the following chapters, I explore the various rituals that
defined life in Celestial Master communities, including the audience

ceremony with which one began and ended each day; the seasonal observances that marked the beginning of the year, the height of summer, and the harvest; as well as the periodic ceremonies that commemorated significant life events and transitions. To do so, I focus on the three primary ritual roles within these communities: the common Daoist citizen; the novice, who was a religious professional in training; and the libationer or Daoist priest, who led each community. First, though, let us consider the ritual settings and environment common to all, as represented by the buildings in which ritual was practiced and the clothing worn during its performance.

The Oratory

In ancient China there were temples (*miao* 廟) established for the ancestors of nobles, but most rituals to the gods of Heaven and Earth seem to have been conducted at an altar constructed in the open. By the early Han, the emperor had taken to building structures for the worship of the gods within the palace. When Emperor Wu had the Sweet Springs Palace constructed, he included a raised chamber where painted images of Heaven, Earth, and the Great One as well as sacrificial implements were placed as a way of summoning them for worship.[1] The Latter Han saw the rise of "chamber cults" (*fangsi* 房祀), shrines for offering worship to the dead who were not one's ancestors, and images of deities of various sorts became more common.[2] The Daoists seem to have eschewed these new developments.

There were two types of ritual structure in early Celestial Master communities, the "quiet room," or oratory (variously written *jingshi* 靜室, 靖室, or *qingshi* 清室), and the parish headquarters, or *zhi* 治. Secular sources also mention a "charity lodge"

---

1. *Shiji* 12/458, 28/1388; *Han shu* 25A/1219.
2. The *Taipingjing* advocates displaying color-coded paintings of the spirits of the five viscera. See *Taipingjing chao yibu* 2/3.

(*yishe* 義舍), but the term is not found in received Daoist sources. It is impossible to say where and for how long such structures might have existed.[3] Beginning in the fifth century, Daoist ritual centers appeared that would eventually develop into a quasi-monastic institution. They were first called *guan* 舘, or "offices," and later *guan* 觀, often translated "abbey" or "belvedere," and were originally places of religious practice for prominent Daoist priests who had attracted the patronage of a ruler or other wealthy individual.[4] Particularly for the early period, information on who lived in these establishments under what sorts of conditions is extremely limited. They were, in any case, very few, a fraction of the Daoist populace.

The *Code of the Great Perfected* says that each family of Daoist believers should have its own oratory:[5]

> When Daoist citizens convert to the faith, each family should establish its own quiet room in the west, facing east.
> 道民入化，家家各立靖室，在西向東。

We have some descriptions of the parish and oratory, including one passage from the *Statutes of the Mystic Capital* that gives the normative dimensions of these buildings:[6]

> Male officers or female officers who administer a parish and register novices should locate their oratories toward the virtue of Heaven, the regions of *jia*, *yi*, *bing*, and *ding* [i.e., east to south]. There are ranks of parish. The oratory in a citizen's home should be eight feet

---

3. There are a few scattered references in Daoist scriptures to *tingzhuan* 亭傳, but it seems likely that these are secular governmental structures like the government post offices that often occur in the same passage rather than descendants of the *yishe*. See *Chisongzi zhangli* 6/23a.

4. See Tsuzuki 2000; Hu Rui 2003.

5. *Yaoxiu keyi jielü chao* 10/4a4–5.

6. *Xuandu lüwen* 15a8–b2; *Yaoxiu keyi jielü chao* 10/4b2–5.

wide and ten feet deep.[7] A mid-level parish should be twelve feet wide and fourteen feet long. A large parish should be sixteen feet wide and eighteen feet deep. The exterior door should face the east, and the incense burner should be placed in the center. If you disobey, for a parish you will be fined one Jupiter-cycle (*ji* 紀) of counters,[8] with points of law determined in accordance with the *Statutes of the Covenant with the Powers*.

男官女官主者籙生安靖於天德者，甲乙丙丁地。治有品第。民家靖廣八尺長一丈，中治廣一丈二尺長一丈四尺，大治廣一丈六尺長一丈八尺。面戶向東，鑪按中央。違，治則罰筭一紀。按如盟威律論法也。

We find another set of dimensions for the oratory in the *Declarations of the Perfected*, but it is noted that this larger oratory (nineteen feet wide) is for "uninhabited wilds of famous mountains and great marshes" and not suitable for populated areas.[9] The same source records alternate names for the oratory: the "thatched hut" (*maowu* 茅屋), the "square eaves" (*fangliu* 方溜), and the "surrounding barrier" (*huandu* 環堵). The first two terms seem merely to describe the building's appearance, but the last links it to a rustic hut mentioned in the *Record of Rites* and in the *Zhuangzi* as the appropriate dwelling for a scholar or a sage.[10] It may also be related to the "essential chamber" (*jingshi*

7. During the third century, a foot was 24.12 centimeters, so this building would be 1.92 meters wide and 2.41 m. deep; the mid-level parish would have been 2.89 m. by 3.38 m.; and the large parish would have been 3.86 m. by 4.39 m.

8. A Jupiter-cycle is the twelve-year period it takes for Jupiter to appear to revolve about the earth.

9. *Zhen'gao* 18/6b–7a. In his note to this passage, Tao mentions an alternate method for constructing the oratory, which in his day was recorded in a text called the *Daoji* 道機, but this text does not seem to have survived. The Tang encyclopedia *Shangqing daolei shixiang* 1/1a cites a "statute" to the effect that the oratory and parish headquarters were the same size, eighteen feet deep and sixteen feet wide, and that this building would be called an oratory if the household were Daoist citizens and a parish if the inhabitant were a master.

10. See *Liji* 42.4, which describes the humble dwelling of a scholar occupying a low office, with a single fence surrounding all four sides. There is considerable dispute as to the length of the fence. In the *Zhuangzi* (H-Y Index edn.,

精室) located near a famous mountain beside an east-flowing stream that Ge Hong promotes as the ideal place for alchemical endeavors.[11]

The Daoist oratory finds attestation in the earliest surviving secular record, the *Summary of Institutions* (*Dianlüe*) recorded by Yu Huan in the first half of the third century:[12] "They add on a 'quiet room' where they place people with ailments and have them ponder their transgressions." Lu Xiujing, writing in the fifth century, affirms the importance of this building and rails against the abuses of this sacred space by the faithful of his day:[13]

> For families who worship the Dao, the oratory is the place where one manifests one's sincerity. Externally, it is separate and removed, not contiguous with other buildings. Inside, it is pure and empty, not defiled with extraneous objects. When opening and closing the gate and door, do not recklessly rush in and out. Mop and sweep it carefully and solemnly, always as if the god is present. Only place there an incense burner, a fragrant lamp,[14] a table for writing memorials,[15] and a writing knife:[16] these four items and no more. It must be plain and clean, costing no more than just

61/23/6 and 78/28/44), it is the home of the "supreme man" (*zhiren* 至人) and of the sage Yuanxian 原憲.

11. Yoshikawa Tadao (1987) argues from this that the oratory was originally an esoteric chamber for magical operations and only later became a site of ritual for Celestial Master Daoists. This does not accord with the evidence, which shows the earliest usage of a similarly named structure is by the Celestial Masters, attested in the second century.

12. *Sanguozhi* 8/264, n. 1.

13. *Lu xiansheng daomenke lüe* 4b3–8.

14. *Wushang miyao* 66/8a–b gives a formula for the fragrant oil that fuels these lamps.

15. *Yaoxiu keyi jielü chao* 11/15a–b specifies that this table must have curved legs and should be 2.4 feet (55.4 cm.) wide, 1.2 feet (27.7 cm.) deep, and eight inches (18.5 cm.) high.

16. Yoshikawa Tadao traces this writing knife back to a "scraper" (*xue* 削), mentioned in the *Zhouli*, that was used to carve characters into wood before there was ink and argues that its continued presence in the oratory was a "forgotten method of antiquity" (1987:135), but, at the time of the founding of Daoism, paper was not common, and silk was expensive, so many documents were still written on bamboo (witness the recently discovered third-century

FIGURE 5. Ink rubbing from a stone-engraved copy of the *Scripture of the Yellow Court* attributed to Wang Xizhi. Eastern Jin dynasty, dated to 356. Wang probably copied this scripture in his oratory. Photo courtesy of The Art Museum of The Chinese University of Hong Kong.

a hundred-odd cash. If compared to those households that engage in heterogeneous profane practices,[17] with their statues on sitting-platforms and pennants and canopies covered with ornamentation, is this not a difference between complex and simple, flowery and unadorned?

奉道之家，靖室是致誠之所。其外別絕，不連他屋。其中清虛，不雜餘物。開閉門戶，不妄觸突。灑掃精肅，常若神居。唯置香爐、香燈、章案、書刀四物而已。必其素淨，政可堪百餘錢耳。比雜俗之家，床座形像，幡蓋眾飾，不亦有繁簡之殊、華素之異耶？

We see here the austerity demanded of Celestial Master sacred space. The highest deity was transcendent and could not be imagined in any fixed physical form. The lower Daoist gods, in reality also just transformations of the pneumas of this ultimate force, the Dao, were too sacred to be depicted except in the mind's eye. This went hand in hand with the Daoist rejection of sacrificial practice and its demotion—if not outright denial—of the sacred character of the gods of the common religion. We might well compare this to the Protestant movement's stripping from its churches of the dense symbolic ornamentation of Roman Catholicism.

Much of the populace in any traditional society was unable to generate a significant surplus of food and so was only one bad crop or other natural disaster away from starvation. The construction of a separate structure devoted exclusively to religious activities

---

Zoumalou documents), and, in any case, a knife is useful to scrape ink off bamboo, paper, or silk as a sort of crude eraser.

17. This phrase, *zasu zhi jia* 雜俗之家, could be interpreted a number of different ways, but Daoist scriptures use it to indicate those who do evil and engage in deviant practices. A Lingbao scripture reports that one of the Twelve Rewards (*shier bao* 十二報) for practicing the Twelve Remembrances (*shier nian* 十二念) is that, "within the 3,600 square *li* surrounding one's dwelling, the bewitching falsities of heterogeneous profane traditions and the goblins that practice scurrilous deception will all at once disappear" 所在住止方圓三千六百里中，妖偽雜俗、姦詐魍魎，一時消滅. See DZ 22 *Yuanshi wulao chishu yupian zhenwen tianshu jing* 3/13b.

would have represented a significant investment of family resources. It was a testament to the fervency of their faith that many peasants did obey this rule. It is hardly surprising that, in Lu Xiujing's day, many did not live up to the ideal, despite his stinging criticism:[18]

> But many of those who worship the Dao today have no oratory. Sometimes they fence off a piece of land and make an altar, but they have never weeded it, and the grasses and rushes pierce the sky. Some have erected a building, but there is no gate or door, and the domestic animals roam or dwell there, with manure and muck up to the knees. Some call it an oratory but use it to store all sorts of household items. Rushing in and out, they let rats and dogs take up residence. To pray to the revered, marvelous Dao in such a setting, is that not truly out of place?
>
> 而今奉道者，多無靜室；或標欄一地爲治壇，未曾修除，草莽刺天；或雖立屋宇，無有門戶，六畜遊處，糞穢沒膝；或名爲靜室，而藏家什物，唐突出入，鼠犬栖止。以此祈尊妙之道，不亦遠耶！

It is interesting to note that some Daoist citizens continued to practice their religion in the open. This would not have been practical for novices and libationers who were able to submit written petitions, but, for penniless, semiliterate Daoist citizens whose primary religious activity was the morning and evening audience rite and the occasional confession, this remained an option.

The Parish

Parishes were originally a clearly defined set of twenty-four, arrayed in the Sichuan basin and centered on a group of three located northwest of modern Chengdu. Central authority was vested in the Celestial Master, who was also the Supervisor of Merit for the most exalted of the parishes, that of Yangping. The

---

18. *Lu xiansheng daomenke lüe* 4b8–5a2.

Code of the Great Perfected preserves a description of the parish buildings of the Celestial Master:[19]

When establishing the parish of the Celestial Master, the plot of land should be eighty-one paces square, modeling itself on the number nine times nine, which is the pneuma of rising yang. In the exact center of the parish is the Hall of the Exalted Void, an area with seven beams and six rooms, spreading out for 120 feet. Atop the central two rooms, build an upper floor for the Terrace of Exalted Mystery. In the center of this terrace place a large incense burner, five feet high, that constantly produces incense smoke. Provide three doors to the east, west, and south, with windows installed beside the doors. There is a walkway wide enough for two horses under a roof below the southern door, resting on a raised pavilion, from which to pay audience to the descendant of the Celestial Master. The Daoist priests from the upper eight parishes, who live their lives in the pure severity of the mountains, can ascend the terrace to pay audience. The other officials, great and small, and the central and external libationers gather in the great hall below to pay audience from afar. Fifty feet north of the Terrace of Exalted Mystery is a Hall of Exalted Transcendence with seven rooms, 140 feet, with seven beams. On the east side is the Chamber of Yang Transcendents and on the west, the Chamber of Yin Transcendents. To the south of the Terrace of [Exalted] Mystery, 120 [feet] away from the terrace and close to the Southern Gate, a five-room, three-beam gatehouse is raised. The eastern room of the gatehouse is the Southern Awe-Propagating Libationers' Lodge. The western room of the gatehouse is the Controllers, Supervisors, and Inspectors of Pneumas Libationers' Lodge. The rest of the small lodges cannot all be described. Each of the twenty-four parishes is like this.

立天師治，地方八十一步，法九九之數，唯升陽之氣。治正中央名崇虛堂，一區七架、六間、十二丈開。起堂屋上，當中央二間上，作一層崇玄臺。當臺中央安大香鑪，高五尺，恒爇香。開東、西、南三戶，戶邊安窗；兩頭馬道廈南戶下、飛格上，朝禮天師子孫。上八大治山居清苦濟世道士，可登臺朝禮；其餘職大

---

19. *Yaoxiu keyi jielü chao* 10/1a–b. Much of this description is obscure. What follows is my best guess as to how it should be interpreted.

小、中外祭酒，並在大堂下，遙朝禮。崇玄臺北五丈，起崇仙
堂，七間、十四丈、七架。東爲陽仙房，西爲陰仙房。玄臺之
南，去臺十二丈，近南門，起五間、三架門室。門室東門，南部
宣威祭酒舍；門屋西間，典司察氣祭酒舍。其餘小舍，不能具
書，二十四治，各各如此。

This would seem quite a grand compound, housing dozens of
religious professionals and serving a huge populace of believers.
It is unclear how much this description resembles any real, historical building. The final statement, that each parish had a similar
complex of buildings, is even more difficult to credit. But this
description does accord with some surviving records, such as the
following account of the founding by the Supreme Lord Lao in Lu
Xiujing's abridged version of the *Daoist Code*:[20]

He established the twenty-four parishes, thirty-six oratory huts,
and 2,400 inner and outer Daoists.

置二十四治、三十六靖廬，內外道士二千四百人。

The early-fifth-century *Code of the Great Perfected* describes
the role of the Celestial Master in appointing these officers:[21]

The code says: After long study and accumulated virtuous deeds, one
receives the mandate to become Celestial Master. He appointed
2,400 male and female libationers, each of whom takes charge of
households and converts [the profane into] citizens.[22] The otherworldly officials are referred to as register [students] and parish
[officers]; this-worldly officers are called ministers and guardians.

科曰：學久德積，受命爲天師，署男女祭酒二千四百人，各領戶
化民。陰官稱爲籙治，陽官號爲宰守。

20. *Lu xiansheng daomenke lüe* 1b.
21. *Yaoxiu keyi jielü chao* 10/1b–2a.
22. See the next chapter for a description of the Daoist citizen, the most
basic member of the Celestial Master church.

Here a comparison is made between the leader of a parish and the administrative head of a commandery or kingdom, the top level of local administration within the state bureaucracy during the Han. This comparison must be somewhat inaccurate, since the Sichuan region was divided into only three commanderies during the Latter Han, but the Shu-Han kingdom of Liu Bei established fifteen commanderies in roughly the same territory. Moreover, the Celestial Master communities included in their fate rosters many non-Chinese minorities like the Ba, who were not included on normal government population rosters. Parishes must have started small but grew rapidly. We can trace some of this geographical growth through changes in the parish system; these seem to indicate expansion toward the east and the north from an original center in the area around Chengdu.

The parish structure would have experienced its first disruption with the move of the Celestial Master to Hanzhong during the period of the theocratic state. Believers came flocking to the new utopia from all over the region, leaving behind their original parishes. It is uncertain how the church initially responded to this problem. Several parishes were moved to the Hanzhong area, including the Yangping parish that was the seat of the Celestial Master, but accommodating newcomers into these parishes would have meant changing their parish registration and perhaps that of their master as well. Ultimately, it seems that at this point the Celestial Masters turned to a new scheme, in which each parish was linked to one of the twenty-eight lunar lodges (*xiu* 宿). An earlier system had linked the parishes to the asterisms by assigning two each to four of the parishes, but now four parishes were added to make a one-to-one correlation.[23]

---

23. The original set of twenty-four was intended to correspond with the twenty-four seasonal nodes (*jieqi* 節氣) of the solar calendar. Those added now included Jushan 具山, Zhongmao 鍾茂, Baishi 白石, and Ganggeng 岡亙 parishes. The *Code of the Great Perfected* (ca. 420 CE) says that outsiders refer to them as Alternate Parishes (*biezhi* 別治), but within the church they are referred to as the Supplementary Parishes (*beizhi* 備治) because they bring the number up to a full twenty-eight. See *Yaoxiu keyi jielü chao* 10/2b.

It is unclear how individuals were assigned to these lunar asterisms and hence to parishes. It may have been geographical, since the field allocation (*fenye* 分野) system of divination had long before established geographical correspondences of all the asterisms. Kou Qianzhi still advocated this system in the fifth century, which suggests that it may have maintained some currency in North China long after its abandonment in the south. Nonetheless, it seems clear that the primary system of organization developed differently, forming a structure that was primarily hierarchical with little or no connection to geography.

The parish system of the mature Daoist church of the mid-fourth century was no doubt diverse, with some parishes serving congregations numbering as many as ten thousand, but the average parish must have been a much more modest affair, staffed by a parish priest and at most a few assistants. This fits well with the description above of a more modest parish building, basically an enlarged version of the oratory. Indeed, as seen in the discussion of the career and promotion of priests below, many individuals making the transition from novice to libationer must have relied on their family oratory as a base of ritual operations until they had gathered a large enough group of parishioners to warrant conferral of a parish register and construction of a parish building.

Archaeologists have not discovered evidence of these structures. Even textual references to them are rare outside the Daoist canon. We know of only one recorded building that might have been a residence of the Celestial Master in South China. During the early sixth century, Xiao Gang 蕭綱 (503–51), the future Emperor Jianwen of the Liang 梁簡文帝 (r. 549–51), built a magnificent structure called the Parish for Summoning the Perfected 招真治 on Mount Yu 虞山 (north of Changshu 常熟 city, Jiangsu) for the twelfth Celestial Master, Zhang Daoyu 張道裕 (fl. 503–15).[24] There is a similar silence, for the most part, concerning the many

24. See Yan Kejun 1958:3, 3029–30 (original pagination, Liang 14/2a–3b). Yan cites Wang Ao 王鏊 (1450–1524), *Gusu zhi* 姑蘇志 30. *Yiwen leiju* 78/1341 records only part of the stele, which seems to have survived into the Ming.

Buddhist institutions that appeared during these centuries, so the silence of secular literature is not anomalous. We must imagine that Daoist oratories and parishes were common features of the Chinese landscape during the Northern and Southern Dynasties, even if the genre conventions of contemporary textual production precluded their mention.

Daoist Attire

Clothing would have been a visible marker of Daoist identity, and there were codes for proper Daoist dress both during the performance of ritual and when off duty.[25] Early Daoist sources have much to say about dress, though it is not always consistent. Certainly, it was considered an important topic. Daoists serve the most exalted deities in the universe and interact with these figures in the course of their ritual activity. For this reason, the clothing they wear during these interactions is special and sacred:[26]

> All Daoist priests and priestesses who wear registers with scriptures, precepts and talismans belted at their waists have celestial documents on their person, perfected beings attached to their physical form, the pneumas of the Dao to protect them, and Transcendent and Numinous Officers[27] on which to call. The garments and hats they wear are called "ritual garb," and each has a divine spirit reverently guarding it.
>
> 凡道士女冠，體佩經戒符籙，天書在身，真人附形，道氣營衛，仙靈依託，其所著衣冠，名爲法服，皆有神靈敬護。

Because Daoists interact with deities as officials using ritual forms and presenting formal documents that closely resemble those

25. On Daoist ritual clothing, see Tanaka 2005:351–70.

26. DZ 1125 *Dongxuan lingbao sandong fengdao kejie yingshi* 3/8a.

27. These are the officers of the register. During the novitiate, one receives either Transcendent or Numinous Officers—depending apparently on the gender of the recipient—up to 75 generals, then receives a full complement of 75 of the other type to make the One Hundred Fifty Generals Register.

of the Chinese governmental administration, Daoist ritual garb is modeled on that of the court and the secular bureaucracy. In *Master Lu's Abridgement of the Daoist Code*, Lu Xiujing remarks:[28]

> The ritual garb of the Daoist resembles the court garb of the [profane] world, where dukes, marquises, gentlemen, and commoners each have their ranks in a five-step system to differentiate noble and mean.
>
> 道家法服猶世朝服，公侯士庶，各有品秩。五等之制，以別貴賤。

Lu continues to describe some of what he characterizes as the "old rules" for ritual attire:

> According to the old rules, one wore an unlined robe with a lined robe and a headscarf; novices wore pants and a jacket. As one of the pledge offerings when receiving a diocese, men would bring an unlined robe with an ink-black headscarf and women, an indigo robe. This explicit written statement should be sufficient to resolve doubts. Turbans, burlap coats, and capes are issued by high Daoists. When performing obeisance, wear burlap coats; when reciting a scripture, wear a cape.[29]
>
> 舊法服單衣袷幘，籙生袴褶。所以受治之信：男齋單衣墨幘，女則紺衣。此之明文，足以定疑。巾褐及帔，出自上道。禮拜著褐，誦經著帔。

Lu thus affirms that by the mid-fifth century there was in place a traditional system of ritual garb that differed according to rank and function. Already in Lu's day Daoists were overstepping these limits, with novices and masters of small dioceses wearing not just capes and coats but hats, trousers, and skirts. Lu also notes that there are exact specifications for the size and number of seams of each garment, although they do not survive.

28. *Lu xiansheng daomen kelüe* 5a.
29. *Lu xiansheng daomen kelüe* 5a.

The *Statutes of the Mystic Capital* preserves a passage dealing primarily with the color of garments that would seem to describe the situation around the fifth century:[30]

Daoist priests, female officers, and register novices who are eighteen *sui* (normally seventeen years) of age or above may receive the great rite. If they are still practicing the external rites, from the time they receive the One Hundred Fifty Generals Register, they may wear yellow ritual garb, robe, and cap. If [they are practicing] the internal [register] rites, those using the *Perfected Text for Spontaneously Ascending to the Mysterious* up to the *Great Cavern Scripture of Supreme Purity* must use purple ritual garb, robe, vest, official tablet, sandals, trousers, and jacket. The official tablet may be held by anyone who has received the ten precepts.[31] When one performs the audience ritual, greets an assemblage, or memorializes a petition, one must have ritual implements, robe, cap, headscarf, burlap cape, official tablet, and sandals.

律曰：道士、女官、籙生，身年十八已上，得受大法。若外法，自受百五十將軍籙已上，堪著黃色法服、衣冠。內法，自然昇玄真文已上，上清大洞已下，須用紫色法服、衣褐，笏履袴褶，其笏但十戒已上，則執之。若朝朝禮謁集及章表，而須法具衣冠幘褐笏履。

Here we see that libationers all dressed in yellow, whereas higher church officers wore purple. Failure to wear ritual garb on appropriate occasions would result, the *Statutes* tell us, in personal disaster extending to three generations of ancestors and one's person being brought before the dread Three Offices for punishment.

30. *Xuandu lüwen* 17a. The use of the term *daoshi* rather than *jijiu* as well as the reference to the *Great Cavern Scripture* would date this passage to no earlier than the late fourth century.

31. The official tablet is still necessary for all Daoist priests, as it was for all secular officials until the fall of the empire in 1911. The passage continues to note that the official tablet was flat and called a "plaque" (*ban* 板) up until the time of the Human Sovereign (*renhuang* 人皇), after which it was renamed *hu* 笏 and became curved, so that its curves and square angles resemble square Earth and round Heaven.

There is evidence that this ritual clothing was noticeable and set Daoists apart from others in society. Consider this anecdote recorded by Tan Daoluan 檀道鸞 (fl. ca. 430) in his *Continued Jin Springs and Autumns (Xu Jin yangqiu* 續晉陽秋):[32]

> Madame Pei, the wife of the seneschal of Huaiyin Yu Yaozi, was adept at correspondence and also consumed elixirs and avoided grain. She always dressed in a yellow robe so that she looked like one who studies the Dao. Sima Daozi would often invite her to his home and was very fond of her talents. Whenever he was banqueting with his subordinates, Pei would also participate, and he would always allow her to converse with his guests and retainers. Everyone thought this was demeaning. Wang Gong once excused himself, saying: "I have heard that the separation of men and women is a major principle of the state. I have never heard of a dissolute woman at the table of the prime minister." Everyone was shocked, and Daozi was mortified.
>
> 檀道鸞《續晉陽秋》曰：初，淮陵內史虞珧子妻裴，以尺牘辯利兼服食絕谷，常衣黃衣，狀若學道。司馬道子常延致，甚悅其才，每與百官飲宴，裴亦預焉。悉令與賓客談，眾人皆為降節。王恭辭曰：「恭聞男女之別，國之大節，未聞宰相之坐有失行婦人。」一坐竦然，道子為慚。

Here we see members of high society mimicking the ritual garb of Daoist libationers. Clearly all present were familiar with the ritual garb of a Daoist, but it was not expected or accepted within high society. It is perhaps relevant that Wang Gong was a devout Buddhist, whereas many of those associated with Sima Daozi were hereditary Daoists. We are unable to trace the exact evolution of these

---

32. *Taiping yulan* 428/2a–b. Cf. the shortened account in *Jin shu* (84/2184.2–4), where the description varies somewhat in the following passage: "The wife of the seneschal of Huaiyin Yu Yaozi, Madame Pei, was conversant in the art of elixirs. She always dressed in a yellow robe so that she looked like a Celestial Master [libationer]. [Sima] Daozi was very fond of her and let her converse with his guests and retainers" 淮陵內史虞珧子妻裴氏有服食之術，常衣黃衣，狀如天師，道子甚悅之，令與賓客談論. The *Jin shu* editors here have understood "student of the Dao" to be a Celestial Master novice. The previous quote from the *Statutes of the Mystic Capital* makes clear that this must refer to a novice or libationer; the Celestial Master himself would wear purple.

styles of ritual dress but can assume that from quite early on the Daoists set themselves off through distinctive attire. Daoist priests, at least, would have been immediately visible in mixed company.

Other sources detail rules concerning the use and care of ritual regalia.[33] Daoists are warned, for example, that they should not carelessly take off ritual clothing. It should not be worn when visiting the privy; instead, it should be placed in a clean, secure place, and the owner should take care to wash his or her hands and feet before donning it again. When washing ritual garb, it should not be mixed with normal clothing, nor should the profane be allowed to touch it. Moreover, it is improper to borrow the ritual clothing of another, so each person must prepare his or her own. Should an item become old or tattered, it should be ceremonially burnt, not discarded, although those living in the remote mountains may bury it. Zhang Wanfu's 張萬福 (fl. 713) *Tract of Code and Precepts for Ritual Garb of the Three Caverns* repeats these points in a list of forty-six rules that stress all the situations where one must wear ritual garb and the few situations where it is inappropriate (while sleeping or resting, while bathing or relieving oneself, when in a defiled place, when in fetters or in prison, when one has bad breath, and so on).[34] We also learn that one should only own three sets of ritual garb and that, once a set of ritual garb is complete, one must announce this to Heaven and make offerings to the Daoist Three Jewels and the various Perfected before accepting and wearing it. Finally, we discover that, if a Daoist does not wear ritual garb, he or she will lose the respect of and in fact be reviled by ten different groups, from heavenly beings down to the mean and lowly.

There were also restrictions on who could wear the most exalted clothing and on what occasions they could wear it, as we see in the following passage from a Tang encyclopedia:[35]

---

33. The following summarizes the rules listed in *Zhengyi weiyi jing* 5b–6a.

34. See DZ 788 *Sandong fafu kejie wen* 7b–10b.

35. *Dongxuan lingbao sandong fengdao kejie yingshi* 3.6a–b. This is a Tang work compiled primarily for monastics, but it preserves the ritual structure and many of the ritual forms from the Six Dynasties.

There are sumptuary rules for each item of the ritual garb of the three caverns worn by Daoist priests and priestesses. . . . The capes in mountain patterns, misty canvas, and auroral streaks—which should not mimic the nine-colored gauze form of a celestial worthy—are worn by the ritual master of great virtue who has ascended to the high seat to preach the great vehicle of the three caverns and extol the marvelous Dao. When one in possession of lofty rites ascends the altar or enters the oratory to proclaim a fête and conduct rituals, acting as leader of prayers, as well as during the regularly observed scriptural rites, or when transmitting the scriptures and precepts as demanded by the solemn rites, it is permitted to don them temporarily, but they should be returned for good when the affair is complete. Except for this situation, they may not be regularly worn. One thousand two hundred counters will be deducted.

道士女冠三洞法服，各有儀制，具如本經。當依法制服，具依下卷。其山文、霞納、暈畫等岐，無擬天尊身上九色離羅之狀，講說三洞大乘，敷揚妙道，陞高座大德法師所服。若具上法，登壇入靜，告齋行道，啓導之首，及常修經法，或傳授經戒，威儀所須，聽臨事暫披，事竟還罷。除此之外，皆不得輒服。減筭一千二百。

The rather elaborate clothing detailed in this passage comes from a mature period of the church, and earlier iterations of ritual garb were probably simpler and more austere. Moreover, the use of distinctive clothing was not limited to formal ritual contexts. The faithful were to wear a much simpler sort of outfit, called "on-duty clothes," during their daily tasks:[36]

Originally, there was no code for the on-duty clothes of Daoist priests and priestesses; now we promulgate one in full. Upper, middle, and lower garments should all be a light yellow color, like the yellow of powdery earth. The yellow should be a light color and the clothing short and small, shaped to fit to the body. While in one's room at

36. *Dongxuan lingbao sandong fengdao kejie yingshi* 3.7a. Cf. Kohn 2004: 120. The differences in our translations are too many to set forth in detail here, but Kohn translates the phrase I take as "on-duty" to mean "prepare [to put on]" in the first instance and "office-holder" in the second.

the abbey or serving one's master out of respect for his or her age and virtue, or adorning scriptures and images, or administering affairs, one should wear this clothing, called "on-duty."

道士女冠執役衣，先不具科，今備出之。其上中下衣皆用淺黃色，若黃屑土，黃作淡色，短小稱身制之。若在觀居房，供養師主，尊年耆德，或修飾經像，執捉營爲，皆服此衣，名爲執役。

Although the full codification of dress took place only during the Tang, after the rise of monasticism, distinctive garb for the performance of ritual was likely a feature of the early church, and there was no doubt some sort of everyday wear for less formal occasions when secular clothing was deemed inappropriate. Color was also surrounded by taboos: the same source informs us that the pants and tops of both male and female Daoist priests should all be the yellow of dust, and all other colors, including white, are forbidden. Bedding also should be this dusty yellow or brown, shoes should be yellow or black, and one should always avoid fancy cloth like damask or gauzy silk.[37] The explicit rationale for the rules was to separate the faithful from the profane.[38] Daoists later became known as "yellow hats" (*huangguan* 黃冠) or "yellow robes" (*huangyi* 黃衣).

37. *Dongxuan lingbao sandong fengdao kejie yingshi* 3.7a–8a. *Zhengyi weiyi jing* 16a adds skirts to the list of clothes and further specifies that the material should in each case be canvas 繒布.

38. For example, *Zhengyi weiyi jing* 16a notes, "If you wear straw sandals or wooden clogs, they must be different from those of the profane."

SIX

The Daoist Citizen

The foundation of the early Daoist church was the Daoist citizen. A citizen (*min* 民) in secular parlance was an individual whose name appeared on the government population roster and who contributed taxes and corvée labor to the state. Similarly, a Daoist citizen was responsible for the annual tithe of grain, five pecks per household. There may have been something parallel to corvée as well; we know that citizens were often called on to help with public works projects such as repairing roads or building bridges, but the sources are ambiguous as to whether such endeavors were undertaken as acts of penance for sins confessed or were normal responsibilities.

There were expectations for the citizens concerning ritual behavior as well, as we see in this passage from the *Statutes of the Mystic Capital*:[1]

> Those citizens who worship the Dao make a vow to take refuge in the Dao until death. They must not doubt with a divided heart, then, turning their backs on the Dao and its virtue, regret their path and return to the profane. This crime is not slight; the disaster will reach to the extinction of the entire family. They also must not licentiously sacrifice to deviant demons. If there is one who transgresses this rule, if he submits a plaque and an account, returning to

---

1. *Xuandu lüwen* 16b.

FIGURE 6a. Yao who want to be ordained must stick a piece of paper with their name on it onto the painting of Lord Lao without glue or adhesive. If it stays, Lord Lao approves and the ordination proceeds. Photo courtesy of Professor R. Hirota, Kanagawa University Yao Research Center.

FIGURE 6b. A Yao Daoist priest transfers spirit soldiers to the initiates as grains of rice. Photo courtesy of Professor R. Hirota, Kanagawa University Yao Research Center.

FIGURE 6c. Yao Daoist spouses being ordained share a bowl of the Rice of Lord Lao 老君飯, symbolizing their new, shared status. Photo courtesy of Professor R. Hirota, Kanagawa University Yao Research Center.

confess at the great parish, and wholeheartedly repents the transgression, that person will escape the calamitous punishment. Those who, knowing this, still offend will be fined the equivalent of one twelve-year period.

奉道之民，誓心至死歸道，不得兩心猶豫，違背道德，悔道還俗。此罪不輕，禍至滅門。亦不得淫祀邪鬼。若有犯者，牒狀歸首太治，專心悔過，得免殃咎。而知者故違，罰等一紀。

Thus, citizenship in a Celestial Master community meant a permanent break with the profane religious world, and divine tribunals punished apostasy. The "deviant demons" referenced here are simply the gods of the popular pantheon, nature spirits, or dead humans revered by locals for their magical efficacy when propitiated with offerings. Traditional community worship typically revolved around such cults, and community membership was defined by participation in periodic rites to the main deity.[2] Fami-

2. Schipper (1977), in a study based primarily on Tainan, Taiwan, demonstrates how earth god temples fulfilled a similar function in late imperial

lies who chose to take refuge in the Dao permanently estranged themselves and their descendants from their local community in favor of a new fellowship of Daoists. The exalted deities of Daoism offered protection from marauding hordes of bloodthirsty demons but at a price: these stern gods demanded unswerving allegiance and punished backsliding and apostasy severely.

Precepts

One of the earliest elements of Daoist belief, documented in the historical accounts of the founding, was a faith in the Three Offices that oversee human conduct. Moreover, we have seen that the primary practice advocated in the *Xiang'er* commentary to the *Laozi* is the observance of a set of rules of conduct called precepts. Precepts defined a code of conduct enforced by the Three Offices according to which each transgression was a sin or crime (*zui* 罪), which could only be absolved in response to a petition, primarily the Personally Written Missive to the Three Offices (*sanguan shoushu* 三官手書) mentioned in chapter 1. These sets of precepts became increasingly complex and demanding as one moved up the hierarchy of the church, but even the lowliest adherent undertook to observe some precepts. These precepts became a defining feature of membership in the Celestial Master church. The *Protocol of the Outer Registers* lists the most basic sets of precepts as follows:[3]

> All those who become Daoist citizens then receive the protective talisman and the three precepts. They advance to the five precepts and eight precepts, and after this they receive a register.
>
> 凡爲道民，便受護身符及三戒，進五戒，八戒，然後受錄。

China. Each temple's area of responsibility was defined by the course of a procession on the god's birthday, and all within those limits were expected to participate in and contribute to the festival.

3. *Zhengyi fawen taishang wailu yi* 11b. The passage is quoted in *Sandong zhunang* 6/3b as coming from the last chapter of the *Ritual Texts of Correct Unity* (*Zhengyi fawen* 正一法文).

It is not easy to identify these sets of precepts, which must have evolved rapidly after the Lingbao revelations familiarized Daoists with Buddhist concepts. Most surviving collections of precepts have been influenced by Buddhist lists and no longer reflect the teachings of the early Celestial Masters. Some, for example, simply identify the Three Precepts with the Three Refuges (*sangui* 三歸), adapting the list of the Buddhist Three Treasures (Buddha 佛, dharma 法, and sangha 僧) to refer to the Daoist Three Treasures:[4]

> The first precept is to take refuge for the person in the Supreme, Limitless Great Dao.
> The second precept is to take refuge for the [inner] gods in the thirty-six volumes of revered scriptures.
> The third precept is to take refuge for the life force in the Mystery-Centered Great Ritual Master.

第一戒者，歸身太上無極大道；
第二戒者，歸神三十六部尊經；
第三戒者，歸命玄中大法師。

The same Tang era compilation lists an alternate version of the Three Precepts that seems more in keeping with early Daoist terminology and is said to "summon the Three Pneumas, Mysterious, Primordial, and Inaugurating":[5]

> The first precept is to carefully recognize karmic affinities; do not forget the fundamental to chase the trivial. The second precept is to carefully guard against even slight selfishness; do not profit yourself at the expense of others. The third precept is to carefully practice diligent conduct; do not mix with the profane and lose your perfection.

---

4. *Sandong zhongjie wen* 1/2a. This work, compiled by Zhang Wanfu, cites the Lingbao scriptures as its source for this version of the precepts. The speaker is the Primordial Heavenly Worthy 元始天尊. The Daoist Three Treasures were the Dao, the scriptures, and the master.

5. *Sandong zhongjie wen* 2/2a.

第一戒者，諦識因緣，勿忘本逐末。第二戒者，諦守少私，勿利
我損物。第三戒者，諦習勤行，勿混俗失真。

Although this set also includes one Buddhist term (translated as
"karmic affinity"), in other respects this list accords well with
early church teaching, especially in the contrast it draws between
the profane and the perfected. It is also followed by a set of five
and then eight precepts, just as in the above quotation from the
Protocol of the Outer Registers.

Many versions of the Five Precepts merely repeat or adapt the
well-known Buddhist Five Precepts against killing, stealing, sexual
misconduct, slander, and intoxicants, but the Five Precepts listed
in the Tang compilation focus on the five senses, often in words
reminiscent of the *Laozi*:[6]

> First precept: The eye should not lust after the five colors; take a vow
> to stop killing and study long life. Second precept: The ear should
> not lust after the five tones; prefer to hear of the good and pursue no
> delusion. Third precept: The nose should not lust after the five pneu-
> mas; use ritual incense and cast away profane defilements. Fourth
> precept: The mouth should not lust after the five flavors; practice
> embryonic breathing and cut off evil words. Fifth precept: The
> body should not lust after the five fabrics; walk a path of diligent
> endeavor in order to accord with the Dao.
>
> 第一戒者，目不貪五色，誓止殺，學長生。第二戒者，耳不貪五
> 音，願聞善，從無惑。第三戒者，鼻不貪五氣，用法香，遣俗
> 穢。第四戒者，口不貪五味，習胎息，絕惡言。第五戒者，身不
> 貪五綵，履勤勞，以順道。

The following set of Eight Precepts is perhaps not the earliest
(number 6 mentions the Three Pure Ones, so it is probably at least
fifth century), but it shows no obvious Buddhist influence.[7] Thus,
we have a set of three, five, and eight precepts presented in succes-

6. *Sandong zhongjie wen* 2/3a–b. The first precept does share with the Buddhist precepts a prohibition against killing.
7. *Sandong zhongjie wen* 2/4a–b.

sion that could plausibly be identified with those mentioned in the *Protocol of the Outer Registers*. The earliest version of these precepts may be lost to us, and we cannot be sure that the early church demanded all of these before conferring the parish register. Nevertheless, it seems likely that some set of precepts, perhaps only an early version of the Three Precepts, accompanied this basic register of the Daoist citizen. We can be confident that they were important to the faithful, as we see in this quotation from the *Scripture of Solemn Deportment*:[8]

> They should proceed to their master to be invested with the parish register, Three Refuges, and Five Precepts. If they do not receive them, then the supervisor of the parish will not record [their names], and the Earth God will not recognize them, will not take charge of the Five Pneumas, and will not inform the Four Supervisors. If they do receive this parish register, then the demon kings will bow down in submission and proclaim themselves subalterns.
>
> 當詣師奉受治籙、三歸五戒。不受之者,則治司不書,土地不明,不攝五炁,不關四司。受此治籙,則魔王拜伏,自稱下官。

The conversion of the profane to Daoism owed much to the supernatural protection afforded by body gods and the ritual services of the community libationers. As the precepts, also enforced by the libationers and body gods, grew in number and complexity, they must have acted together with the grain tithe and other communal responsibilities as a check on overly rapid evangelization, revealing the responsibilities of church membership.

The Daily Audience

Much of the ritual practice that survives from the Celestial Master church was oriented toward novices, masters, and church officers, who could perform elaborate rites for the absolution of sin, the

8. *Zhengyi weiyi jing* 1a.

augmentation of merit, the diversion of calamity, and the correction of celestial records. Later rituals have often overwritten even minor rites that reflect a simpler stage of the church's history, before it had assimilated innovations originating in the Shangqing and Lingbao reform movements of the late fourth century and incorporated ideas and practices that had their ultimate origins in Buddhism. One essential element of daily practice for all Daoist citizens, novices, and libationers was the Entering the Oratory rite (Entering the Parish for libationers), performed every morning and evening. We find perhaps an early reference to this rite in the *Code of the Great Perfected*:[9]

> When Daoist citizens are converted, each family should establish an oratory in the west, facing east. Place an incense burner beneath the west wall. The Celestial Master is the ruler of the Daoist parish. When entering the oratory, first face west, [burn] incense, and visualize the [Celestial] Master. Bow twice, offer incense three times, and verbally express your request. Next do this to the north, then to the east, then to the south. When done, then exit without turning to look backward.
>
> 道民入化，家家各立靖室，在西向東。安一香火西壁下。天師爲道治之主。入靖，先向西香火存師，再拜，三上香，啓願。次北，次東，次南。訖便出，勿轉顧。

We are fortunate that, in addition to the new Entering the Oratory rite revealed by the apotheosized Lady Wei Huacun 魏華存夫人 as part of the Shangqing revelations, Tao Hongjing preserved a copy of the original "Hanzhong" rite, which he knew from a single "ancient document on rice paper" (*guzhi gushu* 穀紙古書). It does not give detailed instructions on how to perform the rite but does preserve the four basic invocations, intoned while rotating counterclockwise, to Daoist deities in the four cardinal directions:[10]

9. *Yaoxiu keyi jielü chao* 10/4a.
10. *Dengzhen yinjue* 3/10b–11a.

The Hanzhong Method for Entering the Parish
and Holding Audience in the Oratory
漢中入治朝靜法

First, face east and say:

I, X, desire life and enjoy living. I wish to beg that you lords and elders allow me to see a prolonged lifespan, extend my years and augment my longevity, to achieve the status of a seed citizen,[11] maintaining myself [as long] as Heaven and Earth. You should, on behalf of my household, cause disasters to be eliminated, the hundred ailments to heal of themselves, deities to attach themselves to our persons, and our hearts and minds to be enlightened.

甲貪生樂活，願從諸君丈人，乞丐長存久視，延年益壽，得爲種民，與天地相守。當使甲家灾禍消滅，百病自愈，神明附身，心開意悟。

Next, facing north:

I, X, want to reform my evil acts and do good. I wish to beg the Most Mysterious Lord of the Superior One to pardon my sins and transgressions, release me from basic demotions, rescue me from disaster and hardship, and keep government officers away. You should arrange that, in whatever direction I turn, metal and stone will open, [catastrophes due to] water and fire will be eliminated, the evil and refractory will submit, and evil sprites will be exterminated or scattered.

甲欲改惡爲善，願從太玄上一君乞丐原赦罪過，解除基讁，度脫灾難，辟斥縣官。當令甲所向，金石爲開，水火爲滅，惡逆賓伏，精邪消散。

Next, facing west:

I, X, am fond of the Dao and delight in transcendents. I wish to beg from the Celestial Master that I obtain what I delight in and accomplish what I undertake. You should cause my heart and mind to be enlightened, my ears and eyes to be sharp, the hundred ailments to be eliminated, and my body to be light and strong.

---

11. As discussed in chapter 2, early Daoists believed that apocalyptic disasters would kill all except the "seed people," who would then survive to see the utopian world of Great Peace.

甲好道樂仙，願從天師乞丐所樂者得，所作者成。當使甲心開意解，耳目聰明，百病消除，身體輕強。

Next, facing south:

I, X, cultivate my person and nourish my nature to restore my years and push back old age. I wish to beg from the Lord of the Dao and Virtue that the pneumas of his enriching grace be distributed through my physical form, causing the pneumas of the Dao to circulate, so that I personally receive his compassionate grace, the many ailments are eliminated, and blessings and luck flock to me. My thoughts are upon the lord of myriad blessings, who will summon for me the cash and wealth of the four directions, ordering my life and promoting my interests so that they are attained in whatever direction I turn.

甲修身養性，還年却老，願從道德君乞丐恩潤之氣布施骨體，使道氣流行，甲身咸蒙慈恩，衆病消除，福吉來集。思在萬福君爲甲致四方錢財，治生進利，所向皆至。

This invocation of spirits in four directions sets out some of the most basic goals of the believing Daoist during the first centuries of the church's existence. Despite the warnings in the *Xiang'er* about greed, there is a frank desire for wealth and worldly success as well as good health, longevity, the elimination of all obstacles, and the avoidance of calamity, including entanglements with government officials. Invulnerability to disaster depends on being a seed citizen, but there is no explicit mention of Great Peace or the impending apocalypse. Health in this ritual encompasses the absence or rapid healing of all illness, the restoration of youthful vigor, and perspicacity of the senses, but also an infusion of pneumas of the Dao and the presence within the body of corporeal spirits. Individuals making this request undertake to reform their conduct, take joy in the Dao, and cultivate their bodies. On the whole, the Hanzhong audience rite can be seen as an all-purpose prayer, affirming one's commitment to the faith, but focusing on the benefits promised through church membership. Such a practice, which must have been near universal in Celestial Master communities, shows that even for the lowest-level members of the faith, ritual practice in the oratory was a vital element of the Celestial Master identity.

The *Scripture of Solemn Deportment* has a section devoted to preparations before entering the oratory.[12] One should attain a peaceful state of mind, avoiding arguments and harsh words. One should straighten one's clothes, wash, chant the appropriate invocation to avoid being punished by the clerks and soldiers of one's register, and prepare everything needed for the upcoming ritual so as not to interrupt it. Entering, one should remove one's shoes, entering first with the right foot. When entering or leaving, one should take care not to look backward or to turn one's back on the place of honor, in the west, where the most exalted deities observed all that went on; later, images of deities came to be placed in this position.

The rites of the oratory were essential to the practice of the Daoists who established the Supreme Purity tradition in the 360s. A revised version of the rite for Entering the Oratory was revealed through the goddess Wei Huacun, who claimed to have been a Celestial Master libationer in life and is recorded in Tao Hongjing's commentary to the *Hidden Instructions for Ascending to Perfection* (*Dengzhen yinjue*).[13] Tao notes that the reason for the great care surrounding this ritual, whether in original or revised form, was not only because the oratory was itself a sacred space and contained sacred objects like scriptures, but because Daoist divinities inhabited it. On entering the oratory, a practitioner should rectify his or her heart, half-close the eyes in the manner still used today for visualizations (*linmu* 臨目), and see arrayed the officer on duty that day, the Zhengyi merit officer, and the emissaries of Officers of the Left and of the Right, altogether four in number, just inside the door, as well as the Dragon Lord and the Tiger Lord on the left and the right, a pair of Incense-Conveying Attendants 捧香使者 flanking the incense burner, and a pair of Oratory-Guarding Jade Maidens 守靜玉女 on either end of the table. We cannot be sure that early Celestial Master adherents followed this exact visualization

12. *Zhengyi weiyi jing* 6a–b.
13. *Dengzhen yinjue* 3/5b–11b. See also Yoshikawa 1987 and Cedzich 1987.

practice, but there must have been a set of visualizations that accompanied the rite. Tao comments:[14]

> If one explores the significance of these [rules], the clerks and supervisors in the oratory are all bureaucrats of the Great Purity [Heaven]. Their investigations are strict and clear, their codes[15] and regulations particularly numerous. If you do not follow the rules, not only will your ritual not move the Heavens, it can also bring blame and disastrous harm.
>
> 尋此之旨，凡靜中吏司，皆泰清官寮，糺察嚴明，殊多科制。若不如法，非但無感，亦即致咎禍害者矣。

At least one member of each Daoist family was supposed to confront these divine beings every day, and every member of the family would have been aware that these awesome officials were constantly on duty in the family oratory. For a Daoist, the gods were never far away; the high gods were approached only through elaborate ritual, but their divine representatives were always close to hand.

The Assemblies

In addition to these rites of audience for the individual or family, Daoist citizens would also gather three times a year for a large communal rite, the Assembly (*hui* 會). A concise introduction to these holy days is provided in *Master Redpine's Petition Almanac*:[16]

> The fifth day[17] of the first month is the Upper Assembly. The seventh day of the seventh month is the Middle Assembly. The fifth day of the

14. *Dengzhen yinjue* 3/6b.

15. Reading *ke* 科 for a character that looks more like *liao* 料. The two are easily confused.

16. *Chisongzi zhangli* 2/5a.

17. The seventh day of the first month, given in the next quotation, is the normal day for this Assembly.

tenth month is the Lower Assembly. On the above days, it is appropriate to submit petitions and make statements of merit. Do not avoid strong winds or violent rain, or the darkenings of the sun and the moon, or the prohibitions and closings of Heaven and Earth. On the day [of the Assembly], the Heavenly Thearch and all the great sages will descend together and assemble in the diocese hall, dividing their forms and distributing their images so that across more than ten thousand miles their response [to the ritual] is identical. On this day, submitting petitions, receiving conferral of ritual registers, men and women circulating virtue and dispensing merit to extinguish disaster and dispel calamity, all these are not prohibited.

正月五日，上會。七月七日，中會。十月五日，下會。右此日，宜上章言功，不避疾風暴雨、日月昏晦、天地禁閉。其日天帝、一切大聖俱下，同會治堂，分形布影，萬里之外，響應齊同。此日上章，受度法籙，男女行德施功，消災散禍，悉不禁制。

Here we see that the Assemblies brought together Daoists and their gods. In this sense, they were similar to the annual festival to the god of the soil (*she* 社) at the root of the Village Drinking Festival discussed in the classics. These village banquets also hosted the local deities and have an even closer tie to the kitchen banquets that Daoists held during the Assemblies, as we shall see below.[18] Unlike the ceremonies of common villagers addressed to their profane gods, Assemblies and other Daoist observances were not subject to taboos and restrictions on when and where they could be held.

The submission of petitions was the most basic ritual behavior of the movement and was regularly followed by a statement of merits (*yangong* 言功) to thank and reward all of the spirits who aided the process. The conferral of registers was also especially appropriate at this time since the Daoist gods were already in attendance. "Circulating virtue and dispensing merit" probably refers to performance of Merging the Pneumas, which was discussed in

---

18. For an instructive tale of the imagined response of deities to events at one of these *she* festivals, see chapter 56 of the *Wenchang huashu*, translated in Kleeman 1994a.

chapter 3.[19] This passage from Lu Xiujing's *Abridgement of the Daoist Code* highlights another aspect of the Assemblies:[20]

> The households of those who worship the Dao are all surveyed and recorded in a roster. Each household has [a master] to whom it belongs, and each year he or she commands them to attend the Three Assemblies, on the seventh day of the first month, the seventh day of the seventh month, and the fifth day of the tenth month. Each citizen gathers at his own parish, where the master is to correct the parish records and roster, dropping the deceased and adding the newly born, correcting the list of names and verifying the number of individuals. He or she will thrice proclaim the Five Commands so that the citizens will know the law. On that day the celestial officers and earthly spirits will all assemble at the master's parish to compare and adjust their documents.
>
> 奉道者皆編戶著籍，各有所屬。令以正月七日、七月七日、十月五日，一年三會，民各投集本治。師當改治錄籍，落死上生，隱實口數，正定名簿。三宣五令，令民知法。其日天官地神咸會師治，對校文書。

In this passage, we see the significance of the Assemblies for the church and the divine bureaucracy. Both depended on accurate and up-to-date rosters of church members to keep track of who was a Daoist and, consequently, merited celestial protection. Heads of households were to bring to the Assembly a current list of family members, the "home record" (*zhailu* 宅錄).[21]

> The home record is the supplementary roster of the citizens. The number of males and females should be recorded therein. The officers in charge of guarding the house take this as their standard in protecting all the members in their activities.

19. The term "dispensing" (*shi* 施) recalls the "mystic dispensation," a euphemism for the rite first employed in the Zhang Pu stele of 173, and the goal, to dispel disaster, confirms this.
20. *Lu xiansheng daomenke lüe* 3a.
21. *Lu xiansheng daomenke lüe* 3a.

宅錄，此是民之副籍，男女口數，悉應注上。守宅之官，以之爲
正，人口動止，皆當營衞。

This record was submitted to the parish libationer, who used it to
adjust the "fate roster" (*mingji* 命籍), something like a parish membership list, and then formally submitted this document to the
Heavenly Bureaus, who adjusted their own records on this basis.[22]
Errors in this process could leave individuals without divine support, as Master Lu points out slightly later in the same document:[23]

Heads of household, bringing the household record, all proceed
to their own parishes, where each is received and recorded in
order to augment and correct the fate roster. On the days of the
Three Assemblies, the myriad gods of the Three Offices select those
who are qualified [for promotion]. If there has been an increase in
population, and it is not submitted, then the Heavenly Bureaus will
not have the [new baby's] name. If the number of mouths decreases,
but they are not removed [from the roster], then the book of names
will no longer be accurate.

籍主皆齎宅錄，詣本治，更相承錄，以注正命籍。三會之日，三
官萬神，更相揀當。若增口不上，天曹無名；減口不除，則名簿
不實。

Inaccuracies in the otherworldly records could have serious consequences when a church member encountered trouble and required

22. The *Scripture of Great Peace* mentions the fate roster, saying: "As for
persons who perform good deeds and have no record of evil, Heaven sees their
good deeds and causes gods, in accordance with this, to transfer their fate
rosters to the bureaucrat(s) who record long life" 行善之人，無惡文辭，天見
善，使神隨之，移其命籍著長壽之曹. The stratification and dating of the
Taipingjing is a complex question, but this may be an antecedent to the Daoist
usage. See Wang Ming 1960:625; Yu Liming 2001:463. Here I follow Yu Liming's punctuation.

23. *Lu xiansheng daomenke lüe* 3b. He further notes (4a) that "The master
on their behalf submits [the fate roster] to the Three Heavens, requesting that
that officer who guards the home will extend protection to those listed on the
roster, expelling disaster and calamity" 師爲列上三天，請守宅之官，依籍口保
護，禳災禍.

a ritual intervention to set things right. Master Lu goes on to tell of the consequences of not reporting deaths, births, and marriages, saying that "as a result there are hundred-year-old adolescent boys and centenarian maidens" and pointing out that, when an individual seeks help from someone other than his or her own master, it seems to the heavenly bureaucrats that this is an unknown individual with no place on the rosters of the faithful. Commands therefore never reach the officials assigned to protect the sufferer's home.[24]

Another aspect of the Assemblies was instruction in the faith. We do not know exactly what the Five Commands (*wuling* 五令) were that were thrice proclaimed at each Assembly (in the next to last quotation), but we can presume that they were moral strictures of some sort, perhaps related to or identical with the Five Precepts that each Daoist citizen was expected to observe.[25] The libationer's role at the Assembly is explained in this passage from the *Statutes of the Mystic Capital*:[26]

> On the auspicious days of the Assemblies, [the masters] appear before the celestial officials, teach and convert the foolish and profane, distribute [acknowledgments of] merit and virtue, and cause the human and spirit [records] to correspond to each other.
>
> 三會吉日，質對天官，教化愚俗，布散功德，使人鬼相應。

Again, the exact nature of the questions posed by the celestial bureaucrats is unclear, but it must have included some sort of information concerning the conduct of the libationers and their flocks in addition to a summary report of additions to and departures from the community.

24. *Lu xiansheng daomenke lüe* 3b. One petition in *Master Redpine's Petition Almanac* enumerates the troops guarding the home as "the three generals, twenty-four clerks, and three hundred thousand soldiers guarding the home" 守宅三將軍、二十四吏、兵士三十萬人. See *Chisongzi zhangli* 5/8a7–8.

25. Lu Xiujing characterizes the content of these addresses as "the enlightened code and orthodox teachings" (*mingke zhengjiao* 明科正教). See *Lu xiansheng daomenke lüe* 2b.

26. *Xuandu lüwen* 15a. On the dating of this text, see Jiang Boqin 1991.

Yet another function of the Assemblies was the collection of the five pecks of rice that were the defined contribution of each Daoist household to the community. Families were encouraged to submit this "heavenly rent rice" (*tianzu mi* 天租米) as early as the first Assembly of the year, and even submission at the second (7/7) would win extra merit, but failure to supply the grain by the last Assembly of the year was a sin meriting severe punishment: "Your [name on the] fate roster will not be submitted to clerks who guard humans; upward it will extend to your ancestors for seven generations, and downward it will flow down to your progeny."[27] Originally, a portion (20 or 30 percent) of this grain was to be transmitted to the parish of the Celestial Master for use by the central administration of the church; given the doubts we have about the existence and authority of the Celestial Master after the diaspora of 215, we cannot say for how long this provision was observed.[28] In any case, the majority of the contribution was retained in the local parish.

The Kitchens

One obvious purpose of the grain contributed at the Assemblies was to feed the religious professionals serving in the parish. Another important use was to supply communal banquets called "kitchens" (*chu* 廚) held at the time of the Assembly. The following passage criticizes libationers who sought to divert these contributions to other purposes:[29]

> The reason why you set up a kitchen on the days of the Three Assemblies is that it allows you to disburse the "rent grain." But recently the many officers have forced the commoners to provide [the food] for the Assemblies. All such actions contravene the code and the canons.

27. *Xuandu lüwen* 11b.
28. The relevant passages are found at *Xiandu lüwen* 11b–12a, 14b.
29. *Xuandu lüwen* 12b.

三會之日，所以供廚，使布散租米，而比者眾官，令使百姓以供
會，此皆不合科典。

Thus, the rice tithe, much like the pledge offerings discussed below, may have been subject to abuse, but these exactions were intended to supply the community with ritual necessities that would benefit all.[30]

We are fortunate that a number of recent publications have explored the ritual preparation, offering, and consumption of food and drink in early China.[31] In this light, we can now see that a periodic ritual event like the village festival to the god of the soil functioned in a number of different ways to situate the village and its members in the cosmos. Socially, it was one of the few events that all members of local society participated in, offering an opportunity to clarify and exhibit the social hierarchy, while also reinforcing bonds of community. Economically, sponsorship by well-off village members permitted a limited redistribution of resources and provided additional nourishment for the most deprived. Morally, it reaffirmed the accepted code of conduct, as exemplary conduct was recognized and misconduct condemned through changes in ritual roles. Spiritually, the sacrifice brought the villagers into direct contact with the deities that oversaw their lives and determined their fate, and established a ritual exchange between mortal and deity of sustaining bloody victuals and auspicious divine blessings that affirmed their continuing relationship. This exchange was effected when the gods consumed the essence of the offering through its scent, then infused it with their blessings (*fu* 福), which community members then incorporated into their persons by consuming the remaining food and drink.

We have seen that a prime tenet of the Celestial Master church since its inception was the rejection of sacrifice as a means of interaction between humans and the divine. Daoists refused to take

30. A passage from the fifth-century *Code of the Great Perfected* suggests that the donated grain went into a Heavenly Storehouse (*tiancang* 天倉) used to supplement supplies in years of famine. See *Yaoxiu keyi jielü chao* 2a.

31. See Boileau 1998–99, 2006; Sterckx 2005, 2011; Brashier 2011.

part in acts of sacrifice or consume their products. This was in part a theological position, based on the belief that Daoists addressed a high level of deity who transcended all such transactional arrangements and could only be swayed through moral conduct, including the proper performance of ritual. It also served to differentiate Daoists from profane nonbelievers. In traditional Chinese society, participation in village ritual was a defining feature of citizenship. Daoist rejection of it must have put them in some sense outside the community.

Despite this condemnation of the ritual acts at the heart of village sacrifice and banqueting, the social value of the communal meal was too great to give up. The Daoists developed their own distinctive communal dining ritual, the Kitchen (*chu* 廚). These kitchen-feasts could be held at any time in response to a current need (*yuanchu* 願廚) or to dispel some harm (*jiechu* 解廚), but an important and even favored occasion for their performance was one of the Three Assemblies. Like most other Daoist activities, these communal feasts escaped the notice of China's standard histories, but references to them in two non-Daoist sources confirm their occurrence and give us some idea of how interested outsiders viewed the rite. The first is from the great occultist Ge Hong. Ge makes no explicit comment about the Daoist religion that was already well established in his day, but he does refer to a Way of the Li Family (*Lijia dao* 李家道) that closely resembles Celestial Master Daoism and may in fact refer to the Celestial Master Daoism practiced by the Li family who ruled the Cheng-Han state in modern Sichuan during the first half of the fourth century:[32]

> There are more than a hundred of these ghoulish Ways; all kill living beings for bloody victuals. Only the Way of the Li Family practices nonaction (*wuwei*) and is a bit different. But, even though they do not butcher animals, every time they offer a blessing meal, there are

32. *Baopuzi* 9/39. For speculation on the identification of this Way of the Li Family with the Cheng-Han state, see Campany 2002:213. On Cheng-Han, see chapter 4.

no limits. They buy everything in the market, striving for bountiful extravagance. They have to buy the finest, freshest goods. Sometimes the kitchen is for dozens of people, and the expense is truly enormous. So they are not unambiguously for purity and economy, and so should also be on the list of prohibited groups.

諸妖道百餘種，皆煞生血食，獨有李家道無爲爲小差。然雖不屠宰，每供福食，無有限劑，市買所具，務於豐泰，精鮮之物，不得不買，或數十人厨，費亦多矣，復未純爲清省也，亦皆宜在禁絕之列。

Ge Hong is much more interested in a Heavenly Kitchen in which Jade Maidens bring down from the Heavens divine foodstuffs guaranteeing immortality.[33] He is not interested in communal ritual as a means of changing one's fate but does mention these Daoist observances and their nonsacrificial character.

Our other external account of this rite, also antagonistic in nature, is Xuanguang's 玄光 (fl. ca. 480) *Discourse on Discriminating Delusion* (*Bianhuo lun* 辨惑論), an anti-Daoist polemic of the late Six Dynasties period:[34]

If there are remnant ethers from the Sinister Way, then [the Daoists] must perform an exculpatory kitchen at the gate to the tomb. Proud of their person and of their secret food, they maintain the attitude of one about to suck a boil.[35] Of old, Zhang Lu held an exculpatory blessing [kitchen] in Hanzhong. He assembled a large group of libationers and demon troopers.[36] They drank more than normal and ended up turning into a drunken mob. The ugly reputation from this incident spread abroad, reaching as far as the Chengdu plain. Liu Zhang admonished them, saying: "Numinous transcendents

33. On this type of kitchen-feast, see Mollier 1999–2000.

34. T2102, 52/49a.

35. This expression, *shunban* 吮班, is otherwise unknown. Chinese doctors (and filial children) were sometimes praised for sucking boils and ulcers to remove the evil elements. Here the sense is that they take pride in their disdain for luxury and the austerity of their diet.

36. This term for Daoist believers is taken directly from historical accounts, such as the *Record of the Three Kingdoms*, quoted in chapter 1, and is not substantiated in any Daoist scripture.

who cultivate their life force treat their bodies well by sticking to pine[nuts] and auroral mist. If you are a glutton, how can you esteem the Dao?" When Master Lu heard this, he was mortified and determined to punish them by making them sweep the roads. Tales abroad in the world say that after this the Daoist priests established standards to forestall this problem. They also set up regulations for the kitchen, limiting it to three pints of liquor.[37] Since the end of the Han, they have been called "wine limiters" (*zhijiu* 制酒).

左道餘氣乃墓門解廚。矜身奧食。懷吮班之態。昔張子魯漢中解
福。大集祭酒及諸鬼卒。酣進過常遂致營逸。醜聲遝布遠達岷
方。劉璋教曰。夫靈仙養命。猶節松霞而厚身。嗜味奚能尙道。子
魯聞之憤恥。意深罰其掃路。世傳道士後會舉標。以防斯難。兼制
廚命酒限三升。漢末已來謂爲制酒。

This tale survives in no other source, and in fact there is no reference to Daoists as "wine limiters" in any surviving source outside the Buddhist canon. The historicity of this scurrilous tale is very much open to doubt,[38] but we can conclude from it that the kitchen was well known to non-Daoists during the fifth century, that it was sometimes performed for the benefit of the recently dead to absolve (*jie* 解) them of sin, and that it was famous for its restraint, with only limited amounts of alcohol and no sacrificial meat served to participants.

It was the meatless aspect of this rite, rooted in the Daoist rejection of blood sacrifice, that set it apart so strongly from traditional communal banquets. It was also this feature that backsliding believers challenged, as we see in this condemnation from the *Statutes of the Mystic Capital*:[39]

37. A pint (*sheng* 升) in the Han dynasty was about 200 milliliters, so three pints would be about 20 percent larger than a standard British pint of ale and probably was not much stronger.
38. Zhang Lu had an independent power base in Hanzhong by the time Liu Zhang replaced his father, Liu Yan, as pastor of Yi province and was responsible for executing Zhang Lu's mother and relatives. It is unclear how much Zhang Lu would have cared about Liu Zhang's opinion or whether they were even in communication. See chapter 1.
39. *Xuandu lüwen* 15a. We see a similar condemnation of Daoists killing living beings for sacrifice in the fifth-century *Lu xiansheng daomenke lüe* 1a.

Recently, the many officials have been killing and cooking domestic animals to supply the kitchens and meetings. This is not in accord with the otherworldly law. To kill the living in search of life is to have departed far from life.

比者眾官烹殺畜生，以供廚會，不合冥法。殺生求生，去生遠矣。

    Kitchen-feasts could be held for a variety of reasons, and their size could vary considerably. A passage preserved from the *Code of the Great Perfected* speaks of an occasional kitchen held in response to the illness of a family member:[40]

If a family has an illness or a cyclical misfortune,[41] they should hold a kitchen-feast for officials and private guests; this is called "feeding the worthies." You should invite pure and worthy Daoist priests of upper, middle, and lower status, numbering ten, twenty-four, thirty, fifty, or a hundred people; it must not be less than ten because this would be insufficient to create blessings.

家有疾厄，公私設廚，名曰飯賢。可請清賢道士上、中、下，十人、二十四人、三十人、五十人、百人，不可不滿十人，不足爲福。

The *Code* goes on to explain that worthy Daoists do not really need much food, nor do they need rich offerings, but the feast is offered to them because they possess the Dao and have many gods in their body. For these same reasons, a single high official in the church could actually count for numerous individuals, according to a formula preserved in the *Statutes of the Mystic Capital*:

An Orthodox Unity Equanimity Pneuma of the Left or Right or higher is equivalent to seven people. A Daoist priest of the Beiqiu

40. *Yaoxiu keyi jielü chao* 12/1a.
41. Cyclical misfortunes (*e* 厄) strike when an individual reaches a certain age. See *Shenxianzhuan*, quoted in *Taiping guangji* 1/2; Campany 2002:198, n. 227.

parish [or above] is equivalent to three people.[42] Those who wear a register with clerks and soldiers or higher are equivalent to two people. Two youths with the Extended Mandate register are equivalent to three people. An unassigned citizen is equivalent to one person.

正一左右平氣以上，一人當七人; 望丘治道士，一人當三人；諸佩籙吏兵以上，一人當二人；更令童子，二人當三人；散民，一人當一人。

Sources are not entirely clear about how often one of these kitchen-feasts should be held. One category of kitchen, usually held at the time of one of the Assemblies, was hosted by local Daoist church officers for the benefit of members of their flock, as we see in this passage from the same text:[43]

Male officers, female officers, leaders [of parishes], and register novices who have made a request for an increase in numbers [of their flock], if by the end of the year they have increased by fewer than ten, set a kitchen-feast for twenty people. If they have increased by thirty or more, set a kitchen-feast for twenty-four. [Even] if it is a million or ten million, [set] no more than a twenty-four-person kitchen-feast. Host one person for each person added, but stop at twenty-four.

男官、女官、主者、籙生，年初願口數，竟歲無十人，設廚二十人。若三十口已上，設二十四人廚。若百千萬口，不過二十四人廚。一口設一人廚，至二十四人止也。

This passage puts some practical limits in the size of the kitchen, since it seems that some parishes could indeed number in the thousands of members, and the logistics of such a large meal would have been daunting.

42. The text reads *wangqiu* 望邱, which seems to be a mistake for the lowest of the twenty-four parishes, which is called either Beimang 北邙 or Beiqiu 北邱. Thus, the *wang* would be a corruption of *mang*, which has been paired with *qiu*.

43. *Xuandu lüwen* 12a–b.

Just as the officers of a parish were expected to provide a kitchen-feast in celebration of an increase in the size of their parish, presumably, at the last Assembly of the year, individual Daoist families were also expected to offer a kitchen in response to the birth of a child:[44]

> If you give birth to a son, hold a superior kitchen; if you give birth to a daughter, hold a medium kitchen. An increase in family size or additional wealth, seeking the protection of a [heavenly] officer, an extension of life, or no trouble through the year are examples of superior kitchens. Seeking to survive a cyclical danger, traveling afar, or seeking a promotion are examples of middle kitchens. Seeking to heal an illness or dispelling a suit before the county prefect, imprisonment, or bondage are examples of an inferior kitchen.
>
> 生男上廚，生女中廚。增口益財，求官保護，延口，歲中無他，上廚之例。求度厄難，遠行，求遷官，廚中之例。求治疾病，消縣官口舌牢獄繫閉，下廚之例。

We see here that, in addition to kitchen-feasts held in celebration of an auspicious event, kitchens were also held to make a request of the divine forces and that the size of such a kitchen depended on the significance of the request. Another statute gives more information on the celebratory kitchen-feasts, including a number of pledge offerings that should accompany the kitchen:[45]

> If you give birth to a son, establish a kitchen-feast for ten people, and [contribute] one hundred sheets of medium petition paper, a pair of writing brushes, a ball of ink, and a writing knife. If you give birth to a daughter, establish a kitchen-feast for five people, and [contribute] a sitting mat and a dustpan. Send these in after a full month.
>
> 生男兒，設廚食十人，中章紙百張，筆一雙，墨一丸，書刀一口。生女子，廚食五人，席一領，糞箕一枚，掃篇一枚。月滿則輸。

44. *Xuandu lüwen* 12a.
45. *Xuandu lüwen* 12b.

Here the pledge offerings reflect a certain stereotyping and reveal the limits of the relatively equal treatment of men and women in the early church.

Pledge offerings were particularly important when making a request in conjunction with the kitchen-feast. Such a kitchen is sometimes termed a "request kitchen" (*yuanchu* 願廚). Much as when making a request through a petition, a request kitchen often had to be accompanied by pledge offerings to demonstrate one's faith, as we see in this passage:[46]

> Male officers, female officers, leaders, and register novices should list the items offered as pledges in the request. For ten people or fewer, 20 feet of offering silk; for more than twenty people, 40 feet of offering silk. Send it in after receiving the favor.
>
> 男官、女官、主者、籙生,條跪願品格,十人以下,跪絹二十尺,二十人已上,跪絹四十尺,蒙恩則輸送。

Here we see another special term, *gui* 跪, meaning a pledge offering. As with the tribute grain in the annual tithe of five pecks of rice, these offerings were meant to supply the needs of the community. Sponsoring a kitchen-feast each year (or each Assembly?) would have been a major expense, as we see in this passage from the *Statutes of the Mystic Capital*:[47]

> Male officers, female officers, and leaders: For a superior kitchen-feast [prepare] five pints of wine and 300 cash [to buy food] per person; for a medium kitchen-feast, four pints and 250 cash per person; for an inferior kitchen-feast, three pints and 100 cash per person.
>
> 男官、女官、主者,上廚,人酒五升,錢三百。中廚,人酒四升,錢二百五十文。下廚,人酒三升,錢一百文。

Because the kitchen was a major ritual as well an important community celebration, it needed religious officiants. Surviving sources

---

46. *Xuandu lüwen* 12b.
47. *Xuandu lüwen* 13b–14a.

speak of three individuals, the Supervisor of the Kitchen (*jianchu* 監廚), the Regulator of the Group (*jiezhong* 節眾), and the Priest of Great Virtue (*dade* 大德).⁴⁸ Each had his or her distinct role, with the Priest of Great Virtue acting as the lead guest in partaking of the banquet. In many ways, the Supervisor of the Kitchen had the greatest responsibility, though it was the Regulator of the Group who was responsible for maintaining order among the guests. The *Scripture of the Ascent to Mystery* records a set of ten matters that the Supervisor of the Kitchen should keep in mind while examining the food:⁴⁹

1. Consider the mercy of the Dao.
2. Consider the mercy of one's master.
3. Consider that the masses are good fields of merit.⁵⁰
4. Consider that the host should take delight in the perfected and distinguish the false so that he or she is able to supply the needs of the worthy and good.
5. Consider oneself fortunate to be able to be one of the staff, occupying a place in the order of Daoists.
6. Considering that the feelings of the host are important, do not allow the group to lightly discuss the virtues and faults [of the food], refusing to partake of those things they do not like.
7. If the host provides foods that are not in accord with the rules, do not permit them to be presented.
8. If there is one among the group who seeks food that is not in accord with the rules, immediately send that person away; do not permit him or her to join in the meal.

48. On these officers, see *Yaoxiu keyi jielü chao* 9/9b, where the first officer is instead termed Supervisor of the Fête (*jianzhai* 監齋). In fact, the ritual banquet held at the end of a *zhai* ritual was essentially the same as the kitchen. The title of the Priest of Great Virtue is reminiscent of the term [Priest of] High Merit (*gaogong* 高功) commonly used for the chief officiant at modern Daoist rituals. It is unclear how these titles relate to Celestial Master ranks, but one supposes that the officers of the kitchen were at least libationers.

49. *Yaoxiu keyi jielü chao* 9/9b, quoting *Shengxuanjing* 昇玄經.

50. This is the Buddhist concept that by accepting gifts one permits the host to accrue merit.

9. When superior and inferior are facing each other, pay sedulous attention to matters of precedence.

10. Do not fear that for those who eat later there will be additions [to] or deletions [from the menu].

一念道恩；二念師恩；三當念眾爲良福田；四當念主人賞別
真僞，能供賢善；五當自慶得在僚隸，備充道流；六當念食
主人意重，勿令眾人輕說美惡，嫌擇不善；七者，主人若設
非法之食，不得令前；八者，若眾中有求非法之食，即便黜
遣，不預食例；九者，上下共相顧望，務盡庠序；十者，無
畏後食，當有增減。

From this list, we can see three points of emphasis in overseeing the kitchen: that status and precedence be observed, that harmony be maintained within the group, and that the rules of the feast, especially the ban on the consumption of meat and smelly foods (*hunhui* 葷穢) referred to obliquely in number 8, be strictly observed.

Let us turn now to the banquet itself. One of the best descriptions of how the kitchen-feast was conducted is found in a passage from the seventh-century *Code of the Thousand Perfected* (*Qianzhen ke* 千真科), preserved in a Tang encyclopedia:[51]

First, [the Supervisor of the Kitchen] personally checks the menu to see that the balance of fruits and vegetables, raw and cooked flavors each is appropriate. Then, he or she examines the time of day by the shadow of the gnomon, or, if the day is cloudy, by reading the clepsydra, in order to determine whether it is the time of the fête. When that time has arrived, he sounds the bell to summon all to eat. Each person sends his or her eating implements into the fête hall. He measures out and places the ranked positions of the seats. When the assembly bell has sounded, he performs a ritual [circumambulation?], praising and requesting. When he is finished praising and requesting, everyone settles into their seats. A course of water is poured, then all commence to eat, with exalted and humble each

51. *Yaoxiu keyi jielü chao* 9/10a–b; *Dongxuan lingbao qianzhenke* 22b–23a. On this text see the entry by Hans-Hermann Schmidt in Schipper and Verellen 2004:1, 576.

in their proper place. He advances and sets down the plate of the Former Master.[52] The Supervisor of the Kitchen kneels upright and raises the plate in front of the seat of the Former Master. The Regulator of the Group sounds the chime once. The [Priest of] Great Virtue at the head of the table chants:

> We present this fête for the Perfected of the Dao and for the race of Daoists, that the Dao Father, the Dao Mother, the Perfected, the Divine, the Transcendents and the Sages, or those who with them pursue the Dao may eat and drink together. May they have long life without limit!

先自檢校廚頭,果菜調和,生熟氣味,並令得所。次看日時圭影,天陰取漏刻,正齋時。齋時至巳,鳴鐘召食。各送食器於齋堂,量坐處位次安置。歛鐘訖,行道歎願。歎願竟,各坐定矣。行水一徧,然始就食,尊卑得緒。前下先師柈。監廚人長跪擎柈於先師座前。節眾人鳴磬子一下。座頭大德祝曰:

> 建齋,爲道真,爲道種、道父、道母、真人、神人、仙人、聖人,或共爲道,同共飲食,長生無極。

After this invocation, the plates are passed, beginning with the seats of the Former Master and the officials in charge of the fête. The servers chant the name of each fruit or dish in a low voice, and the guests hold up their dishes to receive them, taking only what they want to eat. The Priest of Great Virtue at the head of the table is responsible for seeing that each dish makes its way to all of the seats. When all have been served, the Regulator of the Group intones: "Please commence the meal." While food is being distributed, each is offered three times starting from the head seat, and, when the repast is concluded, leftovers are collected from the bottom up. Finally, any leftover grains of rice are collected to be used for the "rice for the masses" (*zhongsheng fan* 眾生飯, see below).

There were detailed and meticulous rules for the conduct of the kitchen-feast, but only a small part of them have come down

52. This "former master" (*xianshi* 先師) is never identified but was probably an empty seat left for founder Zhang Daoling or all preceding Celestial Masters as a group.

to us.[53] These began well before the day of the kitchen. The principal ritual officiants and probably the host as well were supposed to observe a three-day purification ritual, including a fast (*zhai* 齋) and abstention from sex, leading up to the rite and offer a statement of merits three days after its conclusion. The ritual itself was held in the early morning, so participants often assembled the previous evening as we see in this passage from the *Statutes of the Mystic Capital* describing the preparations for an exculpatory kitchen-feast (*jiechu* 解廚):[54]

> Male officers, female officers, register novices, and Daoist citizens: When it is time for an exculpatory kitchen, the head of household purifies himself and observes precepts. The evening before, he invites the guests with words and a calling card. Those who have been invited should all be properly and correctly attired. They should not walk through polluted or defiled areas. All should bathe and wash their hair, and change their skirt, cap, mantel, pants, and tunic. They should not wear skirts, sandals, or revealing robes, showing contemptuous offense to the most perfected. Why is this so? This statute represents the majestic power of the heavenly officers. The gods and transcendents will approach and descend to you. This is no small matter! All should rectify their hearts and visualize [the gods]. You must not speak recklessly or speak of vulgar or other desultory matters.

> 男官、女官、籙生、道民：至於解廚，家主齋戒。宿請客言刺。被請之身，皆嚴整，勿履穢汙。悉沐浴，換易衣裙、幘、褐、袴、褶。不得著裙履露衣，輕冒至真。所以爾者，此律是天官之威，神仙臨降，非小故耶。皆正心存想。不得亂語說流俗不急之事。

The polluted areas to be avoided are places of death like a battle-field, graveyard, or home suffering a recent death as well as menstruating women or other places defiled by blood. The prohibition

---

53. Zhu Faman 朱法滿 (d. 720), the editor of *Yaoxiu keyi jielü chao* (12/1b5), notes that the early-fifth-century *Code of the Great Perfected* contained over ten pages of detailed rules for the kitchen, of which he preserves only a small portion.

54. *Xuandu lüwen* 13b.

would have included the sites of blood sacrifice or other profane rites. Similarly, throughout the rite, participants are encouraged to visualize the Most High and avoid all talk of killing, hunting, fishing, or trapping.[55]

One important principle was hierarchy in the seating arrangement, which was based on rank in the church and then seniority in rank.[56] Only if individuals were ordained to the same rank on the same day was age considered. Surviving passages on seating arrangements, from the late Six Dynasties, include many distinctions that did not exist in the early church, but they do stress the importance of maintaining the proper order of precedence in interactions between Daoists in the upper, middle, and lower seats.[57] Always external ranking and secular office are discounted; status in Celestial Master Daoism was determined solely by rank and date of ordination.

Matters of etiquette were also strictly regulated. The goal was a ritual meal that was simple yet dignified with harmonious interactions appropriate to each individual's station. After all have taken their seats in the proper order, there is to be no talking or laughing, and they should observe the following rules:[58]

> When eating, there is to be no smacking of lips, nor sounds of merriment in drinking, nor spitting, nor burping, nor any clacking of spoons or chopsticks.
>
> 食時，亦不鳴唇，亦無歡飲之聲，亦不咯唾，亦不申聲吐氣，亦不驚匙打筋。

It was also improper to ask for a dish before it has reached one's seat. The Supervisor of the Kitchen alone had the authority to

55. *Yaoxiu keyi jielü chao* 12/2a7–8. If violated, both the host and the guest will suffer three years of ill health.

56. This resembles the rules for banqueting in the Village Wine Drinking described in the *Record of Rites*, where civil rank took precedence over age. See *Liji*, chapter 4; Kleeman 2005b:145.

57. *Zhengyi weiyijing* 5a.

58. *Yaoxiu keyi jielü chao* 9/10b5–7.

make requests of the staff. Those who arrived late were not permitted to enter the feast hall, and anyone who, having eaten to satiety, arose before the formal conclusion of the meal was said to have "startled all in their seats and offended the group" (*jingzuo chuzhong* 驚座觸眾). Eaters were also cautioned to avoid eating more than they had been allotted, not to delay the dishes while they were passed, and not to take too much so that those in the lower seats would not have enough; each of these actions is characterized as "stealing."[59]

After all the remains of the food had been collected, there was one round of alcoholic drinks and one round of water, then the Regulator of the Group would sound the chime once and chant, "This fête-meal has concluded." Then all would leave the hall in order, holding their eating vessels, beginning with the Priest of Great Virtue at the head of the table. All were supposed to return to their rooms to wash up.

The division of the leftovers seems to have been a matter of some consequence. Again it is the Regulator of the Group who had the responsibility of sounding his chime and announcing to all three times:[60]

> I inform everyone: These leftovers from the feast will be available to the host for his unrestricted use. Those who agree, remain silent. Those who disagree, speak up.
>
> 大眾：齋餘長食，充主人無礙用。同者默然，不同者說。

Then anyone who had a special need to feed a parent, teacher, or someone suffering from old age or illness could claim a portion of the leftovers to take home.

The grains of rice collected at the end of the banquet had a special use. Each participant was to set aside seven grains of rice, which was called the Rice for the Masses or the Rice of the Divine Farmer (*shennong fan* 神農飯). To the Daoists, the Divine Farmer,

59. *Yaoxiu keyi jielü chao* 9/13a4–8, citing the *Code of the Thousand Perfected*.
60. *Yaoxiu keyi jielü chao* 9/11a1–2.

also known as the Perfected Who Circulated the Dao (*xingdao zhenren* 行道真人), was ordered at the beginning of the cosmos to taste each plant and tree to discover which could nourish human life. It is out of gratitude for this selfless act that Daoists contribute seven grains of rice, in the belief that each grain can feed a person for a thousand days. Each participant is to intone three magical chants while collecting the seven grains in order to effect this transformation.[61]

Holding these regular feasts at a time when famine was common raised another question for the Daoists: what to do about nonbelievers who came seeking to partake of their bounty. Daoists were famous for their charity; even the standard histories record their "charity huts" that provided emergency food to travelers. But here they had an additional concern, the proper conduct of the kitchen rite.[62]

> If some of the profane come during a fête begging for food, the Supervisor of the Kitchen must ask them if they can observe the fête or not.[63] If they observe the fête, give them food. If they cannot observe the fête, he should [not give them food but instead] explain to them in detail the workings of karma so that they know the source of sin and blessings. This is not because one begrudges the food but in order to make them reflect and understand. To reverently observe the Way of the Dao is the number one compassion. If you do not reveal these words, the masses will accumulate sins.
>
> 若是齋時，俗人來乞食者，監廚之人，即須借問能齋以不。若能齋，與食；若不能齋，深示因果，使知罪福，非爲怯惜，欲令返悟，謹守道法，是第一慈，若不示語，衆生得罪。

61. *Yaoxiu keyi jielü chao* 9/12a. These chants refer to the Supreme Purity Heaven and hence must have been written or edited no earlier than the late fourth century. It may be that this practice of collecting the Rice for the Masses is no earlier. It is in conception similar to Buddhist rites to feed hell beings and other unfortunate souls. The same source continues (9/12b1–5) with two chants to be pronounced when eating morning gruel and another for when rinsing the mouth.
62. *Yaoxiu keyi jielü chao* 9/13b2–5.
63. Presumably, this means observing all the rules of the kitchen, including the limitation on alcohol and the prohibition of meat and sharp flavors.

Thus, the primary function of the kitchen-feast was not nutrition but a communal meal with one's fellow Daoists and some Daoist divinities. It was a ritual unto itself requiring purification rites for kitchen officers beforehand and a statement of merits afterward to thank all the gods and their servants who attended and helped to make it a success. Everyone who participated had to conform to strict rules as to both what they ate and how they ate it, so participation in the rite was sure to win merit. For the host, who bore the primary expense, the rite was either a celebration of an auspicious event that had already occurred or a prayer for some change in the fate of the host or his or her family.

The kitchen provided an alternative to the petition ritual within the early Celestial Master repertoire, less formal than the petition but incorporating merit-making acts on behalf of the client. It did not permit the detailed manipulation of the celestial bureaucracy afforded by the petition, but it did accommodate simpler requests for supernatural protection, healing, or blessings. The function of the kitchen-feast eventually came to be displaced by more elaborate rituals termed Fasts (*zhai* 齋) or Offerings (*jiao* 醮), which incorporated a feast at the end of their ritual program with many of the same rules and procedures as the kitchen. Zhu Faman, writing in the early eighth century, notes that the rite was already rare in his day.[64] We can see in this development a movement away from the universal priesthood of the early church toward a religion of religious professionals with only occasional contact with lay adherents.

64. *Yaoxiu keyi jielü chao* 12/1a5.

SEVEN

The Novice

Many, perhaps most, members of the early Daoist church were Daoist citizens, who undertook three basic precepts and participated in communal rites. As we have seen, such citizens maintained their own ritual space, the oratory, and were responsible for the performance of specific rituals each day and periodically through the year. A sizable proportion of Daoist community members took a further step toward greater participation in the church by becoming novices, who were dubbed "register students" (*lusheng* 籙生). Novices were Daoist priests-in-training. If they completed their course of study, these men and women would becomes masters, responsible for their own groups of citizens and novices, and eventually might come to have their own parishes or even ascend to one of the more exalted offices of the church.[1]

Although one could enter the novitiate at any age, and those who committed a serious infraction of Daoist rules sometimes had to begin the entire process again after climbing well up the ladder of ranks, it seems likely that most novices began their studies as children. Chinese in general considered the age of seven, usually corresponding to six by modern Western counting, to be the age when a child was first able to tell right from wrong and take responsibility for his or her own actions. This was also

---

1. These church offices were marked by conferral of a system of twenty-four Inner Registers, studied by Lagerwey (2005).

the age when one could become a novice. Novices set out on a path that led to direct contact with the exalted deities of the cosmos as well as a variety of lesser spirits, so it was a serious matter, not undertaken lightly.

The Register

The register (*lu* 籙) is first recorded as a document of cosmic significance bestowed on a chosen ruler as a mark of Heaven's favor.[2] For Daoists, however, the register was a document bestowed by a Daoist libationer, written on a long piece of undyed silk and worn at the waist (*peidai* 佩帶).[3] We have seen that a Daoist citizen could gain a parish register by accepting one or more sets of precepts governing his or her conduct. In this chapter I will review the outer registers (*wailu* 外籙) that marked the progress of a Daoist adherent on the way to becoming a libationer or a Daoist priest in charge of a parish. After attaining the status of libationer, one could still be promoted to higher office, first exchanging one's parish for a higher one, then seeking service in the church hierarchy, which was marked by possession of an inner register (*neilu* 內籙). The primary function of a register was to verify the status of an individual within the church, but each new rank was paired with a more complex and demanding set of precepts to be observed. New rank also granted access to higher and more powerful rituals (*fa* 法), which were recorded in scriptures (*jing* 經) and required esoteric talismans (*fu* 符) to activate them. Those registers were sometimes

2. This function of registers in Han apocrypha and classical texts has been explored by Anna Seidel (1983).

3. The Dunhuang manuscript S.203 says that, upon receiving the register, one is to *raoyao santong* 繞腰三通. Schipper understood this to mean that one wrapped it around the waist three times, but Lagerwey thinks that one just passed it around the waist. See Schipper 1985:132; Lagerwey 2005:57. The *Ritual for the Transmission of the Director of Merit Plaque* says that the plaque of the Controller of Merit is placed in a yellow patterned bag 黃紋袋 in the same place as the parish register (*Zhengyi fawen chuan dugongban yi* 正一法文傳都功版儀 2a). This would support Lagerwey's view.

referred to as "scripture, precept, and talisman registers" (*jingjie-fulu*) or "scripture, precept, and ritual registers" (*jingjiefalu*).[4]

As a sacred object conveying access to esoteric texts, talismans, and rituals, the register was the focus of many rules and taboos. This passage from the *Protocol of the Outer Registers* lays out some of them:[5]

The text should be constantly worn at the waist and only removed temporarily. If there is a chance it will be dirtied, you can take it off yourself. Hide the register in a clean place, and be sure not to lose it! If you lose it, there will be punishments as in the ritual code. If you damage it or change it, cleanse it according to the rite. If man and wife both belong to the Dao, [their sexual congress] is not defiling. Wear it and visualize its [officers]; it is even more impermissible to take it off. If you take it off to indulge in licentious behavior, this will further increase the severity of the interrogation.[6] If you enter other [i.e., profane] places, areas of misfortune and death, where you are threatened by demons and bandits, always wear it, and do not remove it. The gods enter into your body; they do not exist on the silk [document]. With the register and talisman[s] on your body, you should keep your master in your heart. Wear it and never abandon it to strengthen your loyalty and integrity. If there is a death or a birth, or you in traveling happen upon a defiled place, always perform an exculpatory exorcism, according to the esoteric teaching of the Most High.

文常佩身，唯欲蹔脫。若兼參染，自可脫之，秘籙淨處，勿令去失。去失有罰，依案科儀。穿壞改易，淨之如法。夫妻同道，非爲淫穢，帶之存之，彌不可脫。脫之爲淫，更增重考。若入餘處凶喪之間，危險鬼賊，恆佩勿脫。神入體中，不存素上。籙符在身，存師在心，帶之不捨，以堅忠信。若有喪產，及行出觸穢，皆即解除，依太上祕教。

4. For the first term, see *Zhengyi weiyijing* 3b; for the second, see *Dongxuan lingbao sandong fengdao kejie yingshi* 5/2b. An example is the *Chuanshou sandong jingjie falu lüeshuo* of Zhang Wanfu.

5. *Zhengyi fawen taishang wailu yi* 11b.

6. Such interrogations were conducted by the Heavenly Bureaus at the Assemblies and when one was being considered for promotion and by the Three Offices after death.

From this we see that pollution was a major concern for early Daoists, but the register could have a prophylactic function in tainted locations. Sexual congress was not defiling as long as it was practiced according to the Merging the Pneumas rite, with its visualization of Daoist deities and pneumas. The register could be temporarily removed for a trip to the privy but had to be stored in a secure, clean location. Even though the register spirits actually existed within the body of the bearer, loss of the physical register was a major disaster. The bearer was as a result reduced to the most basic Renewed Mandate register (described below) and fined according to the level of the register lost:[7]

All those who lose the Renewed Mandate Register are fined five bundles of firewood, three ounces of vermilion [paste for impressing seals], and must offer a "feeding the worthies" feast for three people. [This is a mid-level kitchen.] Those who lose the One General Register are to be fined half a cart of firewood, four ounces of vermilion, and a feeding the worthies feast for five. Those who lose the Ten Generals Register are to be fined one cartload of firewood, five ounces of vermilion, and a feeding the worthies feast for ten. Those who lose the Seventy-Five Generals Register are to be fined two carts of firewood, seven ounces of vermilion, and a feeding the worthies feast for fifty. Those who lose a One Hundred Fifty Generals Register are to be fined three carts of firewood, nine ounces of vermilion, and a feeding the worthies feast for one hundred. Those who lose the Three Officers to the One Hundred Fifty Generals Register, after paying the fine, may receive the Renewed Mandate Register. They can advance according to their merit. If there is one of unusual merit and outstanding virtue, his early promotion is to be determined by the master. In all cases, after paying the fine, the person should bring statements and give pledge offerings just as when they were beginning.

凡失更令，罰薪五束，朱三兩，飯賢三人。皆中廚也。失一將軍，薪半車，朱四兩，飯賢五人。失十將軍，薪一車，朱五兩，飯賢十人。失七十五將軍，薪二車，朱七兩，飯賢五十人。失百五十將軍，薪三車，朱九兩，飯賢百人。失三官至百五十將軍皆

7. *Zhengyi fawen taishang wailu yi* 13a–b.

輸罰畢得受更令，隨功進，若有殊功異德，超復由師。凡輸罰後
操辭送信皆如初。

We cannot ascertain the frequency with which Daoists lost
their registers, but it must have been a significant problem for
them. The last six documents in the *Protocol of the Outer Registers*,
comprising six of twenty-nine pages or around one-fifth of the
text, deal with various situations related to the loss of a register.
Losing an upper-level register, for example, meant a hefty fine plus
the resubmission of all the pledge offerings while working one's
way back up to one's previous position. The responsibilities of the
novice toward his or her master are detailed in the appendix to
this chapter. Let us turn now to the various types of outer registers and their functions.

The first register Daoist children might receive was called the
"renewed mandate" (*gengling* 更令).[8] This register was supposed
to indicate that the child had received the perfected pneumas and
would act in obedience to the dictates of Heaven's mandate for
them (*bing zhenqi shun ming shixing* 稟真氣順命施行). Each
register listed the titles of spirits who could protect and do the
bidding of the wearer, which in the case of the Renewed Mandate register was only nine clerks and soldiers.[9] Still, this was an
important protection; if a child was troubled from birth by many
ailments, the parents could receive it on the child's behalf so that
he or she would have some protection against evil influences. This
register also served to record the child's name with the celestial
bureaucrats and gave him or her the right to enter the oratory or
parish, perform an abbreviated ritual of obeisance, and announce
an urgent need or beg for mercy.[10] If an adult committed a serious
breach of ethics or lost the physical register, he or she would be
reduced to this rank and forced to work his or her way back up

8. See *Yaoxiu keyi jielü chao* 10/5b.
9. One possible referent for these nine officers is the gods of the nine palaces
in the head, as pointed out in Tao Hongjing's commentary to *Dengzhen yinjue*
3/3b.
10. *Yaoxiu keyi jielü chao* 6a5–7, quoting the *Taizhenke*.

through the hierarchy. In this case, the same register was referred to by a slightly different name indicating "extended obedience."[11]

The second register, also received as a child, was the One General Register. It comprised one general together with his cohort of clerks and soldiers. Although the child was ignorant when this register was first received, he or she gradually learned the mystic teachings. An early-fifth-century text tells us that, once you have received the One General Register, "demons will not dare to wantonly kill people."[12] With the help of the officers transmitted through this register, including merit officers, emissaries of the general, his clerks and soldiers, and jade women, the Daoist is, according to the *Protocol for the Inspection of the Register*, supposed to "aid the state by promoting moral transformation and destroy evil so that the supreme Dao will be forever dominant" (*zhuguo xinghua jianmie xionge zhidao chang xing* 助國行化翦滅凶惡至道長興).[13] It is unclear if this register, sometimes referred to as the "Adolescent One General Register," was ever conferred on adults.[14]

Next is the Ten Generals Register. Sources sometimes speak of this as an adolescent register but other times specify that one must be an adult of twenty *sui* to receive it.[15] Its conferral indicated greater abilities and responsibilities. One salient difference: with the Ten Generals Register, the novice received the clerk who delivered petitions to Heaven so that, beginning with this rank, novices

11. The characters remained the same but were read in a different tone. The initial register was, in modern terms, called *gēnglìng*, whereas the replacement register was called *gènglíng*. William Baxter of the University of Michigan (personal communication, August 2009) helped me understand the significance of the *fanqie* spelling provided by the Tang editor Zhu Faman.

12. *Taishang dongyuan shenzhou jing* 7/9a.

13. *Taishang zhengyi yuelu yi* 4b. The functions cited for the following registers are all found here.

14. In the Dunhuang manuscript S.203, studied by Lü Pengzhi (2006), it seems that adults regularly move directly from the Gengling to the Ten Generals Register.

15. See *Taishang sanwu zhengyi mengwei lu* 1a and *Jiao sandong zhenwen wufa zhengyi mengwei lu licheng yi* 13a for the former, *Yaoxiu keyi jielü chao* 10/5b for the latter.

were able to externalize their body gods and employ them to do their bidding.[16] A novice with this rank could therefore submit petitions on behalf of a client (see fig. 7), though presumably the scope of the petition and the gods it called on would be limited. The *Protocol for the Inspection of the Register* says that it allows the bearer to "behead evildoers and reward the good; a myriad requests will be answered as one wishes" 斬惡賞善，萬願隨心.

The Seventy-Five Generals Register was normally awarded to adults. It marked a certain degree of completion, in the sense that one received all of the heavenly soldiers of a certain type. From the One General Register, one would receive either Transcendent Officer (*xianguan* 仙官) or Numinous Officer (*lingguan* 靈官) spirits; reaching this register, one would have a full complement of that type. The distinction between the two types is not completely clear in our sources, as we see in this passage from the *Code of the Great Perfected*:[17]

As for the Seventy-Five [Generals] Register, there are Transcendent and Numinous types. The yin pneumas are Transcendent; the yang pneumas are Numinous. The Numinous are in charge of Earth while the Transcendent are in charge of Heaven. Heaven is in charge of the civil; Earth is in charge of the martial. The martial is in charge of the internal, while the civil is in charge of the external. If one is nurtured within the master's gate and learns from fellow Daoists there, that person should first receive the Numinous Officers; if one lives outside the master's gate, visiting and calling upon others, that person should first receive the Transcendent Officers. After receiving the Transcendent Officers, one should advance and receive the Numinous Officers; after receiving the Numinous Officers, one should advance and receive the Transcendent Officers, so that when added to the previous group it equals one hundred fifty, the register's full complement.

七十五籙，有仙有靈。陰氣仙，陽氣靈。靈主地，仙主天。天主
文，地主武。武主內，文主外。若弘在師門內，伏膺左右，先受

16. See Ōfuchi 1991:382, citing *Dongxuan lingbao sanding fengdao kejie yingshi* 10/5a.

17. *Yaoxiu keyi jielü chao* 10/5b–6a, citing the *Taizhenke*.

FIGURE 7. Detail of a modern painting showing the spirit emissary of the Daoist priest (depicted on the cover) delivering a petition to the Three Officers (*sanguan* 三官). Novices holding the Ten Generals Register or above could send up petitions in this way. Personal collection of Patrice Fava.

靈；在師門外，去來諮稟，先受仙。受仙後，進受靈，受靈後，進
受仙，足前爲百五十，籙滿足也。

One prominent theory[18] is that the two types of register spirits are intended for male and female register students, but in this list the associations do not show a clear correlation. According to traditional views, we would expect males to be associated with yang, Heaven, martial, and outer, but instead transcendent spirits are associated with yin, Heaven, civil, and outer, whereas numinous spirits are associated with yang, earth, martial, and inner. Zhang Wanfu gives a simpler account, saying that the Transcendent Officers are yang and for men, whereas the Numinous Officers are yin and for females; their union, presumably through the Merging the Pneumas rite (see below), produces the Transcendent and Numinous [Officer] One Hundred Fifty Generals Register.[19]

The One Hundred Fifty Generals Register marks the culmination of the outer registers. Investment with this register qualified one for the title of libationer and permitted one to act as a master to households. The *Protocol for the Inspection of the Register* says the spirits of this register empower one to "repel the heterodox men and demons of the four quarters so that disaster and harm are forever extinguished" 辟斥四方不正人鬼，禍害永消. The register comprises seventy-five generals of each type, Transcendent and Numinous. Some sources suggest that this is accomplished by the addition to one's existing Seventy-Five Generals Register of another of the opposite type, but the petition for promotion to the One Hundred Fifty Generals Register translated in the following section indicates that the original register spirits of the Seventy-Five Generals Register are promoted to higher posts, and a new set of mixed spirits is bestowed upon the novice. There is some controversy as to the significance of this register. Schipper, followed by Lü Pengzhi, argues that this conferral was accompanied by the initial performance of the Merging the Pneumas rite of sexual union and that it was effectively a marriage ceremony,

18. E.g., Lü Pengzhi 2006:90.
19. *Chuanshou sandong jingjie falu lüeshuo* 1/3b. Cited in Schipper 1985:132.

uniting a male and a female novice bearing, respectively, Transcendent and Numinous officer registers.[20] There is some evidence for this view in the *Protocol of the Outer Registers*, which speaks of a "mystic dispensation" in connection with this register, but other roughly contemporaneous sources, including those translated below, do not seem to bear out this interpretation.[21] It is possible that such a connection existed at one point in church history, or perhaps in one specific region, but existing sources do not seem capable of resolving this controversy. I will trace the career of the libationer after conferral of this register in the next chapter.

Ordination

A formal ritual of ordination was required for entry into the ranks of novices. This was one of the most widespread rituals in the Celestial Master church and one of the most long-lasting. Two early sources survive that speak about it in detail. The first, in the Daoist canon, is the *Protocol of the Outer Registers*. It collects together a variety of forms to be used in ordination rites, including the actual petition requesting a new ordination rank, but also forms for the Declaration of Merits (*yangong* 言功) that should follow each rite in order to repay all those otherworldly officials who aided in the submission of a petition as well as documents giving thanks after the successful completion of a rite. The second source is an undated and untitled Dunhuang manuscript in the Stein collection, S.203, which has been studied at some length by Maruyama Hiroshi (1990) and Lü Pengzhi (2006).[22] Like the

20. Schipper 1985:131–32; Lü Pengzhi 2006:92–94. Lü points out that Yang Liansheng (1956:21) had already suggested that the Dual Advance Register (*bingjinlu* 並進籙) mentioned by Kou Qianzhi involved men and women uniting in the Merging the Pneumas rite.

21. See *Zhengyi fawen taishang wailu yi* 6a7. Note that this term occurs in the Zhang Pu stele of 173 and elsewhere, as discussed in chapter 2.

22. The selection by Schipper (1985) and Lü (2006) of a line in the middle of the document (*du xianling lu yi* 度仙靈錄儀) as its title is mere conjecture, as is Lü's further identification (2006:79, 83–85) of the manuscript as a quote from

Protocol, this text includes several forms for ritual petitions but also gives detailed instructions on the performance of the rituals through which these documents are to be submitted to the heavenly bureaucrats. I will summarize the course of the ritual and translate a sample of the ritual documents,[23] but first note the formal procedure to be followed in requesting a new register described in the following short passage from the *Correct Unity Scripture of Solemn Deportment*:[24]

> All those who wish to receive the Dao should first proceed to their master's door and sincerely pray, bowing down. If the master agrees to submit a Statement, requesting the various scriptures, precepts, talismans, and registers, write it out according to the rules. Grain for the fast, tokens of faith, ritual garb, and ritual implements should all be prepared. Then ascend the altar to make the announcement, tearing the contract and breaking the covenant,[25] setting out your Statement and self-description. You should always choose a day in the next month; it must not be too frequent or easily agreed to with just a nod.

---

a lost text cited by Zhang Wanfu, the *Zhengyi fawen dulu duzhi yi* 正一法文度籙度治儀. The text is rather a prime example of the type of pragmatic handbook maintained by every Daoist priest for use in ritual and transmitted through the ages from teacher to disciple. There is no reason to think that such a manuscript was copied from one of the few later scriptures whose names were recorded in Tang encyclopedias. Instead, in those sources, one random example of such a handbook from a specific Daoist lineage came into the hands of a later author and was recorded with a specific title that may well have been created at the time of its recording. The manuscript is of Tang date since it reflects the taboo on the personal name of Tang Taizong (r. 626–49) in omitting a stroke in the character *min* 民.

23. The following exposition follows closely the explanation of Lü Pengzhi 2006:103, with modifications based on my own examination of Dunhuang manuscript S.203 in May 2013. See also the exposition in Lagerwey 2005:49–59, which differs from my understanding in several respects.

24. *Zhengyi weiyi jing* 4a.

25. There are scattered references to these contracts and covenants, which were broken in half and half sent to the Heavenly Bureaus, but there is still much we do not understand about their use and function. For an account of the origins of contracts, see Bumbacher 2012:18–21. For one list of the contracts, see *Yaoxiu keiyi jielü chao* 10/7a–b, citing the *Taizhenke*.

凡欲受道，先詣師門，丹禱拜伏。師許投辭，請經戒符籙，書寫
如法。齋糧質信，法衣法物，並備具已。然後登壇啓告，裂券斷
盟，列辭自狀，皆當揀日隔月，不得頻繁，及默許易從。

Thus preparation had to begin at least a month in advance and
depended on the agreement of the parish master. The transmission
was not merely of a register but also of the scriptures and precepts
that accompanied it. Even today transmission from Daoist priest
to disciple is carried on in a similar way, with the priest lending the
disciple the sacred text from which the disciple then makes a personal copy. The Daoist's own copy is burned or buried with him on
his death.[26] The novice must also compose the Statement, a simple
request giving the exact details of his or her native place, age, and
name as well as those of the officiant and any guarantors. The beginning of S.203 is missing but may originally have included some
of these preparations, including the ritual purification during which
meat, sharp-flavored herbs, and sex are avoided.

The ritual commences in the male or female officiant's oratory or parish in a two-stage process.[27] The first day, at either
midnight or noon, the officiant presents a placard (*ci* 刺) notifying
the Heavenly Bureaus of the rite of ordination to be held the next
day. The main ritual was held at dawn on the following day and
involved the submission of a petition (*zhang* 章) that formally requested the conferral of a specific cohort of divine generals, clerks,
and soldiers to the aspirant and their investiture in his or her body.
Both rituals also refer to a tag (*die* 牒), which was a smaller wooden
document listing the names and vital information of the officiant
and aspirant participating in the ritual.[28] Since the two rites are

26. See Schipper 1993:59–60, which is based on Schipper's own apprentice-
ship with a Daoist family in Tainan, Taiwan.

27. The fact that the manuscript is addressed to Daoist priests yet refers to the
site of the ritual as the oratory may mean that by the Tang the parish had become
only a notional ranking system and no longer referred to a distinct building.

28. In the bamboo strips found at Zhangjiashan, *die* is a counter for bamboo
strips, but by this time it may refer to a somewhat larger piece of wood. See
strip 228 of the *Zouyanshu* 奏讞書 in Peng Hao et al. 2007:381. I am indebted
to Michael Lüdke for this reference.

closely parallel, I will first set out the announcement liturgy and then note how it differs from the actual rite of conferral.

The announcement ritual begins when the officiant enters the oratory or parish, offers incense three times, and clacks the teeth, also known as the drums of Heaven (*tiangu* 天鼓), three times to enlist the attention of the spirits. The officiant sings a hymn, "The Most High Mysterious Primordial," which invokes the supreme Celestial Master deity, the Most High Lord Lao. Lü Pengzhi argues convincingly that this is an abbreviated reference to the Uncovering the Incense Burner (*falu* 發爐) rite, which establishes communications with the Heavens.[29] A version of this chant, which Lü argues was influenced by southern occult traditions during the fourth century, is preserved in Tao Hongjing's *Hidden Instructions for Ascending to Perfection*:[30]

> Most High Mysterious and Primordial Lord Lao of the Five Numina: Summon the merit officers and emissaries, the Dragon and Tiger Lords of the Left and Right, the Incense-Bearing Emissaries, and the orthodox gods of the Three Pneumas to quickly ascend and announce to the Most High Mysterious and Primordial Lord of the Dao of the Three Heavens: "I am about to burn incense and enter the oratory for an audience with the gods. I beg that the orthodox pneumas of the Eight Directions be permitted to enter into my body. May that which I announce be rapidly submitted and delivered directly before the Thearch."[31]

太上玄元五靈老君，當召功曹、使者，左右龍虎君，捧香使者，三炁正神，急上關啓三天太上玄元道君：某正爾燒香，入靜朝神。乞得八方正氣來入某身，所啓速聞，徑達帝前。

This is followed by a rite called the Exteriorization of Officers (*chuguan* 出官). It begins with the officiant visualizing (*cun* 存) a

29. See the article by Poul Andersen in Pregadio 2008: 1, 400–401.
30. *Dengzhen yinjue* 3/22b; see Lü Pengzhi 2006:106.
31. In a note to this passage, Tao Hongjing identifies this figure as the Thearch Lord of the Heaven of Great Tenuity 太微天帝君. Parallel texts in other sources record other deities, like the Most Perfected Limitless Dao 至真無極道 found in *Zhengyi zhijiao zhaiyi* 1a, which may in fact be earlier.

huge host of divine representatives emerging from his or her body while chanting:

> I respectfully exteriorize the merit officer and clerk[s] of the Perfected Officer of the Five Appendages[32] within my body, the On-Duty Correct Unity Merit Officer for Healing Disease of the Upper Transcendent and Upper Numinous two [types of] officers, the emissaries of the Officers of the Left and Right, the male and female Clerks for Divine Determination, the Clerk of the Cargo Cart Red Talisman, the Clerk of the Strong Wind Post-Rider, and the Petition-Submitting Post Horseman clerk; let two of each emerge.

謹出臣身中五體真官功曹吏，[出上仙上靈二官直使正][33]一治病功曹官各二人，出左右官使者、陰陽[神決吏、科車赤符吏]、剛風騎置（吏）、驛馬上章吏官各二人出。

The officiant is warned at this point to make sure that each divine officer is visualized with a solemn expression on his or her face, dressed in clearly differentiated ritual garb. Details of their appearance follow:

> The merit officer assigned for deployment is capped[34] with a Vermilion Sunlight turban, wears a [Piercing Heaven hat, and is robed in a singlet of black silk], He wears a dragonhead sword on his belt and carries a log of visitors.[35] The Correct Unity Merit Officer wears a Vermilion Sunlight turban and a singlet with scarlet designs; he has a tiger talisman belted at the waist. All hold jade tablets. The [emissaries of the] Officers of the Left and Right wear Nine Virtues hats,

32. Lagerwey (2005:55), without comment, takes this to refer to the five viscera, but normally it means the arms, legs, and head. It occurs in many early Buddhist sources as well as the mid-sixth-century *Luoyang qielanji* 洛陽伽藍記. See T2092 *Luoyang qielanji* 51/1019a18.

33. Characters in square brackets are missing in the manuscript. Here I supply slightly different characters from those suggested by Lü Pengzhi, based on usages in Celestial Master rather than Lingbao texts. See, for example, *Shangqing huangshu guoduyi* 2b10.

34. Following Lü. The character in manuscript 6040 is a textual variant composed of *mou* ㄙ over *gan* 干.

35. The variant character is a grass radical over *chuan* 傳 or *fu* 傳.

wear Shining Light swords belted at the waist, and hold a banner and a tally. [The merit officers on duty for deployment stand on four sides]; the Correct Unity Merit Officer stands in the middle; the emissary of the Officer of the Left stands holding a banner in the [front; the emissary of the Officer of the Right] stands with the tally upright in the rear; the male Clerk for Divine Determination stands on the left; the female Clerk for Divine Determination stands on the right.

直使功曹弁朱陽之幘戴通[天之冠，衣皂紈單衣]，帶龍頭之劍，持謁簿。正一功曹著朱[陽之幘，衣]絳章單衣。腰帶虎符，齊執玉板。左右官[使者]戴九德之冠，腰帶明光之劍，持幢執節。[直使功曹住立四]方，正一功曹住立中央。左官使者持幢在[前，右官使者]建節在後，陽神決吏立左，陰神決吏立右。

It is unclear to me if these are instructions for the edification of the officiant or if they were actually read as part of the ritual. Either way, they give us rare insight into the visualizations that accompanied the rite. Next the officiant instructs these exteriorized spirits to inform a group of high Daoist deities as to the nature of the ritual to be performed. Some of the spirits must carry with them small writing tables as well as brushes in case they need to correct errors in the petition on the spot:

Pick up the jade writing table and, receiving the words mouthed by your servant, separately announce them to the Perfected Officers, Pneuma Injectors, and inspectors of the local province, county, township, and neighborhood as well as the Lord, General[s], and Clerks of Investigation and Summoning, the Equanimity Lords of the Left and Right Capitals, the Marquis Lords of the Left and Right Capitals, the Left and Right Tiger-Rushing Leaders, the Stewards of the Central Palace, the Lords of the Eight Limits of All Heaven, Law-Enforcing Clerks of the Heavenly August, the various Lords of the Sexagenary Cycle,[36] the Ministers of Indentured Servants of the Four Bureaus, and the retainers of capital officials. May the lords on the left[37] serially inform, the clerks on the right announce in

36. It seems unlikely there is room for the *jiazi* inserted by Lü.
37. Following Lü in omitting the extraneous *you* 右 on the basis of examples cited in his note 276.

order, and the lords of the various offices serially deliver [this peti-
tion], all distinguished by rank, submitting it reverently to the Celestial Master, the Inheriting Master, and the Connecting Master as
well as the female Master Lords who are their spouses and to the
lords, generals, clerks, and soldiers in their service and the lords,
generals, and clerks of the twenty-four parishes, beginning with
Yangping and Lutang.

擎持玉案，銜受臣口中辭語，分別關啓此間厶州縣里中真官、注
炁、監察、考召君將吏、左右都平君、左右都侯君、左右虎
賁將、中宮謁者、周天八極君、天皇執法吏、甲子諸官君、四部
司隸、都官從事。左君歷關，右吏次啓，諸官君歷第，皆以次分
別，謹上啓天師、嗣師[38]、係師、女師君夫人，門下君將吏等、
陽平鹿堂廿四治官君將吏。

The officiant, having exteriorized the gods within his or her
body and commanded them to notify the higher Daoist deities
of the impending ceremony, then goes on to introduce the candidate, relating the province, commandery, county, township, and
village from which he or she hails, identifying his or her rank in
the church as a male or female citizen or novice of a certain age.
Then comes the formal request to the gods:

Now he or she has come to your servant requesting a register of
_____ generals of _____ type. I reverently submit a petition/
placard, on a single sheet, for conferral of a register, which is on the
jade table in this oratory. I request that you with the merit officers
and emissaries verify and inspect this. Your servant reverently and
obeisantly reads this to inform you. _____ kowtows and kneels
with neck outstretched on the ground, facing the petition/placard
in accordance with the rite.

今詣臣求受某官如干將軍籙[39]。謹拜單紙度籙章/刺一通，在此靜
中玉案上。請與功曹、使者對共平省。臣謹伏讀關聞。某叩頭稽
顙伏地，當章/刺如法。

38. Following Lü in excising the extraneous *nüshi* 女師.
39. Lü mistakenly transcribes this character and the same character in the
next sentence as *lu* 錄. The two characters are often confused.

Next the officiant performs the Handling the Placard or Handling the Petition (*cao ci/zhang* 操刺/章) rite. He or she reads the placard (or petition) and clacks the teeth three times, then instructs the perfected officers of the body together with their clerks and twelve writing aides to don formal dress, grind ink, and wet their writing brushes in preparation for their ascent to the Three Heavens. There they will be prepared to correct any mistaken characters and supplement any that have been omitted, observing the progress of the document through the Heavens and making sure that it reaches the appropriate official without being rejected by higher administrators. They are further charged with making sure that the heavenly officers of the register are dispatched in a timely fashion and in the number requested. While the spirits perform this act, the officiant is to crouch on the ground and hold his or her breath. The officiant performs a complex visualization while crouching, in which he or she personally ascends to Heaven to see the petition or placard delivered; since this is internal to the libationer, we will examine it in greater detail in the next chapter.[40]

When the rite is completed, the spirit emissaries are invited to return to their palace offices in the Return of the Officers (*fuguan* 復官) rite:

Your servant has completed the memorialization of information. May the Perfected Officers of the Five Limbs, the merit officers, emissaries, generals, clerks, and soldiers exteriorized from my body all return, entering from the Gate of All Mysteries.[41] Return to within your servant's body and do not leave; do not confuse left or right. Merit officers, emissaries, generals, clerks, and soldiers, each

40. Chang Chaojan (2010) has argued that the earliest Celestial Master rituals did not involve the officiant personally ascending to Heaven, and the visualization referred to here does include some later figures, but it seems likely that this practice was established at least by the end of the fourth century. See chapter 8 for a translation of the visualization rite.

41. The *Yuqing wuji zongzhen Wenchang dadong xianjing* (9/16a) of 1311 identifies this gate with the Hundred Meetings (*baihui* 百會) acupuncture point at the top of the head.

should return to the Central Palace, and to his or her golden hall or jade compartment, there to await your servant's future summons to emerge again and do service, all in accord with former precedents.

臣關奏事竟。所出身中五體真官功曹使者將軍吏兵悉還。從眾妙門而入，還臣中身無離，左右無令錯互。功曹使者、將軍吏兵悉還中宮，各復金堂玉室，須臣後召，復出奉行，一如故事。

After chanting this passage, the officiant again crouches on the ground, clacks his or her teeth three times, then, slightly raising the head, breathes in slowly and swallows the pneumas three times, then bows twice. This marks the end of the Return of the Officers. The officiant then clacks his or her teeth three times and performs the Covering the Incense Burner rite, which is not described. A simple version is preserved in the *Ritual of Initiation of the Yellow Book*:[42]

Let the various officers of the contracts and commands and the various gods of the six Jia, which your servant/maidservant previously exteriorized, having performed their services to the Dao this day, return to the Central Palace.

臣妾所出契令諸官六甲諸神，日行道事，還入中宮。

This concludes the presentation of the placard. This cycle of rites, Uncovering the Incense Burner followed by the Exteriorization of Officers, then the presentation of a petition or other document, followed by the Return of the Officers and Covering the Incense Burner, forms the basic structure of almost all Daoist rituals even today.

The next morning at dawn, the Daoists reconvene to present the formal petition for ordination and to transfer the register together with its complement of divine soldiers. Because the ritual is held at dawn, the first matter of business is the Entering the Oratory rite involving the audience rituals discussed in the previous chapter. This is followed by Uncovering the Incense Burner and the Exteriorization of Officers. Then the officiant reads the

---

42. *Huangshu guoduyi* 23a.

Petition for Conferral of the Register in place of the placard.[43] Manuscript S.203 records three distinct sample petitions,[44] one for a youth receiving the One General Register, one for an adult being promoted from the Renewed Mandate register to the Ten Generals Register, and one for a holder of the Seventy-Five Generals register receiving the One Hundred Fifty Generals Register, the highest register of the novitiate. Here I present in translation the last of these petitions:[45]

> The male /female novice X of a certain commandery, county, and township, so-many years of age.
>
> 厶郡縣鄉[46] 男/女 生厶甲，年如干歲。
>
> [The above-named person had previously received the Upper Transcendent/Upper Numinous Seventy-Five Generals Register. This mortal has served the Dao wholeheartedly, is one whose actions are cultivated and diligent, who loves the Dao and concentrates on advancing. Now he or she seeks promotion and requests the One Hundred Fifty Generals, their clerks and soldiers, including both Upper Transcendent and Upper Numinous officers. I ask that you supply them. Reverently I (submit) this Account.][47]
>
> 右一人先佩上仙或上靈七十五將軍籙。宋人奉道[48]專心，履行脩勲，好道務進。今求遷，請上仙上靈二官百五十將軍吏兵。請給。謹狀。
>
> Your manservant/maidservant _____, libationer of the _____ parish pneuma established by the Celestial Master, Correct Unity

43. The text says to transmit the register itself at this point, but it is clear from the following that this is not correct.

44. Actually, there are four petitions on the manuscript, but the third merely repeats the first with minor variations. See Lü Pengzhi 2006:143, n. 306.

45. This petition is numbered by Lü Pengzhi (2006) as D3.3, transcribed on p. 145. Differences in transcription are recorded in the annotation.

46. Lü Pengzhi, without comment, inserts a character *li* 里, "village," here that is not in the manuscript.

47. This passage is lowered about three characters from the top, perhaps to show that it was to be pronounced orally rather than incorporated into the written petition.

48. The manuscript inserts an open space of three or four characters' length here preceding the character Dao, presumably to express reverence.

Equanimity Pneuma of the Great Mystic Capital, kowtows and bows twice. I submit the following words:

> In reverence, according to the written documents: Your manservant/maidservant at the noon/midnight hour yesterday sent in a placard making a request as [recorded] on the tag. The male/female novice _____, of his master's commandery _____ and county _____, had previously worn the Upper Transcendent or Upper Numinous Seventy-Five Generals Register. This mortal has served the Dao wholeheartedly, is one whose actions are cultivated and diligent, who loves the Dao and concentrates on advancing. Now he or she seeks promotion and requests the generals, clerks, and soldiers of the One Hundred Fifty Generals Register including both Upper Transcendent and Upper Numinous officers. Reverently I submit one petition for your consideration. I request that the superior supervising officials of the Heavenly Bureaus, distinguishing section and priority, send down generals, clerks, and soldiers, each according to left or right [i.e., male or female], to enter into this mortal's body. They should on behalf of _____ dispel disaster and repel evil, and expel the stale pneumas of inferior officials and the reinjections of demonic pneumas. May the former generals, clerks, and soldiers within this mortal's body, in response to this petition, be recommended for promotion to the Heavenly Bureaus. May the affairs investigated by the Lord of Interrogation and Summoning and his clerks be established and those summoned by them present themselves. On behalf of those who have created merit through their efforts, I [now] seek audience to declare their merit and recommend them for promotion in accordance with the regular codes. May they be recorded for appointment in the Central Palace in an appropriate bureau and a stable position. Let them not be disappointed or angry and resentful. You should cause _____, after reception of his or her register, to be happy and content, with the pneumas of the Dao adhering to his or her body as a testament to his or her faith. Full of grace, I hope that the Most High[49] will discern [the facts]. I seek mercy.

49. The name of the Most High is placed at the beginning of a new line to show respect.

泰玄都正一平氣係天師厶治炁祭酒臣稽首再拜。

　上言：謹案文書，臣昨日　子午　時入刺，請如牒。主郡＿＿主縣＿＿[50]男/女　生厶甲先佩上仙或上靈七十五將軍籙。宋人奉道專心，履[51]行脩勤，好道務進。今求遷，請上仙上靈二官百五十將軍籙。謹拜章一通上聞。願天曹上官典者分別課次，下將軍吏兵，各案左右，入宋人身中。當爲甲消災却耶，辟斥下官故炁、復注鬼炁。宋人身中故將軍吏兵隨章受遷天曹，考召君吏所考事立，所召者詣。有功勞者謁爲言功舉遷如常科比。中宮錄署便曹隱職。無令失意悉（＝悉）恨者。當令甲受籙之後，心開意了，道炁附著甲身中，以爲效信。恩惟

太上分別。求哀。

In this petition, the holder of a Seventy-Five Generals Register requests conferral of the One Hundred Fifty Generals Register. I noted above that the Seventy-Five Generals Register was filled with either Transcendent or Numinous spirits, which are associated respectively with yang and yin; this suggests that the former comprised male spirits and the latter female, and many have speculated that this also meant that the former was conferred on male novices and the latter on female, but the evidence is somewhat contradictory. In this early Tang manuscript, such a relationship is not evident but also not excluded. We do not see that the remaining seventy-five spirits, of the opposite type and hence presumably gender, originally belonged to a novice of the opposite sex who also participated in the rite, joining his or her register to the supplicants in a sort of Daoist marriage. If such a relationship ever existed, it does not seem to have survived until this time. Moreover, the previous complement of seventy-five transcendent or numinous spirits is not retained; rather, those spirits were all promoted to heavenly offices and replaced with a new group of

50. The use of a horizontal line resembling the character *yi* 一 to indicate a place to be filled in is unusual. The wording here, where the character *zhu* 主, "leader or ruler," precedes the name of an administrative unit, is not found in received Daoist documents.

51. Lü mistranscribes this character as *shu* 屬.

mixed spirits, seventy-five of each category. The latter half of the petition foreshadows the Declaration of Merits (*yangong*) ceremony to be held three days later.

The text of the petition refers to the tag (*die*), a short document, apparently written on a slip of wood, that accompanied both the placard and the petition. It may be that only this tag was personalized with the names of the individuals involved, whereas the placard and the petition simply said "a certain place" or "person X." Our manuscript preserves the tag that should be used with this petition. We do not know exactly how the document was formatted, but the content is as follows:[52]

The male/female novice _____ of _____ commandery, county, township, and village, _____ years of age, [say, "Summoned by _____ officer-lord"].[53]

Recommended by the male/female novice_____

Household belonging to the parish of the male officer, the libationer _____

The person above previously wore the Upper Transcendent or Upper Numinous [officer] Seventy-Five Generals Register. This mortal has served the Dao wholeheartedly, is one whose actions are cultivated and diligent, who loves the Dao and concentrates on advancing. Now he or she seeks promotion and requests the One Hundred Fifty Generals, their clerks and soldiers, including both Upper Transcendent and Upper Numinous officers. I ask that you supply them. Reverently I submit this Account.

郡縣鄉里男女厶甲，年如干歲。言被厶官神君召。

右一人先佩上仙活上靈七十五將軍籙。宋人奉道[54]專心，履行脩勳，好道務進。今求遷，請上仙上靈二官百五十將軍吏兵。請給。謹狀。

52. Lü Pengzhi (2006) numbers this document D1.4 (p. 142). I largely follow his transcription with differences noted in the annotation.

53. This comment is added in small characters. I suspect it was not a part of the transmitted model document but reflected a contemporary practice, and so it is added orally.

54. The manuscript inserts an open space of three to four characters in length preceding the character Dao, presumably to express reverence.

This tag largely repeats the opening portion of the petition, except that it includes a notation on the deity who has "summoned" the individual. This would seem to be a rather late development in Daoism. The manuscript includes a table for which god summons people according to the month of their birth.[55] Those who do not know their birth month are instructed to use the god for the twelfth month.

This brings us to the actual conferral of the register. The officiant does not perform Return of the Officers but rather clacks the teeth twelve times, then exteriorizes another group of spirits from his or her body, including five each of the Transcendent and Numinous Officers, five each of the Emissaries of the Officers of the Left and Right, five each of the yin and yang Clerks of Divine Decision, and twelve each of seven different groups of officers: Gentleman Clerks, Tiger-Rushing, Evil-Investigating, and Scimitar-Bearing, Charioteer-Archers of the Three Offices, the armored Heavenly Grooms, and the strongmen of the Heavenly Stalwarts. These are all summoned to oversee the transfer of the spirits of the register into the novice's body. The officiant announces:

> Yesterday at the noon/midnight hour, your servant submitted an announcement on a placard, requesting on behalf of the male/female novice _____ and so many others,[56] generals, clerks, and soldiers of a certain type and number as given on the tag. Today they should be dispatched. The on-duty merit officer should select and inspect the clerks and soldiers; the Correct Unity Merit Officer should separate the generals and station each in the body of this mortal. There must be no confusion.
>
> 臣昨日子午 時上刺，啓為 男女 生厶甲如干人各請將軍吏兵種數如牒。今日當下。直使功曹簡閱吏兵，正一功曹分別將軍，付授肉人身中。不得錯乎（＝互）。

---

55. See Lagerwey 2005:58. Lü labels this section, rather curiously, as Do. It does not seem to be a document that is ever directly read or submitted to the Heavens in the course of a ritual.

56. This suggests that more than one person might have been ordained at the same time. If so, each would have had a separate tag, but the placard and petition may have been identical. Lü makes no comment on this phrase.

The officiant then reads the list of spirit officers on the register, and the novice repeats each name, followed by "received" (*shou* 受). Thus, we see that it is really not the physical register that houses these divine officials; instead they are installed directly in the novice's body through this rite.

Registers also contain talismans (*fu* 符) that are needed in order to activate petitions and command spirits.[57] In preimperial times, the word for talisman referred to a tally that was split in half; half was retained by the ruler and the other given to commanders in the field to authenticate commands. Talismans all have a counterpart in the Heavens and authenticate the authority of the Daoist priest who is empowered to use them. The talismans on the register had to be "charged" (*chi* 敕) in order to be effective. To do so, the officiant clacks his or her teeth three times and intones the following spell:

The Most High travels so augustly,
Clerks and soldiers arrayed in order,
The invoked talisman shines forth from the register
    a thousand leagues.
Thousands of demons and myriads of gods dare not face it.
Swiftly, swiftly, in accordance with the statutes.

太上行何皇皇
吏兵羅列有次，
行符從籙千里光，
千鬼萬神不敢當。
急急如律令。

Then the register is placed on the oratory table, and a cup of water is placed in front of it. The officiant summons the cohort of local gods and parish deities to summon the gods of Heaven and Earth as well as the ancestors in three previous generations and the parents from seven previous incarnations to witness the transfer of spirits. The officiant orders that the generals, clerks,

57. See the next chapter for instructions on how to write talismans.

and soldiers to be conveyed be brought forth, and he or she charges them as follows:

> May the generals, clerks, and soldiers of the register be brought and conveyed as a group. From this time forward, they will follow you in moving or stopping, in rising and resting. If _____ should travel through alpine forests, they will repel tigers, wolves, and poisonous insects; if through the rivers and streams, they will repel the wind and waves; if through cities, forts, villages or regions, they will repel the slanders of evil people; if through an area of illness and disease, they will cause disasters to scatter and calamities to disperse; if he or she should enter military ranks, they will repel the naked blades. Pardon all crimes of avarice and greed committed by _____ since the beginning of cognition at age seven until receipt of the register. From Heaven to Earth, let all grant pardon. May the clerks and soldiers support and protect him or her, all according to the rite. Swiftly, swiftly, in accordance with the statutes for living officials in the investigation of demons!
>
> 籙上吏兵一時持度。於今以去，隨行隨止隨臥隨起。厶甲若行山林之中，爲辟斥虎(狼)[58]毒虫。若行江淮，辟斥風波。若行城營里域，辟斥惡人口舌。若行疾(病)[59]之中當使災消禍散。若入軍陣之中，辟斥白刃。原赦厶甲未受籙之前從七歲有識以來所犯心望意貪之罪。從天至地一切原赦。吏兵扶衛一使如法。急急如生官考鬼律令。

Here we see in concrete terms the advantages gained by the recipient of a Daoist register. The spirits of the register accompany one at all times, constantly on guard against a wide range of dangers, including wild beasts, natural disasters, governmental entanglements, epidemic disease, or warfare. The novice is also pardoned for all previous offenses. Left unsaid here is the role of the register spirits in reporting and punishing future misconduct.

Next the officiant returns to the table and prepares to spray

---

58. Following Lü in adding character *lang* to preserve the rhythm of the text.
59. Following Lü in adding character *bing* to preserve the rhythm of the text.

the novice with charmed water. The officiant clacks the teeth three times, then charms the water by taking a sip of the water while reciting the following spell:

> This divine water will arise to push forward the clerks and soldiers, who will be accepted into the body of this mortal. Whether ascending to Heaven or descending into the Earth, he or she will enter fire but not burn, enter water without getting wet, go unharmed beneath a naked blade, and merge into the Dao.
>
> 神水當起，追逐吏兵受入宍人身中。上天下地入火不燃，入水不濡白刃之下不傷。與道合同。

The officiant then sprays the novice with the water three times. This sets the stage for the transfer of the physical register.

The officiant holds the register in his or her left hand (the yang hand) and passes it to the novice. The novice receives it with his left hand if male or her right hand if female, then passes the register around his or her waist three times. Then the novice, who has been facing east, turns to the west and bows twice. Having received the register, the novice turns back to face the officiant, who again binds and charges the spirits by kneeling upright, clacking the teeth twelve times, and intoning:

> May three hundred forty each of the merit officers, emissaries, Gentleman-Clerk Tiger-Rushers, the Corruption-Investigating Hooked-Scimitar Riders, the Charioteer-Archers of the Three Offices, and the armored Heavenly Grooms emerge! May those who emerge be stern of visage, dressed in recognizable garb, and correct in their deportment. Those merit officers and emissaries who tally accounts shall select and review the generals, clerks, and soldiers in the register. After the clerks and soldiers have been transferred, and you have been installed into the body of this mortal, do not commit evil or misbehave. If you disobey the codes and breach your vow, you will be sentenced to suffer a serious wound; the clerks and soldiers will be sentenced first.
>
> 功曹、使者、郎吏虎賁、察奸鈎騎、三官僕射、天騩甲卒等官各三百冊人出。出者嚴庄（＝狀）顯服，正其威儀。對共功曹、使

者簡閲籙上將軍吏兵。從度吏兵之後，付授宍人身中。不犯惡爲
非。一旦違科犯約，坐見中傷。吏兵先坐。

The officiant then performs a final Return of the Officers rite, then, bowing twice, intones the Covering of the Incense Burner incantation. With this, the ritual is complete.

This is not, however, the end of the newly promoted novice's duties. He or she must perform a Declaration of Merits rite three days after the ritual. We get a taste of that in the text of the petition for conferral of the register, translated above, but the actual ritual is not recorded in the S.203 manuscript. Turning to the *Protocol of the Outer Registers*, we find two documents that are to be used to give thanks (*xieen* 謝恩) for a promotion, one of them explicitly three days after the event, as well as a document formally labeled a Declaration of Merits.[60] Here is the Declaration of Merits, in this case for the promotion to the One Hundred Fifty Generals Register but on an accelerated schedule:[61]

> I offer up the following statement: In reverent accordance with the documents, I was born on _____ year, month, and day, when counter-Jupiter was in _____.[62] Owing to good karmic affinities from a previous life, my family had worshipped the great Dao for generations. [If the person has newly converted, say, "My previous sins were profound and grievous, and long I served the Six Heavens," or "I offended[63] against the Perfected and put faith in the profane," or "I did not serve anyone, but having not exhausted my good karmic affinities, I was able to convert to Correct Unity."] Fond of the Dao and delighting in the gods, I ceaselessly practice the utmost sincerity. In truth, I hoped to make some small progress

60. *Zhengyi fawen taishang wailu yi* 5a–9b.
61. *Zhengyi fawen taishang wailu yi* 8b–9b. Tao Hongjing claimed that register spirits were not living beings but rather transformations of the pneumas of the Dao called into existence as needed by the libationer, but this stress on their promotion and inspection (see below) is incompatible with such a view. See *Dengzhen yinjue* 3/22b6–23a3; *Chisongzi zhangli* 2/22a5–7 follows this passage closely.
62. For an explanation of counter-Jupiter, see Wilkinson 2013:515–17.
63. Reading *wei* 違 for the graphically similar *da* 達.

and dared to request to be promoted to the next step. Without my realizing it, the blessings of my previous affinities were rich, and my present teacher's mercy was profound; leaving behind that defiled ilk and being grouped with companions [as virtuous as] pure clouds, I was enlightened with extraordinary methods and located in an unparalleled position. On a certain month and day, my male/female master _____, summoning me for examination according to the code, bestowed upon me, _____, the One Hundred Fifty Generals Register. My clerks and soldiers were shining, and the celestial palace was majestic. The orthodox were assisted and the perverse perished so that both the hidden and the visible reverently submitted. How could a mere weed or insect like me be worthy of this? Unable to support it, I tremble in fear. I reverently bow to present this memorial and express gratitude for your consideration. Prostrating myself, I hope that the bureau(crat)s of the Three Heavens will grant me the special favor of inspecting [the memorial]. My Lord of Interrogation and Summoning as well as the clerks and soldiers of the register of generals that I received have achieved merit in protecting me. Now I visit you in order to declare their merit and recommend them for promotion. Let each increase his salary in accord with the regular codified practices of the celestial bureaus. Assign them to a stable position in an appropriate bureau; let none of them be disappointed. When the affair is complete, all should return to their palaces or homes, all in accord with precedents. Before I received this register, I committed millions of sins and billions of transgressions. Today I request that all be pardoned. Make it so that from now on, in whatever direction I turn my face, metal and stone will open for me, flood and fire will be dispelled, and the thousand ghosts and myriad spirits all will submit and acquiesce. Those I evangelize will convert, those I cure will be healed, and I will receive great grace in order to exhort those who have yet to be enlightened.

Full of grace, I contemplate the Most High . . .

上言：謹案文書，某年某歲月日時生。宿有善緣，世奉大道。（若新化云，宿罪深重，久事六天，或達真信俗。或無所事，未絕善緣，得歸正一也。）好道樂神，至誠無已。實希稍進，敢願超階。不悟先因福厚，今師恩深，捨濁污之類，班清雲之儔，開以拔群之方，處以不次之位。某月某日男女師姓名，依科考召，授

某百五十將軍錄，吏兵光顯天宮，威嚴輔正滅邪，幽顯敬伏。豈
某草蟲所可剋當，不勝感荷屏營，謹拜章謝聞。伏願

　三天曹特降垂省某考召君，并所受將軍錄吏兵，營護有功。
今謁爲言功舉遷，各加其秩，如天曹常科比。署便曹隱（＝穩）
職，無令失意。事訖各還官室，一如故事。某未受錄之前億罪兆
過即日乞丐一切赦貰。令某自今以後，所向金石爲開，水火爲
滅。千鬼萬神，盡爲伏諾，所化者化，所治者差。被受大恩，以
勸未悟。恩惟太上云云。

The object of this ritual is to keep the spirits satisfied by rec-
ognizing their contributions to each ritual event. It was important
to stay on the good side of these register spirits because they not
only were vital for protection but also were charged with oversight of the bearer, as we see in this passage from the fifth-century
Scripture of Divine Spells.[64]

Each Daoist priest has clerks and soldiers in attendance to protect
them. You must not have disobedient conduct for a single day or
night. The clerks and soldiers are supposed to report on people's
faults and sins. Heaven will cause the clerks and soldiers to avoid
the person, leaving his or her body during the night. When the
clerks and soldiers return, they punish the person themselves and
also cause him or her to suffer acute illness. The ill person is interrogated for a long time, which causes him or her to remain un-
healthy. The various sorts of inauspicious events in dreams and
nightmares are caused by clerks and soldiers.

道士自有吏兵侍衛。不得一旦一夕有違。吏兵當告人愆過。天使
吏兵違人夜去身中。吏兵還自誅人。亦令人疾病。病人久考,令人
不健。諸色夢寐不吉吏兵爲之也。

Like soldiers everywhere, the register spirits could also fall
into lassitude and fail to carry out their duties. To avoid this, the
novice or libationer should regularly employ them, by "serving
the register" (*shilu* 事籙), as we see in this passage from the *Protocol of the Outer Registers*:

64. *Taishang dongyuan shenzhou jing* 20/23a–b.

The way to serve the register: Always visualize the officers, taking note of their rank, number, and whether they are civil or military officers. When there is an urgent need, call upon them.

事錄之法,恆存其官，憶識位次，人數少多，文武所主。有急呼之。

For individuals possessing a high-level register, this involved quite a feat of memory, visualizing in detail hundreds of generals and their subordinates. One formal way of doing so was through a rite called Inspection of the Register (*yuelu* 閱籙). Two slightly different versions of this rite survive, both collected by the Five Dynasties Daoist master Du Guangting 杜光庭 (850–933). Both mention a variety of occasions during the year when the rite was to be performed, including one's "birthday" (*benmingri* 本命日),[65] the first (*jiazi* 甲子) and fifty-seventh (*gengsi* 更巳) days of each sexagenary cycle, the Three Assemblies (1/7, 7/7, 10/5), the Three Primes (1/15, 7/15, 10/15), the Five La 五臘 days (1/1, 5/5, 7/7, 10/1, 12/8), the Eight Seasonal Nodes (solstices, equinoxes, and their midpoints), and each new moon.[66] This suggests that each novice or libationer should perform this rite at least fifty-plus times a year, or on average more than four times per month. It seems it was also sometimes advisable to present pledge offerings to the generals on one's register, as we see in this rather cynical comment from the fourth-century *Declarations of the Perfected*:[67]

The Younger Lord [Mao]: I fear that you should make a pledge offering to the clerks and soldiers of us two. Give them a secret treasure that you wear on your body. If you do not, these punks later will not be willing to exert themselves on your behalf.

65. Not the calendrical day one was born but each day sharing the same sexagesimal date; hence, this would occur once each sixty days.
66. See *Taishang sanwu zhengyi mengwei yuelu jiaoyi* 1a and the *Taishang zhengyi yuelu yi* 1a. On these scriptures see Schipper and Verellen 2004:478.
67. *Zhen'gao* 7/8b. See also 18/9b. Mugitani and Yoshikawa (2000:256) misinterpret this passage.

小君曰。我二人吏兵恐宜詭謝。獻以體上之密寶。不爾。小子後
不肯復爲爾用力也。

For the Daoist, then, the generals, clerks, and soldiers of one's register were intimate companions who accompanied one day and night, providing essential protection but also observing one's conduct. They required constant supervision and employment to keep them on their toes and attentive to their duties. This was a big responsibility, especially for a novice who might be as young as six years old.

Promotion

The promotion of a Daoist novice ultimately depended on the opinion of the master, who was responsible for certifying that an individual was of good character and advanced enough in his or her studies to merit promotion. After a certain period of time, a novice would normally be considered for promotion, and particularly talented candidates might be promoted more quickly. This passage from the *Protocol of the Outer Registers* gives a rough schedule of when these offices might be conferred:[68]

> All those who receive the Renewed Mandate Register after five years can advance to the One General; after four [more] years, to the Ten Generals; after three [more] years, to the Seventy-Five Generals; after two [more] years, to the One Hundred Fifty Generals. If during the course of one year one's motivation and conduct are lax and foolish and one makes no substantial progress, the entire year should be repeated. If after three repetitions there is no achievement, he or she does not know to establish virtue and should be left at that level; he or she is totally unsuitable for promotion. If among the candidates there is one who is perceptive and whose talent and wisdom

68. *Zhengyi fawen taishang wailu yi* 11a. Other references to age are confusing. The *Dongxuan lingbao sandong fengdao kejie yingshi* (4/5b) quotes an unspecified protocol that refers to the One, Three, and Ten Generals registers all as "adolescent" (*tongzi* 童子).

are extraordinary, whose merit and virtue surpass the norm, the yearly limits do not apply.

凡受更令，五年得進一將軍，四年十將軍，三年七十五將軍，二年百五十將軍。一年若志行庸愚無長進者，悉又倍年。三倍無功，不知建德直置而已，都不合遷。其中聰明才智秀異，功德超群，不計年限。

It seems that most progressed through these ranks at a regular pace, some especially talented individuals advanced quite rapidly, but some became stalled at a given rank and never advanced beyond it. Thus, a register novice might be of any age, but those actually helping with the ritual workload of the parish, especially those actually presenting as opposed to preparing petitions, were probably near or above the age of maturity, around nineteen years of age.

Advancement was no doubt keyed to acquiring certain skills in writing and composition. A few of the most talented were selected to aid the master in composing documents necessary for the performance of ritual, and they were given the title of "writing clerk" (*shuli* 書吏). How many such clerks a local libationer could appoint was based on the number of households in the master's parish:[69]

According to the laws for masters, a master who has charge of more than ten households should appoint one writing clerk; if more than fifty households, two writing clerks; if more than three hundred households, four; if more than five hundred households, eight; if more than one thousand households, twelve; if more than two thousand households, the number should be calculated on this basis.

案師法：領戶十以上，署書吏一人，五十戶以上署二人，三百戶以上署四人，五百戶以上署八人，千戶以上署十二人，二千戶以上，依此爲率。

Thus, a libationer at the head of a large parish might have a staff of a dozen or more aides, drawn from among his or her novices, who were involved on a regular basis in ritual preparations.

69. *Zhengyi fawen taishang wailu yi* 17b.

This looks rather similar to the practices of modern Daoist troupes, which require at least five persons for the actual performance of ritual but actually often include many others who help out when needed.

Not everyone was suited to be a writing clerk, but all found ways to serve the Dao. Although it was possible for anyone by service to rise through the ranks and become a libationer or higher church officer, depending on one's social and educational background, this service might take a variety of forms:[70]

> Among those who cultivate this enterprise, there are also differences of great and minor. The small, weak, lowly, and insignificant will be employed according to their family status, carrying firewood and fetching water, performing their duties according to their strength. Mid-level persons will attend and protect, clearing a way through the subordinates, sweeping the halls, carrying the incense and candles, grinding ink and checking the brushes, transmitting and translating words.[71] The great possess wealth, honor, and influence; they praise and promote the holy transformation, converting the evil to good and leading others to the master's door. All must exert themselves in pursuing these merits, thus impressing both the hidden and manifest [officials, i.e., those of this world and the other world]. If they do not dare to seek advancement, the master should recommend them. Promotions in register do not depend on age or precedence.
>
> 修此業者，又有洪纖：小弱卑微，擬門驅使，負薪汲水，隨力効勤。中人侍衞，拂拭左右，灑掃庭內，端正香燈，摩研點筆，傳譯語言。大者富貴勢力，讚揚聖化，化惡爲善，導歸師門。必此功勤，感動幽顯。未敢求進，師當薦之。遷籙不依年限隨次。

The master was responsible for assessing the conduct of his or her charges, based not only on service but also on a broader range of moral conduct. The libationer should be liberal in his or her assessment, ignoring minor faults and emphasizing merit:[72]

---

70. *Zhengyi fawen taishang wailu yi* 16b–17a.

71. This is an interesting, and rare, indication of the multiethnic and multilingual nature of Daoist communities.

72. *Zhengyi fawen taishang wailu yi* 16b.

Masters should assess their disciples, calculating their merits and making up for their shortcomings. Minor infractions can be forgiven; great virtues should be commended.

師量弟子，計功補過。小愆可恕，大德宜嘉。

Early masters must have used some guide for assessment, perhaps focusing on the precepts that each novice had undertaken, but these are lost to us now. The *Protocol of the Outer Registers* provides two different rubrics under which the merit of a novice could be assessed, called the Five Virtues 五德 and the Nine Merits 九功. Oddly enough, it then provides two lists for each category. None of them are mentioned in early Celestial Master documents, but some Daoist masters likely used them in assessing their novices by the Six Dynasties period.

The first list of the Five Virtues repeats the traditional list of the Classics, focusing on benevolence 仁, propriety 禮, credibility 信, righteousness 義, and wisdom 智. There is a brief comment on each virtue, which sometimes gives it an unexpected spin, such as the comment for benevolence: "caring for the living and despising killing" (*haosheng wusha* 好生惡殺). For the most, however, this list is quite conventional. Not so the second list of the Five Virtues, which has a decidedly Daoist character:[73]

One: Observe a prolonged fast on dried and vegetarian foods. Do not eat the fat or freshly [killed]. Release the living and rescue the dead, maintaining an impartial, unified heart.

一者長齋乾蔬，不食肥鮮。放生救死，平等一心。

Two: Contribute to and nourish the Three Treasures. Fulfill the requirements for ritual obeisance; be amiable and compliant in serving; avoid indolence and insolence.

二者供養三寶，禮拜盡節，承奉和順，不生息慢。

Three: Be truthful in your words. Practice no deceit; make use of expedient means according to the teachings; do not do violence to other beings to profit yourself.

73. *Zhengyi fawen taishang wailu yi* 15a–b.

三者言語真實，無有虛詐，方便依法，不損物益己。

Four: Clearly distinguish right and wrong. Inquire after your master and friends; distribute charity equitably and correctly; resolve and put aside perverse doubts.

四者辯是明非。諮師問友，布施平正，斷次邪疑。

Five: Be exacting and perceptive in your wisdom. Rely upon the scriptures in what you say; understand comprehensively without obstructions; accord with the Dao in action and repose; do not create your own faith, contravening against both this world and the next.

五者智慧精審。所說依經，經通無礙。動靜會道，不自作一法，違負幽明。

This set of virtues looks rather archaic, with a number of distinct and sometimes only peripherally related topics grouped under a single rubric. The first virtue shows influence from Buddhism in its references to "releasing the living" (*fangsheng* 放生) and to the heart of "impartiality" (*pingdeng* 平等)[74] but also reveals Daoist adaptation in the inclusion of dried meats among fasting foods. The injunction in the last article to not "create your own faith" is also familiar from the *Statutes of the Mystic Capital* and the *Demon Statutes of Lady Blue*.[75]

The Nine Merits are really closer to a list of practices, and both versions of the list are worth examining. Let us begin with the first list of nine, which sees at the center of each practice an "ordering" (*li* 理) of some aspect of the world:[76]

The first [merit] is ordering primal pneumas: hope for and contemplate the formless.

74. On *pingdeng*, "universal, undiscriminating," representing an Indic word like *sāmānya*, see Nakamura 1975:1146–47. The "unified heart" (*yixin* 一心) is also a Buddhist term with many meanings, but, given the signs of Daoist appropriation in this list, we should perhaps not expect a deep understanding of the subtleties of the term on the part of the author. See Nakamura 1975:62 for an accounting of the various Buddhist uses of this term.

75. See *Xuandu lüwen* 17b10 and *Nüqing guilü* 3/4a1.

76. *Zhengyi fawen taishang wailu yi* 13b–14a.

一日：理元炁，願念無形。

The second is ordering the Heavens on high: set your sights on and visualize the great gods.

二曰：理上天，志存大神。

The third is ordering the earth below: preserve quiescence and think of the perfected.

三曰：理下地，守靜思真。

The fourth is ordering the four seasons: follow and accord with them to transform into a transcendent.

四曰：理四時，隨順仙化。

The fifth is ordering the five phases: promulgate and extol the great Dao.

五曰：理五行，宣揚大道。

The sixth is ordering yin and yang: link to and continue the seed of the sages.[77]

六曰：理陰陽，係續聖種。

The seventh is ordering textual documents: praise and glorify the way of the Dao.

七曰：理文書，讚弘道法。

The eighth is ordering the grasses and grains: draw out and prolong the common lifespan.

八曰：理草穀，攝延凡命。

The ninth is ordering possessions and wealth: benefit those below and help them ascend.

九曰：理財貨，利下通上。

All of the activities in the above list can be said to be religious, although some are oriented toward personal self-cultivation, whereas others seem more public in nature—publicizing and popularizing the Daoist movement and aiding the populace physically and financially. The second set of injunctions bearing the name

77. This may refer to the Merging the Pneumas rite.

Nine Merits is also religious in character, but, in place of devotional activities, we find a greater focus on personal practice:[78]

> One: Encourage your coreligionists to meditate upon the body being nonactive, envision the self as wholly pure, and entrust your pneumas to the formless.
>
> 一者：勸諸同志，念身無爲，思身洞白，委炁無形。
>
> Two: Contemplate the form as empty and pure, like jade without impurities.
>
> 二者：守形虛白，若玉無瑕。
>
> Three: Accumulate essence and look within, counting your hairs all the way to your feet.
>
> 三者：積精內視，數髮至足。
>
> Four: Envision the gods of the five viscera; make them appear and converse with them.
>
> 四者：思五藏神，見與言語。
>
> Five: Meditate on summoning the gods of the body, [through them] controlling the four seasons and the body.
>
> 五者：念召體神，使四時五行。
>
> Six: Offer *jiao*-sacrifice to the Six Jia spirits and the Eight Scribes,[79] sending placards with talismans for the gods of the earth.
>
> 六者：醮六甲八吏，符剌地神。
>
> Seven: Employ for errands the many gods of the altars of soil and grain as well as those of the mountains and streams.
>
> 七者：役使社稷山川眾神。
>
> Eight: Practice welcoming the essential pneumas to determine whether statements are true or false.

78. *Zhengyi fawen taishang wailu yi* 15b–16a.

79. Reading *shi* 史 for *li* 吏. The Six Jia are the gods of the six sexagenary days beginning with *jia* 甲. For the Eight Scribes, see Raz 2005. An alternate interpretation would link them with the Eight Emissaries 八使, who are correlated with the eight trigrams of the *Yijing* and are the assistants of the Great One, Taiyi 太一, in ruling both the universe and the body. See entry 13 in *Taishang Laojun zhongjing*.

八者：習延精炁，占說是非。

Nine: Summon spirits to ask them about luck and misfortune.

九者：呼鬼，問以吉凶。

This list, which is notably lacking in Buddhist terminology and hence potentially early, is best understood as practices that create merit. Most are related to self-cultivation and developing the individual practitioner's powers and insights. It was expected that the powers gained would be used in the pursuit of good. The editor of this passage describes the resulting works as able to "rescue the world, aid the state, and support the Mandate, augmenting others and saving yourself" and promises in return a reward in both this world and the next. He is particularly concerned, however, about the pursuit of merits six through nine, which involve contacting external supernatural beings and demanding either service or knowledge from them. He warns:

> There is much perversion in the activities of merits numbers six to nine. If you do not carefully maintain your precepts, you will certainly fall into the [clutches of] hordes of demons. The lowest level of the Dao has these three stages. The methods are extremely perilous, and it is best if you take care with them. When those who are fond of them seek promotion, they should mention this in their statements.
>
> 自六功至九其事多邪，不精持戒，必陷魔群，道之下品，有此三階法甚危險，慎之乃佳。佳者求進，辭略言之。

The perilous mantic methods at the end of the list may have been more prominent in the early church but fell out of favor by the time the *Protocol of the Outer Registers* was edited in the late Six Dynasties. The preferred practice then was meditation and visualization to visit the sacred places and meet the divine beings within one's own body. This practice was comparatively safe and potentially highly rewarding. Despite the danger associated with compelling spirits to do one's bidding, be they local protectors like the Earth God or fearsome demons, libationers had to respond to the needs of their parishioners, who might come to them with all sort of problems, and such actions were still recognized as meritorious. Certainly the spirits summoned to divine good or ill fortune (number nine) must have been restricted to proper Daoist deities, authenticated by the Determiner of Pneumas.

These lists of virtues and virtuous deeds give us some idea of the conduct expected of novices or lower-level libationers looking for promotion to the next register. The evaluation of novices by their masters was facilitated by a quantifiable standard of evaluation rather than just a subjective reckoning according to lists of good deeds. In the following two quotes we see attempts to set forth such a standard, though there is some disagreement over terminology:[80]

> When citizens have three Endeavors, this constitutes one Merit, and three Merits constitute one Virtue. When citizens have three Virtues, then they have differentiated themselves from the norm and are permitted to be appointed to a register. After they have received the register, they must have merits to be promoted again.
>
> 民有三勤爲一功，三功爲一德。民有三德則與凡異，聽得署籙。受籙之後，須有功更遷。

> Converting three people is a Merit; three Merits constitute an Endeavor; three Endeavors constitute an Award. Those with an Award possess virtue and can be appointed to a parish.
>
> 化得三人爲一功，三功爲一勤，三勤爲一勛。勛者有德，仍得署治。

In the second quote we see that, in addition to good deeds, an important way to win merit was to convert a profane person to the Daoist faith. The *Code and Commands of the Most High* (*Taishang keling* 太上科令) gives more examples of ways to earn merit:[81]

---

80. *Lu xiansheng daomenke lüe* 5b; *Zhengyi fawen taishang wailu yi* 19a.
81. *Yaoxiu keyi jielü chao* 12/12b.

Teaching someone to reform three faults can be an Endeavor. Convincing three households to convert can be an Endeavor. Aiding three people who are at the ends of their ropes, orphaned, or widowed also is an Endeavor. Refusing or yielding possessions or not fighting when angry, doing these a full three times is also an Endeavor. Healing three people who have an unresolved fear of committing a sin can be an Endeavor. Other cases like this should be determined on the basis of analogy.

教人改三過，可爲一勤；勸化三戶，可爲一勤；躋施路窮孤寡三人，亦爲一勤；推讓[82]財帛、有瞋不爭，滿三亦爲一勤；憂罪疚、療治三人，可爲一勤。凡如此等，以類求之。

It was the responsibility of the individual master to apply analogic reasoning in assessing the novice's conduct based on the few rather specific examples given above. The assessment must also have differed depending on the rank of the novice and the corresponding set of precepts he or she had undertaken to observe.

Gender, Class, and Ethnicity

The standards of assessment were mindful of the distinctions among individuals made by profane society that influenced how novices were prepared to gain merit within the church, but ultimately any individual might make his or her way through the ranks of the novitiate and emerge as a libationer and master of novices. At that point, only the individual's mastery of Daoist ritual mattered, as we see in this quote from the *Scripture of Solemn Deportment*:[83]

> If someone possesses ritual mastery (*fa*), then he or she is a master. It does not matter if he or she is a slave, servant, or lowly indentured

82. Reading *rang* 讓 for *hu* 護, likely a copyist's error due to graphic similarity, on the basis of a similar quote in *Zhiyan zong* 5/5a. The *Code [and Commands] of the Most High* survives only in a few scattered quotes and may be as late as early Tang.

83. *Zhengyi weiyi jing* 4b.

servant. If they do not bear on their person the precept register, even the most exalted beings in the Heavens cannot be masters; this is because we honor ritual mastery.

有法即師，勿論奴僕下隸。若身無戒籙，天之上尊亦不得師，尊法故也。

The traditional Chinese underclass included both slaves and indentured servants, male and female. Many were members of non-Chinese ethnic groups who had been captured and sold into slavery in China; others were criminals serving set or indefinite sentences of penal servitude. Daoists were not prohibited from owning slaves; there is even a spirit in early lists that can capture runaway slaves and cause them to turn themselves in.[84] Daoists were, however, expected to treat them well, as we see in this quote from the fifth-century reformer Kou Qianzhi:[85]

Male or female novices or Daoist citizens: If you have male or female slaves in your home, you must not call them male slave or female slave; you should refer to them by their cognomen. If they have a fault, you must not beat them without restraint. You should use reason, calling them before you and saying to them: "_____, you did this thing and you deserve to be beaten or fined." Then impose this on them. If you frequently upbraid them, the slaves should correct the sin themselves, without resentful, hateful thoughts.

男女籙生及道民：家有奴婢，不得喚奴婢，當呼字。若有過事，不得縱橫撲打。但以理呼在前，語：《甲乙，汝有此事，應得杖罰。》令受之。若責數，奴婢自當糺罪，無有怨恨之心。

The *Protocol of the Outer Registers* preserves a document titled "Essential Register Received by Menials and Barbarians of the Four Directions" (Xiaren siyi shou yaolu 下人四夷受要籙) that can shed some light on the role of such low-born individuals within the church.[86] It begins with an exhortation from the *Scripture of Great*

84. *Zhengyi fawen jingzhang guan pin* 4/11a.
85. *Laojun yinsong jiejing* 12a–b, paragraph 24.
86. *Zhengyi fawen taishang wailu yi* 4a–5a.

Peace for slave owners to consider manumission for male and female slaves who "obey their lords and master, learn to be good,
and are capable of wisdom" (*shuncong junzhu xueshan neng xian*
順從君主學善能賢).[87] This is followed by two forms, one for
slaves of the Man 蠻, Mo 貊, Di 狄, and Lao 獠 ethnicities who
served in the homes of Daoist citizens, novices, or officers, and
another for members of the "barbarians of the four quarters" (*siyi*
四夷) who had come to settle in China.[88] The Statement to be
offered by members of the first group when requesting a register
reads as follows:

Because in my previous karma my crimes were many, I have now
been born into a lowly state. In my heart, I suffer the hardship will-
ingly and do not dare to bear resentment. [Lowly as] an insect or a
weed, I was fortunate to be able to serve a Daoist household. Hearing and seeing virtuous acts, I sincerely delighted in them. Although
I am lowly and obstinate, I humbly know to use reverent care.
Morning and night I exhaust my efforts. Meek of heart, I do not
dare to malinger. Longing for life and wanting to survive, I humbly
serve my lord, obeying the great household. I look up to and hope
for the aid of the Dao, begging that it will grant me relief. I have
attended to my washing and sweeping in a timely fashion and held
on to every little thing that my lord has bestowed upon me, exchanging them for incense and oil to donate to the parish and oratory. Now I bring the ritual pledges and request to receive a register.
I humbly hope that the enlightened Daoist master will grant me
compassionate completion. Respectfully I make this Statement.

先綠罪深，今生底下。甘苦在心，不敢有怨。蟲草有幸，得奉道
門。聞見善事，誠欣誠躍。某雖卑頑，謬知謹慎。夙夜盡勤，小

87. This passage does not seem to exist in the surviving *Taipingjing*, but
there is a similar passage at *Taipingjing hejiao* 222.

88. The Man and Lao, in particular, were present in Sichuan or on its borders and must have been among those initially converted to the faith. See Kleeman 1998, esp. 11–60 and 204–5. The barbarians of the four quarters are said
in the text to have been born beyond the borders of China or in mountainous
regions beyond Chinese administrative control and to have entered into Chinese civilization of their own volition.

心敢懈。貪生願活、伏事君郎，承順大家。仰希道祐，乞以休
息。時治灑掃，君上賜與之物，豪分撰持，換易香油，給治淨
舍。今賫法信，請受符錄。伏願明師賜垂哀遂。謹辭。

In this evocative passage we see how even servants could devote their service to the Dao. While still in service, they are encouraged to attend the Assemblies to hear the proclamation of the precepts. When such a menial person does receive a register, the master is instructed to record his or her name on a "white roster" (*baiji* 白籍), seal it, and proclaim three times the recipient's Statement. This would seem to be because the individual is establishing a new Daoist household and needs to make sure that the heavenly bureaucrats duly record their name(s) in the roster of the living.[89] This section closes with another injunction: "If there is one with meritorious virtue, a good person will free him and treat him as a worthy citizen." 有功德者，善人放之，依良民也。

The lives of women in medieval China could be far more comfortable than that of a slave or servant, but their actions were still strictly circumscribed in traditional society. Daoism offered them opportunities for education and social advancement without parallel in secular settings. We have seen already that many of the earliest rituals invoke the first three Celestial Masters together with their wives and that the set of diocese/parish offices (*zhizhi* 治職) paired a female officer with a male officer in every rank, whether they were stationed together in large dioceses before the diaspora of 215 or each managed his or her own parish thereafter. The ritual formulae preserved in the *Protocol of the Outer Registers* and

---

89. It may be that this action is intended to remove the new Daoist from the list of those fated to die. *Dongzhen taishang basu zhenjing xiuxi gongye miaojue* 7a records that "if his ghostly name is not removed from the white roster of the Three Offices, after he perishes he will become a lower demon" 三官白籍鬼名不除，滅度之後故爲下鬼. Robinet (in Schipper and Verellen 2004:1, 621) dates this text to the Tang, noting that the text *Gaoshang ke* 高上科 quoted in this passage is otherwise unknown. The text advocates a purely vegetarian diet, but it does have some archaic features, like use of the term "libationer," and may be a bit earlier.

Dunhuang manuscript S.203 make provision for a female as either the officiant or recipient of every level of ordination ritual. The *Protocol* also provides a set of ritual formulae to be used in the petitions of five different sorts of women, which can tell us much about their role in the church.[90] The five possible categories are the maiden, the woman who leaves the family, the married woman, the widow, and the woman who returns to her natal home. All could enter the novitiate and eventually become libationers with register students of their own. I will explore what this material can tell us about the status and role of women in the Celestial Master church.

However enlightened the Daoists were, there is evidence of the traditional preference in favor of males. For example, parents holding a kitchen-feast to celebrate the birth of a child were expected to provide a more elaborate feast with a larger number of guests for the birth of a son than for a daughter. Moreover, petitions for use by women sometimes reflect poor evaluations of the moral status of women that derive ultimately from Buddhism, as we see in the following example of a woman who will "leave the family":[91]

> Because in a previous life my sins were grievous, I was born into a female body. Though malformed, weak, stupid, and obstinate, I do not wish to marry, yet in my parents' home, I have no way to study [the Dao]. Now I vow to entrust my life [to Daoism].
>
> 先緣罪重，生受女身。尫弱愚頑，不願出嫁。在父母家，無由得學。今誓歸命。

The petition for the maiden (*chunü* 處女) represents what must have been the dominant case: a young, unmarried girl who enters the novitiate after attaining the age of seven *sui* (usually six

90. *Zhengyi fawen taishang wailu yi* 1a–4a.

91. *Zhengyi fawen taishang wailu yi* 2a. It is significant that this language is found only in the entry for women leaving the family. Although it does not seem that Daoist women at this time entered a life of celibate monasticism, the term for this category, *chujia* 出家, is closely associated with Buddhism.

years old by our reckoning). As a minor, she is given her basic education by her parents, and it is they who compose the Statement. She remains in her natal home while studying with her master, who is also a woman. When she plans to marry out of the family, she must inform her master or, if she is unavailable, some other high Daoist priest. When she decides to marry, she must also inform her future husband's family about the level of ordination that she has received.

Marriage was normally contracted only between members of the church, preferably those who possessed the same level of register. No doubt this was because they performed rituals together and could not maintain the required secrecy if one was able to employ scriptures and perform rituals that were not permitted for the other. In practice, a complicated situation might require certain ritual interventions, as we see in this passage:[92]

> In the case of a man's wife, there are many different situations. Sometimes she does not wish to marry but is compelled by her revered elders. Sometimes a profane family of high social standing forces marriage upon her. Sometimes they worship the faith, sometimes they worship no one. Any [registers] she previously received should be immediately returned to her master, and the master will then make an Announcement [to Heaven?]. If the husband worships the Dao, she should abandon and change her original surname. If she has not previously received any registers, she should receive those held by her husband.
>
> 凡為人婦，事勢多端：或不欲嫁，尊上逼之。或為貴勢俗家迫取。或侍奉法，或無所奉。先所受者，悉即還師，師即申啓。若夫奉道，捐改本姓。若未有受，隨夫受之。

Thus, marrying into a profane family meant that the new wife had to give up her status within the Celestial Master church along with the body gods and esoteric ritual power of her previous ordination. In contrast, marrying a man with a higher-level ordination meant the new bride would be immediately elevated to his

92. *Zhengyi fawen taishang wailu yi* 2b.

status. Although political or economic factors might compel a family to make other choices, it seems safe to assume that the majority of Daoist marriages occurred between members with similar clerical ranks. Once united in marriage, the couple would receive new registers together.[93]

Women who chose to leave the family without getting married were an unusual case. They resolved to attain a master's position on their own and could possess their own parish, being assigned one of the parish offices designated "of the right." Such unmarried female masters were necessary for all female disciples who did not have a married pair of masters in their community:[94]

> All women who take charge of their own lives and are unwilling to go to someone in marriage should inform their parents that they intend to leave the family to study the Dao. They should either establish their own oratory or join their master's household. A male master who lives alone is not permitted to accept female disciples. If the master is a married woman, then she is called Master Mother. When a female disciple arrives, she can attach herself to the Master Mother. If there is no Master Mother, she should rely on a different female master.
>
> 凡女挺命，不願適人，啓告父母，出家學道，或別立靖舍，或投師門，男師獨立，不得受女弟子，師若婦即號師母，女弟子來，得依師母，無師母者，別憑女師。

Such independent aspirants received special consideration from their masters. Since women had limited financial means, and they had rejected the aid of their natal family, if they were unable to assemble the necessary pledge offerings for ordination, the master was instructed to help them. Such a novice was required to make a special vow not to rescind her decision, under threat of interrogation and torture, but, assuming she remained steadfast

93. See *Zhengyi fawen taishang wailu yi* 20a; *Taishang dongyuan shenzhou jing* 20/24a.
94. *Zhengyi fawen taishang wailu yi* 2b.

in her course, there was a special rite for her to marry at a later date, presumably without the sponsorship of her parents.

The next two cases both involve women whose marriages have ended. The first is the widow. In traditional China, when women went in marriage to a new family, the expectation was that they would become a member of that family and would not return to their natal family. Faced with the sudden death of a spouse, the widow should remain in the married household, serving her deceased husband's parents, if alive, or looking out for the family, if not. The *Protocol of the Outer Registers* sets out the possible situations in some detail:

> There are many different sorts of widow. There are those who are united in marriage, then widowed, and vow not to remarry. There are those who have male progeny and will not leave [the affinal family] because they are aged. There are those who are older and have no son but are wealthy and not willing to go. There are those who are poor, and no one will marry them. There are those who are ill and cannot leave [or] who still have a productive enterprise and do not return to their original home.
>
> 凡寡婦多種：有結帶便寡，誓不重嫁。或有男胤年高不出。或年大無兒，富不肯行。或貧無人娶。或病不能去，尚有產業，不還本家。

Most of these women are in some sense independent financially and are therefore able to avoid remarriage. Remarriage would have meant a new status in the church based on their new husband's register. For those who refused to remarry because of moral beliefs or because they had the economic wherewithal to do so, the novitiate and an independent path to life as a Daoist master must have been a particularly important option.

The final group is women who return to their natal home. This option seems to be primarily for those women whose marriage was interrupted. Divorce was a ready option for males, who could simply cite any of the seven accepted reasons for divorce (*qichu* 七出: failure to produce a son, licentiousness, refusing to serve the parents-in-law, arguing, stealing, jealousy, and serious illness).[95] An alternative rationale is possible as well, the discovery that the fates of the two spouses were in conflict (*nianming xiangke* 年命相剋).[96]

Here again we see that the novitiate provided a place of activity and eventual financial support for individuals who had fallen through the cracks of traditional Chinese society. As with widows and women who leave their natal family without entering into marriage, women forced to return to their natal families could turn to a life in the Daoist clergy as an honorable and sustainable role after rejecting or being expelled from the normative state of a married woman. Among the Celestial Masters, women at all stages of their life, like those of mean birth, found opportunities for social mobility and economic survival that would have been extremely limited if not nonexistent among the profane.

Appendix: "The Codes and Precepts for Disciples in Serving Their Masters"

"The Codes and Precepts for Disciples in Serving Their Masters" 弟子奉師科戒文 is preserved in the *Body of Precept Texts of the Three Caverns*, edited by Zhang Wanfu.[97] Although this list of thirty-six rules for serving the master reached its final state only in the early Tang, it is likely the culmination of a long process. Many of these rules may have been in place for centuries before.

> When disciples have been parted from their master for an entire month, all should don cap and belt, and then, holding their plaque of office, inquire after them. You must not do this in plain clothes. When disciples leave their master to stay elsewhere overnight, they

95. The definition of the seven offenses is taken from the Tang commentary to the *Yili* chapter on mourning by Jia Gongyan 賈公彦 (fl. 750). See *Yili zhushu* (reprint of 1815 Ruan Yuan carved edition) 30/355.

96. *Zhengyi fawen taishang wailu yi* 3b. *Jinsuo liuzhu yin* 12/12b cites this problem as an example of "human disasters" (*renzai* 人災).

97. *Sandong zhongjie wen* 1/4b–6b.

should all bow and kneel upright and should do the same upon their return. Disciples in addressing the master must not refer to themselves as "your disciple"; they should always say their own name. When disciples visit their master, they should not take it upon themselves to sit down; they should seat themselves only when instructed to do so. Disciples should not refer to their master as "the Daoist priest" but rather as "my family priest." Disciples must not offend against the taboo on their master's personal name; if asked persistently, they should respond in a low voice. Disciples must not barge in upon a master; each of them has officials around them in charge of investigating [crimes]. If disciples see that their master has a fault, they should remonstrate with the master while kneeling upright in a remote, hidden place; they must not speak of the master's mistakes and shortcomings in front of others. In speaking with their master, disciples must not speak arrogantly in a loud voice. When sitting with their master, disciples must not be the first to recline or the last to rise. When eating together with their master, disciples must not eat first but are permitted to finish eating first. When making inquiries of a master, disciples should be attired in turban and stole, and grasp an audience tablet as is appropriate to their rank; they must not rush into his or her presence in casual clothes. When disciples follow their master in his or her activities, they must be humble and respectful; they must not be irreverent for even an instant. When disciples serve masters, even if the master is young and the disciple is older, the disciple should always be respectful, treating the master like one's parents, just as if he were a bureaucratic superior or commandery Guardian. They must not rely upon their exalted status to belittle the master. This has far-reaching implications, all set forth in the *Protocol for the Bright Perfected*. If disciples are sitting on the same mat as their master, when the master arises or moves, they must move aside; they must not just keep sitting there unmoved. Even if, before receiving the ritual precepts, a disciple was of the same social rank (*qilei qideng* 炁類齊等) or was already of an advanced age, or if their surname was [already established by] brothers, sons, and grandsons when they received the faith from the master, disciples must always be humble and respectful, referring to themselves by personal name; they must not act in the conventional manner. If a disciple is in a relationship of wearing sackcloth [of mourning] as a relative of the master, then that person must not act as master to the other. Why is this so? When one receives the faith, all is witnessed by one's ancestral parents in the three and seven generations, who come to see their descendant receive [the title]. If he or she breaks the covenant, ancestors nine generations distant will be interrogated, and the harm will fall upon the person of the recipient[98] of the faith. Disciples must not express anger, jealousy, or reproach to the master, or harbor resentment in their breasts. The protocols for these sins are detailed in the *Protocol for the Bright Perfected*.

When disciples proceed to the master to request transmission of the religion (*daofa*), they should be dressed in cap and belt, holding a tablet in hand, and should make the request humbly and meekly; they must not act casually. If disciples are going to be separated from their master for an entire year, they should, on the first day of each month, attired in cap and belt and holding a tablet, perform a ritual three bows and upright kneeling; when finished asking after the master's health, the disciple should bow twice more, altogether performing five bows. When taking leave [of the master], the disciple should do the same to clarify so that all understand [the relationship]. Disciples must not argue with their master or lightly make fun of the master's ideas. In serving the master, disciples should always be respectful; they must not be arrogant or impolite. Punishments [for such behavior] are in the *Protocol of the Bright Perfected*; each of you should pay attention to this.

Disciples must not compete with their master for a meritorious reputation, having no sense of humility. When disciples visit their master, they should ask about what she or he has received; they should not discuss private eccentricities. When disciples are serving their master, should the master return from a long journey, the disciples should come out a certain distance, depending on the length of the journey, to welcome him or her; they must not just sit there peacefully, waiting for the master's arrival. When disciples are traveling with their master, they must not step upon the master's shadow; pay attention to this! When disciples are sitting with their master, they must not accept the obeisance of another. Why is this so? Because in seating there is only one place of honor. Disciples must not secretly act rebelliously, entering into angry conflict

---

98. I suspect this should be the "conferrer" (*shou* 授) of the faith, i.e., the master himself or herself.

with one's master. If disciples must enter or leave [the community] or plan to build something, they should first ask their master about it; they must not act on their own. In serving their master, disciples should all be grateful, loving, reliable, and truthful; they must not harbor doubts or be of two minds. Disciples must not rob or steal or expose things hidden in the master's bags, offending against the master's prohibitions and precepts, or they will be accused of a sin according to the protocols and statutes. Disciples must not betray their master. Pay attention to this. Details are in the text of the *Protocol of the Bright Perfected*.

If disciples live with their master, they must not spit in the master's presence. Pay attention to this. If disciples are waiting upon their master, should they encounter a visitor, the disciples should be at the master's side, waiting upon and protecting the master. They must not sit upon a high seat, as if they were no different from a common profane person; all such conduct is classed as unfilial. Pay attention to this. If a disciple has received a master's ritual enterprise and later achieves mystic virtue such that others look up to him or her, he or she should be humble, remembering his or her own master and not forgetting that master's prior mercy. In serving their master, disciples must not sit on the master's platform or mat; this is an urgent instruction from the divine ministers. All the above are the protocols and statutes for a disciple serving a master, altogether thirty-six in number.

弟子別師經月，皆冠帶執簡問訊，不得白服。弟子別師經宿，皆禮拜長跪，還亦如之。弟子不得向師稱弟子，言皆稱名。弟子詣師，不得專輒而坐，命坐方坐。弟子不得喚師作道士，皆云家師。弟子不得犯師名諱，若人問不止，下聲荅之。弟子不得唐突師，左右皆有司察之官。弟子見師有過失，當於深隱處長跪諫之，不得在人前言師是非醜鄙。弟子與師言，不得高聲大語。弟子與師共室，不得先臥在後起。弟子與師同食，不得在師前食聽在前止。弟子問訊師，皆當隨其所受高下，巾褐執簡，不得趣爾白服。弟子隨師起居行止，皆當謙卑恭敬，不得斯須無敬。弟子事師，師年少，弟子年高，弟子皆應恭敬，譬如官長二千石、父母同等，不得自恃高貴，輕忽於師，其關不小，具在《明真科》。弟子與師同在席坐，師若起動行止，弟子即須倚立，不得安然端坐。弟子先未受法戒，或厼類齊等，或復耆年，或是姓從兄弟子孫，後詣師受法，皆須謙卑恭敬，言皆稱名，不得比常。弟子與師親服總麻者，皆不得相爲師，所以爾者，受法，皆證三曾七祖父母，來監臨子孫所受，若違盟，九祖受考，殃及受法之身。弟子不得忿嫉責怒師主，及懷恨在心，罪科具出《明真經》。弟子詣師請道法，皆當冠帶執簡，謙苦求請，不得趣爾。弟子與師別經年，月朔皆冠帶執簡，禮三拜長跪，問訊訖，復再拜，合成五拜，別亦如之，明各識焉。弟子不得與師爭口，忽忽哂意。弟子事師，皆當恭敬，不得傲慢無禮，罰在《明真經》中，宜各慎之。弟子不得與師爭競功名，無有推讓之心。弟子詣師，當請問所受，不得論及私鄙。弟子事師，師若遠行還，弟子皆當隨路遠近奉迎，不得端坐晏然，待師至，弟子與師同行，不得踐師影，慎之。弟子與師共在座，不得受人跪拜，所以爾者，座無二尊。弟子不得陰行橫勃，忿鬭師主。弟子若出入，及所營作，每先諮問於師，不得自專。弟子事師，皆當恩愛信實，不得猶豫二心。弟子不得竊盜、發泄師器笈中，犯師禁戒，科律得罪。弟子不得背判師主，慎之，具在《明真經》文。弟子與師同處，不得洟唾左右，慎之。弟子侍從師，若值賓客，弟子侍衛師左右，不得高抗大坐，與凡俗無別，皆入不孝，慎之。弟子受師法業，後玄德成就，為人所宗，皆當謙下，存憶本師，勿忘先恩也。弟子事師，不得輒坐師牀席處所，神司之急示也。 右弟子奉師科戒，合三十六條。

EIGHT

The Libationer

"Having studied long and accumulated virtue, [Zhang Dao-ling] received a mandate as Celestial Master. He appointed 2,400 male and female libationers, each of whom took charge of households and converted [the profane] into citizens." Thus states the now lost but widely cited *Code of the Great Perfected.*[1]

The primary religious professional within the Celestial Master church was the libationer (*jijiu* 祭酒). The position is first attested in the Zhang Pu stele of 173 and is noted in the first historical accounts of the movement.[2] The title originally referred to the local elder chosen to offer a sacrifice of wine to the earth at seasonal village celebrations dedicated to the god of the soil but by late Warring States had already evolved into a more general title of respect. When erudites (*boshi* 博士) were established in the Imperial Academy (Taixue 太學) under Emperor Wu of Han, their head was called Libationer, and the term was used in various official titles thereafter but retained its more primitive meaning of local notable.[3] The first historical record of the movement, by Chen Shou, records that libationers were local

---

1. *Taizhenke* (ca. 420), quoted in *Yaoxiu keyi jielü chao* 2b.

2. On the libationer, see also my article in the *Encyclopedia of Taoism* (Pregadio 2008), pp. 550–51. The accounts in the standard histories are translated in chapter 1. For the Zhang Pu stele, see the section in chapter 2.

3. For referents of this term in the Chinese state bureaucracy, see Hucker 1985:130, entry 542.

community leaders similar to county prefects and that those heading larger groups were termed Parish-Heading Great Libationers (*zhitou da jijiu* 治頭大祭酒).[4] The latter term seems to have fallen out of use rather soon, but the distinction is preserved in later internal sources. They regularly call male and female libationers who hold a parish appointment and with it a parish office (*zhizhi* 治職) "male officers" and "female officers" (*nanguan* 男官, *nüguan* 女官), whereas those who merely minister to a number of Daoist households without possessing a parish are called "leaders" (*zhuzhe* 主者). Beginning in the fifth century, libationers were also referred to as Daoist priests (*daoshi* 道士), which is the normal term today for their modern counterparts, but "libationer" continued in use at least into the Southern Song dynasty.[5]

As outlined in the previous chapter, completion of the novitiate, culminating in the conferral of the One Hundred Fifty Generals Register, was the fundamental qualification for a libationer. Libationers in the mature Celestial Master church of the fourth century and later were also hierarchically arrayed according to three different scales: by parish, by parish office, and by register. These hierarchies functioned somewhat differently in the periods before and after the great diaspora of 215 CE; most of our surviving information concerns the period after that momentous event. In this chapter, I trace the development of these ranks and then look at some of the functions of the libationer within Daoist communities. I begin with the first pastoral appointment in the church, that of the itinerant evangelist.

4. We do find this partially confirmed in the *Yangping Parish* encyclical of ca. 220 CE (see chapter 3), which is addressed to, among others, the Parish Libationers (*zhitou jijiu* 治頭祭酒).

5. The term is used frequently, for example, in the *Wushang huanglu dazhai lichengyi* of Liu Yongguang 留用光 (d. 1206).

The Itinerant Evangelist and the Parish Master

Although the One Hundred Fifty Generals Register qualified a person to perform all the basic functions of a libationer, it did not entrust to his or her care any Daoist citizens or novices. It may be that some holders of that register never went on to become a leader, who "led households and converted [the profane into] citizens" (*linghu huamin* 領戶化民), in the classic description of the libationer's duties. Instead, leadership depended on the accumulation of merit and further promotion.

As we saw in the exploration of promotion in the previous chapter, a primary way of gaining merit was the evangelization of nonbelievers, convincing them to join the church by becoming Daoist citizens. The first step for a new libationer was appointment as an Unassigned Pneuma (*sanqi* 散氣) libationer, who can collect households of new believers by recording their names on a "fate roster" (*mingji* 命籍). A libationer who had collected enough names or accumulated sufficient merit by other means would be appointed to a parish and awarded a parish office (*zhizhi* 治職). I will examine this system of parishes and offices in detail below. It seems likely that, before the diaspora, libationers belonged to a single parish determined by their location within the network of parishes that covered the area of early Sichuan province (now comprising the eastern half of modern Sichuan province and the city of Chongqing) and would be promoted through the ranks within it. After the diaspora of 215, the parishes were detached from all geographic moorings and instead functioned as a ranking system themselves, with a specific parish office tied to each parish. It is this mature system of parish ranks that Lu Xiujing describes in the following passage from the middle of the fifth century:[6]

> If among the register clerks there are individuals who are loyal, worthy, earnest, and straightforward, who are cautious and prudent,

6. *Lu xiansheng daomenke lüe* 5b–6a.

fond of the Dao and especially diligent, attentive to precedent and aware of the new, worthy of being entrusted with evangelization, they can be appointed as Daoist priests of Unassigned Pneumas. If amongst these there are individuals capable of pure cultivation, they can be promoted to a position in an Alternate Parish. If amongst those in alternate parishes there are, again, those who are assiduous and earnest, they can be promoted to a position in a Roving Parish. If among those in Roving Parishes there are individuals who are serious and capable, they can be promoted to a position in a Lower Parish. If among those in Lower Parishes there are individuals who are extolled for their merits, they can be promoted to a position in an Accompanying Parish. If among those in Accompanying Parishes there are individuals who meet the standards, all of the Daoist priests in the parish may join in recommending and guaranteeing them, memorializing the Celestial Master's descendant that they may be appointed to one of the twenty-four ranks of parishes, first being invested with one of the lower eight. If they humbly devote themselves to the Dao and achieve merit in promoting evangelization, they may advance to a position in the middle eight. If they rescue and bring order to the myriad clans of the realm, supporting the imperiled and saving the weak, and are able to survive the three fates,[7] they will advance to a position in the upper eight. If they can refine to brightness the pneumas of the Dao, rescue everyone, extinguish demonic pneumas, and cause the myriad clans to submit to them, then they can be installed in the parish offices of the Three Pneumas[8] at Yangping, Lutang, and Heming.

若籙吏中有忠良質朴，小心畏慎，好道翹勤，溫故知新，堪任宣化，可署散氣道士。若散氣中能有清修者，可遷別治職任。若別治中復有精篤者，可遷署遊治職任。若遊治中復有嚴能者，可署下治職任。若下治中復有功稱者，可遷署配治職任。若配治中復有合法者，本治道士皆當保舉，表天師子孫，遷除三八之品，先

7. These are the correct fate (*zhengming* 正命) or received fate (*shouming* 受命), received at birth; the encountered fate (*zaoming* 遭命), for accidental events; and the following fate (*suiming* 隨命), for the results of one's actions. They are first mentioned in the Han apocrypha. See Liu Pansui 1950:49–50.

8. These are the Mysterious, Primal, and Beginning pneumas. They are first mentioned in the *Commands and Precepts for the Great Family of the Dao*, translated in chapter 3.

署下八之職。若有伏勤於道，勸化有功，進中八之職。若救治天下萬姓，扶危濟弱，能度三命，進上八之職。能明鍊道氣，救濟一切，消滅鬼氣，使萬姓歸伏，便拜陽平、鹿堂、鶴鳴三氣治職。

The term Unassigned Pneumas refers to that fact that the bearer has not yet obtained an appointment to a specific parish, at which time one receives a Twenty-Four Parish Pneuma Register (*ershisi zhiqi lu* 二十四治氣籙, not to be confused with the parish register that each Daoist citizen received to show membership in a specific parish). For appointments to lower-level parishes, no doubt the master's voice continued to be decisive, but recommendations from peers were also important. Before the diaspora, the final decision on appointments was made by the Celestial Master, based on records of merit kept by church officers. It is unclear how libationers were evaluated for promotion after the diaspora. This was sometimes a point of contention. The suggestion in the above passage is that for appointment to one of the original twenty-four parishes the recommendation of one's fellows was necessary as well as the approval of the current Celestial Master, but in practice communication over the breadth of China was slow if not impossible, and the authority of one claiming to be the descendant of the Celestial Master may not have been universally recognized.[9]

There is evidence in our sources of contention between these itinerant Unassigned Pneuma libationers and settled masters of parishes. The preface to the *Protocol of the Outer Registers* frames this as a conflict between those willing to go to the homes of their parishioners to preach and perform ritual services, on the one hand, and parish priests who demanded that their followers come to them for instruction, on the other:[10]

9. Kou Qianzhi, living in North China at the beginning of the fifth century, claimed that there had been no living Celestial Master for a long time. See chapter 4.

10. *Zhengyi fawen taishang wailu* yi 1a.

From the devaluation of the Dao inherent in "going to teach" we can understand the regard for Perfection expressed by "coming to learn."[11] [Those who go to teach] are minor masters who, not yet able to establish their own parishes, travel about among the people, devoting themselves to evangelizing others. Their karmic affinity [with the Dao] is fleeting, and they do not feel restrained by the great protocols.

自往教之輕道，明來學之重真。其間小師未能立治，履歷民間，行化自効，因緣暫爾，不拘大儀。

Another passage from the *Notes and Secrets of the Protocol for Transmitting the Scriptures and Precepts* refers to these itinerant pastors as "roving ritual masters" (*youxing fashi* 遊行法師):[12]

In general, when receiving the marvelous teachings, you should always go to your master's household. You must not inconvenience such revered persons by obliging them to go to your humble abode, as if they were itinerant ritual masters whom you could invite any time you please. Coming to study shows that your intention is sincere; if they go to teach, it means you take the endeavor lightly.

凡受妙法，皆詣師門。不得屈尊曲從鄙舍，若遊行法師，延請隨時。來學則志篤。往教則業輕。

One can well imagine that some Daoist families might be attracted by the convenience of a libationer who would come to their abode and perform necessary rituals in the family oratory. Parish priests depended on the stability of their flocks, but the constant ordination of new libationers meant that they were constantly competing to add names to the fate roster. Converting a profane family meant convincing them to forsake the worship of deities that they had trusted for generations and take on onerous responsibilities: the grain tithe, pledge offerings, and observation

11. Compare this passage from the *Record of Rites*: "In the Rites one hears of coming to study, but one never hears of going to teach." See *Liji zhushu*, "Quli" (Taipei, 1974 reprint of 1815 edition), 1.10a.

12. *Chuanshou jingjie yi zhujue* 12a.

of complex precepts. Snatching families of believers from another libationer's flock must have seemed much easier. This passage from the *Statutes of the Mystic Capital* condemns that practice:[13]

> Each male and female officer or leader of households [i.e., itinerant master] has a basic [region] in which to seek [potential] citizens who worship the Dao, but recently the many officers have been ignoring this in accepting the households of others. This is really the fault of the leader. If they cannot convert [new members] with the codes and rules, they just take them [from other parishes]. The foolish citizens know no better and think that they can do this lightly. This ends up letting them come and go as they will, with no regard for the ancient canons. The leader will be accused of a crime meriting seizure [of his or her register], and the citizens will be accused of the transgression of treason. If the master memorializes an account of this, the Celestial Bureaucrats are sure to come.
>
> 男官、女官、主者，尋奉道之民，各有根本，而比者眾官，互略受他戶，寔由主者之過。不能以科法化喻，輒便領受。愚民無知，謂可輕爾。致使去就任意，不遵舊典，主者受奪略之罪，民受叛違之愆。師則以狀言奏，天曹必至。

As we shall see, this was not just a problem of itinerant masters; each libationer constantly sought to increase the number of households under his or her care because doing so was essential to promotion. Lu Xiujing remarks on the uncertainty this introduced into Celestial Master communities of the mid-fifth century:[14]

> Many of the people today who worship the Dao do not attend the Assemblies. Saying it is because the trip is long or that they do not go to this door, they forsake their own master and cross over to some other parish. Only caring about the wine and food, they tempt each other.
>
> 今人奉道，多不赴會，或以道遠爲辭，或以此門不往，捨背本師，越詣他治。唯高尙酒食，更相衒誘。

13. *Xuandu lüwen* 13a.
14. *Lu xiansheng daomenke lüe* 2b.

The reference to parishioners refusing to serve certain masters because of their "door" (*men* 門), or social status, would seem to be a rare reference to the social mobility of libationers born into mean circumstances.

The Parish System

In the earlier discussion of the third-century encyclicals, I touched on some of the church offices that appear there as well as the first record of the parish system. Moreover, we have seen in chapter 5 that our sources record two very different types of parish building, one a large structure with many associated buildings suitable for ritual space and housing for a large number of religious professionals and the other a slightly enlarged family oratory that would accommodate only a single libationer and his or her disciples. We see a similar divergence in the descriptions of parish offices. One account tells us that each parish was assigned twenty-four different offices, each staffed by one male and one female libationer, whereas another account assigns one parish office to each parish. The former, a portion of the *Statutes of the Mystic Capital* now preserved only in a Tang era encyclopedia, gives a fairly detailed description of the duties of each of the offices, as presented below:[15]

No.	Description	Translation
1	監天職：主監亂真戾正也。	Overseer of Heaven: In charge of returning to correctness any disordering of perfection [i.e., heresy or apostasy].
2	督治職：主督察諸	Controller of Parishes: In charge of

15. *Sandong zhunang* 7/17b–19b, citing the *Xuandu zhizhi lü* 玄都治職律, which Wang Chunwu dates to 552 (1996:68). For a different interpretation of these offices, see Cedzich 2009. An error in transmission must be responsible for the presence of twenty-five offices in a list titled "The Twenty-Four Offices" 二十四職品. See the note regarding the Supervisor of Pneumas for one possible solution.

治，正一師性行貪枉不依師法。

controlling and investigating the parishes when a Correct Unity master's nature and conduct is to desire something improper in contravention of the Rules for Masters.

3 貢氣職：主選擇男女官，正一師考察身體瘡瘢，形殘跛躄，務得端嚴質素。

Contributor of Pneumas: In charge of selecting male and female officers. The Correct Unity master investigates whether the body has boils or moles, is disabled or crippled, taking care to find one who is upright, serious, forthright, and honest.

4 大都攻職：主天下屯聚符廟，秦胡氏羌蠻夷戎狄楚越，攻擊不正氣、惡人、逆鬼。盡當分明考錄。

Great Director of Attacks: In charge of talisman temples[16] of local hamlets throughout the realm, whether Chinese, Hu barbarian, Di' barbarian, Qiang barbarian, Man barbarian, Yi barbarian, Rong barbarian, Di barbarian, Chu barbarian, or Yue barbarian, attacking incorrect pneumas, evil people, and rebellious demons. All should be clearly distinguished, interrogated, and recorded.

5 領功職：主天下五方四海、八極十二州、百二十郡國、一千二百縣、萬二千鄉亭市邑屯沙聚石、五嶽四瀆、山川神祇之功賞。直符伐殺萬鬼，盡當了之。

Supervisor of Merit: In charge of rewarding the merit of the deities of the five directions, four oceans, eight extremities, twelve continents, one hundred twenty commanderies and kingdoms, one thousand two hundred counties, twelve thousand communities, cities, oases, and outcroppings, five marchmounts and four rivers, and the mountains and streams of the realm. The talisman-bearer attacks and kills the myriad demons, who should all be exterminated.

---

16. Significance uncertain. Cedzich translates "contractual temple" and interprets the office to be responsible for determining if the gods of such temples "participated in the battle against deviant *qi*" (2009:25). *Dengzhen yinjue* 3/21b counsels employing the Lord Pacifying Heaven 平天君 to attack refractory spirits who accept blood sacrifice in such temples, including the "Camps of the Five Sacred Peaks" (*wuyueying* 五嶽營).

6 都功職：主功勞。錄吏散民義錢穀金銀玉帛、六畜、米物受取出入。管籥倉庫府鬼神之物、禮信，及治殿、作舍、橋道、樓閣、神室，盡主之也。

Director of Merit: In charge of merit and exertion. Records the charity money, grain, gold, silver, jade, and silk; the six domestic animals; and grains received or dispensed by the clerks and unassigned citizens. Administers the spirit objects and ritual pledges in granaries and storerooms as well as parishes, halls, and workrooms; bridges and roads; towers and pavilions; and god rooms. In charge of all of these.

7 領神職：主選擇賢良，貶退偽惡，對會諸氣。諸有犯違，盡主之也。

Supervisor of Deities: In charge of selecting the wise and worthy, and demoting the false and evil, responding to and assembling the various pneumas. In charge of all those who have offended or disobeyed.

8 監神職：主考素所犯狀，結文書，開視利害，縛束謬誤，化諭戒勑。

Overseer of Deities: In charge of investigating the statement of all offenses committed heretofore, compiling it into a document, examining the benefits and harms [engendered thereby], limiting mistakes and errors, and converting and enlightening concerning the precepts and orders.

9 領署職：主選署二十四職名籍功賞，諸職文書，次第校投命籍。

Supervisor of Appointments: In charge of the rewarding of merit in name rosters for the selection and appointment of the twenty-four posts, the documents related to these posts, and the ranking, collation, and submission of the fate rosters.

10 察氣職：主察四方諸氣符瑞徵應。

Investigator of Pneumas: In charge of investigating the auspicious signs and evidential proofs in the pneumas of the four quadrants.

11 平氣職：主質天下之氣，平均四方八極氣候，主之也。

Equalizer of Pneumas: In charge of inquiring into the pneumas of the realm, equalizing the atmospheric phenomena of the four quadrants and eight extremities [of space], and taking command of them.

12　上氣職：主收萬鬼，
　　分別正氣邪精。

Submitter of Pneumas: In charge of collecting the myriad demons and distinguishing the correct pneumas from the deviant sprites.

13　都氣職：主三會吏民
　　請乞治救，分別年
　　紀、郡縣鄉邑，所受
　　官號。

Director of Pneumas: In charge of the requests for healing and rescue at the Three Assemblies, distinguishing age, place of origin, and the official titles they have received.

14　威儀職：主教勑禮
　　制、衣服儀容、法
　　則、起次位，彈邪正
　　非，施行法禮。

Solemn Decorum: In charge of instructing and enforcing the ritual system, [including] clothing, appearance, rules, and seating order; censuring the deviant and correcting the improper; and implementing the rules and rituals.

15　領氣職：主領五色之
　　氣，知其變異氣候，
　　并領知氣職也。一本
　　無領氣職。

Supervisor of Pneumas: In charge of supervising the five-colored pneumas, knowing their deviations and timings, and in charge of the post of Recognizer of Pneumas. [One text does not have the Supervisor of Pneumas post.][17]

16　領決職：主鬼氣男
　　女，被氣傳語。領決
　　教，分別秦夷胡戎狄
　　氏羌，真偽。

Supervisor of Determinations: In charge of spirit pneuma men and women, who are possessed by pneumas and transmit words. Supervises the determination of Teachings, distinguishing among Chinese, Yi barbarian, Hu barbarian, Di barbarian, and Di' barbarian, and between authentic and false [pneumas].

17　四氣職：主諸治投言
　　文書，對會諸治戶籍

Four Pneumas: In charge of documents submitted by the parishes, comparing

17. This may explain why there are twenty-five posts rather than twenty-four. It is unclear whether other versions had twenty-five or eliminated one of the other posts. Cedzich suggests that this extra office may be parallel to the twenty-fifth pneuma of "central heaven" in the human body and consequently explains this post as having "oversight over the other twenty-four ranks" (2009:13, n. 26; 22, n. 44), but it is hard to derive that from this simple record.

	口數，出死入生。	them to the numbers in the rosters of households[18] in the parishes, then removing the dead and entering the newborns.
18	行神職：主布氣宣化，顯明道教。	Circulator of Deities: In charge of distributing the pneumas and propagating conversion to illuminate the Teachings of the Dao.
19	道氣職：主勸化凶逆，化惡爲善。	Pneuma of the Dao: In charge of encouraging the violent and rebellious to convert, converting the evil to the good.
20	聖氣職：主質對文書，歲終功限，謂狀言上者。	Pneuma of the Sage: In charge of investigating and comparing the documents to determine merits at the end of the year. This means to fashion the words into accounts and submit them.[19]
21	承氣職：主承治醫療著功之勳。	Receiver of Pneumas: In charge of receiving the [records of] healings in the parish and recording the notations of merit.
22	典氣職：主典諸職高下次第。	Regulator of Pneumas: In charge of regulating the rank and precedence of the posts.
23	廉平職：主監察廉邪，均平飲食。	Equalizer of Integrity: In charge of overseeing and investigating integrity and deviance, and equalizing food and drink.

18. Cedzich identifies these population rosters with the "household record" (*zhailu* 宅錄) maintained by each family, but cites no evidence for this identification. In the same note, she equates the "record of fate" with the parish register (*zhilu* 治籙), which is certainly incorrect. See Cedzich 2009:23, n. 47.

19. An "account" (*zhuang* 狀) is a document that identifies an individual by place, rank, and sometimes parentage, then sets out a record of his or her accomplishments. Petitions for promotion required the submission of an account together with the petition. Cedzich suggests that the documents referenced here are the petitions submitted through the year (2009:24), which is possible, though we do not know that the petitions were preserved at this time, as opposed to the later practice of burning them, and that the results of this evaluation were eventually sent up to Heaven, which again is possible but is not stated in our text.

| 24 | 行教職：主奉宣師教，勸化愚俗不知法者。 | Circulator of Teachings: In charge of promulgating the Teachings of the master, encouraging the conversion of the foolish profane and those who do not know the rules. |
| 25 | 建義職：主表條功勞，助時伏勤對應退也。 | Establisher of Righteousness: In charge of listing merit and endeavor, aiding those who undertake to strive and responding to those who are losing ground. |

This describes a large, articulated bureaucracy that manages all the tasks of a religious community in medieval China, from recording and evaluating the conduct of church members to managing the church bureaucracy and property, evangelizing and other interactions with profane society, and supervising spirit revelations. Supervision of such an extensive set of church officers would have required a separate level of administration like the Parish-Heading (Great) Libationer mentioned in the earliest historical accounts and in the *Yangping Parish* encyclical. Housing and providing workspace for all of them would have required a very large parish building as well as numerous outbuildings, much as in the description preserved in the *Code of the Great Perfected*.[20] In sum, this system seems consistent with our earliest descriptions of the movement, when the territory of West China was divided into just twenty-four parishes (perhaps dioceses is a better term for such institutions), each of which must have been responsible for thousands if not tens of thousands of Daoist citizens and novices.

We can readily imagine the Celestial Master effectively controlling these twenty-four administrative centers from his seat in the Yangping parish. As libationers earned merit and climbed the ladder of parish offices, they would have been promoted within their own parishes. Two passages speak of the Celestial Master appointing 2,400 libationers, including those working within and outside

---

20. *Yaoxiu keyi jielü chao* 10/1a–b.

parishes (*neiwai* 內外).[21] This is clearly an idealized number, but it would accord well with a system of twenty-four parishes, each staffed by forty-eight or fifty libationers, with a like number ministering to the populace directly in the villages of each parish.

The alternate description of the parish offices is preserved in a quotation of the *Celestial Master's Protocol of the Parishes* 天師治儀, attributed to Zhang Bian 張辯, the thirteenth-generation Celestial Master, who held an official post under the Liang dynasty (502–47). That system can be summarized as follows:[22]

Parish	Post
Twenty-Four Primary Parishes	
Yangping 陽平	Left Equalizer of Pneumas 左平氣
Lutang 鹿堂	Right Equalizer of Pneumas 右平氣
Heming 鶴鳴	Left Extender of Pneumas 左長氣
Liyuan 漓沅	Right Extender of Pneumas 右長氣
Gegui 葛瑣	Left Directing Supervisor 左都領
Gengchu 更除	Right Directing Supervisor 右都領
Qinzhong 秦中	Left Supervisor of Deities 左領神
Zhenduo 真多	Right Supervisor of Deities 右領神
Changli 昌利	Left Director of Oversight 左都監
Lishang 隸上	Right Director of Oversight 右都監
Yongquan 涌泉	Left Overseer of Deities 左監神
Jushan 具山	Right Overseer of Deities 右監神
Chougeng 稠稉	Left Overseer of Inspection 左監察
Benzhu 本竹	Right Overseer of Inspection 右監察
Mengqin 蒙秦	Left Supervisor of Merit 左領功
Pinggai 平蓋	Right Supervisor of Merit 右領功
Yuntai 雲台	Left Overseer of Merit 左監功
Jinkou 瀘口	Right Overseer of Merit 右監功
Houcheng 後城	Left Director of Pneumas 左都氣
Gongmu 公慕	Right Director of Pneumas 右都氣
Pinggang 平岡	Left Contributor of Pneumas 左貢氣

21. See *Lu xiansheng daomenke lüe* 1b; *Yaoxiu keyi jielü chao* 10/1b–2a. The first passage attributes the establishment of the system of twenty-four parishes and 2,400 libationers directly to the Most High Lord Lao.

22. *Shoulu cidi faxin yi* 14a–15a.

Zhubu 主簿	Right Contributor of Pneumas 右貢氣
Yuju 玉局	Left Investigator of Pneumas 左察氣
Beiqiu 北邱	Right Investigator of Pneumas 右察氣

Roving Parish Posts

Emei 峨媚	Left and Right Supervisors of Determinations 左右領決[23]
Qingcheng 青城	Left and Right Promulgators of Authority 左右宣威
Taihua 太華	Left and Right Equalizers of Merit 左右功平
Huangjin 黃金	Left and Right Equalizers of Integrity 左右廉平
Cimu 慈母	Left and Right Circulators of Teachings 左右行教
Ebeng 阿逢	Left and Right Solemn Deportment 左右威儀
Pingdu 平都	Left and Right Receivers of Pneumas 左右承氣
Jiyang 吉陽	Left and Right Establishers of Deportment 左右建儀

In this system, one parish office is assigned to each parish, and the parishes alternate male (left) and female (right) offices, producing two parallel, hierarchically arranged systems for male and female libationers. I believe that this reflects the practice of the mature Celestial Master church after its center of activities was no longer located in Sichuan. The parishes have lost all identification with specific regions of Sichuan and instead function as ranks. Lu Xiujing, in the passage quoted earlier in this chapter, describes a libationer moving from parish to parish as he or she earns merit and wins promotion. It seems unlikely that there was ever a system that required the constant transfer of priests from place to place, because either the households tied to them would have had to move with the libationer or the libationer would have to start over to gather a new flock in each new location. Instead, this system functioned through marking the growth of parishes by changing their names. When a libationer had attracted enough new parishioners

---

23. The original text had *jue* 訣, "secret formula," a graphic error for *jue* 決, "determination."

to warrant a new rank, either through evangelization of the profane or perhaps by attracting dissatisfied parishioners from neighboring parishes, he or she would be reassigned to a new, higher parish with a different parish office. We find confirmation of this union of parishes and parish offices as a unified ranking system in texts like the *Ritual for the Transmission of the Director of Merit Plaque*:[24]

> The Celestial Master said: A Correct Unity Daoist priest who has achieved merit in serving the Dao should be appointed to a parish office. The priest will be recommended and promoted according to his or her achievements, with no impropriety, culminating in Yangping [parish].
>
> 天師曰：正一道士奉道有功，應補治職。隨功舉遷，不得叨妄，極於陽平。

Here a libationer advances from parish to parish, taking on new parish offices with each step, until he or she reaches the highest parish, Yangping. Lu Xiujing, after describing the path of advancement from parish to parish in the passage cited above, complains that people of his day vied to possess the largest parish, equating parish size with rank.[25]

We can trace to a limited degree in our sources the course of this transformation from regional parish to parish as rank. The pivotal period was the autonomous Daoist kingdom established by the third Celestial Master, Zhang Lu, in the Hanzhong region from around 191 to 215 CE. The establishment of this kingdom itself must have destabilized the parish system as Daoist believers flocked to Hanzhong, which many thought would be the utopian realm of Great Peace. The first step was the addition of four new parishes, called Separate Parishes (*biezhi*) or Supplementary Parishes (*beizhi*), so that the now twenty-eight parishes could be equated with the twenty-eight lunar lodges.[26] This meant that

24. *Zhengyi fawen chuan dugongban yi* 1a.
25. *Lu xiansheng daomenke lüe* 7a.
26. *Yaoxiu keyi jielü chao* 10/2b, citing the *Code of the Great Perfected*, tells us that Separate Parish was the external name and Supplementary Parish the

individuals could be assigned to a parish not on the basis of the location of their residence but based on the time of their birth. It is uncertain whether this system was ever fully implemented, or, if so, how long it continued in use, but it maintained a certain appeal in North China, because Kou Qianzhi tried to reestablish this system in the fifth century.

The final nail in the coffin of the old parish system was the great diaspora of 215, when Zhang Lu surrendered to Cao Cao.[27] Then Daoist households were resettled across the breadth of North China. Although Zhang Lu was treated well by Cao Cao, he died soon thereafter. It is unclear to what degree the central church administration survived, and the physical distances separating the faithful must have presented a formidable obstacle to efficient communication. The *Yangping Parish* encyclical complains:[28]

> Since the Jian'an period or the first year of Huangchu (196–220), all the various leaders and libationers have cited a Teaching[29] to create their own parish. They no longer obtain them according to the former rules of the Dao.
>
> 從建安、黃初元年以來，諸主者祭酒，人人稱教，各作一治。不復按舊道法爲得爾。

Similar complaints are made in the encyclical issued in 255, titled *Commands and Precepts for the Great Family of the Dao*, which cites the year 231 as a key transition, after which "the various postings have each been self-appointed."[30] This chaotic situation must have continued for some time as Daoists turned to spirit revelations called Teachings to justify the establishment of parishes.

---

internal name for the parishes of Jushan 具山, Zhongmao 種茂, Baishi 白石, and Ganghu 岡互.

27. Described in detail in chapter 3.

28. *Zhengyi fawen tianshi jiao jieke jing* 21b; see also chapter 3.

29. For this specialized usage of *jiao* 教, referring to a spirit communication from a dead church leader or Daoist deity, see below.

30. *Zhengyi fawen tianshi jiao jieke jing* 17a; see chapter 3.

We see this situation reflected in the following passage from the *Statutes of the Mystic Capital*:[31]

> Recently I have noticed that some of the many officers and the commoner Daoist citizens, in the absence of a master, have set up their own religion. Some are very far from their home parish, scattered across the wilds of the four directions; they award titles and confer registers upon each other on their own authority, commandeering citizens and converting [profane] households, wielding power and wealth as they please. Some go just far enough from their parish that they are cut off; the abandoned pledge offerings of the tithe-paying citizens accumulate year after year, until someone appropriates them for himself rather than transmitting them on up [to the Celestial Master]. They create their own religion and do not accept [orders from anyone], turning their backs on the codes of the netherworld. They act inconsistently; this tendency manifests in myriad ways: the Correct religion does not shine forth, true and false become indistinguishable, the timings of the pneumas become confused and disordered, pernicious evil flourishes, and one meets with disaster and torture. How could this not be painful [to consider]?
>
> 竊尋比頃以來眾官百姓道民，或有無師而自立法；或去本治遼遠，布於四野，私相號授，領民化戶，威福自由；或有去治不遠而致隔絕，至於租民脆物，通廢積年，私自沒入己，不傳奏上，自作一法，無所稟承，背違冥科。前後非一，其事萬端。致使正法不明，真偽無別，氣候錯亂，妖惡滋生，罹災被考，豈不痛哉。

We have few sources from this period of Daoist history, but the movement experienced explosive growth, becoming a significant force all across North China. It is not surprising that Daoists had to improvise.

It was probably during this period of disruption and loss of central control that the practice of hereditary succession took hold. Given the prominent role of the family in Chinese society, it is perhaps not surprising that it proved impossible to eradicate this custom. Today Daoist priests normally transmit their positions to

31. *Xuandu lüwen* 17b–18a.

their children, though they sometimes send them for a time to train with another family.[32] Kou Qianzhi, writing around 415 in North China, railed against this practice:[33]

> Lord Lao said: In the world today there are those who follow their forefathers in serving the Dao. Creating their own religion, they perform rituals using incense and lamps in their homes. There are also those who follow their forefathers in taking up the office of libationer; the commoners in their ignorance think that when a father dies, the son inherits and no longer belongs to the Correct. Both the household master and the common citizens are guilty of licentious sacrifice. Their heterodox commands are numerous and diverse! Their heterodox commands are not the Unity [faith].[34]
>
> 老君曰：世間有承先父祖事道，自作一法，家宅香火。復有承先祖作祭酒之官者，民戶無知，言父死子係， 更不正屬。戶師民氓，同婬祠。邪令眾雜，邪令非一。

Even Kou Qianzhi, however, agrees that, if the descendant is "pure, discerning, and intelligent, and practiced in dealing with demons" 清徹聰明閑練鬼事, he or she can go to a proper master and be ordained in order to succeed the father.[35] The *Statutes of the Mystic Capital* is even more matter-of-fact in relating the hereditary nature of Daoist parishes:[36]

> According to an imperial rescript: As for the master to whom a Daoist priest, female officer, Daoist citizen, or novice is attached, when

---

32. This fosterage system was perhaps in practice in our period. The *Zhengyi weiyi jing* 4b says that "you must not transmit to anyone who shares an ancestor of the same surname within nine generations."

33. *Laojun yinsong jiejing* 12b, paragaraph 25.

34. Here the previous statement has already informed us of the multiplicity of their improper commands, so I understand this *yi* 一, like the preceding *zheng* 正, to be a reference to the common epithet of the Daoist faith, which was regularly then, and still is today, proclaimed to be Correct and Unitary (Zhengyi 正一).

35. *Laojun yinsong jiejing* 6b–7a, paragraph 8.

36. *Xuandu lüwen* 11a.

the father dies, the son succeeds, and, when an elder brother perishes, the younger brother succeeds. If it is not a legitimate progeny, he cannot inherit. In a case where the son is a young minor, there should be an adult who takes charge of the parish; when the son is grown, then he will establish a parish just as before. If there is no one to succeed as leader, then you should seek out the [former master's] roots to reattach to his superior. You must not attach yourself to a stranger.

制：道士、女官、道民、籙生、百姓所奉屬師者，父亡子繼，兄沒弟紹，非嫡不得繼。或兒息小弱，當大人攝治，兒長則立治依舊。若無人承領，則尋根本上屬，不得他人屬。

Here we see that hereditary control of a parish is not just acceptable but correct, in accordance with the commands of the Heavenly Thearch, and to be disrupted only temporarily if the heir is a minor. In this respect, at least, Daoism by the end of the Six Dynasties had already reached the mature form we still find today among nonmonastic Daoist priests.

The Libationer and Spirit Revelation

The Celestial Master church was founded, all early accounts tell us, by a spirit revelation to Zhang Daoling in 142 CE.[37] The earliest record of the church, the Zhang Pu stele, records a spirit revelation from the Heavenly Elder sanctioning the promotion of a group of libationers. The two encyclicals of the third century, *Yangping Parish* and *Commands and Precepts for the Great Family of the Dao*, were revelations from a dead Celestial Master, probably Zhang Daoling.[38] Thus, spirit revelation was an important source of religious truth and approval during the early centuries of church history.

One of the early church offices mentioned above (number 16),

---

37. See chapter 2.

38. For a translation and discussion of the Zhang Pu stele, see the beginning of chapter 2. For the two encyclicals, see chapter 3.

the Supervisor of Determinations (*lingjue*), was specifically in charge of a group of spirit mediums called "spirit pneuma men and women" (*guiqi nannü* 鬼氣男女), who are possessed by these pneumas and transmit messages from them. The Supervisor of Determinations is charged with determining the nature of these messages: the ethnic identity of the revealing spirit and whether the revelation is true or false. It may be that only messages from Chinese spirits were considered authentic, but given the multi-ethnic nature of the early church, we cannot assume this. We do not find the Supervisor of Determinations anywhere in our received material, but there is a church office called Determiner of Pneumas (*jueqi* 決氣) that seems to be an alternate name for this official. This officer was indeed intimately tied to spirit revelation, as we see in the following passages from the third-century encyclicals:[39]

Why am I so anxious? I am anxious to turn the people of the parish about. The Determiner of Pneumas has sent down Teachings, telling you all what Lord Lao, the Most High, has passed on, that he wants to make all of you take care, to earnestly exert yourselves, and further to exhort yourselves, for the sake of the Dao, to maintain all of the principles, and to encourage the commoners to convert.

吾有何急？急轉著治民。決氣下教，語汝曹輩。老君、太上轉相督，欲令汝曹人人用意，勤心努力，復自一勸，爲道盡節，勸化百姓。

The Dao has again and again saved your lives, sometimes speaking to you through the Determiner of Pneumas, sometimes having a former official or commander correct you, and yet you do not believe. This is so lamentable.

道乃往往救汝曹之命，或決氣相語，或有故臣，令相端正，而復不信，甚可哀哉。

39. The first quote is from the *Yangping Parish* of ca. 220; the second from the *Commands and Precepts for the Great Family of the Dao* of 255. See *Zhengyi fawen tianshi jiao jieke jing* 21b, 14b–15a, respectively.

In these passages, the Determiner of Pneumas is a church official transmitting messages called Teachings (*jiao* 教) from the spirits. We have one complete example of such a Teaching, the "Teaching of the Celestial Master" translated in chapter 3, but we have also seen in the previous section references to libationers who "have cited a Teaching to create their own parish" (*cheng jiao zi zuo yizhi* 稱教自作一治).[40] Whether conveying high moral directives or practical instructions on the administration of the church, messages from the deceased Celestial Masters or other high officers seem to have been an important source of guidance for members of the early church. In the hands of church elders, they could have been a significant aid in galvanizing followers to pursue reforms or simply increasing group cohesion, but they also offered a way for Daoists who had fallen out of contact with the central administration of the church through the vicissitudes of a disordered age to gain divine guidance on pressing local or personal matters. Either way, these documents, written in the first person and claiming the authority of revered figures in the church, would have played an important role in shaping church teachings. It is uncertain how long this practice continued, but Du Guangting, writing in the tenth century, records a "Petition for Daoist Priests Seeking Release from Faults" that apologizes for "citing a Teaching to speak recklessly" (*cheng jiao wang yu* 稱教妄語).[41]

Finally, spirit communication played a vital role in the evaluation of candidates for promotion. A variety of gods and spirits were responsible for overseeing the conduct of Daoists. The most intimate were the officers, generals, clerks, and soldiers of one's register who dwelt in one's own body and accompanied one through all activities. They were externalized and dispatched to notify the perfected officers of the Daoist bureaucracy at all levels of the locality and region (*jun xian xian li zhong zhenguan* 郡縣鄉里中真官), comprising the Lords of Pneuma Injection

40. *Zhengyi fawen tianshi jiao jieke jing* 21b.
41. See the "Daoshi jieguo zhang" 道士解過章, in *Taishang xuanci zhuhua zhang* 2/2b.

(*zhuqi* 注氣), Inspection (*jiancha* 監察), and Interrogating and Summoning (*kaozhao* 考召); sometimes even the local earth god and other chthonian spirits (*tudi lingqi* 土地靈氣) were notified.[42] Gods with local jurisdiction like the God of the Hearth (*zaojun* 灶君), the Director of Fates (*siming* 司命), and the Earth God (*sheshen* 社神) were also tasked with gathering information on the individuals within their assigned areas and reporting to the Heavenly Bureaus. In the final stage of the conferral of a new register, the master summons the Four Lords of Interrogation and Summoning, who are responsible for summoning the relevant gods, who, in turn, question and interrogate the lower-level spirits as to the conduct of the candidate. In the "Placard and Petition for Promotion in Register," the master announces the result of this investigation:[43]

> I reverently dispatched the merit officers, emissaries, and Lords of Interrogation and Summoning, together with their clerks, to examine the mortal, in order to determine his situation and disposition. X is a good choice.
>
> 謹遣功曹使者、考召君吏，考覈肉人，審知情實。某應良選。

We do not know how the master received the report of these officers. Today it would be common to cast divination blocks, but in medieval China it could have come in the form of a vision, a spoken message, or some other mantic means. In any case, a report from the spirits in some form was necessary for every ordination ritual. Thus we see that the multitude of spirits, high and low, that surrounded the Daoist priest and populated his or her body did not merely protect and observe but also communicated the knowledge of the spirit world.

---

42. See *Zhengyi fawen lubu yi* 15b.
43. "Jin lu ci zhang" 進籙刺章, in *Zhengyi fawen taishang wailu yi* 10a.

The Libationer as Judge

In a traditional teacher-disciple relationship, the teacher functioned very much like a parent and hence had the authority to discipline his students. Daoist masters had even greater authority, because they represented the Daoist Heavens. The precepts disciples accepted as part of their ordination rank in the church were their code of conduct, as we see in the following passage from the *Protocol of the Outer Registers*:[44]

All those who transgress the precepts, whether they rebel against their admonishments, join with other Daoists to put faith in heterodox forces, or mix their worship and put faith in the profane, this represents a lack of fidelity and a betrayal in their heart of hearts, foolish confusion and doubt, and a deep entanglement in misleading hindrances. The master should admonish such individuals three times. If they can truly change and preserve the One without confusion, then they will be effective in summoning the gods. If after three admonishments such persons do not reform, this is rebelling against the Dao and opposing one's revered master; according to the rules, they should be stripped of their registers. If such people have transgressed against the Perfected by worshipping the profane or serving no one, the master may take pity on them and not blame or reprimand them for their former actions. If they respond with resentment and go to serve another, abandoning the root and pursuing the branch, though they may claim to be worshipping the Dao, in fact they are offending against the orthodox code. The master should transfer the various officers [assigned in their registers]; this may not be permitted. If as time passes they know enough to express regret and again establish exceptional merit, then beg to return, they should be permitted to advance according to their virtue. If they become angry and flee, not turning in their registers and talismans, the master should not harshly demand them; just transfer the officers.

凡違戒者，背負鞠言，恊道信邪，雜事信俗，此爲不專，中心懷二，愚迷猶豫，惑障纏深。師三誨之，必能改革，守一不惑，召

44. *Zhengyi fawen taishang wailu yi* 12b.

神有效。三誨不悛，是爲叛道，乖逆師尊，法應奪籙。違真倸
俗，及無所事，師慈愍之，不追咎責。怨對事他，棄本逐末，雖
名奉道，實犯正科。師移諸官，不得容受。積久知悔，更立殊
功，乞還聽許，依德昇遷。若瞋恚委遁，不輸籙符，師勿苦求，
但移而已。

Several points merit mention here. First is the relative leniency of Daoist law, granting three pardons before imposing punishment. This striking feature of the movement had already been noted by Chen Shou in his historical account of the movement in the *Record of the Three Kingdoms*.[45] Second is the prominence of religious crimes such as putting faith in the profane. The punishment is also religious in character, canceling registers and thereby demoting miscreants within the church. This punishment would have had immediate consequences since the wrongdoer would lack the supernatural protection necessary in a chaotic and dangerous world. Because of the unique structure of the Daoist church, with each master teaching a common curriculum across the breadth of China, an evildoer could seek to avoid punishment by bringing his or her register to another master and seeking membership in that master's flock. The home master held the trump card in such situations: he or she could submit a petition removing the individual's inner-dwelling gods and soldiers. Ultimately, the register was revealed to be a meaningless strip of cloth and the miscreant was bereft of spiritual aid.

Although primary authority for meting out punishment lay with the master, there was provision for a degree of consultation if the individual did not respond to exhortation:[46]

If [members] internally transgress against the otherworldly officials, the master and friends should remonstrate with them. If they continue to do it and do not follow their advice, they should in all cases be stripped of registers. The severity of the offense should be assessed

45. See *Sanguozhi*, "Weishu" 8/263.
46. *Zhengyi fawen taishang wailu yi* 13a.

in detail, with the master and friends discussing it. The commands and rules must be appropriately applied; both hidden and manifest [powers] value knowing [all the facts]. If the mistake of breaking the precepts continues, the master will suffer the same fate.

內犯陰官，師友諫喻，苟作不從，皆宜格奪。輕重詳量，師朋評議，令法取允。幽顯貴知。破戒謬濫，師資格同。

Here we see that misconduct by a novice was a serious matter; failure to deal with it could result in the punishment for the offense being applied to the master as well. If the precept breaker was already a libationer, the consultation would have included other libationers who had studied with the same master.

Infractions against secular laws also were of concern to the Daoist community and had to be dealt with by the master. As we see in the following passage, the master did have the resources to intervene:[47]

Further, if one externally transgresses against the officials of the mortal world, committing an offense worthy of execution or corporal punishment, this is also a betrayal of the Dao, and all such persons should be stripped of registers. After being beaten in order to redeem the punishment, the person can be absolved through submission of a memorial. If someone who is innocent suffers corporal punishment, announce this fact [to Heaven?] and do not strip him or her of registers.

又外犯陽官，死罪從刑，即是負道，皆應奪籙，鞭笞贖罰，章奏解之。刑而枉者，啓告勿奪。

Offenses against the legal code were necessarily offenses against the moral code of the Daoists, but the punishment was different. Even minor offenses against the legal code could result in mutilating punishment and a period of penal servitude. If, however, the lawbreaker was a Daoist, he or she would be demoted by confiscation of the register and would be subject to both physical

47. *Zhengyi fawen taishang wailu yi* 12b.

punishment and a fine, but the master would release the individual from the entanglements of the secular legal system through submission of a petition. Moreover, if the Daoist was wrongly accused, an announcement would be made to the spirits to this effect, and he or she would suffer no harm. In the mind of Daoists, at least, the heavenly code superseded that of the state.

The Libationer as Pastor

Among the many roles fulfilled by the Daoist libationer, none was more important than that of pastor to the households inscribed on his or her fate roster. Members of these families could come to the libationer with a wide range of problems. The libationer was expected to do everything possible to aid them, as we see in this exhortation from the *Statutes of the Mystic Capital*:[48]

> If there are people who come to you announcing they have a serious illness or are threatened by misfortune, you should do everything possible to rescue them. You must not burden them with your private matters, recklessly speaking of disasters and curses to seek favors from others. If you accept these [favors], this is a sin that will decrease your accumulated store [of merit].
> 百姓有疾病厄急歸告之者，當匍匐救之。不得以私事託設，妄說禍祟，求人意氣。受取皆計減爲罪。

Thus, the libationer must not only spare no effort to aid his or her parishioners but also make no improper demands of them in return for this service. This recalls the second half of the Pure Bond, that "the master does not accept money" (*shi bushou qian* 師不受錢). As a limitation on this injunction, the same source includes the following warning:[49]

48. *Xuandu lüwen* 14a–b. Cf. Yang Liangsheng 1956:27; Yang would emend *jian* 減 to *zang* 贓.
49. *Xuandu lüwen* 14b–15a.

You should carefully select those whom you rescue. You must not act in an unprincipled fashion, besmirching the pure void. In converting [people] to become citizens, always inspect the Statements they pen, questioning or rejecting their statement about the circumstances. You should ascertain that all in the household, young and old, agree; only then should you transmit the conversion and rescue them according to the code.

當詳擇救民，不得苟且，塵穢清虛。化民皆檢其墨辭，質却情狀。令家內大小和同，然後宣化，依科救之。

Here the libationer accepts the claims made in the Statement (*ci* 辭) only after inspecting it carefully, rejecting improper requests, and making sure that all in the household agree with the requests. Since almost all illnesses or other misfortunes had their roots in sinful behavior by some member of the family, the libationer was also to use this opportunity to preach to them concerning proper conduct.

Having listened to the parishioner's problems and confirmed the parishioner's Statement, the libationer would suggest a response. Usually this involved the performance of some sort of ritual, but it also included moral exhortations and penance. In the early days, the most common advice was almost certainly reflection upon one's faults, followed by repentance expressed in the Personally Written Missive to the Three Offices and sometimes acts of penance akin to modern community service, such as repairing the local roads or bridges.[50] The simplest requests could be voiced orally in the family oratory during the morning or evening audience rite, but the head of household might still want advice as to how to phrase such a request, whether pledge offerings were necessary, or what deity to call upon.

As an intermediate step, the libationer might counsel the family to offer a request kitchen (*yuanchu*), preparing a meal for a certain number of members of the community and dedicating the merit earned thereby to a specific purpose, be it restoring the health of a

---

50. See chapter 1 for a discussion of early references to these practices in external sources.

family member, assuring a good harvest, or simply forestalling misfortune in the coming year.[51] The kitchen-feast often took place at the parish, and the vessels for the meal could be borrowed there. The libationer was responsible for offering a kitchen-feast at the time of the Assemblies, drawing upon the food tithed by his or her parishioners to supply the meal.

Petitions

The most important responsibility of the libationer was the composition and ritual submission of petitions (*zhang* 章) to the Heavenly Bureaus. The crafting of a petition took considerable expertise, some of it technical knowledge, such as which gods to petition and how to write the document (discussed in detail below), but also the social skills needed to discover the root cause of misfortune or disharmony in the home of someone who came to the libationer in need. Based on my field work in Taiwan, it appears that this aspect of the Daoist priest's life has not changed over the centuries.

Petitions to celestial bureaucrats, unlike oral requests made during the audience ceremony, could only be offered by certain members of the early church. Through petitions, church members realized their goals of longevity, health, fortune, and salvation. The foundational Personally Written Missives to the Three Offices, through which all members confessed their sins, repented, and begged forgiveness, were submitted by placing them on a mountain, burying them in the earth, and sinking them into a body of water. The petition, by contrast, was delivered directly to the heavenly bureaucrats by supernatural beings that were summoned out of the body of the officiant through a rite called the Exteriorization of Officers (*chuguan*).[52] These officers were not part of the psycho-physical constitution of all human beings, like the body gods detailed in the *Scripture of the Yellow Court*, but rather

51. For more detail on kitchens, see Kleeman 2005b and chapter 6.
52. For an example of this rite, see chapter 7.

were conveyed to the Daoist through an ordination ritual conferring a register.

This complex of registers, register spirits, and petitions is so basic to Celestial Master Daoism, so early, and so universal that it is definitional. Its ubiquity alone suggests that it could not have been created after the dispersion of Daoist believers at the fall of the Hanzhong state in 215 CE. We also have the testimony of Tao Hongjing, who quotes extensively from the *Protocol of the Twelve Hundred Officials*, a text listing the celestial deities to be invoked in a wide variety of specific contexts in order to attain desired goals, and explicitly attributes this work to the Hanzhong period church.[53] These officials could only be invoked through a petition, the petition could only be delivered by the spirits of the register, and the spirits could only be obtained through the conferral of a register by an accepted religious professional who was already in possession of a more exalted register. For all these reasons, we can safely assume that the entire complex was present at least in the time of Zhang Lu, if not already during the time when Zhang Daoling served as Celestial Master.[54]

Rules for Submitting Petitions

Master Redpine's Petition Almanac is the primary repository of surviving petitions. Its table of contents lists 134 different petitions, of which 66 are extant. The work has been dated variously from the end of the Southern Dynasties to the Tang or even Song dynasty, but, whatever the date of its latest material, it contains some authentically early petitions, including some that may derive from the Hanzhong kingdom.[55] Identifying and accurately dating these early works is difficult. Still, with the exception of a few relatively specialized petitions preserved in scriptures on ordination, such as those presented in the previous chapter, the *Petition*

---

53. On this text, see Wang Zongyu 2009a, 2009b; Cedzich 2009.
54. Lü Pengzhi makes this argument in a clear and convincing way (2008:25).
55. See Verellen 2003a, 2004.

Almanac is the only source that sheds significant light on this aspect of the early church's ritual practice.

On the basis of surviving examples of petitions, it is clear that they follow a certain pattern. A member of the community comes to the libationer, describes a problem, and requests help. The libationer first sets forth this series of events on the basis of the Statement of the supplicant, then gives an analysis of why there should be intervention, and finally requests divine aid, often indicating which supernatural agents should be assigned to deal with the matter.[56] The first part of the petition is described in detail in the following passage from *Master Redpine's Petition Almanac*:[57]

> Whenever one wishes to memorialize a petition, first prepare the Statement. List the place of origin, the name of the native village, the rank, surname and name, age, the number of family members surviving, their sexes and ages, the pledge offerings that they brought according to the Daoist code, the ritual master to whom they have come requesting that a petition be memorialized, that they humbly beseech compassion, and that you are making a special report on their behalf.
>
> 凡欲奏章，先具辭疏，列鄉貫、里號、官位、姓名，年幾，并家口、見存眷屬、男女、大小等，令依道科，齎某法信於某處，詣某法師，請求章奏，伏乞慈悲，特爲關啓。

One key purpose of this careful identification of the client was to avoid bureaucratic mishaps that might result in the petition being directed toward the wrong individual. Given the small number of common surnames and given names, such clerical snafus were already a concern in the common religion of the third

56. Although this information may have been conveyed verbally initially, it was recorded in a written document, which is invariably referred to in petitions by the phrase *jin an wenshu* 謹按文書 ("reverently, in accord with the written document . . ."). It is unclear whether it was the responsibility of the client to bring this document or if the libationer recorded it on the basis of oral testimony.

57. *Chisongzi zhangli* 1/18b6–10.

century BCE, when a document recorded an improper death owing to such an error.[58]

Writing the Petition

The *Petition Almanac* includes a small number of essays that directly address aspects of the petitioning process. They can be rather technical in nature and are difficult to date, but they are worth careful consideration. Tao Hongjing criticized libationers of his day for often failing to comply fully with these instructions, but they did provide a model for all to emulate.[59] One such essay is titled "How to Write a Petition":[60]

When writing a petition, do not mix the brush or inkstone [with those used for other purposes]. Grind the ink, turning to the left forty-nine times; do the same when regrinding.[61] When writing "for your consideration," write it an inch below the phrase "I bow twice." The phrase "your servant" is separated from the line "for your consideration" by three lines. The phrase [beginning] "Great Purity" should be separated from "your Servant X" by three lines. The record of counter-Jupiter [i.e., year of birth] should be separated from "Great Purity" by three lines. If the writing of the petition is completed and you are interrupted by a minor matter, you cannot send up the petition for an entire year.[62] If you have not added the small

58. See Li Xueqin 1990; Harper 1993.

59. *Dengzhen yinjue* 3/13a–b. *Zhengyi fawen taishang wailu yi* and the Dunhuang manuscript S.203 (both discussed in the preceding chapter) provide similar normative models for training students. Such documents must have circulated widely, even if they were not always followed exactly.

60. *Chisongzi zhangli* 2/3b–4b; much of this is repeated in *Yaoxiu keyi jielü chao* 11/14a–b, where it is attributed to the *Statutes of the Mystic Capital* 玄都律. Cf. Cedzich 1987:83–84.

61. In his *Secret Essentials for Ascending to Perfection*, Tao Hongjing notes that you turn to the left to mimic the progression of the twelve lunar mansions across the ecliptic toward the east (when facing south). See *Dengzhen yinjue* 3/12b.

62. It is uncertain what sort of "minor matter" is intended here, presumably something ill-omened or inauspicious. There is a parallel to this passage and the

characters [at the end of the petition], you can send up the petition after a month. The small characters at the upper register should be 3.5 inches [from the top]; in the middle register, 4.5 inches; in the lower register, 5 inches; it cannot be more than this. If you let people with much to say write 1.5 inches more, this is wrong. If the petition reaches the counter-Jupiter part and you are at the end of the paper, it cannot be sent up. If [the page] has a line of the main text, then it is acceptable. If it is two lines, you can add another sheet of paper. As for wrong or missing characters, in a small petition, there must not be more than three; in a large petition, you can estimate the [permissible] number according to this standard. When writing a petition, leave eight-tenths of an inch margin at the top; on the bottom, there should be room for a column of ants. When writing a petition, spread a kerchief on the table; do not let the petition come into contact with the table. Do not let your robe rest on top of the petition or let it fall to the ground. When you enter the oratory to write a petition, do not let common people make a ruckus, discuss other matters, or use profane language. When writing a petition, do not let the brush touch the water or your mouth. You should close your mouth; you must not eat anything or breathe on [the petition] 氣衝. When writing a petition, wash your hands first, and write it facing north. If your person has been polluted by exposure to a dead body, you must not write a petition. You must not write incorrect or incomplete characters; the paper must not be ripped or torn; and you must not drink wine, eat meat, or smell of onions. You should straighten your robes and cap. You must not write a petition while naked or exposing yourself. You must be completely reverent and respectful. You must not write a petition while squatting. After finishing it, you should proofread it one time and only then memorialize it. The character "your servant" (*chen* 臣) must not come at the top of a line. You must not end a line with "living" or start a line with "dead" (*si* 死). The character "demon" should not come at the top of a line. You should not break between the characters of someone's name. You must not let anyone [unauthorized] peek at the petition or touch it. The date following "Great Purity" cannot be written in advance; it must be added just before [memorializing]. If you are submitting a petition about an

---

next couple of lines of text in *Yaoxiu keyi jielü chao* 11/11a6–b2, where it is attributed to the *Statutes of the Mystic Capital*. Unfortunately, that version is equally opaque.

urgent matter, you should use a red-ink brush to write the title.[63] If you submit a petition to drive away a demon, you should use vermilion to write the name of the Correct Unity disciple. If it is a petition to cure an illness caused by deviant forces, use green paper. The lords and clerks of the Three Offices value green. If it is an illness caused by a pneuma-injecting demon and you make a demon-binding petition, write it in vermilion on green paper. After the petition has been memorialized, burn it in the parish building. Combine by pounding [the ashes] with two-tenths of an inch of true vermilion, then combine with honey to make a pellet; at dawn the next morning, enter the oratory, bow twice, and swallow one. Anyone on the point of death will live. Do not let anyone know about this. If you enter the oratory to write a petition because of illness, then burn incense in all four directions.

書章筆硯勿雜用。研墨左轉四十九。重磨亦然。「以聞」去「再拜」下一寸。「臣姓」去「以聞」隔三行。「太清」去「臣姓」三行。「太歲」去「太清」三行。若書章已成而有小事，經年不可上。若未下細字，經月可上。細字上度三寸五分；中度四寸五分；下度五寸。不得過此。今人多言一寸五分，非也。章至「太歲」紙盡，不可上。若有主行，即可。若兩行，可全紙續之。錯誤脫字，小章不過三字；大章以意量之。書章上讓八分，下通蟻走。書章以巾敷案上。不得令著床。勿以衣著章上及落地。書章入靜不得常人亂鬧、論及他事、臭穢之言。書章不得以筆點水中及口。當閉口。不得有所食及氣衝。書章淨洗手向北書。身經殗穢，不得書章。書不得敗字不成。紙不得破裂。不得飲酒、食肉。薰穢。當整理衣冠。不得裸露書章。當須匍匐恭敬。不得蹲踞書章。畢，先校讀一遍，然後奏之。「臣」字不得上行頭。不得懸「生」露「死」。「鬼」字不得居行首。不得抽破人姓名。不得令人竊讀、觸動。太清日月不得預下當在臨時。若急事上章，當用朱筆題署。若上逐鬼章，當朱書所上正一弟子姓名。若治邪病章，用青紙。三官君吏貴在青色。若痒氣鬼病作繫鬼章朱書青紙。章奏了於治中燒。和真朱二分，擣和蜜爲丸。平旦入靖，再拜服之。垂死皆活。莫令人知。若因病入靖書章，即四面燒香火。

63. The passage from this sentence to the end is also found in *Yaoxiu keyi jielü chao* 11/11b6–12a4, where it is attributed to an early Shangqing document, the *Biography of Lady Wei* 魏夫人傳.

These directions describe the exact format to use for the petition, which is, after all, a formal request to be presented to some of the most powerful bureaucrats in the cosmos. Mistakes when writing had to be corrected but even so had strict limits. As in the case of the petition for promotion in the previous chapter, supernatural officers were sent along with the petition to correct any mistakes or omissions not caught by the libationer. The document itself was sacred and could be defiled through inappropriate treatment, such as letting it touch the ground or writing the document while not properly attired. Even today, the formal documents used in Daoist rituals are long, complex affairs subject to a variety of rules and taboos.

How to Submit a Petition

Just as the beginning of a petition was essential because it set out the details about the supplicant and the problem to be remedied, the ending was where the religious officiant identified himself or herself, noted the date and place the ritual was performed, and specified the recipient. One surviving passage describes how the reading of this part was to be performed:[64]

> When you submit a petition, you should altogether bow four times. In order to finish reading the petition, even the line with the date is essential. You must have a correct heart and perform the ritual in the proper way. The way to read the small characters is to kneel with body straight and use a small voice that can barely be heard. In the rite there is no provision for lifting it from the table while reading. You should read the small characters in just one breath.

> 若上章一通，前後可四拜。讀章竟，太歲皆當緊要。須正心整頓取法也。讀細字法，長跪下聲，出口而已。法無擎案讀者。讀細字一氣耳。

64. *Yaoxiu keyi jielü chao* 11/14b3–5, where it follows immediately upon the end of a passage identical to that cited above, here attributed to the *Statutes of the Mystic Capital.*

Tang Daoist encyclopedias like the *Excerpts from the Precepts and Statutes for Ritual Codes Essential to Cultivation* (*Yaoxiu keyi jielü chao*) of Zhu Faman preserve a variety of information on the practice of writing petitions. Much of it derives from two sources, the *Statutes of the Mystic Capital* and the *Code of the Great Perfected* (*Taizhenke*). The *Statutes of the Mystic Capital* is an authentically early work, dating to the early years of the church, but, like many traditional scriptures, it was also added to and otherwise modified in subsequent centuries. The *Code of the Great Perfected* actually derives from a Shangqing milieu, but its attention to Celestial Master ritual testifies to the fact that the Shangqing revelation represented a reform movement within the Celestial Master church rather than a new religion. We cannot be sure that all of these regulations existed from the beginning of the church, but we can exclude later developments, such as taboos on the timing of ritual performances and elements derived from Buddhist practice.

A good example of such regulations is the following paragraph from the *Statutes of the Mystic Capital*, which sets out standards of behavior in the parish and principles to follow when submitting petitions.[65]

When entering the parish to submit a petition, all should stand upright and hasten their steps.[66] Showing deference to those around them, they should be serious, respectful, and most reverent. Men and women must not mingle or commit the fault of gazing improperly. If one disobeys the statute, the fine is three ounces of jade. You must not submit a petition for someone who has committed the Ten Evils or the Five Rebellions.[67] The phrasing should be substantial and not

65. *Yaoxiu keyi jielü chao* 11/11b. The second half of this passage is also found in *Chisongzi zhangli* 1/19a.

66. During auspicious rituals, movement was by quick, small steps to show reverence.

67. The Ten Evils (*shie* 十惡) involve prohibitions on drunken debauchery, slander, irreverence to the teacher or faith, stealing and revealing scriptures, unreturned borrowing, killing for food and duplicity, unfilial or ungrateful behavior, careless recitation of scripture, acting angrily toward others, and distorting the scriptures. See *Taishang dongxuan lingbao zhihui zuigen shangpin dajie jing* 1/6b–7a. For the Five Rebellions, see chapter 3, n. 61.

ornamented, workmanlike and not stylized, simple and not flashy, honest and not hypocritical, straightforward but not unrestrained, discriminating but not intricate, supple but not defiled, pure and not muddled, true and not deviant, selectively concise and exuding credibility; then it will move Heaven and Earth, motivate the spirits, who will take it up to the Heavenly Bureaus, and the response will arrive immediately.

入治上章，皆正身趨步，科次左右，肅恭致敬。不得男女雜錯，妄視謬誤。違律，罰玉三兩。不得爲十惡、五逆之人上章。辭質而不文，拙而不工，朴而不華，實而不僞，直而不肆，辯而不煩，弱而不穢，清而不濁，真而不邪，簡要而輸誠，則感天地、動鬼神，御上天曹，報應立至。

Thus, mingling of the sexes was inappropriate in this ritual context, and the style of the petition was intended to set it apart from all temporal compositions. We see a similar concern with mixing in the following passage, also from the *Statutes*, but here it is the mixing of petitions from people of different status that presents a problem:[68]

Petitions on behalf of Daoist priests and female officers, officials of the province or county, commoners and Daoist citizens should not be mixed or memorialized together. Their official ranks are different. Those who disobey will be tortured by illness for fifty days. Daoist priests and female officers who present petitions at feasts or assemblies must carry official tablets and wear hempen coats; their ritual garb should be neat and in good repair. If submitting a petition to cure an illness, the host must not kill living beings to feast the Daoist priest. If the Daoist priest knows about this and still eats them, the master and the host will bear the same penalty, losing two Jupiter-cycles [i.e., twenty-four years] of fate counters. When submitting the petition, the household members, young and old, must not be disorderly, speaking in loud voices so as to scare the chickens and rouse the dogs, or the ritual pneumas will be unsettled. If one disobeys this statute, the fine will be one Jupiter-cycle [twelve years] of fate counters. After the petition has been memorialized, you

68. *Yaoxiu keyi jielü chao* 11/13a–b.

must not leave the document in a profane home; because it contains the name of the Most High. It should be burnt in the tenth month of the following year. If one disobeys this statute, the fine will be one Jupiter-cycle [i.e., twelve years] of fate counters. If one memorializes a petition while under the influence of alcohol, the fine is to suffer illness for one thousand days and lose five years of one's lifespan.

律曰：道士女官、州縣官人、百姓道民等章，並不得參雜，同共奏呈。官位不同。違者，考病五十日。道士女官齋會呈章，要須笏褐法服整頓。若上章治病，主人不得殺生飴道士。道士知而故食者，師與主人同罰，減筭二紀。上章之時，家中大小不得歷亂，高聲大語，驚雞動犬，則法氣不安。違律，罰筭一紀。章奏了，不得放縱文書在俗人家。爲有太上名字。至一年十月即燒。違律，罰筭一紀。若承酒氣奏章，罰病一千日，減五年壽。

Here the distinction would seem to be among three major groups—Daoist officers, local officials, and common citizens—but without distinction between male and female, or Daoist and non-Daoist. The significant index is rank, and representatives of the state are accorded a rank below church officials but above mere members of the church or peasants. This statute probably derives from a later period and a region where predominately Daoist communities were rare and Daoists were often employed to perform rituals on behalf of non-Daoists. One indicator of this is the use of the term "Daoist priest" rather than "libationer"; this becomes common no earlier than the fifth century. An important distinction is still maintained, however, between the profane and the faithful: the ritual documents used in the petition ceremony must not be shown to or left in the care of profane individuals, even though they had requested, paid for, and benefited from the ritual that employed these documents. Only members of the church might see them.

This passage is followed by a number of miscellaneous rules, also taken from the *Statutes*.[69] These prohibit the submission of petitions during a storm or continuous rain, or when the liba-

---

69. *Yaoxiu keyi jielü chao* 11/13b7–14a2.

tioner suffers from one of the "six acute illnesses" (*liuji* 六疾).[70] Another rule, which might reflect increasing Buddhist influence, prohibits the submission of petitions after having consumed wine, meat, or the "five aromatic vegetables" 五辛 (onions, chives, garlic, leeks, and ginger). Intermixed with these is a passage on the writing medium. Normally petitions were written on paper, which is why paper was the most common pledge offering, but this rule says that, for cases of several deaths in a row or release from banishment to an inauspicious tomb (*muzhe* 墓謫), the petition could be submitted on a wooden plaque (*muzha* 木札). The significance of this distinction is not clear.

Another issue discussed in this material is the direction that one should face when submitting a petition. The early oratory was supposed to face east, and most ritual was performed at the table facing toward the east, or occasionally with the officiant turned around to face the deities of the oratory where they were enshrined in the west. This was a departure from non-Daoist Chinese ritual, which placed the secular ruler and sacred deity both in the north, with the yang force of the southern sun shining in their faces.[71] The *Code of the Great Perfected* gives the most straightforward instructions:[72]

When memorializing a petition, face east. Later, to memorialize and display a petition, you should in both cases face north. If ordaining someone during the daytime, face east to split the contract.[73] When making a request to the stellar lodges for someone's life at noon and

70. These are illnesses involving chills, fever, the extremities, the digestive system, the mind, and the heart. See *Chunqiu Zuozhuan zhengyi*, Duke Zhao 1, 31b.

71. Sterckx, however, points out that, at a traditional banquet, the guest of honor sat facing east. See Sterckx 2011:39, n. 136, citing *Shiji* 107/2844.

72. *Yaoxiu keiyi jielü chao* 11/12a1–4.

73. A contract (*qi* 契) typically was written twice on a single board or other writing material, then split in half, with each party to the contract retaining one-half, which could be reunited when demanding execution or acknowledging completion of the contract. In the case of Daoist contracts, the other party was divine and that half of the contract was presumably conveyed by burning and held in heavenly storehouses for reference.

midnight or making a request with an emergency petition, in both cases face north and visualize the Great Thearch. If it is not a great petition to the stellar deities, or a major ritual where one ascends the altar, or an emergency petition for arresting or expelling, one need not submit it in the open.

奏章向東，其後奏及露章，並向北。白日授度，向東破契，子午請命星宿請急章，皆向北，存大帝。自非星宿大章、登壇大事，并收捕驅除急章，不煩露上。

Other passages are more complex, as we see in the three following quotations, all from the *Statutes of the Mystic Capital*, though probably not all of the same date:[74]

To cultivate blessings and extend your years, dispel disaster and harm, or suppress the hundred ailments, submit the petition facing east. To gain release from the tomb, eliminate a reprimand, open your heart and make hearing and sight perspicacious, or pass through disasters and survive cyclical dangers, submit the petition facing west. If you disobey this statute, you will fall ill for one hundred days. For an acute ailment from which only one out of a hundred survive, submit the memorial facing north. To cultivate your person and nourish your life force, or enrich your wealth and status, submit the petition facing south.

修福延年，消卻災害，厭百病，皆東向上章；解墓除責，開心聰明，過災度厄，皆西向上章；違律，病百日。疾病百死一生，北向上章；修身養命，溫潤富貴，皆向南上章。

When submitting a petition to apologize for a sin, family members old and young face north and first apologize to the Thirty-Two Heavens. The entire family, young and old, with hair unbound and hands crossed [like a prisoner], faces north and confesses transgressions to the petition. For disobeying this statute, the penalty is ten days of illness.

上章謝罪，家中大小，北向先謝三十二天。舉家大小，散髮交手，北向對章首過。違律，罰病十日。

74. These passages are preserved in *Xuandu lüwen* 21a and 20b (first and third, respectively) and in *Yaoxiu keyi jielü chao* 11/12a–b (first and second).

If a petition dispels acute illnesses, face the Gate of Demons [NE]; if it dispels disaster and cyclical danger, face the Door of Earth [SE]; if it seeks longevity or seeks fortune, status, wealth, and benefit, face the Gate of Heaven [NW]; if it dispels slander and curses, face the Gate of Humans [SW]. To suppress tigers, face *yin* [ENE], to suppress snakes, face *si* [SSE]. In this way you will combine your power with that of the Heavenly Dipper and be greatly auspicious. For disobeying this statute, the penalty is one hundred days worth of fate counters.

章，消疾病，向鬼門；消災厄，向地戶；求長生、求富貴財利，向天門；消口舌咒咀，向人門。厭虎向寅，厭蛇向巳，與天罡并力，大吉。違律，罰筭百日。

These sources indicate that the orientation of ritual activity depended on its nature and goal. It is uncertain if this was true in the early church. The first passage could be early, but the second mentions the Thirty-Two Heavens, which dates it no earlier than the late fourth century, and the third passage, which uses directions like Gate of Heaven that are tied to the system of the Eight Trigrams, is clearly a product of Daoism after the incorporation of southern occult traditions.[75] It may be that all of these ascriptions of specific directions to rituals appeared after the development of the round, three-tiered altar in the open that was used for Lingbao *zhai*-rituals.

The other major restraint on rituals elaborated in these texts concerns days on which the ritual cannot be performed. This seems curious in light of the declaration that the Three Assemblies are observed on the designated days, regardless of the climactic conditions or occult indications.[76] These taboos must be

---

75. These terms for the four intermediate directions (NW, SW, SE, NE) are found first in texts compiled during the Latter Han, such as the *Wu Yue chunqiu* 吳越春秋, under the first year of King Helü (514 BCE). They were associated by this time with the Eight Trigrams and are also prominent in the *Taipingjing*, which was incorporated into Daoism during the fifth or sixth century. See Zhou Shengchun 1997:4/39–40.

76. *Chisongzi zhangli* 2/5a. See chapter 6 and the treatment of land contracts buried in fifth- and sixth-century tombs below.

later, but their emergence cannot be dated with precision. They are of two types, focusing either on the day of the month or on the date in terms of the cycle of sixty days denoted by ten heavenly stems and twelve earthly branches. The first chapter of *Master Redpine's Petition Almanac* lists specific days of the month that are auspicious for submitting a petition and others that are lucky for observing a fast. Another section provides comments for each day of the sixty-day cycle, stipulating which sorts of ritual activity are auspicious and which contraindicated. There is also a list of specific hours of each day when the Gate of Heaven is open or closed. The second chapter lists a number of other groups of taboo days, like days when Yin Killers are present 陰殺所在 or the Killing the Master taboo days 殺師忌日. Hemerology was commonly employed in China to schedule all sorts of activities, but observing all of these rules would have made planning a ritual difficult indeed.

In the discussion of the ordination ritual in the preceding chapter, I described submitting a petition for promotion, including a key stage when the officiating libationer crouched on the ground and recited a spell as the gods externalized from his or her body carried the petition up to the Heavenly Bureaus. This seems to have been the norm for the first two centuries or more of the church's existence,[77] but eventually, perhaps after the revelation of the Supreme Purity texts with their focus on visualization, it became common for the libationer to visualize himself or herself accompanying the divine emissaries up to the Heavens to watch the delivery of the petition. This process, as depicted on the cover, is described in a text called "Visualization" (*cunsi* 存思) from the *Code of the Great Perfected*, preserved in *Master Redpine's Petition Almanac*:[78]

> After completing the Handling [of the Petition], crouch on the floor in front of the writing table. Visualize scarlet-red pneumas emerging

77. Chang Chaojan 2010.
78. *Chisongzi zhangli* 2/24b–25a. I benefited from a discussion of this text with Lennert Gesterkamp in November 2009. See also the summary of this paragraph in Lü Pengzhi 2010:2, 1279, and the translation in Cedzich 1987:95–97.

from your heart and ascending to Heaven. In an instant it will be as if you have traveled one hundred *li* [ca. 40 kilometers]. The scarlet-red pneumatic path billows before you; on both sides is unblemished darkness, featuring only many bejeweled trees. Suddenly you see a yellow path, which is the Yellow Path of the Sun and the Moon [i.e., the ecliptic]. Crossing directly the Yellow Path and [continuing] five or six *li*, you will see in the distance purple clouds beclouding all. Proceeding directly to the purple clouds, you will see the Gate of Heaven. The gate is eighteen feet high. Your various attendants must all stay there. Take the petition to the gate, accompanied by only General Zhou, the on-duty merit officer, and the Petition-Transmitting Jade Lad. To the west, greet the Correct Unity Ritual Master of the Three Heavens, Zhang Daoling. After bowing twice, completely set forth the circumstances of the petition. The Celestial Master will bow nine times, then proceed to enter from the Phoenix Pavilion Gate. After a moment, a transcendent lad wearing a vermilion robe and dark hat will emerge and go to the Petition-Transmitting Jade Lad. He will receive the petition from [the Jade Lad's] hands and enter the gate. After a moment, he will come back out and lead you in to meet the Most High. The Most High sits facing the hall, wearing a Nine-Colored Cloudy Auroral cape and a Nine-Virtue hat, attended on his left and right by two dark-clothed Perfected. You will also see the Great One, wearing a vermilion robe and dark crown, who will present the petition to the Most High. The Most High will peruse the petition. Then the Great One, having received the intention of the Most High, will sign the document below the "Jade Ruler of Great Purity," writing, "Approved." When this is complete, you will see another transcendent lad who will accept the petition on the right side of the steps and give commands to the emissary of the Bureau on duty that day. Mentally bow twice, then take leave of the Most High and depart through the gate. Bow twice again and take leave of the Celestial Master. Together with the perfected officers who submitted the petition, leap down and return to the place where the petition was submitted. Then rise and proclaim, "It has been submitted for consideration."

操復畢，便於案前伏地，便存赤紅炁從己心中出，上昇天。俄頃如經歷百里。赤紅炁路蕩蕩。兩邊無瑕翳，惟多寶樹。忽見一黃道，即日月黃道也。直過黃道五六里，遙見紫雲隱隱。直到紫雲，見天門。門度一丈八尺，諸侍衛悉住。唯與周將軍及直使功

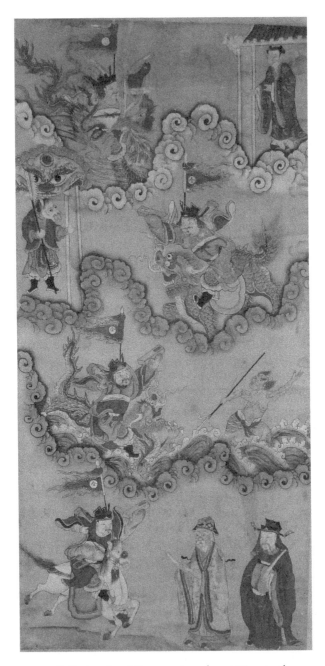

FIGURE 8. Emissaries deliver copies of a petition to the
Four Realms: the Heavens, the Earth, the Watery Realm,
and the World of Men. 60 × 124 cm. Personal collection
of the author.

曹、傳章玉童擎章表至闕門之下。西謁見正一三天法師姓張名道
陵。載拜訖,具陳章表事由。天師九拜,即往鳳凰閣門之下入。
須臾,有一仙童朱衣玄冠出,就傳章玉童,手中接章表入,少
頃,復出,引入見太上。太上著九色雲霞之帔,戴九德之冠,當
殿而坐。左右二玄真人侍衞。又見太一著朱衣玄冠,呈太上章
表。太上一覽,太一承太上意,署太清玉陛下,作依字。了,又
見一仙童,收章表於右陛,分付今日日直曹官使。心載拜,辭太
上出門。又載拜,辭天師。同奏章真官扑躍而迴至奏章之所。便
起稱以聞。

Although there may be some influence in this document from
the Supreme Purity movement, it retains basic Celestial Master
features, with the Most High Lord Lao as the supreme deity and
Celestial Master Zhang Daoling playing a key role in admitting
officials into his presence. Modern Daoist priests in Taiwan still
perform a visualization similar to this at the key point in the presentation of a petition, called the *fuzhang* 伏章 ([submission of] the
petition while crouching down), as part of a Daoist Offering ritual.[79] Modern practice is to burn the petition immediately at the
conclusion of the ritual, but in the early church the petitions were
stored safely, away from insects and dirt, until a certain number
accumulated, at which time all were burned together in a rite
called "Ending the Petitions" (*duanzhang* 斷章).[80]

Types of Petition

Petitions varied depending on the problem to be resolved and
the method chosen to address it. The following passage from the
Code of the Great Perfected details the order of petitions to be submitted in dealing with an illness. Since all illness was attributable
to supernatural causes, this was a vital issue for all libationers,

79. See Schipper 1982:134; Hsieh Tsung-hui 2008:72–73.
80. See *Chisongzi zhangli* 2/26b–27b, citing *Taizhenke*. The note suggests
that, if many petitions are submitted, they should be burned when a hundred
have accumulated; otherwise, they should be burned each year in the tenth
month, perhaps implying the last Assembly of the year.

who held the health and well-being of their flocks in the phrases of their petitions. The earliest formulation of such a list might have been simpler, but the passage still gives us a good idea of the factors that were understood to cause illness and the methods used in combating them:[81]

> For the various acute ailments, first submit a petition with a Confession Account. If there is no improvement, submit a Petition to Release from Interrogation. If there is no improvement, submit a Petition for Release from the Punishment for Sins of the Deceased. If there is no improvement, submit a Petition for Promotion. If there is continued decline, submit a Petition to Repel Killers and Arrest Infusing Demons. If there is further decline, submit a Great Petition for Release from Calamities and Cyclical Dangers. If there is still no relief, submit a Petition for Release from the Punishment of Five Generations of Tombs. If there is still no relief, submit a Petition for Supporting the Enfeebled and Those [Suffering from] Epidemics and Great Cyclical Dangers. If there is still no improvement, submit a Petition for Returning the Cloud Soul and Restoring the White Soul. If there is still no improvement, submit a Petition Settling the Tomb and Releasing from the Wasting Harm of the Five Soils.[82] If there is still no improvement, submit a Petition Settling the Tomb, Quelling Gods, and Expelling and Arresting Demons. If there is still no improvement, submit a Petition for Separating and Releasing from Internal and External Great Interrogations. If there is an acute worsening, submit a Releasing Petition to Beg for One's Life at Noon and Midnight and Repel Death from the Three Offices. If there is progress and relapses, submit a Petition Apologizing to the Thirty-Two Heavens Above. If it becomes critical, submit the Eighty-One Petitions That Contribute Pledge Offerings to Redeem Life, as well as Plucking out the Fate, as well as [Lighting] Candles

81. *Yaoxiu keiyi jielü chao* 11/10b–11a.
82. The Five Soils can refer to the different types of soil that make up the earth—the soils of forests, marshes, hills, riverbanks, and depressions—or to the five colors of soil (green, red, white, black, and yellow), corresponding to the five directions, which were combined to make a sacred altar to the soil. See *Kongzi jiayu*, "Xiang Lu," in Chen Shike 1987:1/1; Cai Yong, *Duduan* (Siku quanshu edn.) 2/9a. Whichever the exact referent, here it probably refers to the soil that was disturbed in the construction of a tomb.

and Lamps, as well as Releasing from and Driving Back Connections [to the Dead], as well as [Lighting the] Five Lamps, as well as the Twenty-Eight Asterisms, as well as Discerning the Asterism, as well as Releasing from the Great Infusions of the Deceased. If there is no disastrous disease, you must not wantonly demand this petition. Those who transgress this will be adjudged according to the Three Punishments.[83]

諸疾病，先上首狀章；若不愈，又上解考章；若不愈，更上解先亡罪讁章；若不愈，上遷達章。故沉，上卻殺收注鬼章；復沉頓，上解禍厄大章；復不差，上解五世墓讁章；復不差，上扶衰疫大厄章；復不愈，上還魂復魄章；復不愈，上安墓、解五土耗害章；復不愈，上安宅鎮神、驅除收鬼章；復不愈，上分解中外大考章。若急困，上子午請命、并卻三官死解章；若進退，上仰謝三十二天章；大危篤，上贖命交貤，又拔命，又燭燈，又解退復連，又五燈，又二十八宿，又審宿，又分解先亡大注，復八十一章。無災病，不得妄求此章。犯者，三刑論。

This passage shows that multiple causes might give rise to illness. The first suspect is personal sin and is dealt with through a confession, then a release from supernatural investigation into one's actions. Several petitions deal with one's deceased ancestors, who may have been accused or convicted of misconduct. Some deal with nefast influences from their tombs, either because the tombs are poorly sited or constructed, causing the dead suffering, or because their construction offended against spirits of the earth. Cyclical disasters are really just luck, a matter of timing, but there are also active demonic agents who might spread disease and misfortune and need to be driven off or seized. If all else fails, one can try to purchase redemption through offerings or rituals, and in the end there is a giant kitchen-sink sort of ritual where you toss everything imaginable at the disease. Performing this entire cohort of rituals would have been both time-consuming and expensive.

83. This passage also appears in the second chapter of *Chisongzi zhangli* (18b–19a), with the same attribution. There the passage ends with a threat of the "two punishments," and a commentary explains these as sweeping a road and repairing a bridge, both punishments mentioned in the *Shenxianzhuan* biography of Zhang Ling.

The passage mentions fourteen distinct petitions used to treat illness, followed by a mass ritual encompassing eighty-one different petitions, which it does not enumerate. The first chapter of *Master Redpine's Petition Almanac* (1/1a) speaks of a set of "three hundred great petitions," but that work preserves far fewer.[84] Other sources preserve a few more, especially the petitions surrounding ordination in the *Protocol of the Outer Registers* and the Dunhuang manuscript S.203. Du Guangting records twenty-eight petitions in use at the end of the Tang.[85]

A review of these petitions can tell us much about the ritual life of the early church, the sort of problems church members encountered, how they conceptualized them, and how they thought to respond to them. One large category was clearly illness; we have seen in the quotation above the numerous causes of illness. Other aspects of human physiology were also addressed through petitions. For example, we find (4/12a–16b) a series of four petitions related to children, including the Petition to Protect the Embryo 保胎章, the Petition to Hasten Birth 催生章, the Petition to Use Upper Brightness to Survive Cyclical Dangers 小兒上光度厄章 (for children plagued by bad dreams), and the Petition to Protect Infants and Youths 保嬰童章.

Another major focus of these petitions is the dead and their relationship to the living. The best-known example of this is the Great Petition for Sepulchral Plaints 大冢訟章, which has been studied by Maruyama (1986) and Nickerson (1997, who also provides a full translation of the first of two petitions with this title). A sepulchral plaint is a lawsuit lodged by a dead person with one of the Three Offices against a dead relative for an offense committed against the complainant either in this world or in the other world. The party being sued is often interrogated under torture and sometimes found guilty and a penalty assessed. At either stage, the

84. See Zhang Zehong 2000; Verellen 2004. Zhang believes that there were originally 1,200 at the founding of the Celestial Masters in 142, comprising the content of the *Protocol of the Twelve Hundred Officials*, which most other scholars believe was instead a list of supernatural officials to be employed in petitioning rituals.

85. See *Taishang xuanci zhuhua zhang*.

deceased may turn to living relatives for assistance or may be commanded by the court to repay the complainant through the assets, material or living, of these relatives. The most common notification involves a demonic infusion, which will result in the illness, misfortune, and/or death of a living member of the family. The petition seeks to sever these ties between living and dead by resolving the judicial entanglements of the other world, if possible, and denying their influence on living relatives, if not. Many sorts of worldly suffering were attributed to such lawsuits from the grave. A particularly well documented case involved the Xu 許 family at the center of the Shangqing revelations and a deceased wife, Tao Kedou 陶科斗, who was punished for the immoral actions of a Xu family member of the previous generation and sought to take the life of a Xu family infant to extricate herself from the lawsuit.[86]

How to Draw a Talisman

Talismans (*fu* 符) play a special role in Daoism as magical symbols that link this world and the heavenly realms. The efficacy of a talisman relies on the fact that it re-creates a sacred symbol that exists in the other world and permits one to draw upon divine forces and apply them to a this-worldly problem. The design itself is secret and can only be drawn after considerable training by someone adept at calligraphy, but the talisman is only a design unless it is "charged" (*chi* 敕) through the recitation of a spell that establishes the link with the divine. Talismans are often included in petitions but can also be independently displayed or burnt. Daoist priests often suspend the ashes in water to make a potent liquid that is useful in a variety of ways. Priests transmitted talismans together with registers to give the ordained individual the authority to command the spirits and perform the rituals conveyed by the register. *Master Redpine's Petition Almanac* preserves

86. This incident is explored in considerable detail in Bokenkamp 2007.

the most detailed instructions in an early source on how to draw an effective talisman.[87]

The rite begins with a purification of the ritual space. This is done by facing the cyclically dominant direction, determined by the season or month of the year, clacking the teeth, pronouncing a spell to charm a sword and water while visualizing the stars of the Dipper, and then spraying the water from the mouth. This is followed by a personalized spell to summon the Daoist spirits:

Generals Tang, Ge, and Zhou, Perfected of the Original Mandate:[88] Now the man [or woman] _____ suffers from an acute illness and has made an appeal to your servant, asking for rescue and protection. Your servant, in accordance with Daoist rites, will respectfully give a perfected talisman of the Dao to _____ to swallow or wear at the belt. I request that you command the perfected officers, the talisman-bearing emissaries, and the millions of ranks of Daoist pneumas to descend, in accordance with my spell, and enter into this talisman, there to circulate deities and deploy pneumas that will search out malefic sprites, execute demonic raiders, and rescue heavenly men [i.e., Daoists].

元命真人唐葛周三將軍：今有男女某甲疾病，告訴向臣，求乞救護。臣謹依道法，以道真符與某甲吞帶。當願勑下真官直符使者，百千萬重道氣，隨禁降入符中，行神布氣，搜索邪精，誅戮鬼賊，救濟天人。

The officiant then visualizes the deities of the oratory or parish floating on a roiling, multicolored cloud of perfected pneumas just

87. The following description is based on *Chisongzi zhangli* 2/1b–3a. The specific deities invoked in this example are no earlier than the fourth century, but the basic procedure is probably much earlier. It follows closely the instructions in *Dengzhen yinjue* 3/14a.

88. These three generals, corresponding to the heart and two kidneys and representing the primal essence of water and fire, are in charge of the diagrams and forms in the Dipper and appear for the conferral of registers, Declarations of Merit, and other rites. They are the subject of their own register, the Register of the Generals of the Three Primes, which is usually listed just after the One Hundred Fifty Generals Register. It is not, however, mentioned in *Lu xiansheng daomenke lüe*. See *Zhengyi xiuzhen lüeyi* 5b; Cedzich 1987:96, n. 180.

in front of the priest's writing table. These include the Talisman-Bearing Lads, clad in vermilion robes and green skirts, to the left and right, and the Talisman-Circulating General, dressed in vermilion robes and black cap with a sword at the waist and holding an axe, flanked by two more Talisman-Bearing Lads dressed in yellow with a red cape, carrying swords. Directly in front of the priest's face are the sun and the moon, less than a foot away, shining down upon the cup of vermilion ink to be used in the ceremony. The seven stars of the Dipper are atop the priest's head, with the Dipper's handle projecting forward over the cup of vermilion ink like the bill of a cap. The priest chants three times, "I unite my light with the sun of the Heavenly Thearch." Then, visualizing the pen that has been dipped in the vermilion ink as a flying snake, the priest holds his or her breath and writes the talisman.

The talisman, written in vermilion ink, is surrounded by a rectangular frame written in black. Depending on the situation to be addressed, the ink may be mixed with special ingredients like tiger bone or crushed pearl. The actual writing is done while silently incanting the following spell, which summons gods from all parts of the body to aid in the task:[89]

I respectfully command the Perfected Officers of the Five Appendages within your servant's body: the *hun*-soul will become the Heavenly Father, the *po*-soul will become the Earth Mother, the head will become the Duke of Thunder, the hair will become the black clouds, the top of the head will become the shining stars, the brain gate [fontanel?] will become the Vermilion Sparrow, the eyebrows will become the unicorn, the eyes will become the sun and the moon, the nose will become the Tiger-Rushers, the upper lip will become the Earl of the Wind, the lower lip will become the Rain Master, the tongue will become Inspector General of the Nine Provinces, the throat will become the Nine-Story Tower, the left cheek will become the Grandfather of the East, the right cheek will become the Grandmother of the West, the ears will become Distant-Hearing Transcendent Lads, the neck will become the Heavenly

89. *Chisongzi zhangli* 2/2b–3a.

Pillar, the shoulders will become the Vajra, the elbows will become the Strongmen, the left arm will become the Great General Repelling Di Barbarians of the Jade Compass, the right arm will become the Great General Destroying the Di Barbarians of the Jade Transverse, the palms will become fire chariots, the fingers will become armored troops, the liver will become the Green Thearch, the lungs will become the White Thearch, the heart will become the Red Thearch, the kidneys will become the Black Thearch, the spleen will become the Yellow Thearch, the intestines will become the Yellow Dragon, the gall bladder will become the Great One, the bladder will become the Earl of the River, the blood will become the Water Officer, the sinews will become the Heavenly Mainstay, the bones will become the Earthly Mainstay, the body hair will become the Net of Heaven, the feet will become white horses. The three officers walking before them will each lead a force of seven billion, riding in great chariots. All will emerge from your servant's body and aid your servant in writing the talisman, circulating pneumas to crush and kill violent demons, goblins, monsters, evil demons, and malefic pneumas. Quickly, quickly, in accordance with the statutes and commands commanded orally by the Most High.

謹勑臣身中五體真官，魂爲天父，魄爲地母，頭爲雷公，髮爲黑雲，頂爲明星，腦門爲朱雀，眉爲麒麟，眼爲日月，鼻爲虎賁，上脣爲風伯，下脣爲雨師，舌爲九州都督，喉爲九層樓臺，左頰爲東王公，右頰爲西王母，耳爲仙童遠聽，項爲天柱，肩爲金剛，肘爲力士，左臂爲璇璣卻狄大將軍，右臂爲玉衡破狄大將軍，掌爲火車，指爲甲卒，肝爲青帝，肺爲白帝，心爲赤帝，腎爲黑帝，脾爲黃帝，腸爲黃龍，膽爲太一，膀胱爲河伯，血爲水官，筋爲天網，骨爲地網，毛爲天羅，足爲白馬，前步三官，各領七千萬眾，乘駕大車，並從臣身中出，助臣書符行炁，破殺兇魔，魍魎魖魅，惡鬼邪炁，急急如太上口勑律令。

This formidable force of body gods with the three generals in the van, each leading a huge army, must be visualized in their appropriate clothing and holding appropriate weapons or other symbols of power in order to produce a talisman charged with magical power. The talisman can then be used in a variety of ways, posted on the sufferer's wall, pasted on his or her body, suspended in lustral water, or burned to transfer it into the ethereal realm.

Pledge Offerings

The greatest expense for the supplicant in presenting a petition with its talismans was the pledge offering (*guixin, xinwu*). As the name suggests, these represented the sincerity of the supplicant, rather than recompense for the libationer. As we see in the following quotation, they originally consisted only of items actually used in the preparation and offering of the petition or the operation of the parish, and hence contributed to operating expenses:[90]

> The Connecting Celestial Master Lord Zhang said: Whenever you proceed to the parish to request a petition, for a major one, [bring] one hundred sheets of paper, two writing brushes, and one ball of ink; for a minor one, fifty sheets of paper and one brush. This is to supply the leader when writing the petition, for laying out the draft, and for repairing mistakes, and does not exceed the limits for pledge offerings. Moreover, the rules for petition pledge offerings should all be clearly observed. If a petition is not fixed by a pledge offering, it cannot be used. After the petition has been memorialized, if the pledge-offering goods are too many, they should be distributed to the poor. You should practice hidden virtue.[91] The master should not use all of them. If calculating in tenths, the master should expend only three-tenths. The code of Heaven is extremely strict, and those who offend against it will have a crime before the Three Offices, the misfortune will reach to the ninth generation, and they will forever be a lower demon. Take care! Take care!

> 係天師張君曰：凡詣治請章，大者，紙百張，筆二管，墨一丸；小者，紙五十張，筆一管。此給主者書章起草，換易陋誤，不開信限也。且章信之法，宜明各遵之。章無信定，未可用。奏章已後，其信物多可施貧者，宜行陰德，不可師全用之。十分爲計，師可費入者，三分而已。天科甚嚴，犯者獲罪於三官，殃及九祖，永爲下鬼，慎之慎之。

90. *Yaoxiu keyi jielü chao* 11/9b–10a. The first part of this quote is paralleled in *Chisongzi zhangli* 1/18b.

91. Hidden virtue (*yinde* 陰德) refers to the merit that is accumulated in the other world when someone performs a meritorious act that is not immediately rewarded in the temporal realm. For an early example of the term, see *Han shu* 71/3046.

In Zhu Faman's compilation, this passage is preceded by a lengthy list of specific petitions and the rather more elaborate pledge offerings that are appropriate for each; the first chapter of *Master Redpine's Petition Almanac* contains a similar list. In addition to items mentioned above, there are other pledge offerings that seem necessary for the operation of the parish, like incense 香, oil and wax for lamps and candles, a writing knife 書刀 used for erasures, woven mats 席 for sitting on, vermilion paste 朱砂 for imprinting seals or writing in red, and plain silk 素, used for writing registers. Some of these items were expensive, however, and certain petitions demand items like a pair of gold bracelets that would have been ruinously expensive for a peasant family. There are two places in the *Petition Almanac* where this issue is discussed. The first is in the opening essay, which takes the form of a discussion between an interlocutor, Master Redpine, and the Heavenly Elder Pingchang 天老平長:[92]

> Whenever people are told to memorialize a petition, they must first prepare a pledge offering. The gods illuminate the proceedings, demanding sincerity of heart. If there are absolutely no pledge offerings, then the deities will not accept [the petition] and will reprimand you for your parsimony and miserly heart. He also said: Petitions do not have exact pledge offerings. The wealthy and fortunate increase them, the poor and straitened decrease them. Sometimes there is a high official from a rich family who in his heart desires merit but cherishes wealth and possessions, so he imitates a poor person in providing pledge offerings; this will not benefit him in his endeavors. The Code says: If there is a poor person from a humble background who seeks to request an Offering with the presentation of a petition, the master should provide pledge offerings on his or her behalf. Although the old petitions each detailed what should be used, in general there were three [classes]: the Son of Heaven, the kings and lords,[93] and the commoners. Since they are not the same

92. *Chisongzi zhangli* 1/1b–2a; the same passage occurs, attributed to a Code 科, in *Wushang huanglu dazhai lichengyi* 10/11a–b.

93. It is unclear who exactly is intended by this term. Kings were at this time usually members of the royal family, and the three highest bureaucratic offices

in status, the requirements for each are different. You cannot lump them together and make no distinction.

凡曰奏章，先須備信，神明鑒燭，冀質誠心。若都無信，即神明不納，責子有慳鄙不捨之心。又云：章無的信，富饒者增之，貧窮者減之。或有官高富足之家，心希功德，而恡惜財物，便效貧窮之人，出信如此，亦無益於有為。科云：有寒棲貧乏之人，求請章醮，師爲代出法信。舊章雖各具所用，大抵有三：天子、王公、庶人。且尊卑不同，品目各異，不可般混而無分別。

Thus, some sort of pledge offering is mandatory to confirm one's sincerity. Even though the ritual codes specify a distinct constellation of items for each petition, in practice they were to be tailored to the economic means of the supplicant. A later section in the same chapter (1/18a–b) elaborates on the different pledge offerings expected from the three classes mentioned above. For example, when cash is specified, the Son of Heaven uses golden coins, kings and lords use silver, and commoners use bronze; for a pledge offering of rice, the Son of Heaven would offer 72 liters, a king or lord, 48 liters, and a commoner, 24 liters; a pledge offering of oil would mean 24 liters for the Son of Heaven, 12 liters for a king or lord, and 4.4 liters for a commoner.

Rituals for the Dead

Postmortem care of the dead has been a primary concern of the Chinese since the oracle bone inscriptions that mark the beginning of Chinese history. They were focused on determining the status of the royal dead, appeasing discontent among them, and thereby avoiding or ameliorating any misfortune. Royal burials are the only monumental architecture to survive from archaic China. Although archaeological discoveries have shed much light on mortuary practice in Han and later China, we know compara-

---

were sometimes referred to as the "three lords" (*sangong* 三公), but, since it here contrasts with commoners, perhaps the term is meant to refer more broadly to elites.

tively little about funerary ritual beyond what we can infer from tomb finds and the occasional literary reference to elite practice.

The Latter Han dynasty saw many innovations in mortuary practice that are significant for understanding popular belief. These include land contracts (*maidiquan* 買地券) for the purchase of a tomb from the divine authorities as well as bottles or urns with spells and occasionally talismans intended to prevent demonic infusions. These grave-quelling texts (*zhenmuwen*) or infusion-dispelling texts (*jiezhuwen*)[94] have two goals: to eliminate any punishment due to the deceased for breaking taboos concerning digging in the earth and to separate the dead and the contagion of death from the living. In the already highly bureaucratized world of these documents, the deceased is formally transferred from the population rosters of the living to those of the dead. This is sometimes also reflected in tomb decoration, where the local head of the neighborhood (*tingzhang* 亭長) is seen standing in an open door, welcoming the deceased into their new home.

At its inception, Celestial Master Daoism did not envision its members dying at all; instead they would live to see the advent of a world of Great Peace, where the seed people would potentially live forever. Only sin, in the form of offenses against the precepts, could cause illness, and only a failure to properly repent of these sins would result in death.[95] The traditional bureaucracy of the world of the dead was identified with the "stale pneumas" (*guqi* 故氣) of the lower Six Heavens. The quasi-demonic officials of the netherworld were subordinate to the Three Heavens and their representatives, the Three Offices.[96] Protection from these

94. On land contracts, see Kleeman 1984; Seidel 1987. On grave-quelling texts, see Wu Rongceng 1981.

95. The passage in the *Xiang'er* commentary describing individuals whose vital organs survive a transition through the Great Yin to reemerge among the living (discussed in chapter 2) may have been a provisional response to those who died during this formative period.

96. See Kleeman 2011. This is the clearest reason why the Han mortuary documents discussed above are not Daoist or the direct source of Daoism, pace

nefast forces was available through confession and repentance, expressed through the famous Personally Written Missives to the Three Offices.

Daoists eventually developed more elaborate ritual procedures to deal with negative influences from the dead. A direct attack from the spirit of a dead human could be deflected by the spirits on one's register or those overseeing one's dwelling. More troubling were irate ancestors or those wronged by one's ancestors who sued in the otherworldly tribunals for justice or revenge. A lawsuit lodged against an individual with one of the Three Offices could result in the punishment of living descendants by illness, misfortune, or death. Although the proximate source of the trouble might be a demon, it was in the service of legitimate authority, so it could not be countered simply by deploying one's own protector spirits. Instead, one had to appeal to a libationer, who would draft a sepulchral plaint petition (*zhongsong zhang* 冢訟章).[97]

One way to forestall such problems was to submit a petition at the time of death that recorded a wide variety of possible errors committed by the deceased and request pardon for all of them at once. *Master Redpine's Petition Almanac* preserves one such petition, titled Petition on Behalf of the Deceased to Confess, Repent, and Redeem Sins and Release from Reprimand (Wei wangren shou hui shuzui jiezhe zhang 爲亡人首悔贖罪解譴章). The petition begins by recounting the Statement from the survivors of the deceased:[98]

> X was the descendant of a low-grade officer. Fated to live a certain number of years, she [or he] encountered the great transformation [i.e., death]. Bringing pledge offerings, we attached ourselves [to the Dao] in order to protect and heal ourselves. Receiving the kindness of sheltering security, young and old were fortunately consoled. But

Zhang Xunliao (1996, rep. in Zhang and Bai 2005:1, 107–32). See also Hsieh Shuwei 2010:737–38.

97. On the sepulchral plaint petition, see above as well as Maruyama 1986; Nickerson 1997; Lai Chi-tim 2002b.

98. *Chisongzi zhangli* 6/11a–12b.

because we were obstinate and foolish, with many failings in serving the Dao, this has brought interrogation and punishment. Recently it has been difficult, with not a single matter going right. Person Y has suffered illness, and since then . . .

某乙素以下官子孫，運會有年，遭逢大化。操信制屬，以自保治，蒙恩覆蓋，大小慶慰。而以頑愚，修奉多違，以招考罰。頃來轗軻，凡百無善。某身疾病，從來云云。

The Statement would have continued to list specific problems encountered by living family members. The libationer assesses the problem, setting out all the transgressions the deceased may have committed:

Humbly reflecting upon this, I think it must derive from a sprite or curse. I fear that the deceased X while alive committed a sin, was disloyal or unfilial, was lacking in benevolence or compassion, was jealous of her [or his] spouse, scolded or cursed, called upon Heaven or Earth or upon the divine spirits [in vain]. Perhaps she robbed or stole out of a desire for wealth, acted severely or unreasonably, was not constant in her actions, without a single good deed to bring about this great torture that left her bound before the Lord of the Earth. I fear that after perishing she received a heavy sentence so that her soul is suffering torture, bound before the Three Offices, sentenced to corporal punishment and indentured labor, her painful suffering so extreme that she cannot bear the pain and misery, to the point that she implicated the living. This has caused her family to suffer repeatedly so that the disasters are without end, and both living and dead endure hardship and disgrace from which they cannot extricate themselves. With these pure sentiments they have entrusted themselves to the pneumas of the Dao. They now have fully listed the sins [that the deceased] committed while alive and, setting them forth, proceeded to the parish, bringing with them _____ as offerings in order to establish the sincerity of their hearts and to redeem the myriad sins that X committed while alive.

伏自考思，精祟所由。恐亡人某生時犯罪，不忠不孝，不仁不慈，娌情嫉妬，罵詈咒詛，牽天引地，叫喚神靈。或貪財盜竊，枉剋非理，改動所作，凡百無善，致收大考，繫身后土。恐亡歿之後，被受重謫，魂魄考對，結在三官，徒刑作役，楚毒備至，不堪困苦，逮累生人，致令某家基考復注，殃禍不絕，生死困辱，不自解免。元元之情，憑恃道氣。某今備條某生時罪狀，首列詣治，并賫某物，以立心信，拔贖某生時所犯百萬之罪。

Having affirmed the sincerity of the deceased survivors and noted that they have followed proper procedure in bringing appropriate pledge offerings, the libationer then makes a formal request for divine aid in resolving the problem:

Your servant is stubborn and benighted and does not understand the pneumas of the spirits. Reverently I have received the Statement of _____ and, prostrating myself, submitted a petition for your consideration. I only hope that the Most High Great Dao and the administrators in the service of the Celestial Master will extend a special, compassionate mercy in examining that which I have memorialized. I beg that, in accordance with the Most High's system of confession and repentance, you will grant a harmonious solution to problems encountered by the deceased _____ of _____ family, dispelling the torture and reprimand. I again dispatch the merit officers and emissaries to bring the pledge offerings of _____ to the distant Bureaus of the Three Heavens. Pardon and forgive her for all infractions while alive, erase the assigned punishment, and quash the case. I respectfully request the Perfected Talisman of Great Mystery and the conferral of the Rescript of Lady Blue. [May] the Subterranean Two-Thousand Bushel [Officers], the Tumulus Assistant, the Earl of the Tomb, the Twelve Gods of the Sepulcher, the Twenty-Four Prisons of Mount Tai, the Great Prison of the Central Capital, the Northern Prison of the Heavenly One, the Nine-Level Prisons of August Heaven, the Three Offices of Heaven, Earth, and Water, the Marquis of the River, the Earl of the River, their aides, assistants, clerks, and so forth, all release the souls of the deceased, allowing them to return to and attach themselves to the skeleton of her corpse. Absolve her of any sentence for imprisonment or labor so that in the midst of her torment she may attach herself to the harmonious, pleasant realm of the Heavenly Bureaus above. Cut off cursed infusions and delete [her name] from the Roster of Death. If, while alive, she offended against the Five Covenants or

Seven Oaths,[99] so that they entangle and constrain her and will not release her, I beg that all will release and free her. Let her family from now on live and die in peace and security. Let her household grow and prosper and serious illnesses be expelled as proof of her sincerity. I look to the Most High, full of grace, to use discernment, and I beg for mercy.

臣以頑闇，不明鬼氣。謹承某辭，伏地拜章上聞。唯願 太上大道、天師門下典者，特垂愷悌之恩，察臣所奏。乞依 太上首悔之制，為某家亡人某隨事和釋，解散考譴。重遣功曹使者，賫某信儀，遙詣 三天曹。按某生時所犯，隨原料剔，削除刑名，絕滅事目。謹請太玄真符、攝下女青詔書、地下二千石、丘丞、墓伯、十二塚神、泰山二十四獄、中都大獄、天一北獄、皇天九平獄、天地水三官、河侯、河伯、將佐掾吏等，一切放某等魂魄，使還附尸骨。免離囚徒困苦之中，得上屬天曹和樂之地。斷絕殃注，滅除死籍。若某生時有犯五盟七詛，更相拘牽，結逮不解者，某乞丐一切解罷釋散。某家從今以去，令生死安穩，門戶隆利，疾病除差，以為效信。恩惟 太上分別。求哀。

Thus, we know a bit about the ritual interventions that were possible for a Daoist after death, but we have very little information concerning the actual disposition of the dead. It seems there was a taboo against dying among the profane:[100]

Whether a Daoist priest, female officer, libationer, or novice, they bear on their person the precepts of the faith. If one should die, it must be in an oratory or abbey parish. It must not be in the home of a profane person.

99. These covenants and oaths are mentioned repeatedly in surviving petitions but are seldom explained. A Tang dynasty Shangqing text, the *Daomen jingfa xiangcheng cixu* 3/14a, explains that the Five Covenants refer to the Five Teachings 五教 (i.e., the "Confucian" virtues of benevolence, duty, propriety, wisdom, and credibility), and the Seven Oaths (sometimes referred to as the *wushi* 五誓 or *wuzhou* 五咒) refer to blood oaths taken to the Dao, heavenly gods, earth spirits, human ghosts, the sun, the moon, and the stars to observe these teachings.

100. *Xuandu lüwen* 17b. This prohibition may well be ancient, but the mention of an abbey indicates this formulation must be no earlier that late Six Dynasties or early Tang.

道士、女官、祭酒、籙生，身任法誡。若死，要在靖宇觀治，不
得在俗人舍宅。

We have found no identifiably Daoist burials until the fifth
century, but this is perhaps not surprising since Daoism appears
to have been a largely aniconic tradition until about that time.
Daoists might have followed traditional Chinese methods for the
encoffinment and burial of the deceased. However, the following
passage would contradict this:[101]

> When encoffining the corpse, place it in a burlap bag and, sending
> it into the mountains, forests, meadows, or marshes, simply bury it
> in the earth. You must not raise a burial mound, plant a tree on the
> tomb, or build an embankment around it.
>
> 几[102]棺布囊舉尸，送山林藪澤，入土而已，不得立墳，封樹丘壠。

It is uncertain how ancient this practice is, but it is said that
the fifth-century master Lu Xiujing, author of an abbreviated version of the Celestial Master code, requested this sort of burial.[103]
The passage that follows indicates that the Daoist's register, contracts, and sword should also be placed in a burlap bag and buried
with him or her. Such a burial in the wilds would be difficult to
locate, but, should we find such a burial, we might also find an
authentic register from the early church.

We are not, however, totally lacking in evidence for Daoist
burials. In 1977 a tomb in Changsha, Hunan, produced a land
contract for a fifty-nine-year-old man named Xu Fu 徐副, who
had been reburied (in a larger tomb) on December 24, 433.[104] It
opens by invoking the talisman of the Newly Emerged Most High
Lord Lao (*xinchu taishang laojun* 新出太上老君) in summoning

101. *Zhengyi weiyi jing* 19a.
102. Reading *fan* 凡 for the graphically similar *ji* 几.
103. See *Lishi zhenxian tidao tongjian* 24/10b. More conventional funerary and burial practices are preserved in chapter 14 of the Tang era *Yaoxiu keyi
jielü chao*.
104. See Wang Yucheng 1993; Zhang Xunliao and Bai Bin 2005:846–51.

the chthonian deities. The text identifies Xu as a "male officer libationer of Daiyuan parish, holder of the Yellow Book Contract" (*nanguan jijiu Daiyuan zhi huangshu qiling* 男官祭酒代元治黃書契令).[105] Daiyuan is one of the Accompanying Parishes (*peizhi* 配治). The Yellow Book Contract presumably means that this libationer has completed the Merging the Pneumas rite. The land contract is in many ways similar to those of the profane in calling on many members of the subterranean bureaucracy to accept him into their care and laying out the underground scope of the territory belonging to Xu that they should guard for him. There is one distinctive passage, however, that shows the survival of ancient Daoist practices nearly three centuries after the church's founding:

> In accordance with the Daoist religion of the various[106] lords and elders of the Most High, we did not dare to choose the time or select a day, and did nothing to avoid any of the subterranean prohibitions or taboos. The Dao circulated correct pneumas; we did not consult the tortoise or milfoil.
>
> 遵奉太上諸君丈人道法，不敢選時擇日，不避地下禁忌。道行正氣，不問龜筮。

Here the family of the deceased libationer affirms that it followed the teaching of the church not to use mantic means to select the day of burial, nor did it seek to avoid the wrath of deities of the earth, who are in the service of the Dao. Finally, it did not use either oracle bone divination or *Yijing* divination to ascertain that the burial site or time was auspicious. Instead, it buried the deceased's plaque of office (*ban* 板), demanding that the gods of the underworld give repose to his form (*an qi shixing* 安其尸形) and protect the living (*lihu shengren* 利護生人). The contract further promises that the survivors will perform a Declaration of Merit rite in terms very similar to those we have seen in preserved templates for such a rite:

105. Wang Yucheng misreads the character *nan* 男 as *jie* 界, which is graphically similar.
106. This *zhu* 諸 may be a mistake for the graphically similar *lao* 老.

On the auspicious days of the Three Assemblies, on behalf of the Attendant of the Tumulus and the other gods, we will offer a Declaration of Merit recommending them for promotion so that the salary and emolument of each shall be increased in accordance with the code of the Heavenly Bureaus.

至三會吉日當爲丘丞諸神言功舉遷，各加其秩祿，如天曹科比。

Any spirit who does dare to interfere with the deceased or his family is threatened with prosecution under the authority of the Spirit Code of the Mystic Capital (*xuandu guilü* 玄都鬼律). In place of the final exhortation in all official documents, "Quickly, quickly, in accordance with the statutes and commands" (*jiji ru lüling* 急急如律令), we find this final statement:

Clearly receive and carry out [these instructions], all in accordance with the statutes and commands of the Limitless Great Dao of the Great Purity Mystic and Primordial Upper Three Heavens, the Most High Lord Lao, and of the imperial rescript of the subterranean Lady Blue.

明承奉行，一如太清玄元上三天無極大道、太上老君、地下女青詔書律令。

It is rare to find such Daoist language inscribed on a land contract,[107] but we can well imagine similar statements being made orally and written on paper Daoist petitions throughout the period covered by this study. Thus the libationer watched over his flock from birth, when the newborn was first inscribed on his parish fate roster, until long after death, when the deceased was settled peacefully in the other world.

---

107. Of the thirty-eight land contracts from the Three Kingdoms through the Sui dynasty discussed by Zhang and Bai, five closely resemble Xu Fu's and another seven are identifiably Daoist because the deceased is identified as a Daoist citizen, or a Daoist deity like Lord Lao or Lady Blue is invoked. See Zhang Xunliao and Bai Bin 2005:3, 843–78. The practice was especially popular from the mid-fifth century on.

Epilogue

The sort of communal Daoism described in the preceding chapters, with its system of rituals, assemblies, precepts, and fate rosters, did not end abruptly at the close of the Six Dynasties. Such a form may have survived throughout imperial China, and it survives in a uniquely transformed state among some modern Yao communities. Nonetheless, by the end of the Six Dynasties, the Daoist religion was undergoing many different types of change. In this short epilogue, I will set out some of the forces at play and briefly sketch the current state of living Daoism, to show how the Celestial Master tradition lives on today in Chinese communities across the world.

The two greatest challenges to the Celestial Master ritual system came from a series of scriptural revelations in Southeast China during the late fourth century. The Maoshan revelations of the 360s introduced important occult beliefs and practices that flourished at the time in South China but that members of the early church had considered heterodox. The new techniques included the use of herbs and mineral-based elixirs as well as focused meditations on the adept's body and on astral deities. They involved meditative journeys within the body and to the stars. We also see in these texts the first assimilation of certain Buddhist ideas, including postmortem punishment in hells and something like reincarnation. These ideas eventually expanded the repertoire of the Daoist priest, but Lu Xiujing's *Abridgement of the*

Daoist Code indicates that, at least during the fifth century, the mainstream of Celestial Master Daoists continued to reject these methods in favor of purely ritual responses to medical and other problems. Moreover, the early-fifth-century *Code of the Great Perfected* (*Taizhenke*) shows that followers of these new revelations continued to be ordained through the Celestial Master novitiate and maintained Celestial Master–style parishes, attended Assemblies, and observed Celestial Master precepts.[1] Moreover, the original revelations were swathed in secrecy, transmitted only to a very small group. The forgeries of Wang Lingqi spread more widely. It is not clear whether anyone organized a Maoshan or Shangqing lineage of Daoist masters before the Tang.[2] The series of Shangqing patriarchs enumerated in the *Filiation of the Perfected* (*Zhen xi* 真系) is a retroactive re-creation of the early Tang. By the high Tang, it seems there was a recognized lineage of Shangqing patriarchs, such as Sima Chengzhen 司馬承禎 (647–735), who interacted regularly with the court and literati in the capital, but Shangqing Daoism remained primarily of interest to elite intellectuals, with no connection to the average Daoist believer. In the Tang, Shangqing scriptures were consolidated into one stage of a ranked ordination system that required all members first to pass through Celestial Master ordinations as well as those of lower-ranked scriptural groups before receiving a Shangqing register. In the same period, the mature Shangqing system of texts and practices was codified as a school.

Most Shangqing practices were intended for the spiritual development and transformation of the individual adept, not for communal ritual, but certain elements were adapted for mass use and survive today in the Offering, or Jiao ritual. The Celestial Master petition was originally transmitted by spirit emissaries, but priests of that movement came to adopt a Shangqing ritual centering on the priest visualizing himself ascending to Heaven

1. See the assemblage of all surviving quotes from this work in Ōfuchi 1997: 473–505.

2. On the transmission of these early scriptures, see Strickmann 1977, 1979, 1982b.

and meeting with exalted Daoist deities.[3] Another example is the ritual for untying the knots of fate (*jiejie* 解結), which began as a solitary, meditative rite but evolved into a public portion of the Offering for a deceased person.[4] The Lingbao, or Numinous Jewel, scriptures, revealed beginning in the 390s, like the earlier Shangqing revelations incorporated not only elements of southern occult tradition dating back to the Han, but also many elements of Buddhist doctrine and ritual practice.[5] Their impact on Daoist ritual practice at all levels was far-reaching and permanent. In Lingbao ritual, the preliminary purification rites, the actual request presentation in the form of a petition, and the subsequent kitchen banquet of thanksgiving were integrated into a single ritual, initially termed Fast (*zhai* 齋) and later called the Offering (*jiao* 醮) or Rite of Cosmic Renewal. Although the Buddhist-inspired purpose of this ritual program was universal salvation, it kept significant elements from Celestial Master ritual. For example, the "audience" rites (*chaoli* 朝禮), including those constituting the "spontaneous audience" (*ziran chao* 自然朝), are transformations of the Celestial Master audience ritual that each citizen household was expected to perform morning and night, with actions directed to the four quarters expanded to the Buddhist ten directions and incorporating Buddhistic confessions.

A more dramatic change over these centuries was the shift in the focus of the ritual from the individual or household to the entire community and, indeed, the cosmos. Although there was already in the Shangqing scriptures mention of a new place of the dead called Fengdu 豐都, the Lingbao scriptures introduced the Buddhist concept of hells as a series of trials through which each deceased soul was judged and punished.[6] No longer did you and your priest have to deal with the particular problems of an ancestor confronting a sepulchral lawsuit in the other world. Now your

3. Lü Pengzhi 2010:1279.

4. See Lagerwey 1987:187–88. In Lagerwey's example, it occurs on the second day of a three-day Offering, after Paying Homage to the Three Treasures 拜三寶.

5. On Lingbao ritual, see Lü Pengzhi 2010:1280–1302.

6. See Bokenkamp 1997:373–404; 2007; Robinet 1997:153.

ancestor was just one of the masses of dead needing salvation from unlimited pain and suffering. Lingbao provided Daoist versions of a rite of universal salvation that responded to this urgent need. The belief in reincarnation and posthumous punishment in the other world became firmly rooted in the Chinese consciousness, at the latest by the Tang, in spite of fundamental contradictions with the system of ancestral sacrifice that remained a fixed feature of conventional elite Chinese life. The simple Celestial Master petition ceremony was no longer sufficient to respond to the needs of the Daoist lay population.

The introduction of extended, elaborate rites of universal salvation fundamentally altered the relationship of the Daoist priest to the average believer and, with it, the character of Daoist communities. As they spread through China, living side by side with non-Daoists, many of them lost their exclusivity and communal character. Even where communal Daoism survived, individual rites confronting specific problems were replaced with universal rites addressing all conceivable problems at once. Moreover, whereas the individual Daoist citizen in the early church was expected to perform rituals like the personal confessions and the daily audience rites for themselves, turning to the parish priest only for more involved problems, now followers of Daoism became largely a laity served by a distinct class of priests who monopolized the intercessory role. Lingbao was a distinct rank in the mature Tang system of registers through which Daoism was integrated into a whole, but it seems that by the Song dynasty Lingbao-type ritual became the norm for all Daoist priests.

The next major innovation in Daoist ritual practice was the development of Thunder Rites beginning in the Song. These rites claimed to invoke the power of celestial thunder for exorcism. A distinguishing feature was the transformation of the officiant into a powerful deity who then wields divine powers to expel demons. Although some have theorized that these rites were practiced by a new class of religious professional, the ritual master (*fashi* 法師), who was located somewhere between the Daoist priest and popular ecstatic performers like spirit mediums in terms of class, literacy, and cost, a recent study has shown that exorcistic titles were often added on as supplements to the formal title of Daoist rank (*fawei* 法位) in Song Daoist records.[7] Thunder rituals are still common among Celestial Master priests throughout China.

Today priests who identify themselves with the Correct Unity or Celestial Master tradition are found in every province of China as well as in Taiwan, Hong Kong, Singapore, and other Chinese communities throughout the world. Believers refer to them by a wide variety of local terms, which link them to disparate ritual traditions from Daoist history. They practice an equally diverse array of rituals derived from these traditions. The set of ritual forms and practices adopted by an individual Daoist troupe (*dao-tan* 道壇) is hereditary and unique to that lineage of Daoists, though there are broad similarities across regions and even to some degree across China.

Taiwan was the site of most twentieth-century field work on living Daoism, and hence its Daoism is best understood. Taiwan is a complex example, because it was colonized from the seventeenth century on by Chinese immigrants from several distinct regions of Southeast China, including Quanzhou and Zhangzhou in Fujian as well as the Hakka populations of southern Fujian and northern Guangdong. The Daoists of northern and southern Taiwan have similar ritual programs except that northern Taiwan Daoists do not perform rites for the dead. Those in the north refer to their tradition as Correct Unity, but in the south they use the term Numinous Jewel. Both perform the grand, multiday Offering rite as well as rites addressing mundane problems similar to those that fall mainly in the province of the exorcistic (*fashi* 法師).

A focus of recent scholarship has been living Daoism in mainland China. Lagerwey has traced the Daoist tradition of northern Taiwan to Hakka communities in Fujian, but it is difficult to be sure of ecclesiastical lineages for more than a few generations. A new type of evidence has been discovered recently in rural Hunan province: Daoist statuary containing documents that record their creation, the creating artisan, and the Daoist priest who ritually

7. See Sakai 2008.

enlivened the statue.[8] By collecting statues in a given region from diverse epochs, one can begin to trace lineages of Daoist priests through the centuries. In the mixed Daoism of western Hunan, a single individual will hold registers derived from the Daoist, Buddhist, and exorcistic traditions, performing services from each as needed.

Our understanding of the evolution of communal Daoism has also benefited from research into the Daoism practiced among the Yao ethnic group of South China and mainland Southeast Asia.[9] The Yao still maintain communal practice. All members of the community pass through an ordination ritual and hold a Daoist rank, which determines the local status hierarchy. Both men and women receive cohorts of spirit generals for their protection, and spouses unite their spirit generals in a symbolic ritual called "grain of Lord Lao" (*Laojun fan* 老君飯) that replicates in many ways the functions of the ancient Merging the Pneumas rite.[10] The Yao ritual tradition is complex, with both Thunder Rites and more traditional Celestial Master rituals. How Daoism was transmitted to the Yao is unclear, but its survival there suggests that the communal Daoism of the early Celestial Master church described in the preceding chapters never wholly disappeared from the Chinese world. Just as much of the Daoist canon remains to be studied, local traditions of Daoism exist in profusion across the face of China, waiting to be explored. With each new site and each new text deciphered, we deepen our understanding of Daoism. It is my hope that future scholars of Daoism will build on the preliminary conclusions of this work to extend and recast our understanding of Daoism and its vital role in Chinese civilization.

8. This field was pioneered by Patrice Fava (2014) and furthered by Alain Arrault (2010), together with Mark Meulenbeld, David Mozina, and others.

9. On Yao Daoism, see Hirota 2007; Maruyama 2011.

10. In this rite, bowls of rice from the husband and the wife are tied together in a symbolic merging of the two companies of troops.

Bibliography

Texts from the Daoist Canon

Baopuzi neipian 抱朴子內篇 [The master who embraces simplicity, inner compilation], DZ 1185.

Chisongzi zhangli 赤松子章曆 [The petition almanac of Master Redpine], DZ 615.

Chuanshou jingjie yi zhujue 傳授經戒儀註訣 [Annotations and secret formulae for the Protocol for the Transmission of the Scripture and Precepts], DZ 1238.

Chuanshou sandong jingjie falu lüeshuo 傳授三洞經戒法籙略說 [Summary explanation of the transmission of the Three Caverns scripture, precepts and ritual register], DZ 1241.

Daodian lun 道典論 [Discourse on the institutions of the Dao], DZ 1130.

Daomen dingzhi 道門定制 [Established institutions for Daoists], DZ 1224.

Daomen jingfa xiangcheng cixu 道門經法相承次序 [Daoist procedures for transmitting the scriptures and rituals], DZ 1128.

Dengzhen yinjue 登真隱訣 [Hidden instructions for ascending to perfection], DZ 421.

Dongxuan lingbao qianzhenke 洞玄靈寶千真科 [Cavern Mystery Numinous Jewel Code of the Thousand Perfected], DZ 1410.

Dongxuan lingbao sandong fengdao kejie yingshi 洞玄靈寶三洞奉道科戒營始 [Cavern Mystery Numinous Jewel Three Caverns Foundation for the Codes and Precepts for Serving the Dao], DZ 1125.

Dongzhen huangshu 洞真黃書 [Cavern Perfection Yellow Book], DZ 1343.

Dongzhen taishang basu zhenjing xiuxi gongye miaojue 洞真太上八素真經修習功業妙訣 [Marvelous formulae for cultivating and practicing the merit karma of the Grotto-perfection Most High's perfected scripture of the eight elementals], DZ 1321.

Gaoshang shenxiao yuqing zhenwang zishu dafa 高上神霄玉清真王紫書大法 [Great Ritual of the Purple Book of the Perfected King of Jade Purity of the Lofty Exalted Divine Empyrean], DZ 1219.

Jiao sandong zhenwen wufa zhengyi mengwei lu licheng yi 醮三洞真文五法正一盟威籙立成儀 [Protocol for the appointment to the register of the Correct and Unitary Covenant with the Powers for the five rites of Offering to the Perfected Writs of the Three Caverns], DZ 1212.

Laojun bianhua wuji jing 老君變化無極經 [Scripture of Lord Lao's limitless transformations], DZ 1195.

Laojun yinsong jiejing 老君音誦戒經 [Scripture of the intoned precepts of Lord Lao], DZ 785.

Lu xiansheng daomenke lue 陸先生道門科略 [Master Lu's abridgement of the Daoist Code], DZ 1127.

Nüqing guilü 女青鬼律 [Demon Statutes of Lady Blue], DZ 790.

Sandong fafu kejie wen 三洞法服科戒文 [Writ of the codes and precepts for ritual garb of the Three Caverns], DZ 788.

Sandong zhongjie wen 三洞眾戒文 [Writ of the collected precepts of the Three Caverns], DZ 178.

Sandong zhunang 三洞珠囊 [Pearl satchel of the Three Caverns], DZ 1139.

Santian neijie jing 三天內解經 [Scripture of the inner explanation of the Three Heavens], DZ 1205.

Shangqingdao lei shixiang 上清道類事項 [Categorized terms of the Way of Supreme Purity], DZ 1132.

Shangqing huangshu guoduyi 上清黃書過度儀 [Supreme Purity Yellow Book of the rite of initiation], DZ 1294.

Shoulu cidi faxin yi 受籙次第法信儀 [Protocol for the organization and pledge offerings for receiving a register], DZ 1244.

Taipingjing 太平經 [Scripture of Great Peace], DZ 1101.

Taishang dongxuan lingbao jieye benxing shangpin miaojing Yuanshi tianzun shuo Fengdu miezui jing 太上洞玄靈寶結業本性上品妙經元始天尊說豐都滅罪經 [Most High's Cavern Mystery Numinous Jewel marvelous scripture, upper chapter for resolving karma and the original nature, the scripture of Fengdu for exterminating sin pronounced by the Promordial Heavenly Worthy], DZ 345.

Taishang dongxuan lingbao tianzun shuo jiku jing 太上洞玄靈寶天尊說濟苦經 [Most High's Cavern Mystery Numinous Jewel scripture of the Celestial Worthy expounding on saving from suffering], DZ 375.

Taishang dongxuan lingbao zhihui zuigen shangpin dajie jing 太上洞玄靈寶智慧罪根上品大戒經 [Most High's Cavern Mystery Numinous Jewel scripture of the great precepts of the upper chapter on wisdom and the roots of sin], DZ 457.

Taishang dongyuan shenzhou jing 太上洞淵神咒經 [Scripture of divine spells piercing the abyss], DZ 335.

Taishang ganyingpian 太上感應篇 [Most High's fascicle on retribution], DZ 1167.

Taishang huangting neijing yujing 太上黃庭內景玉經 [Most High's jade scripture of the inner landscape of the Yellow Court], DZ 331.

Taishang huangting waijing yujing 太上黃庭外景玉經 [Most High's jade scripture of the outer landscape of the Yellow Court], DZ 332.

Taishang jingjie 太上經戒 [Scriptural precepts of the Most High], DZ 787.

Taishang Laojun jinglü 太上老君經律 [Scripture and Statutes of the Most High Lord Lao], DZ 786.

Taishang Laojun zhongjing 太上老君中經 [Central scripture of the Most High Lord Lao], DZ 1168.

Taishang sanwu zhengyi mengwei lu 太上三五正一盟威籙 [Register of the Most High's Three and Five Correct and Unitary Covenant with the Powers], DZ 1208.

Taishang sanwu zhengyi mengwei yuelu jiaoyi 太上三五正一盟威閱籙儀 [Protocol for the Offering to review the register of the Most High's Three and Five Correct and Unitary Covenant with the Powers], DZ 796.

Taishang xuanci zhuhua zhang 太上宣慈助化章 [Most High's petitions for disseminating compassion and aiding transformation], DZ 617.

Taishang zhengyi mengwei falu 太上正一盟威法籙 [Most High's ritual register of the Correct and Unitary Covenant with the Powers], DZ 1209.

Taishang zhengyi yansheng baoming lu 太上正一延生保命籙 [Most High's correct and unitary register for extending life and protecting the lifespan], DZ 1216.

Taishang zhengyi yuelu yi 太上正一閱籙儀 [Most High's correct and unitary protocol for reviewing the register], DZ 797.

Taizhen yudi siji mingke jing 太真玉帝四極明科經 [Scripture of the bright code of the four extremes], DZ 184.

Wushang huanglu dazhai lichengyi 無上黃籙大齋立成儀 [Protocol for the performance of the Supreme Yellow Register Great Fast], DZ 508.

Wushang miyao 無上秘要 [Supreme secret essentials], DZ 1138.

Xuandu lüwen 玄都律文 [Statutes of the Mystic Capital], DZ 188.

Yaoxiu keyi jielü chao 要修科儀戒律鈔 [Excerpts of codes, protocols, precepts, and statutes that must be followed], DZ 463.

Yuanshi wulao chishu yupian zhenwen tianshu jing 元始五老赤書玉篇真文天書經 [Primordial Five Elders scripture of the Heavenly writing, the perfected writs of red writing on jade fascicles], DZ 22.

Yuanshi wuliang duren shangpin miaojing sizhu 元始無量度人上品妙經四註 [Four commentaries on the Primordial's Limitless top-class marvelous scripture of salvation], DZ 87.

Yunji qiqian 雲笈七籤 [Seven slips from the cloudy portfolio], DZ 1032.

Yuqing wuji zongzhen Wenchang dadong xianjing zhu 玉清無極總真文昌大洞仙經註 [Commentary to the transcendent scripture of the great cavern of Wenchang, limitless controller of the perfected of Jade Purity], DZ 103.

Zhen'gao 真誥 [Declarations of the perfected], DZ 1016.

Zhengyi chuguan zhangyi 正一出官章儀 [Correct and unitary protocol for petitions exteriorizing the officers], DZ 795.

Zhengyi fawen chuan dugongban yi 正一法文傳都功版儀 [Protocol for transmitting the Director of Merit plaque of the Correct and Unitary Ritual Texts], DZ 1211.

Zhengyi fawen falubu yi 正一法文法籙部儀 [Protocol of the ritual register section of the Correct and Unitary Ritual Texts], DZ 1242.

Zhengyi fawen jingzhang guanpin 正一法文經章官品 [Chapter on officers for scriptures and petitions of the Correct and Unitary Ritual Texts], DZ 1218.

Zhengyi fawen shilu zhaoyi 正一法文十籙召儀 [Summoning protocol for the ten registers of the Correct and Unitary Ritual Texts], DZ 1210.

Zhengyi fawen taishang wailu yi 正一法文太上外籙儀 [Protocol of the outer registers], DZ 1243.

Zhengyi fawen tianshi jiao jieke jing 正一法文天師教戒科經 [Ritual Texts of Correct Unity: The Scripture of precepts and codes, Teachings of the Celestial Master], DZ 789.

Zhengyi tianshi gao Zhao Sheng koujue 正一天師告趙昇口訣 [Oral formulae announced to Zhao Sheng by the Correct and Unitary Celestial Master], DZ 1273.
Zhengyi weiyi jing 正一威儀經 [Correct and unitary scripture of proper deportment], DZ 791.
Zhengyi zhijiao zhaiyi 正一旨教齋儀 [Correct and unitary protocol for the fast of the essential teachings], DZ 798.
Zhiyan zong 至言總 [Miscellany of supreme sayings], DZ 1033.

Traditional Texts

Chunqiu Zuozhuan zhengyi 春秋左轉正義. Shisanjing zhushu (Wuyingdian edn.). Canton: Guangdong shuju, 1871 rep. of 1739.
Hanyu dazidian 漢語大字典. 8 vols. Chengdu: Sichuan cishu, 1986–90.
Quan Tang shi 全唐詩. Beijing: Zhonghua, 1960.
Songtuo Chunhuage tie 宋拓淳化閣帖. Beijing: Zhongguo shudian, 1988.
Yiwen leiju 藝文類聚. Ed. Ouyang Xun 歐陽詢. Shanghai: Shanghai guji, 1965.

Modern Texts

Alberts, Eli. 2006. *A History of Daoism and the Yao People of South China.* Youngstown, NY: Cambria Press.
Andersen, Poul. 1981. *The Method of Holding the Three Ones: A Taoist Manual of Meditation of the Fourth Century A.D.* Studies on Asian Topics 1. Copenhagen: Curzon Press.
———. 1994. "Talking to the Gods: Visionary Divination in Early Taoism (The Sanhuang Tradition)." *Taoist Resources* 5:1–24.
Arrault, Alain 華瀾. 2008. "Analytic Essay on the Domestic Statuary of Central Hunan: The Cult to Divinities, Parents and Masters." *Journal of Chinese Religions* 36:1–53.
———. 2010. "La société locale vue à travers la statuaire domestique du Hunan." *Cahiers d'Extrême-Asie* 19, 2010 [2012]: 47–134.
Asad, Talal. 1993. *Genealogies of Religion: Discipline and Reasons of Power in Christianity and Islam.* Baltimore: The Johns Hopkins University Press.
Bai Bin 白彬. 2010. "Religious Beliefs as Reflected in the Funerary Record." In Lagerwey and Lü 2010: 2, 989–1074.
Bai Bin and Dai Lijuan 代丽鹃. 2007. "Shicong kaogu cailiao kan *Nüqing guilü* de chengshu niandai he liuxing diyu" 试从考古材料看女青鬼律的成书年代和流行地域. *Zongjiaoxue yanjiu* 2007.1:9–17.
Baopuzi neipian 抱樸子內篇. Zhuzi jicheng edn. Shanghai, 1935.
Barrett, Timothy H. 2005. "Chinese Religion in English Guise: The History of an Illusion." *Modern Asian Studies* 39.3:509–33.

Benn, Charles D. 1991. *The Cavern-Mystery Transmission: A Taoist Ordination Rite of A.D. 711*. Honolulu: University of Hawai'i Press.

Beyer, Peter. 2011. "Historical Observation in the Sociology of Religions: A View from within the Communicative Networks of Two Scientific Disciplines." In Barbara J. Denison, ed., *History, Time, Meaning, and Memory: Ideas for the Sociology of Religion*, 79. Leiden: Brill.

Bo Yi 柏夷 (Stephen R. Bokenkamp). 1999. "Tianshidao hunyin yishi 'heqi' zai shangqing lingbao xuepai de yanbian" 天師道婚姻儀式「合氣」在上清靈寶學派的演變. *Daojia wenhua yanjiu* 16 (1999): 241–48.

Boileau, Gilles. 1998–99. "Some Ritual Elaborations on Cooking and Sacrifice." *Early China* 23–24:89–123.

———. 2006. "Conferring Meat in Archaic China: Between Reward and Humiliation." *Asiatische Studien* 60.4 (2006): 737–72.

Boltz, William G. 1982. "The Religious and Philosophical Significance of the 'Hsiang erh' *Lao Tzu* in the Light of the *Ma-wang-tui* Silk Manuscripts." *Bulletin of the School of Oriental and African Studies* 45.1:95–117.

Bokenkamp, Stephen R. (see also under Bo Yi). 1983. "Sources of the Ling-pao Scriptures." In Michel Strickmann, ed., *Tantric and Taoist Studies in Honour of R. A. Stein* 2:434–86. Brussels: Institut belge des hautes études chinoise.

———. 1996–97. "The Yao Boduo Stele as Evidence for the 'Dao-Buddhism' of the Early Lingbao Scriptures." *Cahiers d'Extrême-Asie* 9 (1996–97): 54–67.

———. 1997. *Early Daoist Scriptures*. Berkeley: University of California Press.

———. 2002. "The Salvation of Laozi: Images of the Sage in the *Lingbao Scriptures*, the Ge Xuan Preface, and the 'Yao Bodao Stele' of 496 C.E." In Li Zhuoran 李焯然 and Chen Wancheng 陳萬成, eds., *Daoyun xufenlu* 道苑續紛錄: *A Daoist Florilegium*, 287–314. Hong Kong: Commercial Press.

———. 2007. *Ancestors and Anxiety: Daoism and the Birth of Rebirth in China*. Berkeley: University of California Press.

Brashier, Kenneth. 2011. *Ancestral Memory in Early China*. Cambridge, MA: Harvard University Press.

Bu Qiuxiang 卜香秋. 2005. "Tang Song shiqi de yishe" 唐宋时期的邑社. *Qinghai shifan daxue xuebao (Zhexue shehui kexue ban)* 110 (2005.3): 65–68.

Bumbacher, Stephen. 2000. *The Fragments of the* Daoxue zhuan: *Critical Edition, Translation, and Analysis of a Medieval Collection of Daoist Biographies*. Frankfurt: Peter Lang.

———. 2012. *Empowered Writing: Exorcistic and Apotropaic Rituals in Medieval China*. St. Petersburg, FL: Three Pines Press.

Cahill, Suzanne. 1993. *Transcendence and Divine Passion: The Queen Mother of the West in Medieval China*. Stanford: Stanford University Press.

Campany, Robert Ford. 2002. *To Live as Long as Heaven and Earth: A Translation and Study of Ge Hong's "Traditions of Divine Transcendents."* Daoist Classics 2. Berkeley: University of California Press.

———. 2003. "On the Very Idea of Religions (In the Modern West and in Early Medieval China)." *History of Religions* 42.4 (May 2003): 287–319.

———. 2005. "The Meanings of Cuisines of Transcendence in Late Classical and Early Medieval China." *T'oung Pao* 91:1–57.

———. 2009. *Making Transcendents: Ascetics and Social Memory in Early Medieval China*. Honolulu: University of Hawai'i Press.

Cao Qunyong 曹群勇. 2011. "Lun Mingdai Tianshidao zhi fulu" 論明代天師道之符籙. *Zongjiaoxue yanjiu* 2011.1:222–25.

Cedzich, Ursula-Angelika. 1987. "Das Ritual der Himmelsmeister im Speigel früher Quellen: Übersetzung und Untersuchung des liturgischen Materials im dritten chuan des *Teng-chen yin-chüeh*." Ph.D. dissertation, Julius-Maximilians-Universität, Würzburg.

———. 1993. "Ghosts and Demons, Law and Order: Grave Quelling Texts and Early Taoist Liturgy." *Taoist Resources* 4.2:23–35.

———. 2001. "Corpse Deliverance, Substitute Bodies, Name Change, and Feigned Death: Aspects of Metamorphosis and Immortality in Early Medieval China." *Journal of Chinese Religions* 29:1–68.

———. 2009. "The Organon of the Twelve Hundred Officials and Its Gods." *Daoism: Religion, History, and Society* 1:1–93.

Chang Chaojan (Zhang Chaoran 張超然). 2003. "Rudao yu xingdao: Zhao Sheng yixi Tianshi jiaotuan de huangchi jiaofa" 入道與行道:趙昇一系天師教團的黃赤教法. *Taiwan zongjiao yanjiu* 3.1:49–87.

———. 2010. "Tianshidao jijiu qinzi shangtian chengzhang?" 天師道祭酒親自上天呈章? *Tianwen: Chuantong wenhua yu xiandai shehui* 2010:171–87.

———. 2011. "Killing Spirits from the Dead: The Object of Exorcism in Medieval Daoist Funeral Rites." In Florian C. Reiter, ed., *Exorcism in Daoism: A Berlin Symposium*, 11–30. Wiesbaden: Harrassowitz Verlag.

Chard, Robert L. 1995. "Rituals and Scriptures of the Stove Cult." In David Johnson, ed., *Ritual and Scripture in Chinese Popular Religion: Five Studies*, 3–54. Publications of the Chinese Popular Culture Project 3. Berkeley, CA: Chinese Popular Culture Project.

Chavannes, Édouard. 1905. "Les pays d'Occident d'après le Wei lio." *T'oung pao* 6:519–71.

Chen Guofu 陳國符. 1963 [1949]. *Daozang yuanliu kao* 道藏源流考. 2 vols. Beijing: Zhonghua.

Chen, Jack W. "On the Act and Representation of Writing in Medieval China." *Journal of the American Oriental Society* 129.1:57–71.

Chen Jinfeng 陳金鳳. "Yuan Shizu chongfeng Longhushan Tianshi Zhang Zongyan de zhengzhi yiyun" 元世祖崇奉龍虎山天師張宗演的政治意蘊. *Yichun xueyuan xuebao* 35.10 (Oct. 2013): 11–15, 88.

Chen Shike 陳士珂. 1987. *Kongzi jiayu shuzheng* 孔子家語疏證. Shanghai: Shanghai shudian reprint of 1940 Commercial Press edn.

Chen Yinke 陳寅恪. 1932. "Tianshidao yu binhai diyu zhi guanxi" 天師道與濱海地域之關係. *Bulletin of the Institute of History and Philology* 3.4: 439–66.

———. 1950. "Cui Hao yu Kou Qianzhi" 崔浩與寇謙之. *Lingnan xuebao* 11.1: 111–34.

Csikszentmihalyi, Mark. 2000. "Han Cosmology and Mantic Practices." In Kohn 2000:53–73.

———. 2002. "Traditional Taxonomies and Revealed Texts in the Han." In L. Kohn and H. D. Roth, eds., *Daoist Identity: History, Lineage, and Ritual*, 81–101. Honolulu: University of Hawai'i Press.

Cutter, Robert Joe and William G. Crowell. 1999. *Empresses & Consorts: Selections from Chen Shou's Records of the Three States with Pei Songzhi's Commentary*. Honolulu: University of Hawai'i Press.

De Meyer, Jan. 2006. *Wu Yun's Way: Life and Works of an Eighth-Century Daoist Master*. Leiden: Brill.

Dubs, Homer H. 1942. "An Ancient Chinese Mystery Cult." *Harvard Theological Review* 35:221–40.

Dudink, Adrianus. 2004. "*Nüqing guilü.*" In Schipper and Verellen 2004: 1, 127–29.

Eichhorn, Werner. 1954. "Description of the Rebellion of Sun En and Earlier Taoist Rebellions." *Mitteilungen des Instituts für Orientforschung* 2.2:25–53 and 2.3:463–76.

———. 1955. "Bemerkungen zum Aufstand des Chang Chio und zum Staate des Chang Lu." *Mitteilungen des Instituts für Orientforschung* 3:291–327.

———. 1957. "T'ai-ping and Tai-p'ing Religion." *Mitteilungen des Instituts für Orientforschung* 5:113–40.

Eskildsen, Stephen. 1998. *Asceticism in Early Taoist Religion*. Albany: State University of New York Press.

Espesset, Grégoire. 2002a. "Criminalized Abnormality, Moral Etiology, and Redemptive Suffering in the Secondary Strata of the *Taiping jing.*" *Asia Major*, 3rd series, 15.2:1–50.

———. 2002b. "Revelation between Orality and Writing in Early Imperial China: The Epistemology of the *Taiping jing* [Scripture of Great Peace]." *Museum of Far Eastern Antiquities Bulletin* (Stockholm) 74:66–100.

———. 2004. "A vau-l'eau, a rebours ou l'ambivalence de la logiques triadique dans l'ideologie du *Taiping jing.*" *Cahiers d'Extrême-Asie* 14:61–94.

Esposito, Monica. 2000. "Daoism in the Qing." In Kohn 2000:623–58.

———. 2001. "Longmen Taoism in Qing China—Doctrinal Ideal and Local Reality." *Journal of Chinese Religions* 29:191–231.

Fan Ning 范寧. 1980. *Bowu zhi jiaozheng* 博物志校證. Beijing: Zhonghua.

Farmer, J. Michael. 2001. "What's in a Name? On the Appellative 'Shu' in Early Medieval Chinese Historiography." *JAOS* 121.1:44–59.

———. 2007. *The Talent of Shu: Qiao Zhou and the Intellectual World of Early Medieval Sichuan*. SUNY Series in Chinese Philosophy and Culture. Albany: State University of New York Press.

Farmer, Steve, John B. Henderson, and Michael Witzel. 2000. "Neurobiology, Layered Texts, and Correlative Cosmologies: A Cross-Cultural Framework for Premodern History." *Bulletin of the Museum of Far Eastern Antiquities* 72:48–90.

Fava, Patrice. 2014. *Aux portes du ciel, la statuaire taoïste du Hunan*. Paris: Les Belles Lettres.

Fu Xiaojing 傅晓静. 2003. "Lun Tangdai xiangcun de minjian jieshe" 论唐代乡村的民间结社. *Shandong shifan daxue xuebao (Renwen shehui kexue ban)* 山东师范大学学报（人文社会科学版）48.6:83–86.

Fukui Kōjun 福井康順. 1974. "Kōkin shūdan no soshiki to sono seikaku" 黄巾集団の組織とその性格. *Shikan* 89:18–31.

Ge Zhaoguang 葛兆光. 1999. "Huangshu, heqi yu qita—Daojiao guoduyi de sixiangshi yanjiu" 黃書合氣與其他--道教過度儀的思想史研究. *Gujin lunheng* 2:62–76.

Geertz, Clifford. 1973. *The Interpretation of Cultures: Selected Essays*. New York: Basic Books.

Girardot, Norman. 1983. *Myth and Meaning in Early Taoism*. Berkeley: University of California Press.

Goodman, Howard. 1994. "Celestial-Master Taoism and the Founding of the Ts'ao-Wei Dynasty: The Li Fu Document." *Asia Major*, 3rd series, 7.1:5–33.

Goossaert, Vincent. 2001. "The Invention of an Order: Collective Identity in Thirteenth-Century Quanzhen." *Journal of Chinese Religions* 29:111–38.

———. 2004. "The Quanzhen Clergy, 1700–1950." In John Lagerwey, ed., *Religion and Chinese Society*, 699–772. Hong Kong: Hong Kong Chinese University Press and Paris: École française d'Extrême-Orient.

———. 2007. *The Taoists of Peking, 1800–1949: A Social History of Urban Clerics*. Cambridge, MA: Harvard University Asia Center.

Gu Baotian 顧寶田 and Zhang Zhongli 張忠利. 1997. *Xinyi Laozi xiang'er zhu* 新譯老子想爾注. Taipei: Sanmin shuju.

Haloun, G[ustav]. 1949. "The Liang-chou Rebellion 184–221 A.D." *Asia Major*, new series, 1.1:119–32.

Harper, Donald. 1985. "A Chinese Demonography of the Third Century B.C." *Harvard Journal of Asiatic Studies* 45.2 (Dec. 1985): 459–98.

———. 1987. "The Sexual Arts of Ancient China as Described in a Manuscript of the Second Century B.C." *Harvard Journal of Asiatic Studies* 47.2 (Dec. 1987): 539–93.

———. 1993. "Resurrection in Warring States Popular Religion." *Taoist Resources* 5.2:13–29.

———. 1999. "Warring States Natural Philosophy and Occult Thought." In Michael Loewe and Edward L. Shaughnessy, eds., *The Cambridge History of Ancient China: From the Origins of Civilization to 221 B.C.*, 813–84. Cambridge: Cambridge University Press.

He Qimin 何啓民. 1978. *Wei-Jin xuanxue yu tanfeng* 魏晉玄學與談風. Taipei: Xuesheng shuju.

Hendrischke, Barbara (Barbara Kandel). 1985. "How the Celestial Master Proves Heaven Reliable." In G. Naundorf, K.-H. Pohl, and H.-H. Schmidt, eds., *Religion and Philosophie in Ostasien: Festschrift für Hans Steininger*, 77–86. Wiirzburg: Konigshausen und Neumann.

———. 1991. "The Concept of Inherited Evil in the *Taiping jing*." *East Asian History* 1991.2:1–30.

———. 1992. "The Taoist Utopia of Great Peace." *Oriens Extremus* 35:61–91.

———. 2000. "Early Daoist Movements." In Kohn 2000:134–64.

———. 2004. "The Place of the Scripture on Great Peace in the Formation of Taoism." In John Lagerwey, ed., *Religion in Chinese Society*, 249–78. Hong Kong: Chinese University Press and Paris: École française d'Extrême-Orient.

———. 2006. *The Scripture on Great Peace.* Berkeley: University of California Press.

———. 2009. "Divinaton in the *Taiping jing*." *Monumenta Serica* 57:1–70.

———. 2012. "Religious Ethics in the *Taiping jing*: The Seeking of Life." *Daoism: Religion, History, and Society* 4:1–52.

Hendrischke, Barbara and Benjamin Penny. 1996. "The 180 Precepts Spoken by Lord Lao." *Taoist Resources* 6:17–29.

Hirota Ritsuko 広田律子. 2007. "Chūgoku Konanshō no Yaozoku no girei ni midasu Dōkyō no eikyō" 中國湖南省のヤオ族の儀禮に見出す道教の影響. *Tōhō shūkyō* 110:57–81.

Hong Kuo 洪适. 1983. *Lishi Lixu* 隷釋 隷續. Beijing: Zhonghua.

Hsieh Shu-wei (Xie Shiwei 謝世維). 2010. "Shouguo yu chanhui: Zhonggu shiqi zuigan wenhua zhi tantao" 首過與懺悔:中古時期罪感文化之探討. *Qinghua xuebao* 40.4:735–64.

Hsieh Tsung-hui (Xie Conghui 謝聰輝). 2008. "*Duren jing* zai Taiwan 'fuzhang' yijie de yunyong neihan" 《度人經》在台灣「伏章」儀節的運用內涵. In Florian C. Reiter, ed., *Foundations of Daoist Ritual: A Berlin Symposium*, 71–83. Wiesbaden: Harrassowitz Verlag.

Hu Rui 胡銳. 2003. "Lun Nanbeichao shiqi Daojiao gongguan zhi fazhan yu tedian" 論南北朝時期道教宮觀之發展與特點. *Zongjiaoxue yanjiu* 2003.2: 104–7.

Hu Wenhe 胡文和. 2004. *Zhongguo Daojiao shike yishu shi* 中國道教石刻艺术史. 2 vols. Beijing: Gaodeng jiaoyu.

Hucker, Charles O. 1985. *A Dictionary of Official Titles in Imperial China.* Stanford: Stanford University Press.

Ishihara Akira and Howard S. Levy. 1970. *The Tao of Sex.* New York: Harper and Row.

Jiang Boqin 姜伯勤. 1991. "*Xuandu lü* niandai ji qi suo jian Daoguan zhidu" 玄都律年代及所見道官制度. *Wei Jin Nanbeichao Sui Tang shi ziliao* 11:50–58.

Kalinowski, Marc. 1985. "La transmission du dispositif des neuf palais sous les Six Dynasties." In Michel Strickmann, ed., *Tantric and Taoist Studies in Honour of R. A. Stein* 3:773–811. Brussels: Institut belge des hautes études chinoise.

———. 2008. "Les livres des jours (*rishu*) des Qin et des Han: La logique éditoriale du recueil A de Shuihudi (217 avant notre ère)." *T'oung Pao* 94:1–48.

Kaltenmark, Max. 1979. "On the Ideology of the *T'ai-p'ing ching*." In Welch and Seidel 1979:19–52.

Kamitsuka Yoshiko 神塚淑子. 1993. "Nanbokuchō jidai no Dōkyō zōzō: shūkyō shisōshiteki kōsatsu wo chūshin ni" 南北朝時代の道教造像ー宗教思想的考察を中心に. In Tonami Mamoru, ed., *Chūgoku chūsei no bunbutsu*, 225–89. Kyoto: Kyōto daigaku jinbun kagaku kenkyūjo.

Kandel, Barbara (see also under Hendrischke). 1979. Taiping jing, *the Origin and Transmission of the "Scripture on General Welfare": The History of an Unofficial Text.* Hamburg. Mitteilungen der Gesellschaft für Natur- und Völkerkunde Ostasiens 75, 1979.

Kikuchi Noritaka 菊地章太. 2009. *Shinjugyō kenkyū: Rikuchō Dōkyō ni okeru kyūsai shisō no keisei* 神呪経研究：六朝道教における救済思想の形成. Tokyo: Kenbun shuppan.

Kleeman, Terry. 1984. "Land Contracts and Related Documents." *Chūgoku no shūkyō, shisō to kagaku: Makio Ryōkai hakushi shōju ki'nen ronshū* 中国の宗教思想と科学：牧尾良海博士頌寿記念論集, 1–34. Tokyo: Kokusho kankōkai.

———. 1994a. *A God's Own Tale: The Book of Transformations of Wenchang, Divine Lord of Zitong.* Albany: State University of New York Press.

———. 1994b. "Licentious Cults and Bloody Victuals: Sacrifice, Reciprocity and Violence in Traditional China." *Asia Major*, 3rd series, 7.1 (1994): 185–211.

———. 1998. *Great Perfection: Religion and Ethnicity in a Chinese Millennial Kingdom.* Honolulu: University of Hawai'i Press.

———. 2002. "Ethnic Identity and Taoist Identity in Traditional China." In Livia Kohn and Harold D. Roth, eds., *Daoist Identity: History, Lineage, and Ritual*, 23–38. Honolulu: University of Hawai'i Press.

———. 2005a. "The Evolution of Daoist Cosmology and the Construction of the Common Sacred Realm." *Taiwan Journal of East Asian Studies* 2.1 (June 2005): 89–110.

———. 2005b. "Feasting without the Victuals: The Evolution of the Daoist Communal Kitchen." In Roel Sterckx, ed., *Of Tripod and Palate: Food, Politics, and Religion in Traditional China*, 140–62. New York and Hampshire, UK: Palgrave MacMillan.

———. 2007a. "Daoism in the Third Century." In Florian C. Reiter, ed., *Purposes, Means and Convictions in Daoism: A Berlin Symposium*, 11–28. Wiesbaden: Harrassowitz Verlag.

———. 2007b. "Shoki kyōkai shiryō to shite no Dōkyō no rinri kihan ni tsuite" 初期教会資料としての道教の倫理規範について. Trans. Mori Yuria. *Tōyō no shisō to shūkyō* 24:1–26.

———. 2009. "Michi no kyōkai wo sadameru: shoki Dōkyō kyōdan ni okeru shūkyōteki aidentiti" 「道」の境界を定める―初期道教教団における宗教的アイデンティティ. In F. Tanaka and Terry Kleeman, eds., *Dōkyō to kyōsei shisō* 道教と共生思想, trans. N. Kikuchi, 36–52. Tokyo: Taiga shobō.

———. 2010a. "Authority and Discipline in the Early Daoist Church." *Daoism: Religion, History and Society* 2:37–64.

———. 2010b. "Community and Daily Life in the Early Daoist Church." In John Lagerwey and Lü Pengzhi, eds., *Early Chinese Religion*, part 2: *The Period of Division (220–589)*, 1:395–436. Leiden: Brill.

———. 2011. "Exorcising the Six Heavens: The Role of Traditional State Deities in the *Demon Statutes of Lady Blue*." In Florian C. Reiter, ed., *Exorcism in Religious Daoism: A Berlin Symposium*, 89–104. Asien- und Afrika-Studien der Humboldt-Universität zu Berlin 36. Wiesbaden: Harrassowitz Verlag.

———. 2012. "'Take Charge of Households and Convert the Citizenry': The Parish Priest in Celestial Master Transmission." Special Issue: Affiliation and Transmission in Daoism: A Berlin Symposium. *Abhandlingen für die Kunde des Morgenlandes* 78:19–39.

Knoblock, John and Jeffrey Riegel. 2000. *The Annals of Lu Buwei: Lu Shi Chun Qiu: A Complete Translation and Study.* Stanford: Stanford University Press.

Kobayashi Masayoshi 小林正美. 1990. *Rikuchō Dōkyoshi kenkyū* 六朝道教史研究. Tokyo: Sōbunsha.

———. 2003. *Tōdai no Dōkyō to Tenshidō* 唐代の道教と天師道. Tokyo: Chisen shokan.

Kohn, Livia. 1995. *Laughing at the Tao: Debates among Buddhists and Taoists in Medieval China.* Princeton: Princeton University Press.

———, ed. 2000. *Daoism Handbook.* Leiden: Brill.

———. 2004. *Cosmos and Community: The Ethical Dimension of Daoism.* Cambridge, MA: Three Pines Press.

Kroll, Paul W. 1985. "In the Halls of the Azure Lad." *Journal of the American Oriental Society* 105.1 (Jan.–Mar. 1985): 75–94.

Lagerwey, John. 1981. *Wu-shang pi-yao: Somme taoïste du VIe siècle.* Publications de l'École française d'Extrême-Orient 124. Paris: École française d'Extrême-Orient.

———. 1987. *Taoist Ritual in Chinese Society and History.* New York: Macmillan.

———. 1992. "La ritualité chinoise." *Bulletin de l'École française d'Extrême-Orient* 79.2:359–73.

———. 2005. "Zhengyi registers." In *ICS Visiting Professor Lecture Series. Journal of Chinese Studies* (Hong Kong), special issue, 35–88.

———. 2007. "The Old Lord's Scripture for the Chanting of the Commandments." In Florian C. Reiter, ed., *Purposes, Means and Convictions in Daoism: A Berlin Symposium,* 29–56. Wiesbaden: Harrassowitz Verlag.

Lagerwey, John, and Lü Pengzhi, eds. 2010. *Early Chinese Religion.* 2 vols. Leiden: Brill.

Lai, Chi-tim (Li Zhitian) 黎志添. 1998. "The Opposition of Celestial-Master Taoism to Popular Cults during the Six Dynasties." *Asia Major,* 3rd series, 11.1:1–26.

———. 1999. "Daoism and Political Rebellion during the Eastern Jin Dynasty." In Cheung Hok-ming and Lai Ming-chiu, eds., *Politics and Religion in Ancient and Medieval Europe and China,* 77–100. Hong Kong: Chinese University Press.

———. 2002a. "The *Demon Statutes of Nüqing* and the Problem of the Bureaucratization of the Netherworld in Early Heavenly Master Daoism." *T'oung Pao* 88:251–81.

———. 2002b. "Tian, di, shui san guan xinyang yu zaoqi Tianshidao zhibing jiezui yishi" 天地水三官信仰與早期天師道治病解罪儀式. *Taiwan zongjiao yanjiu* 2.1:1–38.

Legge, James. 1895. *Mencius. The Chinese Classics,* vol. 2. Oxford: Oxford University Press.

Lévi, Jean. 1983. "L'abstinence des céréales chez les taoïstes." *Études chinoises: Bulletin de l'Association française d'études chinoises* 1:3–47.

Li Bujia 李步嘉. 1992. *Yuejueshu jiaoshi* 越絕書校釋. Wuchang: Hunan daxue chubanshe.

Li, Gang. 2010. "State Religious Policy." In Lagerwey and Lü 2010: 1, 193–224.

Li, Jianmin. 1999. "Contagion and Its Consequences: The Problem of Death Pollution in Ancient China." In Yasuo Otsuka, Shizu Sakai, and Shigehisa Kuri-yama, eds., *Medicine and the History of the Body*, 201–222. Tokyo: Ishiyaku EuroAmerica.

Li Song 李淞. 2002. *Chang'an yishu yu zongjiao wenming* 长安艺术与宗教文明. Beijing: Zhonghua.

Li Xueqin 李學勤. 1990. "Fangmatan jianzhong de zhiguai gushi" 放马坦简中的志怪故事. *Wenwu* 1990.4:43–47.

Libbrecht, Ulrich. 1990. "Prāna = pneuma = ch'i?" In *Thought and Law in Qin and Han China: Studies Dedicated to Anthony Hulsewé on the Occasion of His Eightieth Birthday*, ed. Wilt L. Idema and Erik Zürcher, 42–62. Leiden: Brill.

Lin Feifei. 2014. "Liu-Song Wudi yu Tianshidao." *Baoji wenli xueyuan xuebao* 2014.1:36–41.

Lin, Fu-shih 林富士. 2001. "Luelun zaoqi Daojiao yu fangzhong shu de guanxi" 略論早期道教與房中術的關係. *Bulletin of the Institute of History and Philology* 72.2:233–300.

Lippiello, Tiziana. 2001. *Auspicious Omens and Miracles in Ancient China. Han, Three Kingdoms and Six Dynasties*. Monumenta Serica Monograph Series 39. Sankt Augustin, Nettetal: Steyler Verlag.

Liu Lin 劉琳. 1984. *Huayangguo zhi jiaozhu* 華陽國志校注. Chengdu: Ba Shu shushe.

Liu Pansui 劉盼遂. 1950. *Lunheng jijie* 論衡集解. Taipei: Shijie.

Liu, Ts'un-yan (Liu Cunren 柳存仁). 2006. "Was Celestial Master Zhang a His-torical Figure?" In Benjamin Penny, ed., *Daoism in History: Essays in Honour of Liu Ts'un-yan*, 189–253. London and New York: Routledge.

Liu Yi 劉屹. 2002. "Kou Qianzhi de jiashi yu shengping" 寇謙之的家世與生平. *Hualin* 華林 2:271–81.

———. 2005. *Jingtian yu chongdao: Zhonggu jingjiao Daojiao xingcheng de sixiangshi beijing* 敬天與崇道：中古經教道教形成的思想史背景. Beijing: Zhonghua.

———. 2006. "*Hua Yuntaishan ji* yu Dong Jin de Zhang Daoling chuanshuo" 《畫雲台山記》與東晉的張道陵傳說. *Yishushi yanjiu* 藝術史研究 8:29–51.

———. 2011. "Early Mediaeval Concepts of Demon Troops, Discussed with the Focus on Wang Ningzhi's Request for Demon Troops to Provide Support." In Florian C. Reiter, ed., *Exorcism in Religious Daoism: A Berlin Symposium*, 51–68. Asien- und Afrika-Studien der Humboldt-Universität zu Berlin 36. Wies-baden: Harrassowitz Verlag.

Liu Zhaorui 劉昭瑞. 2004. "Shuo tiangong yu Kou Qianzhi de 'jinglun tian-gong'" 說天宮與寇謙之的靜輪天宮. *Shijie zongjiao yanjiu* 2004.3:55–63.

———. 2005. "'Laogui' yu Nanbeichao shiqi Laozi de shenhua" 《老鬼》与南北朝时期老子的神化. *Lishi yanjiu* 2005.2:172–79.

———. 2007. *Kaogu faxian yu zaoqi Daojiao yanjiu* 考古發現與早期道教研究. Beijing: Wenwu.

Lo, Vivienne. 2014. *How to Do the Gibbon Walk: A Translation of the* Pulling Book *(ca 186 BCE)*. Cambridge: Needham Research Institute Working Papers.

Lü Pengzhi 呂鵬志. 2006. "Tianshidao shoulu keyi: Dunhuang xieben S203 kaolun" 天師道授籙科儀—敦煌寫本S203考論. *Bulletin of the Institute of History and Philology, Academia Sinica* 77.1 (Mar. 2006): 79–166.

———. 2008. *Tangqian Daojiao yishi shigang* 唐前道教儀式史綱. Beijing: Zhonghua.

———. 2010. "Daoist Rituals." In Lagerwey and Lü 2010: 2, 1245–1351.

Ma Chengyu 馬承玉. 2005. "*Zhengyi fawen tianshi jiao jieke jing* de shidai ji yu *Laozi xiang'erzhu* de guanxi" 正一法文天師教戒科經的時代及與与老子想爾注的關係. *Zhongguo daojiao* 2005.2:12–16.

Makita Tairyō 牧田諦亮, ed. 1973–75. *Gumyōshū kenkyū* 弘明集研究. 3 vols. Kyoto: Jinbun kagaku kenkyūjo.

Mansvelt-Beck, B. J. 1980. "The Date of the *Taiping jing*." *T'oung-pao* 66:149–82.

Maruyama Hiroshi 丸山宏. 1986. "Shōitsu dōkyō no jōshō girei ni tsuite— 'chōshōshō' o chūshin to shite" 正一道教の上章儀禮について—冢訟狀を中心として. *Tōhō shūkyō* 68 (Nov. 1986): 44–64.

———. 1990. "Shōitsu Dōkyō no juroku ni kansuru kisoteki kōsatsu: Tonkō shutsudo monjo Sutain nizerosangō wo shiryō to shite" 正一道教の受籙にかんする基礎的考察:敦煌文書スタイン203号を史料として. *Tsukuba Chūgoku bunka ronsō* 10:39–61.

———. 2000. "Girei to kotoba" 儀礼と言葉. In Tanaka Fumio et al. 2000: 144–68.

———. 2004. *Dōkyō girei monjo no rekishiteki kenkyū* 道教儀礼文書の歷史的研究. Tokyo: Kyūko shoin.

———. 2011. "Chūgoku Konanshō Ranzanken Yao-zoku no tokai girei monjo ni kansuru jakkan no kōsatsu" 中国湖南省藍山県ヤオ族の度戒儀礼文書に関する若干の考察. In Horiike Shinobu 堀池信夫, ed., *Chi no Yūrashia* 知のユーラシア, 400–427. Tokyo: Meiji shoin.

Maspero, Henri. 1981. *Taoism and Chinese Religions*. Trans. Frank Kierman. Amherst: University of Massachusetts University Press.

Mather, Richard. 1958. "The Landscape Buddhism of the Fifth-Century Poet Hsieh Ling-yun." *Journal of Asian Studies* 18.1:67–79.

———. 1979. "K'ou Ch'ien-chih and the Taoist Theocracy at the Northern Wei Court 425–451." In Welch and Seidel 1979:103–22.

McGuire, Meredith. 2008. *Lived Religion: Faith and Practice in Everyday Life*. New York: Oxford University Press.

Michaud, Paul. 1958. "The Yellow Turbans." *Monumenta Serica* 17:47–127.

Miyakawa Hisayuki. 1971. "Son On Ro Jun no ran ni tsuite." *Tōyōshi kenkyū* 30:1–30.

———. 1979. "Local Cults around Mount Lu at the Time of Sun En's Rebellion." In Welch and Seidel 1979:83–101.

Mollier, Christine. 1990. *Une apocalypse daoïste de Ve siècle: Le livre des incantations divine des grottes abyssales.* Paris: Collège de France.

———. 1999–2000. "Les cuisines de Laozi et du Buddha." *Cahiers d'Extrême-Asie* 11:45–90.

———. 2006. "Visions of Evil: Demonology and Orthodoxy in Early Daoism. In Benjamin Penny, ed., *Daoism in History: Essays in Honour of Liu Ts'un-yan*, 74–100. London and New York: Routledge, 2006.

———. 2008. *Buddhism and Taoism Face to Face: Scripture, Ritual, and Iconographic Exchange in Medieval China.* Honolulu: University of Hawai'i Press.

Mugitani Kunio 麥谷邦夫. 1985. "*Rōshi Sōjichū* ni tsuite" 『老子想爾注』について. *Tōhō gakuhō* 57:75–107.

Mugitani Kunio and Yoshikawa Tadao 吉川忠夫. 2000. *Shinkō kenkyū* 真誥研究. Kyoto: Kyōto daigaku jinbun kagaku kenkyūjo.

Nakamura Hajime 中村元. 1975. *Bukkyōgo daijiten* 佛教語大辞典. 3 vol. Tokyo: Tōkyō shoseki.

Nickerson, Peter. 1994. "Shamans, Demons, Diviners, and Daoists: Conflict and Assimilation in Medieval Chinese Ritual Practice (c. A.D. 100–1000)." *Taoist Resources* 5:41–66.

———. 1996. "Taoism, Death, and Bureaucracy in Early Medieval China." Ph.D. dissertation, University of California, Berkeley.

———. 1996b. "*Abridged Codes of Master Lu for the Daoist Community.*" In Donald S. Lopez, Jr., ed., *Religions of China in Practice*, 347–59. Princeton: Princeton University Press, 1996.

———. 1997. "The Great Petition for Sepulchral Plaints." In Stephen R. Bokenkamp, *Early Daoist Scriptures*, 230–74. Berkeley: University of California Press, 1997.

———. 2000. "The Southern Celestial Masters." In Kohn 2000:256–82.

———. 2006. "'Let Living and Dead Take Separate Paths': Bureaucratization and Textualization in Early Chinese Mortuary Ritual." In Benjamin Penny, ed., *Daoism in History: Essays in Honour of Liu Ts'un-yan*, 10–40. London and New York: Routledge.

Obi Kōichi 小尾郊一. 1955. "Rantei shi kō" 蘭亭詩考. *Hiroshima daigaku bungakubu kiyō* 7:224–49.

Ōfuchi Ninji 大淵忍爾. 1964. *Dōkyōshi no kenkyū* 道教史の研究. Okayama: Okayama daigaku kyōsaikai shosekibu.

———. 1974. "On *Ku Ling-pao Ching.*" *Acta Asiatica* 27:34–56.

———. 1978–79. *Tonkō dōkyō: Mokurokuhen* 敦煌道経：目録篇, *Zurokuhen* 図録篇. Tokyo: Fukutake.

———. 1979. "On the Formation of the Taoist Canon." In Welch and Seidel 1979:253–68.

———. 1991. *Shoki no Dōkyō* 初期の道教. Tokyo: Sōbunsha.

———. 1997. *Dōkyō to sono kyōten: Dōkyō shi no kenkyū sono ni* 道教とその教典：道教史の研究　其の二. Tokyo: Sōbunsha.

Orsi, Robert A. 2003. "Is the Study of Lived Religion Irrelevant to the World We

Live In?" Special Presidential Plenary Address, Society for the Scientific Study of Religion, Salt Lake City, November 2, 2002. *Journal for the Scientific Study of Religion* 42.2 (June 2003): 169–74.

———. 2005. *Between Heaven and Earth: The Religious Worlds People Make and the Scholars Who Study Them*. Princeton: Princeton University Press.

Peng Hao 彭浩, Chen Wei 陳偉, and Kudō Motoo 工藤元男, eds. 2007. *Ernian lüling yu Zouyanshu: Zhangjiashan ersiqihao Hanmu chutu falü wenshu shidu* 二年律令与奏讞书：张家山二四七號漢墓出土法律文獻釋讀. Shanghai: Shanghai guji.

Petersen, Jens O. 1989–90. "The Early Traditions Relating to the Han Dynasty Transmission of the *Taiping jing*." Parts 1 and 2, *Acta Orientalia* 50:133–71, 51:173–216.

———. 1990. "The Anti-Messianism of the Taipingjing." *Journal of the Seminar for Buddhist Studies* 3:1–36.

Poo, Mu-chou. 1993. "Popular Religion in Pre-Imperial China: Observations on the Almanacs of Shui-hu-ti." *T'oung Pao* 79.4–5:225–48.

———. 1998. *In Search of Personal Welfare*. Albany: State University of New York Press.

Pregadio, Fabrizio. 1991. "The *Book of the Nine Elixirs* and Its Tradition." In *Chūgoku kodai kagakushi ron* 中国古代 科学史論 [Studies on the history of ancient Chinese science], ed. Yamada Keiji 山田慶児 and Tanaka Tan 田中淡, 2:543–639. Kyoto: Kyôto Daigaku Jinbun Kagaku Kenkyüjo, 1991.

———. 2006. *Great Clarity: Daoism and Alchemy in Early Medieval China*. Stanford: Stanford University Press.

———, ed. 2008. *The Encyclopedia of Taoism*. 2 vols. London: Routledge.

Puett, Michael. 2002. *To Become a God: Cosmology, Sacrifice, and Self-Divinization in Early China*. Cambridge, MA: Harvard University Press.

———. 2004. "Forming Spirits for the Way: The Cosmology of the *Xiang'er* Commentary to the *Laozi*. *Journal of Chinese Religions* 32:1–27.

Rao Zongyi 饒宗頤. 1991. *Laozi Xiang'er zhu jiaozheng* 老子想爾注校證. Shanghai: Shanghai guji chubanshe, 1991; amended reprint of 1956 Hongkong Suji shuzhuang edn.

Raz, Gil. 2004. "Creation of Tradition: The Five Numinous Treasure Talismans and the Formation of Early Daoism." Ph.D. dissertation, Indiana University.

———. 2005. "Time Manipulation in Early Daoist Ritual: The East Well Chart and the Eight Archivists." *Asia Major*, 3rd series, 18.2:27–65.

———. 2008. "The Way of the Yellow and the Red: Re-examining the Sexual Initiation Rite of Celestial Master Daoism" *Nannü* 10.1:86–120.

Ren Naiqiang 任乃強, ed. 1987. *Huayangguo zhi jiaobu tuzhu* 華陽國志校補圖註. Shanghai: Shanghai guji chubanshe.

Robinet, Isabelle. 1984. *La révélation du Shangqing dans la histoire du taoïsme*. Paris: Publications de l'École française d'Extrême-Orient.

———. 1989. *Méditation taoïste*. Paris: Dervy.

———. 1997. *Taoism: Growth of a Religion*. Stanford: Stanford University Press.

Robson, James. 2009. *Power of Place: The Religious Landscape of the Southern*

Sacred Peak [Nanyue 南嶽] *in Medieval China*. Cambridge, MA: Harvard University Asia Center.

Rogers, Michael C. 1968. *The Chronicle of Fu Chien: A Case of Exemplary History*. Berkeley: University of California Press.

Sælid Gilhus, Ingvald. 2004. "The Animal Sacrifice and Its Critics." In Barbro Santillo Frizell, ed., *Man and Animal in Antiquity*, 112–16. Proceedings of the conference at the Swedish Institute in Rome, Sept. 9–12, 2002; Projects and Seminars 1. Rome: The Swedish Institute in Rome.

Sakai Norifumi 酒井規史. 2008. "Nan-Sō jidai no dōshi no shōgō: Kyōroku no hōi to dōhō no shokumei" 南宋時代の道士の称号—經籙の法位と「道法」の職名. *Tōyō no shishō to shūkyō* 25:115–34.

Sasaki Satoshi 佐　木聡. 2009. "*Josei kiritsu* ni mieru kishinkan oyobi sono juyō to hatten" 『女青鬼律』に見える鬼神観およびその受容と発展. *Tōhō shūkyō* 113 (May): 1–21.

Sawa Akitoshi 澤章敏. 1987. "Gotōbeidō seiken to Hanjunman" 五斗米道政権と板楯蛮. *Shikan* 116:2–15.

———. 1994. "Gotōbeidō seiken no soshiki kōzō" 五斗米道政權の組織構造. In Dōkyō bunka kenkyūkai 道教文化研究會, ed., *Dōkyō bunka e no tenbō* 道教文化への展望, 131–52. Tokyo: Hirakawa shuppan.

Schafer, Edward H. 1977. *Pacing the Void: T'ang Approaches to the Stars*. Berkeley: University of California Press.

Schipper, Kristofer M. 1975a. *Concordance du Houang-t'ing King: Nei-king et Wai-king*. Paris: École française d'Extrême-Orient.

———. 1975b. *Concordance du Tao-tsang: Titres des ouvrages*. Paris: École française d'Extrême-Orient.

———. 1977. "Neighborhood Cult Associations in Traditional Tainan." In G. William Skinner, ed., *The City in Late Imperial China*, 653–76. Stanford: Stanford University Press.

———. 1982. *Le corps taoïste*. Paris: Fayard.

———. 1985. "Taoist Ordination Ranks in the Tunhuang Manuscripts." In Gert Naudorf, Karl-Heinz Pohl, and Hans-Herrman Schmidt, eds., *Religion und Philosophie in Ostasien (Festschrift für Hans Steininger)*, 127–48. Königshausen: Neumann.

———. 1993. *The Taoist Body*. Trans. Karen C. Duval. Berkeley: University of California Press.

———. 1994. "Purity and Strangers: Shifting Boundaries in Medieval Taoism." *T'oung Pao* 80:61–81.

———. 2000. "Le pacte de pureté du taoïsme." *École pratique des hautes études, Section des sciences religieuses: Annuaire* 109:29–53.

Schipper, Kristofer M. and Franciscus Verellen, eds. 2004. *The Taoist Canon: A Historical Companion to the Daozang*. 3 vols. Chicago and London: University of Chicago Press.

Seidel, Anna K. 1969. *La divinisation de Lao Tseu dans le taoïsme des Han*. Publications de l'École française d'Extrême-Orient 71. Paris: École française d'Extrême-Orient.

———. 1969–70. "The Image of the Perfect Ruler in Early Taoist Messianism: Lao-tzu and Li Hung." *History of Religions* 9.2–3:216–47.

———. 1983. "Imperial Treasures and Taoist Sacraments: Taoist Roots in the Apocrypha." In Michel Strickmann, ed., *Tantric and Taoist Studies in Honour of R. A. Stein* 2:291–371. Brussels: Institut belge des hautes études chinoise.

———. 1984. "Taoist Messianism." *Numen* 31.2:161–74.

———. 1987. "Traces of Han Religion in Funeral Texts Found in Tombs." In Akizuki Kan'ei 秋月觀英, ed., *Dōkyō to shūkyō bunka* 道教と宗教文化, 21–57. Tokyo: Hirakawa.

———. 1988. "Early Taoist Ritual [Ursula-Angelika Cedzich, *Das Ritual der Himmelsmeister im Spiegel früher Quellen*]." *Cahiers d'Extrême-Asie* 4.1:199–204.

Shao Mingsheng 邵茗生. 1962. "Ji Mingqian to Bei Wei Zhongyue Songgao lingmiao bei" 記明前拓北魏中岳嵩高靈廟碑. *Wenwu* 1962.11:21–27.

Shiratori Yoshio 白鳥芳郎. 1975. *Yōjin monjo* 傜人文書. Tokyo: Kōdansha.

Sivin, Nathan. 1976. "On the *Pao P'u Tzu Nei Pien* and the Life of Ko Hong (283–343)." *Isis* 60:388–91.

———. 1978. "On the Word 'Daoist' as a Source of Perplexity." *History of Religions* 17:303–30.

———. 2010. "Old and New Daoisms." *Religious Studies Review* 36.1 (March 2010): 31–50.

Stein, Rolf A. 1963. "Remarques sur les mouvements du taoïsm politico-religieux au IIe siècle ap. J.C." *T'oung Pao* 50:1–78.

———. 1979. "Religious Taoism and Popular Religion from the Second to Seventh Centuries." In Welch and Seidel 1979:53–82.

Sterckx, Roel, ed. 2005. *Of Tripod and Palate*. New York: Palgrave Macmillan.

———. 2011. *Food, Sacrifice, and Sagehood in Early China*. Cambridge: Cambridge University Press.

Strickmann, Michel. 1977. "The Mao Shan Revelations: Taoist and the Aristocracy." *T'oung Pao* 63:1–64.

———. 1979. "On the Alchemy of T'ao Hung-ching." In Welch and Seidel 1979: 123–92.

———. 1982a. "The Tao among the Yao." In *Rekishi ni okeru minshū to bunka* 歷史に於ける民衆と文化, ed. Sakai Tadao Sensei koki shukuga kinen no kai, 23–30. Tokyo: Kokusho kankōkai.

———. 1982b. *Le Taoïsme du Mao Chan: Chronique d'une révélation*. Mémoires de l'Institut des Hautes Études Chinoises 17. Paris.

———. 1990. "The Consecration Sutra: A Buddhist Book of Spells." In Robert E. Buswell, Jr., ed., *Chinese Buddhist Apocrypha*, 75–118. Honolulu: University of Hawai'i Press.

———. 2002. *Chinese Magical Medicine*. Ed. Bernard Faure. Stanford: Stanford University Press.

Stuart, G. A. 1911. *Chinese Materia Medica: Vegetable Kingdom*. Shanghai: American Presbyterian Missionary Press.

Tanaka Fumio 田中文雄. 2000. "Girei no kūkan" 儀礼の空間. In Tanaka et al. 2000:93–115.

————. 2005. "Dōkyō hōfuku kō" 道教法服考. In Fukui Bunga hakase koki tai-
shoku kinen ronshū kankōkai, ed., *Fukui Bunga hakase koki kinen ronshū:
Ajia bunka no shisō to girei* 福井文雅博士古希記念論集：アジア文化の思想
と儀礼, 351–70. Tokyo: Shunjūsha.

Tanaka Fumio, Maruyama Hiroshi, and Asano Haruji, eds. 2000. *Dōkyō no kyōdan to girei*. Vol. 2 of *Kōza Dōkyō*. Tokyo: Yūzankaku shuppan.

Tang Changru 唐長孺. 1954. "Fan Changshen yu Badi ju Shu de guanxi" 范長生
與巴氏據蜀的關係. *Lishi yanjiu* 4:115–21.

————. 1983. "Wei Jin qijian beifang Tianshidao de chuanbo" 魏晉期間北方天
師道的傳播. In *Wei Jin Nanbeichao shilun shiyi* 魏晉南北朝史論拾遺, 218–
32. Beijing: Zhonghua.

Tang Yongtong 湯用彤. 1991. *Lixue, Foxue, Xuanxue* 理學、佛學、玄學. Beijing:
Beijing daxue.

Taniguchi Fusao 谷口房男. 1976. "Shindai no Teizoku Yōshi ni tsuite" 晉代の氏
族楊氏について. *Tōyō daigaku bungakubu kiyō* 東洋大学文學部研究紀要 30:
31–57.

Thompson, Laurence G. 1989. "On the Prehistory of Hell in China." *Journal of
Chinese Religions* 17 (Fall): 27–41.

Troeltsch, Ernst. 1912. *Soziallehren der christlichen Kirchen und Gruppen*. Trans.
Olive Wyon as *The Social Teaching of the Christian Churches*. London: Allen
and Unwin, 1931.

Tsai, Julius N. 2005. "Identity in the Making: Ritual, Lineage and Redaction in
the *Jinsuo liuzhu yin*." *Journal of Chinese Religions* 33:61–76.

————. 2008. "Reading the *Inner Biography of the Perfected Person of Purple
Solarity* (Ziyang zhenren neizhuan): Religion and Society in an Early Daoist
Hagiography." *Journal of the Royal Asiatic Society*, series 3, 18.2:193–220.

Tsuzuki Akiko. 2000. "Tōdai chūki no Dōkan: Kūkan, keizai, kairitsu" 唐代中期
の道観―空間. In Yoshikawa Tadao, ed., *Tōdai no shūkyō*, 269–96. Kyoto:
Hōyū shoten.

Verellen, Franciscus. 2003a. "Tianshi dao shangzhang keyi: Chisong zi zhangli
he Yuanchen zhangjiao licheng li yanjiu" 天師道上章科儀一《赤松子章曆》
和《元辰章醮立成曆》研究. In Lai Chi Tim, ed., *Daojiao jingdian yu Zhongguo zongjiao wenhua*, 37–71. Hong Kong: Zhonghua.

————. 2003b. "The Twenty-Four Dioceses and Zhang Daoling: The Spatio-
Liturgical Organization of Early Heavenly Master Taoism." In Phyllis Granoff
and Koichi Shinohara, eds., *Pilgrims, Patrons, and Place: Localizing Sanctity in
Asian Religions*, 15–67. Vancouver: University of British Columbia Press.

————. 2004. "The Heavenly Master Liturgical Agenda according to Chisong
Zi's Petition Almanac." *Cahiers d'Extrême-Asie* 14:291–343.

————. 2005. "Guérison et redemption dans le rituel taoïste ancien." *Comptes-
rendus de l'Academie des inscriptions et belles-lettres* 147.3:1029–47.

————. 2006. "The Dynamic Design: Ritual and Contemplative Graphics in Daoist Scriptures." In Benjamin Penny, ed., *Daoism in History: Essays in Honour
of Liu Ts'un-yan*, 159–86. London and New York: Routledge.

Wang Chunwu 王純五. 1996. *Tianshidao ershisi zhi kao* 天師道二十四治考. Chengdu: Ba Shu shushe.

Wang Guowei 王國維. 1984. *Shuijingzhu jiao* 水經注校. Ed. Yuan Yingguang 袁英光 and Liu Yinsheng 劉寅生. Shanghai: Shanghai renmin chubanshe.

Wang Ka 王卡. 1997. "Huangshu kaoyuan" 黃書考源. *Shijie zongjiao yanjiu* 1997.2:65–73.

Wang Liqi 王利器. 2002. *Yanshi jiaxun jijie* 顏氏家訓集解. Xinbian zhuzi jicheng edn. Beijing: Zhonghua.

Wang Ming 王明, ed. 1960. *Taipingjing hejiao* 太平經合校. Beijing: Zhonghua.

———. 1985. *Baopuzi neipian jiaoshi* 抱朴子內篇校釋. Beijing: Zhonghua.

Wang Yongping 王永平. 2002. *Daojiao yu Tangdai shehui* 道教与唐代社会. Beijing: Shoudu shifan daxue chubanshe.

Wang Yucheng 王育成. 1991. "Wuchang Nan-Qi Liu Ji diquan kefu chushi" 武昌南齊劉覬地券刻符初釋. *Jiang-Han kaogu* 1991.2:82–88.

———. 1993. "Xu Fu diquan zhong tianshidao shiliao kaoshi" 徐副地券中天师道史料考释. *Kaogu* 1993.6:571–75.

Wang Zongyu 王宗昱. 1999. "Daojiao de 'liutian' shuo" 道教的"六天"說. *Daojia wenhua yanjiu* 16:22–49.

———. 2009a. "*Chisongzi zhangli* de chengshu niandai" 《赤松子章曆》的成書年代. In Florian C. Reiter, ed., *Foundations of Daoist Ritual: A Berlin Symposium*, 207–16. Wiesbaden: Harrassowitz Verlag.

———. 2009b. "*Zhengyi fawen jing zhangguanpin* jiaokan" 正一法文經章官品校勘. In Zheng Kai 郑开, ed., *Shuibian yun qi: Daojiao wenxian yanjiu de jiuxue xinzhi* 水扁云起 道教文献研究的旧学新知, 51–100. Beijing: Shehui kexue wenxian chubanshe.

Welch, Holmes, and Anna Seidel, eds. 1979. *Facets of Taoism: Essays in Chinese Religion*. New Haven: Yale University Press.

Wile, Douglas. 1992. *Art of the Bedchamber: The Chinese Sexology Classics*. Albany: State University of New York Press.

Wilkinson, Endymion. 2013. *Chinese History: A New Manual*. Cambridge, MA: Harvard University Asia Center.

Wu Jinhua 吴金华. 1990. *Sanguozhi jiaogu* 三国志校诂. Huaiyin: Jiangsu guji chubanshe.

Wu Rongceng 吳榮曾. 1981. "Zhenmu wen zhong suo jiandao de Dong Han daowu guanxi" 鎮墓文中所見到的東漢道巫關係. *Wenwu* 1981.3. Reprinted in *Xian-Qin Liang-Han shi yanjiu* 先秦兩漢史研究, 362–78. Beijing: Zhonghua, 1995.

Wu Zhen 吳真. 2014. "Zhengyi jiaoquan xiangzheng 'Tianshi jian' de xingqi yu chuanshuo" 正一教权象征「天师剑」的兴起与传说. *Huanan shifan daxue xuebao* 2014.3:28–36.

Xiao Yunzhong 肖云忠. 2007. "Zhengyidao Tianshi chuancheng zhidu chutan" 正一道天師傳承制度初探. *Zongjiaoxue yanjiu* 2007.1:154–58.

Yamada Toshiaki 山田利明. 1999. *Rikuchō Dōkyō girei no kenkyū* 六朝道教儀礼の研究. Tokyo: Tōhō shoten.

———. 2000. "The Lingbao School." In Kohn 2000:225–55.

Yan Kejun 嚴可均. 1958. *Quan shanggu sandai Qin Han Sanguo Liuchao wen* 全上古三代秦漢三國六朝文. 4 vols. Beijing: Zhonghua.

Yang Hongnian 杨鸿年. 1985. *Han Wei zhidu congkao* 汉魏制度从考. Wuchang: Wuhan daxue chubanshe.

Yang Liansheng 楊聯陞. 1956. "Laojun yinsong jiejing jiaoshi" 老君音誦誡經校釋. *Zhongyang yanjiu yuan, Lishi yanyu yanjiu suo jikan* 28.1:17–54.

Yang Minkang 楊民康 and Yang Xiaoxun 楊曉勳. 2000. *Yunnan yaozu Daojiao keyi yinyue* 雲南瑤族道教科儀音樂. Taipei: Xinwenfeng.

Yasui Kōzan 安居香山. 1979. *Isho no seiritsu to sono tenkai* 緯書の成立とその展開. Tokyo: Kokusho kankōkai.

———, ed. 1984. *Shin'i shisō no sōgōteki kenkyū* 讖緯思想の総合的研究. Tokyo: Kokusho kankōkai.

Yasui Kōzan and Nakamura Shōhachi 中村璋八, eds. 1971. *Jūshū Isho shūsei* 重修緯書集成. Tokyo: Meitoku shuppansha.

Yoshikawa Tadao 吉川忠夫. 1987. "Seishitsu kō" 「静室」考. *Tōhō gakuhō* 59: 125–62.

———, ed. 1998. *Rikuchō Dōkyō no kenkyū* 六朝道教の研究. Kyoto: Shunjusha.

Yoshikawa Tadao and Mugitani Kunio 麥谷邦夫, eds. 2000. *Shinkō kenkyū: Yakuchū hen* 真誥研究：譯注篇. Kyoto: Kyōto daigaku jinbun kagaku kenkyūjo.

Yoshioka Yoshitoyo 吉岡儀豊. 1976. "Rikuchō Dōkyō no shumin shisō" 六朝道教の種民思想. In *Dōkyō to Bukkyō* 3:221–84. Tokyo: Kokusho kankōkai.

Yu Liming 俞理明. 2001. *Taipingjing zhengdu* 太平經正讀. Chengdu: Ba Shu Shushe.

Yu Wanli 虞萬里. 2001. *Yufangzhai xueshu lunji* 榆枋齋學術論集. Nanjing: Jiangsu renmin chubanshe.

Zeng Chao 曾超. 2008. "Baren zhanbu xingshi kao" 巴人占卜形式考. *Tongren xueyuan xuebao* 同仁学院学报 10.3 (2008.5): 66–72.

Zhang Huasong 張華松. 2004. "Handai Chengyang Jing wang shen congbai shimo kao" 汉代城阳景王神崇拜始末考. *Qi-Lu wenhua yanjiu* 2004:141–50.

Zhang Xiangwen 張祥穩. 1996. "Chimei yuanyou xintan" 赤眉緣由新探. *Chizhou shizhuan xuebao* 1996.2:59–62.

Zhang Xunliao 張勛燎. 1996. "Dong Han muzang chutu de jiezhuqi cailiao he Tianshidao de qiyuan" 東漢墓葬出土的解注器材料和天師道的起源. *Daojiao wenhua yanjiu* 9:118–48.

———. 2010. "Daoist Stelae of the Northern Dynasties." In Lagerwey and Lü 2010: 1, 437–544.

Zhang Xunliao and Bai Bin 白彬. 2005. *Zhongguo daojiao kaogu* 中國道教考古. 6 vols. Beijing: Xianzhuang shuju.

Zhang Zehong 張澤洪. 2000. "Zaoqi zhengyidao de shangzhang jidu sixiang" 早期正一道的上章濟度思想. *Zongjiaoxue yanjiu* 2000.2:22–29.

———. 2005. "Bei Wei daoshi Kou Qianzhi de xin Daojiao lunxi" 北魏道士寇謙之的新道教論析. *Sichuan daxue xuebao (Zhexue shehui kexue ban)* 138 (2005.3): 41–47.

———. 2012. "Zaoqi Tianshi shixi yu Longhushan Zhang Tianshi sijiao" 早期天師世系與龍虎山張天師嗣教. *Shehui kexue yanjiu* 2012.6:122–28.

Zhong Guofa 鍾國發. 2008. "Du Zigong yu Jiangdong Tianshidao" 杜子恭與江東天師道. *Chuantong Zhongguo yanjiu jikan* 2008:46–63.

Zhou Shengchun 周生春. 1997. *Wu Yue chunqiu jijiao huikao* 吳越春秋輯校彙考. Shanghai: Shanghai guji.

Zhou Xibo 周西波. 2003. *Du Guangting Daojiao yifan zhi yanjiu* 杜光庭道教儀範之研究. Taipei: Xinwenfeng.

Zhuang Hongyi 莊宏誼. 1986. *Mingdai Daojiao Zhengyi pai* 明代道教正一派. Taipei: Xuesheng shuju.

———. 2010. "Li zhi wei diwang shi: Kou Qianzhi de zongjiao lixiang yu shijian" 立志爲帝王師：寇謙之的宗教理想與實踐. *Furen zongjiao yanjiu* 21:21–51.

Zürcher, Erik. 1959. *The Buddhist Conquest of China*. Leiden: Brill.

———. 1980. "Buddhist Influence on Early Taoism." *T'oung Pao* 66:84–147.

Index

Page numbers in italics refer to a definition or a primary discussion of a term.

Harvard-Yenching Institute Monograph Series
(titles now in print)